The Mediocre Infantryman's Guide to Ranger School

Andrew Goldsmith

© 2025, Andrew Goldsmith

All rights reserved. No part of this publication may be reproduced or distributed in any form or by any means without written permission, except in the case of brief quotation embodied in critical articles and reviews that include credit to the author and source.

Library and Archives Canada Cataloguing in Publication
Goldsmith, Andrew, author
The Mediocre Infantryman's Guide to Ranger School / Andrew Goldsmith

Issued in print and electronic formats.
ISBN: 978-1-998501-44-1 (paperback)
ISBN: 978-1-998501-45-8 (ebook)

Cover Design: Stefan Prodanovic
Interior Design: Winston S. Prescott
Double Dagger Books Ltd.
Toronto, Ontario, Canada

www.doubledagger.ca

This book is dedicated to the elite warriors of the 75th Ranger Regiment and U.S. Army Special Forces. No one fought harder or sacrificed more during the 2001 to 2021 United States wars in Iraq and Afghanistan. It was an honor to share in the Ranger School struggle with some of you.

And to my beloved wife and children, who have no choice but to listen to my ranger stories.

[INSERT TABLE OF CONTENTS]

FOREWORD

I was what you would call a "hungry ranger," perpetually hungry, mind constantly on my belly, twenty-four hours a day.

I could deal with the cold, the near-constant pain, Ranger Instructor mind games, and leading patrols, but boy, was I hungry, all the time. That's why I will never forget that wonderful evening in Florida Phase when I stumbled out of the patrol base after midnight to relieve my bladder only to stumble upon what can only be described as an MRE massacre. It was a burnt-out field strewn about with hundreds of flame-kissed, sun-whitened prepackaged Army snacks and main meals. The vacuum-sealed food was of indeterminate age and the packaging was starting to deteriorate. Many of them were too burned by fire to eat, most were already scavenged by crows, pigs, and rodents, but fortunately for me, I was able to find two largely unsinged and unopened entrée meals, which I gleefully shoved into my cargo pocket.

I had struck Ranger gold. There was no man happier in our ranger platoon that night, I guarantee it.

Back at the patrol base, I immediately wolfed down both entrees cold like an animal. Not only was I not planning on sharing, but the extra, unauthorized food was illicit contraband, and if I was caught by a Ranger Instructor I would be in big trouble. Full, for the moment, I resumed my position besides my winter warming fire for some well-deserved rest. Unfortunately, within moments, my stomach was in severe pain, roiling with torment, certainly brought on from eating the trash food moments before. However, because I had not slept more than one or two hours a night in days, I naturally went deeply and soundly to sleep.

Three hours later, I awoke at 4:00 a.m. with one of my boots melted onto my foot and half of a pant leg burned off up to the knee. Burned and blistered flesh extended from my ankle to my groin. Apparently, I slept with my leg in the fire, and I didn't even feel a thing.

Welcome to Ranger School.

But with only days left in the final field problem, a week from the finish line, after enduring and suffering so much, there was no way I was going to let a little thing like a burned leg stop me from completing the mission, finishing Ranger School, and earning that goddamn Tab. If I told an RI about it, if I sought any medical attention, at the very least I would have to repeat or recycle a phase, or worse, be kicked out for several rules violations including eating unauthorized food and being careless with my warming fire. I couldn't chance this, not when my burns were just one more injury stacked upon a dozen others, including an inflamed and swollen Achilles tendon, a post-surgical ankle, a cellulitis racked knee, and near-constant pain in my back, knees, neck, and shoulders.

No, there was nothing I could do other than suck it up and carry on the mission. After all, no matter the conditions, no matter the odds, as Corporal Andrew Goldsmith will show you in his epic tale of grit and fortitude, rangers complete the mission, that's just what they do.

No matter what.

I can tell you that Ranger School lived up to the hype. I went to the course in 2010 as a twenty-seven-year old sergeant first class. An elder statesmen with years of Army experience, I was the second oldest ranger in my class, so naturally, I was known as the "old guy." I had more preparation than most for the course, having spent my team leader and squad leader time in the mountains of Korea, three years as a platoon sergeant, and two-years on deployment to Iraq. Yet, like many others in Ranger School, I was a little lost, very ill-prepared, and rapidly broken down physically and mentally by the relentless stress, injury, and hunger inflicted by the course.

That is what Ranger School is designed to do after all, take away every conceivable advantage, comfort, and status from the individual, to show him who he really is. From special forces operator to Airborne Ranger to freshly-minted lieutenant alike, Ranger School breaks everyone down to the lowest common denominator, only then to see if we have what it takes to lead other desperate, hungry, wounded men in ranger operations in the field.

I was a recently-arrived platoon sergeant in a mechanized infantry company in 2007 when I sent Goldsmith, a Corporal team leader at the time, to Ranger School. Due to seemingly endless back-to-back deployments to Iraq, troop shortages, and the "Stop-loss" policy which retained soldiers years beyond their agreed-upon enlistment dates, morale at our unit was at an extraordinarily low point. I wanted to re-motivate the men, to fire them up about something other than deployments to Iraq, and more than that, I needed leaders to help lead the platoon, people who could excel outside the norm, for our upcoming deployment to Iraq, which I knew would be full of challenges. I figured sending some platoon "champions" to prestigious Army schools like Airborne and Ranger School, would be a good way to accomplish both goals.

And although I had just met the guy, Goldsmith was at the top of my list. A red-headed, two-hundred-and-twenty-pound cage fighter who had a blackened ear when I first met him, he was both intimidating and yet more humble than I expected. He had a lot of energy, loyalty to his men and the mission, and little leniency for laziness in others or himself. He got things done, with little tolerance for the bullshit in-between, and would not hesitate to stand up for himself.

I sent Goldsmith, or Andrew as I now call him, to Ranger School because I knew he could hack it, physically and mentally. Little did I know it would give him so much trouble. In a way, I almost feel sorry for sending him.

Almost.

That's because if I never sent him, you, the reader, would not be in possession of a book as hard-hitting, realistic, and informative as this one. This book is about Goldsmith's unique, epic, oftentimes hilarious, and utterly absurd struggles and triumphs in earning his Ranger tab, but in a way, it's about every ranger's journey, every person's journey, as they transition from innocence to adulthood or, in this case, a "ranger." In this masterful narrative, which reads like a novel, he captures the Ranger School experience, in its totality: the self-doubt, the suffering, the humor, the triumph, from a ground-level grunt's perspective. Goldsmith is unabashedly honest, irreverent, and insightful, describing the experience for the reader not as an untouchable, unrelatable super soldier, but as the "everyman," someone we can all relate to, someone just like ourselves.

Goldsmith expertly captures the madness of Ranger School in all its glory and infamy, and deeply immerses the reader into a world that few will ever see. His guide truly immerses the reader into every gut-wrenching step of the course, expertly shows the timeless Ranger School experience for what it is, something undeniably raw, real, and extraordinary, an unparalleled warrior rite of passage that cannot help but transform someone physically, mentally, and morally, a course which has been described by many of its attendees as worse than actual combat.

Yes, as Goldsmith will describe in this book, Ranger School, like other extreme circumstances in life and war, lives up to the hype. And that is why a guide like this is so valuable, for everyone. Whether you are a prospective ranger student, military servicemember, business leader, armchair general, young adult seeking their calling in this world, or just someone looking for a fascinating tale, about a bizarre, yet true, world, chock-full of adventure, adversity, and triumph. Most importantly, its overall message: that when you have a purpose, you can put up with almost any hardship, is one that we can all to take to heart when confronting the great challenges in our lives.

Several years after attending Ranger School, I was privileged enough to serve as the Operations Sergeant Major for the Ranger Training Brigade, a position that had me overseeing and bearing responsibility for all the air and land training and operations within the brigade including Airborne School, Ranger School, Pathfinder School, Jumpmaster School, and others. I was fortunate to be able to see "behind the curtain" of Ranger School, to see all the moving pieces, preparation, and safeguards that went into making the experience so impactful for students, how the Ranger Instructors and other cadre pushed us all to our absolute limits, miles beyond where we previously thought we could go, all the while, without actually killing us.

I was honored to play my small part in continuing the Ranger legacy and to be in the presence of ranger heroes and legends, some of the finest fighting men our nation has ever produced. Men like Medal of Honor recipient Colonel Ralph Puckett, a silent, humble warrior who stood tall and regularly attended Ranger events well into his nineties, in order to ensure the torch was properly passed to future generations. Men like Command Sergeant Major Victor Ballesteros, who exemplifies the Ranger spirit, a consummate warrior who treated my family like his own when we were going through the roughest period of our lives.

Ranger School as an institution, since its establishment in 1950, has specialized in creating the type of stress, deprivation, and hardship that only combat, natural disaster, or deep personal loss can create. The extremes of Ranger School creates an experience with endless lessons for soldiers and civilians alike. I know this because I still learn and reflect upon the lessons I learned in Ranger School daily. Like Goldsmith, I believe that the transmission of these experiences and lessons should not be limited to the select one or two thousand rangers who graduate the course every year, but should be shared with anyone facing challenges or struggle in their own life, that is, all of us.

Goldsmith may only be a self-avowed "mediocre infantrymen," a buck sergeant with two combat tours to Iraq almost two decades ago, but I cannot think of anyone more qualified to write this book. Not only did he survive the course and earn his Ranger Tab, but he was a professional and tactically sound small unit leader, well-versed in infantry doctrine and tactics, and a rock solid trainer and leader of men in combat. Since leaving the Army, he has made deep study into military doctrine, tactics, and history, and knows more about the subject of warfare than almost anyone I know. More than that, although he did some pretty stupid things under my command (didn't we all?), he has subsequently proven to be a very bright and successful writer, lawyer, business, and family man who exemplifies what it means to lead and conquer in life with a ranger spirit.

So, without further ado, I will stop flapping my gums and simply encourage you, the reader, to get started on an epic journey, the quest to earn the coveted Ranger Tab. Prepare yourself for an experience, a true adventure, one that will test your stamina, endurance, health, your sanity, and more than anything else, your will. If you are ready to learn what it takes to be a ranger, well then, ladies and gentleman, put on your big-boy pants, find your courage, and prepare to embrace the suck, because your Ranger School journey is about to begin. Good luck.

You are going to need it.

Sergeant Major (ret.) Dennis Tripp

PROLOGUE
WELCOME TO RANGER SCHOOL

Rule #1: Ranger School will suck.

12:57 a.m.
Aid Station, Camp Rogers
Fort Benning, Georgia
Day 5 of Ranger School

"This may hurt a bit," the fat, acne-scarred medic tells me. "In fact, it's going to hurt a lot."

He jabs a hypodermic needle filled with some sort of purplish solution into the juicy mass of the largest blister on the bottom of my right foot. For a long, agonizing thirty seconds, it feels like a wasp injecting me with venom.

Curse these cruel, incompetent medics!

The pain is bad. I can't help but writhe on the hospital bed, emitting low animal groans and grating my teeth.

"Fuck me!" I turn to see a tall ranger student in the gurney bed next to me getting the same "treatment," injections of tincture of benzoin into our blisters to essentially glue the flesh together, reducing pain and causing them to heal. The extreme-sporting world calls the procedure a "hot shot."

"Sweet Mary, Mother of Jesus!" My neighbor shouts and laughs maniacally. "What in the hell are you quacks doing to me?!"

After most of the pain from my own injection subsides, I look up reluctantly at my torturer.

"You ready for more?" he asks me, "Or have you had enough, ranger?"

I want to punch the tab-less, nineteen-year-old peon in the mouth, but all I can manage is a nod and a lame reply. "Just fix as many as you can and do it quickly."

I endure a second, third, fourth, fifth, and finally sixth jolt of pain as the medic successively jabs the needle tip into the largest blisters on the soles of my feet. Each time the tincture of benzoin burns fiercely for about a minute. After the sixth injection I tell him to stop – I cannot take it anymore.

I don't know this yet, but all this pain will be for nothing, because the medic has botched the job. He should have drained my blisters first. If that were the case, the tincture of benzoin would, in theory, help the separated skin to bond together and ultimately cut down on my pain and healing time. But, through some combination of incompetence, laziness, or malice, my medic chose not to do so.

"All patched up, ranger."

I put on sweat-stained socks and lace up my boots over blisters filled near to bursting with purple-hued blood and pus. The burning fluid continues to slosh around inside, causing fresh pain.

I hobble out of the aid station in even worse shape than when I entered, every step a painful and brutal shock to my psyche. After only a few steps, the pain drops me to my hands and knees.

My pride as a man, as an infantryman, commands that I get up and walk the mere six hundred feet back to the barracks, where the rest of the men in Ranger Class 01-08 are already sleeping. Wake up is less than three-and-a-half hours away, at four a.m. in the morning, and there is no time to waste.

But I can't do it. After taking a few limping and tip-toeing steps, the searing pain in my feet forces me to drop to my hands and knees again. All I can do is crawl forward.

A painful and humiliating cycle begins. I walk a few steps, drop to my knees in agony, and crawl a few meters forward, before pride compels me to rise to my feet again. Embarrassed and in great pain, tears of desperation start falling onto the concrete and gravel beneath me.

Fortunately, no one sees me. It is half past midnight, and Camp Rogers, the home of 4th Ranger Training Battalion, is a ghost town. I am completely and utterly alone, just me and my thoughts.

What was I thinking! Me! A mediocre infantryman from a regular Army unit... whatever made me think I could ever hack it here, in Ranger School?

A mere twenty-four hours ago, it was a different story. I was riding high, feeling strong and confident. I was practically breezing through the first few days. I was an Iraq War veteran, a corporal about to make sergeant in an infantry squad, twenty-two years old and in the best shape of my life. I was selected ahead of my peers to attend the U.S. Army's most challenging and celebrated leadership course because my leaders thought I had the skill and ability to handle it.

But now, reality is hitting hard because my feet, the most important thing to an infantryman, let alone a ranger student, are beaten down, riddled with blisters, and now swollen from defective hotshot injections. Now, every step is a trial of fortitude. My two-hundred-and-ten-pound body applies pinpoint pressure to the nickel and quarter-sized blisters. With each step, the searing purple mixture sloshes around inside my wounds and burns with renewed intensity. Worse yet, with each step, they feel ready to burst, to explode even, with each... and every... step.

So, I drop to the ground and crawl, like a baby, inching my way over to the barracks, fully knowing how absurd and pitiful I must look, but with no other choice.

After several minutes, the doors to the Charlie Company barracks are no more than two hundred feet away, but traversing this petty distance may just be the greatest challenge I've faced in my army career.

I turn towards the night sky, hands clasped together in supplication, and speak aloud to any deity that would hear my pathetic cries.

"Please, God, if you are listening... please, please, help me get through this thing. Not the whole thing, not all of Ranger School, just tonight. Just help me get back to my bunk tonight, so that I can get some sleep. Get me through tonight... that is all I am asking."

Other than the low buzzing of streetlights, there is nothing but silence. No miracle appears.

So, I start crawling forward again.

I make it a few dozen feet further before my formerly pious mood transforms into a vitriolic rage at my condition and the hostile, indifferent universe. Most of all, I think about my "comrades," my fellow ranger

students, mere strangers who know and care nothing about me. They are fast asleep at this very moment, all of them, other than the two fireguards, momentarily numbed to the perpetual suffering of Ranger School. They are blissfully unaware of the pitiful, yet titanic struggle enfolding a mere two hundred feet from them. They are at peace, sleeping soundly and warm in their bunks, and I hate them for it.

    I hate them for the extra hour of sleep they are getting over me. I hate them for not having the terrible blisters I do. I hate them for having actual friends and battle buddies to rely upon. I hate them for having abilities and knowledge greater than my own. I hate them for actually belonging here, in Ranger School.

    Now that I am among the doomed and the dying, I envy the living.

    In an emotional frenzy, one last time, I cry out to a higher power:

    Please, God… ALL I WANT IS A MERE THREE HOURS OF SLEEP TONIGHT! IS THAT SO MUCH TO ASK?

    But my cries to the heavens bring no relief. I know now that I am truly and utterly on my own here, a mediocre infantryman, lost in Ranger School.

    But fortunately, dear readers, you do not have to be.

Ranger Goldsmith did not have a guide. He did not know the answers to even the most basic of Ranger School questions such as: Why am I here? What are the rules to this place? What challenges will tomorrow bring? But mostly, how can anyone, even you, the reader, survive and ultimately thrive in the U.S. Army's most austere leadership course?

Well listen up, rangers, because this humble grunt is going to reveal all the secrets that he wished he knew about Ranger School, back when he was that sad sack of garbage, a tab-less wonder with terrible prospects and little hope of success, crawling and crying his way to a lonely bunk. Please allow me to serve as your guide, and show you how even the most naive and unprepared young infantryman can do the seemingly impossible: pass U.S. Army Ranger School and earn the coveted Ranger Tab.

So, without further ado, ladies and gentlemen... welcome to Ranger School.

Part I - "Crawl"

RAP Week and Darby Phase

Camp Rogers and Camp Darby, Fort Benning, Georgia

Days 1 – 20

[I]n the daytime the heat has consumed me, and at night the cold has gnawed at me, and sleep has fled from my eyes.
— **Genesis 31:40**

Ranger, noun – *definition: a specially selected and highly-trained light infantryman specializing in small-unit raids, ambushes, and other combat missions deep inside enemy territory.*

Rule #2: Endure the suffering; earn the Tab.

Chapter 1:
"Not for the Weak or Fainthearted"

Rule #3: Do not show up to Ranger School tired, hungry, or alone.

2353 Hours (11:53 p.m.)
October 2007
Fourth Ranger Training Battalion Headquarters, Camp Rogers
Fort Benning, Georgia
Day 0 of Ranger School

I show up to Ranger School tired, hungry, and alone.

Tired, because the taxi driver drops me off at Camp Rogers a few minutes shy of midnight, the night before the start of the course.

Hungry, because I have eaten clean and exercised insatiably in preparation for the days ahead. I have easily lost ten pounds and an inch off an already trim waistline in the last three weeks.

And I am alone, because I am a vanilla infantryman in the U.S. Army, a mediocre one even, an "eleven-bravo," a grunt, a straight leg, non-airborne, mechanized "baby tanker." I am not a member of a Ranger Regiment, a green beret, an infantry officer, or even a light infantry Airborne stud. I am a mere corporal in a regular army unit and, here at Ranger School, this makes me an

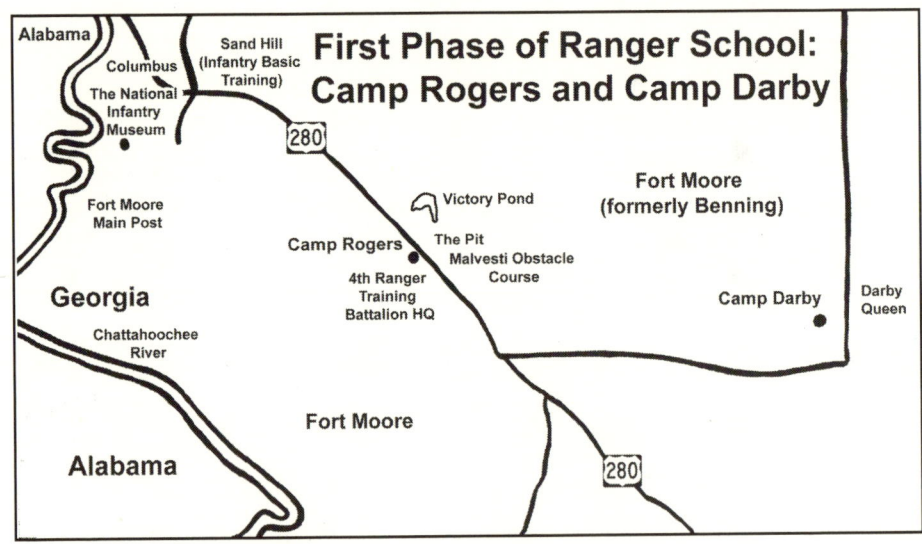

outlier, doomed to solitude and friendlessness, a true nobody.

But fortunately, I do not know that yet.

I should be sleeping right now, I tell myself as I shoulder my duffle bags and drag them the short distance to 4th Ranger Training Battalion headquarters to officially check into Ranger School.

I stop walking when I see a bronzed plaque affixed to a granite rock

and adorned with a giant Ranger Tab. The plaque commemorates the ranger students who perished in their attempt to complete this course. No less than twenty-eight physically fit young men at the peak of their health, some of the finest soldiers in the nation, are listed here. They fell off obstacles in the very first days of the course or died of exposure to the elements or drowned in the Florida swamps, or otherwise found their premature,

2 | THE MEDIOCRE INFANTRYMAN'S GUIDE TO RANGER SCHOOL

unexpected end, here, where I am now. They sought the Tab and never returned. Ranger School killed them.

What did they die for? The Ranger Tab, a 2 3/8" by 11/16" arch made of cloth and inscribed with the word, "RANGER." It is worn on the left shoulder above the uniform's unit patch and confers a unique status, aura, and respect to the wearer. The Tab sets him apart from his peers as a specialist in light infantry tactics, a capable leader, and most importantly, a tough son of a bitch who is aggressive in battle. The Tab can only be earned by completing Ranger School, a sixty-day master course in pain and suffering that has not significantly changed since the 1950s, a training course that many report to be more difficult and stressful than actual combat.

Back home, in my mechanized infantry company, the Tab is my ticket to increased admiration, respect, and greater responsibilities. Earning it will be a true test of mettle but also a unique opportunity to follow up on the dream every young infantryman has at his recruiting station: painting my face green, wading through a swamp, and being a ranger! This is my chance to show others, but more importantly myself, that I am who I think I am: a hardcore infantryman, tough, strong, and lethal, someone who lives up to his highest ideals and dares to be great, a hero even.

A ranger.

Most people, even civilians, have at least heard about U.S. Army Ranger School. They may have some passing familiarity with its difficulty and dark legend, maybe even seen a documentary about it on the History Channel. In the Army infantry, everyone knows about the course, or at least, we think we do. It conjures up images of obstacle courses and rope climbing, commando skills and zodiac boats, living in the bush, shooting bad guys, eating and sleeping very little, and most of all, flying around in helicopters and jumping out of airplanes.

That's the kind of stuff I wanted to do when I joined the Army as an intellectually gifted, but emotionally and morally unsettled, red-haired, six-foot, two-hundred-pound, nineteen-year-old infantryman three years ago. After becoming disillusioned with school, fighting and partying too much, and getting in trouble in my late adolescent years, I was ready for a change, a mission, a purpose. And boy did I get it. After Basic and Infantry Training, a year training up with my unit as a humble machine gunner, a year in Iraq running patrols, doing raids, and getting shot at and blown up periodically, I am a different person, despite being just a regular old infantry grunt.

Like many others who joined the infantry, deep in my little boy's heart, I longed to go to Ranger School, but after basic training, barely surviving as an ignorant peon at my unit, deploying overseas, and living the already Spartan life of an infantryman, like most everyone else, I basically let that dream die.

Yet here I am.

What everyone knows for certain is that the Ranger Tab is not freely given. Renowned for its difficulty and deprivation, Ranger School is surrounded by dark tales of woe: high failure rates, minimal rations, prolonged exposure to the elements, and sleeping so little rangers start hallucinating and talking to trees.

Ranger School, as the motto so aptly states: "Not for the weak or fainthearted."

I break my attention away from the memorial plaque, take a deep breath, and resume my short walk to headquarters. I drop my bags at the entrance, pull open the swinging door, and enter 4th Ranger Training Battalion to officially check in.

There is a lone, bored sergeant seated on desk duty reading a car magazine. Otherwise, the building is deserted. The sergeant does not appear to notice me.

"Ahem," I clear my throat, "Corporal Goldsmith, Fourth Infantry Division, reporting for Ranger School." My chest swells with pride just saying the words.

"Sign in here," the sergeant keeps reading his magazine as his hand motions toward a clipboard on the counter.

There is no going back now, I say to myself as I jot down my name and signature.

"Hey, Sergeant," I ask tentatively, conditioned by three years in the Army to fear asking dumb questions, "just where is everyone?"

The desk sergeant sighs as he reluctantly breaks his attention away from his magazine to look me in the eyes.

"Most people check in in the morning, but there are a handful of guys sleeping in the barracks across the street tonight. Just make sure you are out on the field in your PT uniform with all your duffel bags, ready to go, by zero-three-hundred hours tomorrow morning."

"Roger, Sergeant." A darting glance at my Timex watch informs me that it is now past midnight. I will be lucky to get two-and-a-half hours of sleep tonight.

Great planning, Goldsmith. I re-shoulder my duffel bags, cross the street, and walk the short distance to the barracks. Inside, half of the lights are still on as I trudge past rows of bunk beds with a handful of sleeping bodies occupying them. I find an empty lower bunk for myself, pull out my sleeping bag, and set my alarm for 2:45 a.m. I take the initiative to turn off the room's overhead lights before laying my head down and shutting my eyes for a few hours of much-needed rest.

But sleep will not come, not tonight, not when I need it the most, not when I am starting Ranger School in a matter of hours. Ten minutes after I shut the lights off, new students, heedless of anyone else, arrive and flick the light switches back on again. Indeed, soldiers continue to trickle into the barracks all through the short night. The noise and commotion, overhead lights, and the angst and anticipation of the upcoming trial keeps my mind racing for well over an hour before I eventually drift off into cheap, fitful, anxiety-ridden sleep.

0245 Hours (02:45 a.m.)
The Barracks, Camp Rogers
Fort Benning, Georgia
Day 1 of Ranger School
Hours of Sleep Last Night: 1.5 hours

Beep-Beep-Beep-Beep. Beep-Beep-Beep-Beep. Beep-Beep-Beep-Beep.

My watch alarm goes off into my right ear after what feels like a half-hour of sleep. The overhead lights are still on in the barracks. I feel lousy with lack of sleep, but fortunately, the excitement and anticipation of the day to come gets me up and moving quickly.

Time to report for Ranger School, Goldsmith.

I run a razor over my face, brush my teeth, put on my Army-issue physical training shorts and t-shirt, grab my duffel bags, and walk the short distance to an open field a short distance away.

I drop my bags on the grass and take a seat with two dozen other students who got there before me. The temperature is barely above freezing, and I can clearly see my breath when I exhale. No one is excited to be up three hours before the sunrise in a t-shirt and shorts to sit down and shiver in a dew-soaked field. We are mostly silent, alone with our thoughts in the darkness, as other men slowly start trickling in. By three-forty-five a.m., there are three hundred young men assembled in the field, and not a single woman. It is 2007, after all, and Ranger School will not have its first female attendees for another eight years.

A few of the younger soldiers crack jokes or chatter nervously, but most of the group remains silent in the chill morning air. We are cold, nervous, homesick, and look boyish and awkward with our freshly shaven heads. While nearly everyone looks in shape and physically strong, in the dim night lighting, at this ungodly hour, many also look pale, timid, filled with self-doubt, even scared.

The first Ranger Instructors, or "RIs," as we call them, start gathering in the area. They wear black sweatshirts and extremely high-cut black shorts, or "ranger panties," that expose their thickly muscled thighs. They start issuing orders through bullhorns to corral us into four separate "Companies" of about eighty men each. I am assigned to Charlie Company.

Suddenly, at four a.m., stadium lights abruptly turn on and an RI lets off a loud siren sound on his blowhorn. The light and noise jolt the chilled, half-dozing ranger students awake. A blond-haired, hulking, Adonis of an RI wearing the shortest ranger panties I have ever seen climbs onto a platform and shouts into his bull horn.

"Cadre, get these rangers formed up and ready to go. Prepare to conduct the Ranger Physical Training Assessment."

Finally! The Ranger PT Test, the first "go or no-go" event in Ranger School. A large proportion of the class will wash out here, on the very first event and within the first hour of Ranger School. I am determined not to be among them.

Three-hundred-and-forty ranger students line up around "The Pit," a circular enclosure padded with wood chips and edged with railroad ties. To exit it successfully, we need to execute forty-nine perfect push-ups and fifty-nine sit-ups in two minutes each. I pass both the push-up and sit-up portions of the test by doing the bare minimum and standing up. There is no need to do any more.

Up next is the five-mile run, which must be completed in forty minutes or less. This is the task I have dreaded and prepared for more than any other. I usually weigh two-hundred-and-twenty-five pounds and running has never been my strong suit. Yet I manage to maintain a consistent, moderate pace throughout the five-mile course, following and then pushing past the pace man before managing to cross the finish line with ninety seconds to spare.

It is anti-climactic to pass the five-mile run so easily, an event which I greatly feared failing prior to showing up to Ranger School. Almost as an afterthought, I saunter over to the pullup bars to bust out six excruciatingly slow pullups.

"Up... down... one. Up... down... two. Up... up... and... down..."

After the RI finally counts to six, I drop to the ground.

"You are a 'go' at this station, ranger," he tells me. "Stand over there."

Despite barely sleeping last night, I am enthused and filled with energy. I have just conquered the first pass-or-fail test of Ranger School, and I barely broke a sweat. But a surprisingly large number of students, at least forty, have not. They are formed up into ranks and marched off to the Recycle barracks. Some of them will linger around here for weeks until the next class forms up, others will exit the course for good. One thing is certain, they will not be graduating with Ranger Class 01-08.

The rest of us, three hundred students now, are marched inside a large classroom and ordered to sit down behind many rows of long tables.

I am only seated for a moment when an RI bellows out loudly, "ON YOUR FEET!" causing all three hundred of us to scramble to the position of attention: heels together, back straight, arms pinned to our sides. A square-jawed, crusty-looking colonel with gray hair, a 3rd Ranger Battalion combat scroll, jump wings, pathfinder badge and, of course, a Ranger Tab, walks up to the podium at the front of the classroom. At his signal, an RI in the back of the room turns on a projector and the lights are dimmed.

"Good morning, rangers! Welcome to Ranger School and congratulations on making it this far in the course."

The colonel's introductory remarks garner a few scattered "Hooahs!" from the audience.

"And don't worry, men, this is going to be the only time you will be subjected to a PowerPoint presentation. After all, this is Ranger School."

A few of us respond with nervous, forced chuckles.

"In fact, there is only one thing every one of you must remember in the next two, three, four or six months, however long you are here, and that is this: earn the Tab. It is that simple, earn the Tab. Now, I want all of you to say it with me."

"Earn the Tab." We intone the mantra aloud.

"Louder! Not like a bunch of fucking sissies! Earn the Tab! Loud and proud!"

"Earn the Tab!" We say it louder.

"Again!"

"EARN THE TAB!" Me and three hundred other rangers fill the room with a mighty roar.

"Good, good. Now, let's get on with the presentation. Here's some numbers for you…"

The colonel's slide tells us that three-hundred-and-forty students showed up for Ranger School this morning, a little over two hours ago, and now three hundred remain. A second one shows the average attrition rates for the various events that take place in Ranger Attrition Phase or, "RAP Week:" the land navigation course, ruck march, obstacle courses, as well as skills testing and the Combat Water Survival Test. Another slide gives us all a stark reminder of something we already know: that half of us that start this course will not complete it; we will return home without a Tab.

The colonel goes on to briefly describe our operational environment before addressing our strategic goal of disrupting and destroying our shadowy, fictional, insurgent enemy, the Aragon Liberation Front, the "Opfor." To do so, our ranger companies will utilize basic and timeless small-unit infantry tactics of movement, reconnaissance, ambushes, and raids to find, fix, and kill them wherever they operate, whether that be deep in the woods, high in the mountains, or in a swamp.

"But before we can do all that, rangers, we have to see if you have what it takes to join the campaign."

"That is the purpose of RAP Week, rangers," the colonel explains, "to see if you possess the required ability, stamina, maturity, and resilience to make it through the rest of this demanding course. Sadly," the colonel pauses and lifts his gaze for emphasis, "many of you sitting in this room do not."

In Ranger School, they tell it to you straight. As I will learn repeatedly, there is no sugar-coating the truth here, and our feelings do not matter.

"In Ranger School, we grade you against the standard, the Army standard, and if you fail, it is only because you have failed yourself, because your leaders have failed you, because you have never actually been held to those standards."

Damn, I think, as a cold shiver runs down my spine.

"And remember, you all volunteered to be here. It is a privilege and an honor simply to be sitting where you are now. Don't you forget that. Our nation has and continues to be at war with an enemy that wants to see us all dead and our way of life destroyed. Seize this opportunity to learn some useful skills, to sharpen your leadership abilities, and to make yourselves, your families, and your units proud. Above all, earn the Tab so you can get back out there and do what you do best: close with and destroy the enemy. You understand me, rangers?"

Yes, Sir!

"Endure the suffering... EARN THE TAB!" The colonel shouts.

"EARN THE TAB!" Three hundred rangers yell in response.

"ON YOUR FEET!" An RI shouts out. We spring up again to the position of attention. The auditorium is silent as the colonel executes a left face and abruptly marches out of the classroom.

Several RIs march us out of the classroom and separate us into our four assigned ranger companies, now numbering about seventy-five men each. They give us twenty minutes to eat breakfast, a Meal Ready to Eat or "MRE," in a grass and gravel strewn field.

At 8:00 a.m. an RI orders Charlie Company to assemble.

"Look at the man in front of you." The RI tells us as he pairs us off. "Get to know him and get to know him well. He is your Ranger Buddy, your better half. You will do everything together, you will go everywhere, and I mean everywhere, together. If he is taking a shit, you are taking a shit; if he is having a bad day, you will be having an even worse one."

My ranger buddy and I look each other in the eyes and exchange quick downward nods. His name tape reads, "TOBIRI."

"Now," the RI pulls up his shirtsleeve and looks at his watch, "you have ten minutes to learn everything you can about each other, where he's from, what he does in the big Army, who or what he fucks, everything. You will be tested. Go!"

"Nice to meet you, ranger buddy." I say to Tobiri.

"Heck of a place to meet," he responds affably, "but nice to meet you too, Goldsmith."

"Is your name pronounced, toe-beery?"

"More like two-bree. It's Norwegian, but everyone calls me toe-beery, so you can, too."

Tobiri may have Norwegian roots, but he does not look much like a Viking. Far from it, he stands barely five foot six inches tall, has a slim build, and does not look particularly strong or athletic. The hair stubble adorning his plain, square-shaped face is so blond it is almost white. His appearance is only remarkable for a prominent brow and an upper lip that resembles a duck bill. He is soft-spoken, unassuming, and not in any way intimidating, the antithesis of who I thought would be attending this course. He is also thirty years old, which in Ranger School, makes him an old man.

Based on first impressions, I do not expect him to survive the week.

"What brings you to Ranger School, Tobiri?" I ask him.

"I'm a lieutenant with the combat engineers. I am almost done with my initial training, and this is my last stop before I report to my first unit. I figured I'd earn my Ranger Tab to make it more likely that I will pick up a platoon command instead of riding a desk for my first assignment. What do you do, Goldsmith?"

"I'm a team leader in an infantry company."

"Really? Cool!" Tobiri seems genuinely impressed. "What unit are you in? Eighty-Second Airborne, Hundred and First, Tenth Mountain?"

"I'm with the Fourth Infantry Division."

Tobiri gives me a blank stare.

"We're, uh... mechanized infantry. We ride around in Bradleys and Humvees."

"Oh." Tobiri sounds a little disappointed. "Have you been overseas?"

"Yeah, a year in Iraq, and when I am done here, I get to go back and do it all over again."

"Really? I'm sure you can teach me a lot about the infantry then," Tobiri humbly states before adding, "I am glad I have you as my ranger buddy."

"All right! That's enough!" A gruff speaking RI interrupts everyone's meet and greet. "You love birds can share your bedtime secrets later, on your own time. Company... Atten-shun! "

As we stiffen our spines and pin our arms to our sides, three more Ranger Instructors appear out of nowhere and arrange themselves menacingly around us.

"This is when the fun begins, rangers! Open your bags and dump 'em, all of them, on the ground. Yes, all of them, rangers! Go ahead, empty your duffle bags, turn out your pockets, take off your soft caps, everything you've got! All of it, in the dirt, let's go!"

The RIs are conducting a layout, the first of many brutal and stressful layouts in Ranger School. They want to see if the students have brought along all the required items listed in a detailed, four-page packing list. If we have neglected to bring even one necessary item, we can be instantly dismissed from the course. I have two large Army-issue duffel bags packed near to bursting with uniforms, cold weather gear, combat boots, t-shirts, socks, notepads, pens, batteries, and a hundred other miscellaneous items. I have checked and re-checked that I have everything on the list multiple times, I am 99.99% certain I have everything, but I am still intensely nervous that somehow, something got lost or stolen along the way.

The RIs are also looking for extra items that are not on the packing list. All such items are presumed to be unauthorized and viewed with suspicion, while others are strictly forbidden.

"If you have contraband, meaning cigarettes, chewing tobacco, snuff, tobacco in any other form, alcohol, coffee, stackers or other diet pills, caffeinated gum, unauthorized prescription medication, illegal drugs, cell phones, outside food or drink, books, magazines, newspapers, or anything else that you know or even think you should not have, now is the time to give it up. No questions asked, rangers, as long as you do it now. This is your one-and-only amnesty period, utilize it men! All contraband can be placed in the receptacle located to my right."

In response to this warning, every fourth or fifth ranger starts nervously shuffling around amongst their piles of gear and clothing, anxiously fingering concealed cans of chewing tobacco and cigarettes.

"Should I toss it now or keep it?" The nicotine-dependent rangers have a hard choice to make. A handful of them accept the RIs offer of amnesty, depositing cans of Copenhagen Long-Cut and Marlboro cigarettes into the box, but others resolve to hold onto their illicit stores, at least for now, reasoning that it is worth the risk.

"Anyone else?" The RI asks us after a few moments. "I know some of you are holding out on me."

No one in Charlie Company makes a move.

"Well then, rangers, from this moment forward, if contraband is discovered, you will recycle or be removed outright from the course. This is your last chance, rangers, five, four, three..."

Beads of cold sweat hit the ground, but no one makes a move.

"... two... one. All right, then, rangers." The word "rangers" exits the RIs mouth with obvious contempt. "Let's get this party started. Hold up four ACU or BDU shirts. I said hold them up! High over your heads! Let's go!"

The former contents of our duffel bags, hundreds of items for seventy-five rangers, are heaped in great, disordered piles on the ground. After the Ranger Instructor calls out an item on the packing list we frantically search through our mounds, grab it, and hold it up over our heads. After one of several RIs arrayed around us confirms our possession of the item, they signal us to throw the item back into our duffel bags.

"You all move like nuns fuck! Hurry... Up! We do not have time for this shit! Flashlight with red lens, hold it up now!"

Hundreds of items need to be checked and, according to the RIs, we are short on time. Every man in Charlie must locate and display every item demanded by the RI within seconds. The slightest delay or inability to locate an item results in shouts, threats, and invariably a brutal "smoking" as if we were back in infantry boot camp.

"Rangers, you have five seconds to hold your flashlights up. Five, four, three... you know what, just get down, all of you, just get down. Front leaning rest position, MOVE!"

The RIs cannot hit us, not anymore, but they can collectively punish us by making all of us do endless calisthenic exercises while verbally abusing us. The RIs push us far past muscle failure with repeated sets of push-ups, flutter kicks, mountain climbers, and Hello Dollies. It makes the weak ones amongst us want to quit.

"On your feet, rangers." We clamber clumsily to our feet again, muscles quivering, lungs aching. "Hold up eight, yes count them eight, T-shirts. Hurry the fuck up, rangers! Lots to do today!"

Have to find eight T-shirts! I scream to myself. Four, five, six, seven... goddamnit! Where is my eighth T-shirt!

"Hurry... the... fuck... up... rangers! Goddamnit, I said 'HURRY!' It should not take this long to pull out eight T-shirts. You know what, just get down and push... everyone, push! Yeah, that means you too, shit-for-brains! You goofy motherfucker! Get the fuck down and push! 1, 2, 3..."

The RIs keep stressing that we are dangerously short on time, but it seems that for every other item on the packing list, we are dropped to the ground for five or ten minutes of physical torment. We beat our faces into the ground and pump our legs beneath us like pistons. Great puddles of sweat form beneath us, sharp gravel digs into our palms. We wince with pain and self-pity while questioning our life choices. Meanwhile, the RIs continue to berate us, insult our manhood, and dare the cowards amongst us to quit. Throughout all this chaos, our piles of gear and clothing become increasingly mixed up with our neighbors.

"Push ups, go!" We assume a plank position and start moving our chests up and down. "Flutter kicks, go!" We turn onto our backs and move our legs up and down. "Mountain climbers, go!" We get back on our hands and knees and start climbing a steep, imaginary peak. "Push ups, go!" We get back into plank position and start beating our faces into the ground again, and on and on it goes.

I have been through some arduous layouts in my three years in the infantry, but this is proving to be the worst yet. The RIs seem to enjoy keeping up the pressure and torturing us. It all seems so unnecessary, unjust even, because if they just took a calmer approach to it, it would be done in half-an-hour. But that appears not to be the point.

The point they are hammering home is this: it doesn't matter who we are, what rank we have, or where we came from, the Ranger Instructors, the ones with the Tabs, are the bosses here. The rest of us are all equally worthless.

"All right, fuck sticks. On your feet! Gore-Tex cold weather boots, one pair. Hold them up, high over your head's rangers!"

"This is fucking stupid." I overhear a slim, short-statured, baby-faced soldier from the Ranger Regiment mutter as he brushes off dirt and gravel from his backside. "My team leader never told me it would be this dumb." His name tape says "LEON." He is a second-generation Cuban American from Florida and, as I will shortly learn, he is fond of cursing and telling stories of striking people in Iraq with the barrel of his rifle, what he affectionately calls "muzzle thumping."

"I hear you, Leon, but keep your voice down." Newton, a handsome, broad-shouldered, and square-jawed twenty-year-old, also from the Ranger

Tribes of Ranger School

The "Bat Boys" - Private First Classes and Specialists from the 75th Ranger Regiment - young, fit, unbreakable, and aggressive, if immature and arrogant; many have a combat tour or two with their Ranger Battalion; there is no quit in them and they stick togther; easily one-third or more of a typical Ranger School class.

Lieutenants or "LTs" - Newly commissioned officers and recent graduates of various branch training courses, mostly infantry, but also some engineer, tanker, and cavalry scout lieutenants. Another third of the class, in the main, the LTs are older, wiser, and better planners than the other ranger students; however, most have little field experience and no combat experience.

Special Forces - The storied "Green Berets," long-tab wearing, snake-eating, operators . . . some of the finest trained, most highly skilled, and experienced men the Army has to offer. They attend Ranger School in small numbers, with most squads having one or two. Purportedly accustomed to deprivation and suffering, they are the most respected and trusted students in Ranger School, true badasses and capable dudes, for the most part . . . .

Ranger Instructors or "RIs" - The instructors, guides, evaluators, and bosses of Ranger School. Generally senior non-commissioned officers with a smattering of officers, all of whom have earned their Tabs, they are equal parts tormentor, teacher, disciplinarian, nemesis, manipulator, and mentor to the ranger students. They are with us 18-22 hours of the day, teaching us, shepherding us, hazing us, putting us under stress, seeing if we have what it takes to be rangers.

And finally, the Randoms - Everyone else in Ranger School, a motley assortment of paratroopers, aged non-commissiooned officers, airmen, Marines, outright POGs (support soldiers) like cooks, logistics, and ordinance officers, and, of course, me, a non-airborne infantryman from a mechanized infantry company. Renegades without a larger tribe to adhere to, the randoms are a mixed-bag, some are popular and well-liked, others are friendless outcastes. Many are doomed to failure.

Regiment whispers back as he thrusts his boots over his head. "Just remember what we are here for and who we represent."

The soldiers from the elite 75th Ranger Regiment, most of whom are still in their teens, are the most populous, motivated, and easily the most arrogant residents of Ranger School. Collectively known as "bat boys," because they come from the three Ranger Battalions, it is a nickname they carry with pride and distinction, as they repeatedly demonstrate to the rest of us. Generally, they are extremely physically fit, loud-mouthed, and intensely devoted to each other. They are vetted and highly trained members of the world's most elite light infantry unit, Airborne Rangers, and arguably, the best prepared students at the course. Long steeped in the ranger tradition and coached by team and squad leaders who have already earned their Tabs, they are well informed about the school's demands, tasks, and schedule. They have also already completed the Ranger Regiment Pre-Ranger course, commonly considered an extra phase of Ranger School, to better prepare themselves.

There are four bat boys in our squad: Leon and Newton, who have already formed a tight bond with each other, and Jenson and Salvador, who are equally thick as thieves. Jenson is tall, lanky, brown-haired, and slightly buck-toothed, a good-old-boy with a deep-southern accent and coarse manners. After knowing him for only a few hours, I already detest him. Salvador, in contrast, is a short, stocky second-generation Puerto Rican from Brooklyn. More friendly and laid-back than the average bat boy, he stands out for having a large, highly visible skull in a sombrero tattooed on his neck. Both have already been at Ranger School for months. This is Jenson's second attempt at RAP Week and Salvador's third.

The bat boys have compelling reasons to stay in the course. You are not a real "ranger" in the 75th Ranger Regiment, and cannot command troops at any level, until you have earned your Ranger Tab. What's more, they will not be able to stay in their elite units if they return without earning their Tabs. Failing the school and getting kicked out of their beloved Regiment, being banished from their tribe and stripped of their identity, is a fate worse

Ranger Regiment vs. Ranger Tab

Ranger Regiment	Ranger Tab
• Member of the 75th Ranger Regiment, an elite airborne light infantry and special forces unit.	• Graduate of US Army Ranger School, the Army's preeminent leadership and small unit tactics course.
• Assigned to a Ranger Battalion: training and deploying overseas to conduct ranger operations to kill and capture our nation's enemies.	• Ranger-qualified leaders serving throughout the army in many types of special forces, conventional infantry, and even non-infantry units.
• Members wear the tan beret and the Ranger Scroll, earned after passing the Ranger Regiment selection program.	• After successful completion of Ranger School, graduates wear the Ranger Tab on their left shoulder.
• Must be airborne qualified to be in the Ranger Regiment.	• Usually airborne qualified, but not required.
• The only "real rangers," at least, according to the bat boys.	• Also a "ranger," but with humility and deference owed to the badasses of the Ranger Regiment.
• Composed of three battalions of airborne light infantry, two formed in 1974 and the third in 1984.	• Ranger School and the Ranger Tab were established in 1951 during the Korean War.
• A Scroll and Tab wearing member of the Ranger Regiment is a "made" man, a leader of elite soldiers in one of the preeminent military units in the world.	• A Tab wearing ranger is accorded deference and respect Army wide and expected to look, act, and lead like a ranger.

ANDREW GOLDSMITH | 15

than death to the typical bat boy. Accordingly, no one has more to lose in Ranger School than the bat boys and they are committed to stay the course, no matter how long it takes or how stupid things get.

As much as I hate to admit it, despite their immaturity and obvious contempt for the rest of us, the bat boys are pretty badass, and I respect them greatly.

"All right, fuck sticks, hold up two polypro shirts, that's right, two polypro shirts... hurry the fuck up, rangers. You have five seconds before I will drop you again!"

"Man... they're just being stupid on purpose." I overhear Fulton, the squad's lone green beret muttering as he shakes his head and holds up two polypro shirt tops. "Whatever. Play the game, man. Only sixty more days and a wake up."

The bat boys may be badass, but to an ordinary infantryman like me, the handful of Special Forces soldiers in our company, the "green berets," are legends, and I hold them in awe. Army Special Forces soldiers come to Ranger School to better learn small unit infantry tactics, hone their leadership skills, help their promotion prospects, and further set themselves apart as some of the world's best-trained and most elite soldiers.

The green berets here at Ranger School are primarily younger buck and staff sergeants in their twenties. Many, but not all of them, have combat tours to Iraq and Afghanistan under their belts. They are phenomenally well trained and presumably more inured to hardship than the rest of us, even the bat boys. Many of us assume their experiences in special forces selection, training, and combat will make their time at Ranger School easier to handle and that compared to the rest of us, they will cruise through the course.

But this belief, like many of our assumptions in Ranger School, would prove to be mistaken.

Even the bat boys respect Fulton who, they whisper, is a staff sergeant medic in a Special Forces Alpha Team. He bears himself like many in his tribe, quiet and aloof, rarely talking to the rest of us, and seeking companionship with his own kind. Fulton is tall and lean, moves swiftly and silently, betrays little emotion, and usually wears a subtle, knowing grin on his relaxed, youthful face. His eyes, when one can see them through the brim of his lowered soft cap, are wide open and intelligent.

By spontaneous and unspoken consensus, Fulton is recognized as the squad's leader and role model. I feel honored to be attending a course with someone like him.

"M4 magazines, seven, hold them up." The RIs patience grows increasingly thin as the layout extends past an hour. "Seven fucking mags, damn it! Hold 'em up, right now!"

As I hold up seven rifle magazines, I can see Lieutenants Tobiri and Sven rummaging around frantically through their piles in search of their own.

"Oh!" The RI grasps his heart with false indignation. "Looks like two lieutenants who don't have their magazines in order, imagine that."

The RI leading the layout, a sergeant first class with over ten years of service, would usually have to defer and salute to these newly minted commissioned officers, but here, in Ranger School, where rank does not matter, he can berate them as he sees fit.

"Do you butter bars have seven magazines or not?"

Tobiri and Sven stare dumbly and meekly back at the RI before continuing to rummage through their piles. Wisely, they choose to remain silent.

"How in the fuck are you supposed to lead men in combat when you can't even properly pack a duffle bag? My heart weeps for the future of the Army." Again, the RI mock clutches his non-existent heart. "Goddamnit, we don't have time for this! Front-leaning rest position... MOVE!"

Leon moans out, "Fucking LTs!" as every man in Charlie Company grumbles for the twentieth time as we drop down to our hands and knees again.

Other than the bat boys, second and first lieutenants, or "LTs," form the second largest contingent at Ranger School, about a third of the class. These college-educated young men are the "nobility" of the modern U.S. Army, they are its future platoon leaders, company commanders, and field-grade officers. Coming straight out of several months-long training schools like the Infantry Basic Officer Leader Course, most have little experience with the real Army outside of the schoolhouse. Almost none have combat experience.

The vast majority of the LTs are in the infantry branch, but there is a smattering of engineers, tankers, and other branches scattered throughout the class. The LTs tend to be older than the average ranger student, usually being in their mid to late twenties, with some even pushing thirty. While short on practical army and combat experience, the LTs bring a welcome level of maturity and intelligence to the course.

Infantry LTs have little choice and are expected to attend Ranger School as preparation for leading a platoon of infantrymen in combat. A Tab significantly increases their odds of commanding a platoon after arriving at their units, rather than riding a desk as a staff officer. The Tab is also useful for gaining the instant respect of their men, an acceptable substitute for experience and shared hardships.

Our squad has three lieutenants, Tobiri and Sven, both combat engineers, and Dale, the twenty-year-old boy wonder infantry officer. Dale is well-spoken, confident, intelligent, and motivated. He graduated high school at sixteen and obtained his bachelor's degree in political science as well as a commission in the U.S. Army in his nineteenth year. Now, after preparing for years, he has his chance to live out a life-long dream by attending Ranger School and earning his Tab.

Standing well over six-feet, Dale is tall, lean, has pale white skin with dark freckles on his face, and black hair stubble. He looks older than his tender age of twenty and speaks clearly, slowly, often in a dull monotone. Few of us in the squad have any doubts that he will be a judge or a senator one day. Like many in the squad, I instantly dislike him.

Our squad has another officer, McCormick, a thirty-five-year-old staff Captain from a Special Forces group. McCormick is the old man of the squad and many of his colleagues have questioned the wisdom of his attending Ranger School so late in his Army career. Not only does he have a wife and kids at home, he is nearly twice as old as some of the bat boys and a rare non-infantry or combat arms soldier, also known derogatively as a "pog," or person other than grunt. Other than intensely clear and expressive blue-gray eyes, there is nothing remarkable about McCormick's appearance. He is of average height and build with sandy blond hair and beard stubble.

Right now, after five minutes of flutter kicks with no rest, McCormick is increasingly inclined to agree with his colleagues. But though there are far easier ways in life to have a midlife crisis, McCormick is resolved to conquer the Ranger School challenge.

"Recover! That means, on your feet shitbags! Let's go! One headlamp, optional… Hold it up if you got it. High over your heads, rangers."

After surveying the men arrayed around me, there is no doubt that I am a lone infantryman cast adrift in a sea of bat boys, lieutenants, and green berets. I am a member of a small, silent minority; with no connections, no relationships, and few advantages over anyone else. Nearly everyone else can rely on other members of their tribe to help them through the challenging days ahead. They have pre-existing networks and knowledge imparted by others who have charted a similar path. As the lone regular grunt in my squad, however, I have no friends or allies, and worse yet, I know nothing.

More importantly, each member of these groups has individual and communal reasons for being here, for enduring the inevitable struggle and suffering to come. If the bat boys fail the course, they will get kicked out of their beloved Regiment. The LTs, they will ride a desk instead of commanding a platoon, grounding their Army career before it can even get started. The green berets, they'll suffer raised eyebrows and reputational harm in an elite organization where reputation truly matters.

But me, I am still not really sure why I am even here. I came here with three weeks notice because of a lucky break. All I know is, whatever the challenge, I must keep going, as long and as far I can, even if it means enduring something as stupid as this layout.

Fortunately for me, and as the coming days will prove, Ranger School does not really care about which tribe we come from and who we were before we came here. As we pack up the last of our items into our duffel bags, and an RI drops us to the ground, to the push-up position for the hundredth time, he delivers one final message.

"Start pushing, rangers, and don't count off this time. Now listen, I want you all to get it through your pea-sized brains that it does not matter who you are in the big Army or what elite unit or high-speed schoolhouse you just came from. I don't give a rat's ass if you are an absolute legend at your unit, I don't care how many terrorist cocksuckers you've killed, and I give less than two shits about the fact that outside of this course, I may have to salute you and call you 'Sir.' Airborne Ranger, Green Beret, Lieutenant-fucking-Jerk-Off, son of the famous General 'Who-Gives-A-Shit,' none of it matters to me, or anyone else here. The fact of the matter is you are all equally worthless tab-less losers. All of you will be judged the same way, to the same standards, and under the same conditions. Understand, rangers?"

"Roger, Sergeant!" The Company grunts in unison, our arms quivering and our foreheads dripping sweat.

The RIs speech somehow makes me feel a little better. I am alone, I am nothing, but in a way, so is everybody else.

"Enough of this. On your feet!" The RI abruptly shouts out. "Rangers, you have," he looks at his watch, "one minute to stow away any remaining gear. Then, you will sling your bags onto your back and prepare to follow me. Get ready to move out."

Thank the ranger gods, I tell myself. After more than two hours of frantic movement, collective punishment, and public humiliation from the RIs, the hellish layout is over. Only two rangers out of seventy-five in Charlie Company failed to bring all the required items on the packing list. One of the RIs pulls them aside and walks them over to the Recycle barracks.

Now that we have finished the layout, it is time to collect even more gear, this time it is "TA-50," the decades-old basic issue of rucksacks, load-bearing equipment, pouches, Kevlar helmets and other patrol gear that will practically become a part of ourselves in the coming weeks. We are also individually issued Ranger Handbooks, the master text of Ranger School and the infantry Bible, which we are expected to carry on our persons, at all times.

The sun is high in the sky by the time the supply sergeant finishes the gear issue. The RIs tell us to hurriedly drop off our duffel bags and rucksacks back at the barracks. They then march the entire class off to an open clearing in front of long rows of bleachers. We take our seats, packed tightly together shoulder to shoulder, as another gray-haired, angular-jawed, stiff-backed, and scary-looking colonel steps up to a podium.

"ON YOUR FEET!" An RI yells out loudly.

Two-hundred-and-ninety rangers shoot up to the position of attention.

"Good afternoon, men, or should I say, rangers. Take your seats. Welcome to Ranger School. I hope my RIs have been showing you a good time."

He smiles and pans his eyes across the class, but few of us chuckle.

"A serious crowd, huh? Good, just the way I like it. Now, I want all of you to look to your left... Go on, do it..."

When I turn to the left, I see my ranger buddy, Tobiri. He gives me a nod and a small smirk.

"Good, now, look to your right..."

To my right is Fulton, the green beret. He nods his head up and down and gives me a thumbs up.

"Good. Now, of the three of you," the colonel continues, "at least one and maybe two of you will not pass this course."

This colonel's speech is not as motivational as the first colonels was.

"That's because there are many ways to fail, gentlemen. You can no-go a RAP week event, screw up your patrols, piss off your buddy and fail Peers, mouth off to one of my instructors, have a negligent discharge, earn too many major- or minor-minuses, commit a safety violation, recycle any phase more than once..."

The old salt shows no signs of slowing down.

"You could lose a sensitive item, get injured or pick up an infection, accumulate too much sick call time, miss too much training, fight another student, fall asleep pulling security, get caught with contraband, eat unauthorized foods or outside of authorized mealtimes, fail to complete the course within six months..."

And then the kicker.

"... or just turn yellow and quit."

The colonel spits this last one out with obvious distaste.

"Yes, rangers, there are many ways to fail Ranger School. Committing any of the above enumerated offenses will at a minimum cause you to recycle a phase, risk a Day One recycle, or even cause your removal from the course outright."

He forgot to add, "covered in shame."

"But many of you can succeed," the colonel's voice suddenly changes in tone, "and many of you will succeed if you stay the course, remember where you came from, and keep faith in yourselves, and your classmates. Those who really want their Tabs, those who earn them, every single day, will become rangers. Is that understood, men?"

"Yes, Sir!" The entire class shouts.

"Outstanding! Well then, Ranger Instructors, prepare these men for the Combat Water Survival Test."

"ON YOUR FEET!" An RI shouts out again. We rise and stand at the position of attention as Colonel #2 walks off out of sight.

"You heard the colonel, rangers! Form up by companies and prepare to move out!"

We march the short distance to Victory Pond, the location of the second pass-fail event of RAP Week, the Combat Water Survival Test.

If you can swim, are not unduly afraid of the water, and can at least hide your fear of tall heights, then the water test is no big deal. The tasks themselves are not that difficult, so long as the ranger can look confident and self-assured while doing them. The RIs are watching us closely to make sure we do not panic during any portion of the test. If we do, we can be instantly cut from the course.

Knowing how to swim and not fear the water is important, because Ranger School will have us traversing swamps and marshlands, walking neck deep through streams and rivers, and moving at night during winter thunderstorms. Several rangers have died of drowning in the past, four during one tragic day in 1995, those who are weak swimmers need to be weeded out early, before they become a danger to themselves.

Charlie is the last company to go through the test. After I have been standing around for an hour-and-a-half, it is finally my turn to climb hand-over-hand up a thirty-foot, narrow, rebar metal ladder that brings me to the top of a platform perched over Victory Pond. Here, I am presented with a long, thin balancing log to walk across.

It is difficult to keep my balance as I walk across the log as well as the narrow stairs awkwardly placed in the middle of it. Two RIs yell at me to move quickly across the obstacle while simultaneously taunting me about being scared and falling into the waters below.

For a few seconds, I almost lose my balance and sway nervously over the abyss, but according to Newton, a bat boy who knows these types of things, it is practically impossible for someone to lose their balance and tumble into the pond below. Something inside most of us will simply not allow it to happen. Few, if any, rangers in each class will actually fall off the log, one merely has to look forward and walk confidently.

And that is what I do. Like every other ranger in the class today, I make it across the log beam without falling, and heave a sigh of relief. The hard part done, I gorilla hang from a thick manila rope, slide my body a few meters along it to touch a large wooden Ranger Tab, hang from my palms for a moment, ask an RI's permission to drop, and then await his command to do so. With the RI's consent, I plummet twenty-some feet into the chill waters of Victory Pond.

The second part of the test requires that I swim less than the length of a pool on my side carrying a rubber rifle above the water. It is easy for those who can swim, but soon after I finish, I see a ranger several students behind me panic and toss his weapon into the pond. He even requires the assistance of an RI to get out of the water. He is instantly kicked out of the course.

The third and final task is "The Slide for Life," a pulley-operated zipline that has us flying above the surface of Victory Pond connected to a 200-foot-long rope cable. We climb another narrow, rebar ladder to get to the starting platform. A single RI is there at the top to give us some brief instructions. He concludes by telling me, "Don't fuck up or you can die," before telling me to grab the handles and "Go! Go! Go!"

I fly fast along the steel cable, legs dangling in the air, high above the surface of the water. For a few seconds, I feel nothing but exhilaration and pure joy, like I'm invincible even. Then an RI on the shoreline waves some brightly colored flags. I raise up my legs parallel to the surface of the water, just as the other RI instructed. The RI waves the flags again. I release my grip on the handles and plunge into the water below.

I must have done it correctly because I emerge from the water unhurt, and no one is yelling at me.

Back on shore, I shiver in my soaking wet uniform and boots and slowly drip dry. It is a crisp October afternoon, and the sun is going down. But despite the chill, I feel cleansed, invigorated, and for the first time today, truly awake. I soak up the sun's final warming rays as the last rangers go through the swim test. Soon enough, it dips below the horizon, signaling the end of our first day of Ranger School.

And I am still here. For now, at least, the ranger gods are smiling down on me.

But I am fooling myself. The day is far from over, rangers train through the night. After a hot dinner in the chow hall, which I ravenously devour without leaving a scrap of food, two RIs order us to the barracks to give us some instruction on land navigation. This is in preparation for tomorrow morning's first pass-or-fail event: the land navigation course. After the PT test, this event has the highest failure rate in RAP Week.

This is followed by several hours confusedly preparing, fixing, modifying, and tying down our rucksacks and load-bearing vest in accordance with vague and contradictory standards laid down by, and then repeatedly changed, by the RIs.

By the time Charlie Company finally finishes tying down our gear it is past midnight. Only then do the Ranger Instructors finally leave our barracks for good. Before they do, they order us to conduct basic hygiene before bedding down for the night. Jenson and a few other long-haired bat boys shave their heads with two sets of clippers that run continuously for close to an hour. Someone draws up a "fireguard roster," a list composed of sixteen pissed-off rangers who have been selected to pull successive two-man, fifteen-minute guard shifts through the remaining hours of the night. It takes more than an hour for the bulk of Charlie Company to finally clamber into their bunks and settle down for sleep.

It is 1:30 a.m. when some blessed, considerate soul finally turns the lights off.

1:30! Dear God! I despair in the darkness. Wake up is 3:00 a.m. tomorrow. I'll be lucky to get one-and-a-half hours of sleep tonight!

Oh well, I sigh and take a deep breath, just like last night, I guess.

But despite the lack of sleep, I remain optimistic. I have passed almost effortlessly through the first day of Ranger School. I have already seen dozens of others fail where I have succeeded, my body is healthy and sound, and I was lucky enough not to draw a guard shift tonight. I may be physically exhausted, mere seconds from deep, dreamless sleep, but for a few seconds, I am truly happy.

Day One of Ranger School is done, and I, the most mediocre of infantrymen, am still here. Maybe I have what it takes to survive here, maybe I can actually earn my Tab, maybe, just maybe, I belong.

Little did I know, we were just getting started.

Chapter 2: "RAP Week"

Rule #4: Do not excel; do the bare minimum.
Rule #5: Take care of your feet.

0354 Hours (3:54 a.m.)
Camp Rogers Training Area
Fort Benning, Georgia
Day 2 of Ranger School
Hours of sleep in the last forty-eight hours: 3 hours

Two-hundred-and-eighty-five rangers sit on the cold ground, just off a dirt trail, shivering in the night's darkness. We all bob our heads sleepily, most of us losing the battle to stay awake. The sun will not rise for several more hours. I am desperately tired after only getting three hours of sleep in the last two nights but the butterflies in my stomach manage to keep me semi-conscious.

It is officially Day Two of Ranger School, and the first assigned task is the land navigation course, where I will be tested on my ability to use a compass and map to navigate through the woods.

"Land nav" has never been my strong suit and in fact, at my unit back home, I have a bit of a reputation for getting lost.

I do not despair, however, instead I decide to focus on the basics. I think back upon my land nav training in boot camp, at my unit, and last night, the fundamental skills: orienting the map, getting a compass reading, dead reckoning, pace counts, terrain association, and all the rest. I hope it will be enough to pass this course.

Despite my anxiety and the harsh cold, it is growing increasingly difficult to keep my eyelids open. I slip inexorably to sleep, my head resting on the back of my folded arms.

Two minutes later, at 3:58 a.m., the murmurs and whispers of other rangers briefly wakes me from my slumber, but then I fall asleep again.

A minute after that, at 3:59 a.m., an RI standing close by shouts out, "On your feet, rangers. Prepare to begin the land navigation course." Other RIs start handing out packets of papers to all of us.

"Remember rangers, anyone caught talking from here on out until he finishes the land nav course," the RI sternly reminds us, "will not only fail RAP Week, but he will be kicked out of Ranger School for good on an honor violation. Is that clear, rangers?"

They don't want us to cheat. We must find our own points and cannot check our answers against anyone else. We grunt and nod our heads affirmatively as we tighten our boot laces and adjust the primitive GPS tracking harnesses we wear over our uniforms.

"Go ahead and open your packets," the RI tells us. "You should have a map, the grid coordinates to five points, and a space to record the code associated with those points. Go ahead and find your points, rangers. You have four hours to do it. Go!"

Time is ticking, but before I move off heedlessly into the woods, I sit down to plot the location of points two, seven, eleven, sixteen, and twenty-three on my map, and then select the best route to find them.

I pull out my old-fashioned army flashlight for the first time and turn it on. It has a special lens on it so that all that comes out is red light, which is supposedly more difficult for other people to see in the darkness. The only time we are allowed to use our flashlights during the course is when we are sitting or standing absolutely still, either checking our maps, taking a compass reading, or reading the code off the point placards. If we walk with the flashlight on, and an RI sees us, we will instantly fail the course.

It only takes a few minutes to plot my points and one minute more to decide on the quickest route to find the four closest points. I have no illusions about collecting the fifth point. Locating the fifth point would earn me a minor-plus, and this tempts the most motivated and cocksure of us rangers, but I am seasoned enough to know that a smart ranger does only the bare minimum to pass each task, and no more. During RAP Week at least, the goal is to be mediocre.

And being mediocre is something I can do.

Most of my peers have already left on their journey by the time I rise, take one last compass reading, and plunge into the murky woods to find my first and closest point, point number eleven.

It is still very dark in the Fort Benning woods at four in the morning, and we are not using night vision. I must rely solely on my natural sight and other senses to briskly, yet cautiously, travel cross-country through unfamiliar woods, over and through brush, around tree roots, up and over small hills, ridgelines, and depressions. I must avoid any roadways, trails, or paths I happen to stumble upon, as utilizing any established route is yet another way to fail.

To know how much distance I have traveled, I count every other step. When my count reaches seventy-two, I know I have walked approximately one hundred meters. This is called keeping a "pace count." Along with frequent compass readings, it allows me to "dead reckon" my way to my first point, only eight hundred meters, half a mile, from the course start point.

As I get closer to where the first point should be, I grow increasingly worried that it may be difficult to locate the exact point placard in this darkness. After all, I have no idea what it will look like and, according to the bat boy rumor mill, the RIs will sometimes conceal or move certain points to make them more difficult to spot.

But I do not worry for long. By the time I get to within one hundred meters of my first point, I see two or three red flashlight beams bobbing and weaving on some object ahead of me.

That's about where my point should be, my slow, sleep-deprived brain says, then it dawns on me. Hey! That must be my first point! I waste no time in rushing off excitedly towards the light beams.

And bless the ranger gods, it is point number eleven! After waiting behind two other rangers who were there before me, I turn on my red-lens flashlight and write down the point's code on my answer sheet. I then step off to the side to consult my map and compass to find the next point.

Soon, I am off again, walking in the darkness. Before I go too far, I see another collection of red-light beams dancing around something two-hundred meters to the left of my position.

My ass you can't see red light in the darkness, I think to myself. It sure

ANDREW GOLDSMITH | 27

made it easy to find that first point...

It is at that moment that a brilliant plan forms in my mind.

The sun won't be up for another hour-and-a-half, at least. Screw a strict-pace count! I need to move faster, while it's still dark. There is no reason I cannot knock out another point, or even two, just like I took care of that last one. I just need to get somewhat close to my point, and then, in this darkness, the red light of my competent peers will do the rest.

There is no time to waste, I must move fast if I want to capitalize on the darkness. All I need to do is get close, perhaps one hundred or two hundred meters away from each point, and then, simply walk towards the light.

I start running the course, racing against the sunrise, covering ground twice as fast as I was before. I move nimbly around brush, over tree roots, and up and down hillsides. I dodge pine trees, large and small, battering away their branches and twigs with my forearms. It is pitch black and not yet five-thirty-in-the-morning, but I am wide awake now, and even having a little fun.

And miraculously, the plan works. I am about a hundred meters away from point number twenty-three when I see the warm, reassuring glow of two red-lens flashlights. They guide me straight to the point placard. It says "23" in large black letters. I have now collected half my points, I have two-and-a-half hours more to collect two more.

My third point is a little less than a mile away. Jogging at a good pace, I make it there in less than half an hour.

Hot damn, I'm killing this thing! I tell myself as I jot down the code for point number sixteen on my answer sheet. Only one more to go and I still have two hours! But unfortunately, the horizon is beginning to lighten up with the rapidly approaching sunrise. Like the other rangers, I stow away my now useless flashlight. I am going to have to find my fourth and final point on my own, the proper way.

I start walking, not running, again, keeping an accurate pace count, taking frequent map and compass checks, ensuring that I do not veer off course. I carefully travel the twelve hundred meters to where I think my fourth point, number seven, is located.

Yet, I am dismayed upon my arrival to see nothing but a small, empty clearing with no sign of a point placard.

Oh, no! How did I miss the point?! I scream at myself. It should be right here, or close by, or maybe over there ... Damn it!

I do not allow myself to despair long, quickly I start weighing my options.

Should I start fanning out in circles around the area? Or perhaps the wisest course is to just chalk this point up as a loss and go try to find the fifth point instead?

But to do that I have to know where I am, and I cannot even be sure of that now.

Damn these deceptive Ranger School maps! Despair returns. I should have trained more, I should have paid better attention to my drill sergeant, I should have studied the Ranger Handbook instead of sleeping last night, I should have...

Another ranger student stumbles into the clearing behind me, interrupting my pity party. He does not seem to notice me as checks his map and walks silently past me. He enters the wood line just past the small clearing to our front.

Crunch, crunch, crunch. I cannot see him any longer, but in the calm dawn forest quiet, I can still hear his boots stomping leaves and crashing through undergrowth. But then, after five, ten seconds, it stops. Nothing but silence.

A moment passes and it resumes. *Crunch, crunch, crunch,* the noise steadily growing louder. The ranger reemerges into the clearing again before walking silently past my position. As he passes, I see a pleased expression on his face.

Like someone who just found another point.

I dash off excitedly into the trees and, lo and behold, there it is, a placard prominently displaying "7" in bold, black letters. I drop to my knees and clasp my palms together in gratitude to the powers above before quickly jotting down the code onto my answer sheet. I had overestimated how far I had traveled. All I had to do was walk another thirty meters and I would have found it on my own.

All that matters now is that I have my four points, enough to pass the land nav course. The only thing left to do is to make it back to the start point, about a "klick," or a kilometer away, and I still have an hour and twenty minutes to do it. I banish any lingering temptations to go for that fifth, extra point as I take one final compass reading and strike a bearing for the start point.

This should be a piece of cake, and it is. After walking for five minutes, I run into and start skirting a rough dirt road that takes me almost the entire

ANDREW GOLDSMITH | 29

way back to the start point. Along with two other rangers with the same idea, I stay at least twenty meters away from the road so that the RIs cannot say I am using it.

Back at the start point, I hand in my answer sheet to the two RIs sitting at a folding table.

One of them checks my numbers against a laminated answer sheet. He makes four checkmarks and throws my sheet on top of a short stack of others.

"Nice work, ranger. You are a go at this station. Grab an MRE and hang out in that clearing over there until all your buddies come in."

Wow. Not only have I just gamed the dreaded land navigation course and finished with an hour to spare, but an RI just gave me some positive feedback and spoke to me like I was a real person. Other than the five-mile run, the land nav course was the Ranger School test I feared the most. I am pleasantly surprised and greatly relieved to put it behind me.

I am among the first dozen rangers to complete the event. I join Fulton the green beret and a few others at a prime sun-lit spot. Leaning up against a pine tree, I enjoy a leisurely meatloaf and gravy MRE breakfast, savoring every vacuum-sealed bite.

There are forty minutes left in the course when I lick the last bits of gravy off my MRE spoon and slide my patrol cap down low over my eyes. Plenty of time for a decent nap.

I am fucking doing this thing, I think to myself before drifting off into sweet slumber, I am crushing Ranger School.

A few hours later

But it is Ranger School that ends up crushing me, a few hours later, when we do Combatives in the Pit. Combatives is the Army's hand-to-hand combat fighting system, a synthesis of Brazilian jiu-jitsu, judo, striking, and weapons techniques. The Pit is an imposing 150-foot wide circular fighting arena lined with sandbags and filled with wood chips. I may love jiu-jitsu and fighting back home but there is nothing enjoyable about the brutal training in the Pit.

The RIs issue instructions and demonstrate moves from a raised demonstration area in the middle of the Pit. To warm up, they make us run laps, fireman carry our buddies, and perform flutter kicks, push-ups, and mountain climbers until we are all sweating hard and breathing heavy. Then

"The Pit"

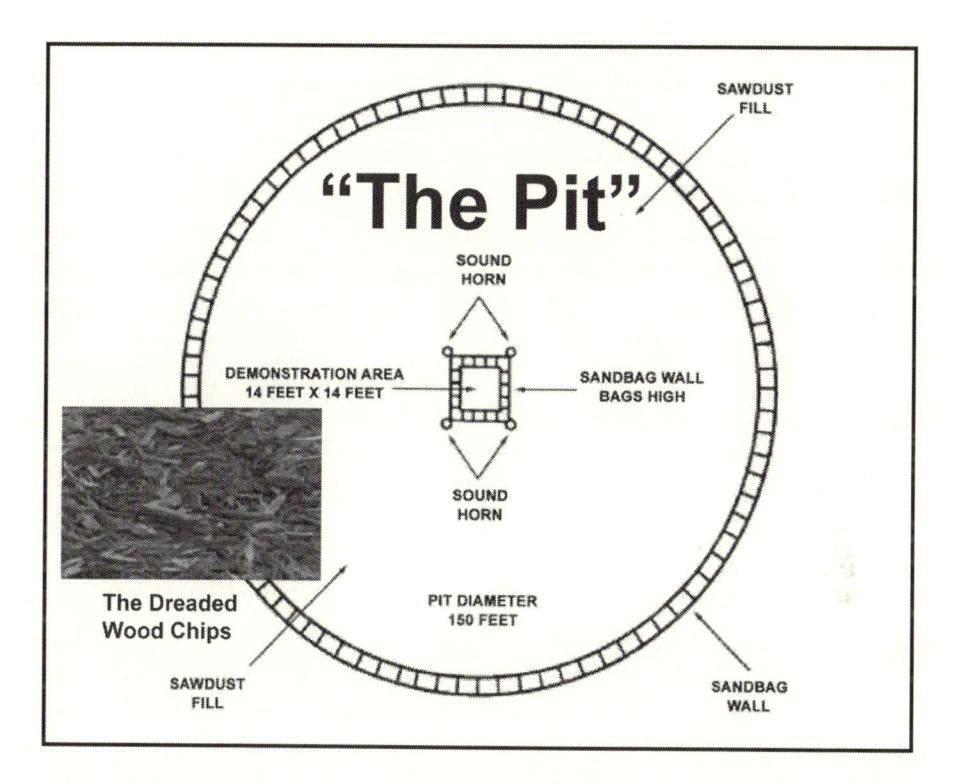

- SAWDUST FILL
- SOUND HORN
- DEMONSTRATION AREA 14 FEET X 14 FEET
- SANDBAG WALL BAGS HIGH
- SOUND HORN
- The Dreaded Wood Chips
- PIT DIAMETER 150 FEET
- SAWDUST FILL
- SANDBAG WALL

they have us crowd around the raised platform, packed as tightly together as possible, so that I can feel five or six other rangers squirming around me. They demonstrate throws, positional controls, chokes, and joint locks. They show everything two or three times before telling us to go execute it with our partners. We do the move five, ten, fifteen times, until the RI says time, and we must do it with feeling, with gusto.

Or else.

The RIs pair me up with some poor bat boy half my size. I can feel him struggling to throw my weight around, which makes me feel bad for him. On the plus side, it's easier for me to have a smaller partner and it feels good, in a petty way, to best a bat boy in something.

While it is painful to be thrown to the ground, repeatedly, especially by an unskilled and exhausted opponent, the worst part about our time in the Pit, what torments my very soul, are the translucent, nearly invisible tiny little wood chip splinters boring their way into my skin. After every throw, every crash, every scuffle in the chips, more and more of the little guys are driven into the exposed flesh of my arms, back, face, neck, legs, and stomach.

Everywhere.

Hundreds, thousands of minuscule splinters rub, burn, and itch in equal measure. The unpleasant sensation is all I can think about as I mindlessly obey the RI's commands and execute techniques on my hapless training partner. I do my best to move as little as possible to minimize the itching and pain, but under the circumstances, it is impossible.

I have never craved a shower more badly. I have gone weeks in Iraq without bathing, endured countless heat rashes and weeks of prickly heat, but never has my skin felt so miserable. One, two, three hours pass, but we keep training, without pause, other than the occasional one-minute water break. Everyone is tired, everyone is breathing hard, everyone is sore.

And the whole time, my skin feels like it is on fucking fire.

The Pit fucking sucks.

By the third hour of training, the only thought that keeps me moving forward is knowing that no matter how bad I have it, the agonies of my small-framed training partner must be worse. I hear him grunt, strain, and curse my bulk as he executes every move. I do my best to encourage him, but he does not want to hear it. Hatred leaks out of his tired, dejected eyes.

After four straight hours in the Pit, Combatives is finally over. The RIs tell us to form up by companies and march back to the barracks. The sun is just starting to go down. Every ranger in the class silently cheers. There is nothing in life I want more right now than a hot shower to wash these infernal splinters out of my skin.

But the showers can wait, the RIs have other plans for us, additional ways to keep us busy, to keep us moving, from sunup to long past sundown. First, there's chow, which I am grateful for, then we get classes from the RIs about disassembling and assembling machine guns, calling in artillery strikes, and utilizing radios, then the RIs have us practicing these skills, for hours and hours, until well past midnight.

Only then are we finally allowed to shower, and boy do we take advantage of it. By the time the last wood chip splinters are washed down the drain and everyone is dressed and in bed, it is past 1:00 a.m., again. Wake up tomorrow is at four.

Worse, tonight I have to pull a guard shift, a terrible one, too, the 1:40 a.m. to 2:00 a.m. shift. It makes little sense to try to sleep for twenty minutes before rising again, so I pull out a pocket-sized book, The Tao Te Ching, technically contraband, and read a few passages.

Soon enough, me and another accursed ranger sullenly patrol the barracks hallway, pacing up and down between the bunks of our deeply sleeping comrades. We use flashlights to see in the darkness. Time passes slowly and I am depressed at the prospect of getting less than two hours of sleep tonight, again.

But alas, we must maintain a "fireguard." It serves to ensure the barracks is not burnt down in the night, with all of us in it. Guards deter thieving, prevent suicides, and make it just a little bit harder for any ranger to run away. It also ensures that someone is awake at 4:00 a.m., to wake us up, before the RIs have to do it themselves.

The hard way.

So, I do my duty, I keep walking, slowly and silently, angry, and spiteful at my sleeping fellows, until 1:55 a.m., when I wake up the two poor rangers on the next shift.

By 2:02 a.m., they are both sitting up sleepily in their bunks. One of them gives me a head nod, meaning, "Go to sleep, we got this."

He does not need to tell me twice. Within seconds my boots are off, and I am crawling under my blanket.

God help me, I say to myself as I lay my head down, I do not think I can take too many more days like this. Are they ever going to let us sleep?

Yet, I made it through Day Two of Ranger School, in one piece, and arguably, ahead of the pack. Not only am I surviving, but other than the merciless sleep deprivation, I am thriving.

With a confident heart and a smile on my lips, I am sound asleep in seconds.

0404 Hours (4:04 a.m.)
The Barracks, Camp Rogers
Fort Benning, Georgia
Day 3 of Ranger School
Hours of Sleep in last three days: 5 hours

Waking up at 4:00 a.m. is hard, brutally hard, and only getting harder by the day. I have to will my eyelids open; they want to stay shut so badly. I am not sure how much longer my brain and body can function with this little sleep. Three years in the infantry has inured me to sleep-deprivation, but not like this. I wonder when the RIs will let us sleep more than an hour or two at night.

Maybe they never will.

The rangers of Charlie Company reluctantly embrace Day Three of Ranger School. We know the routine by now. We have twenty minutes to shave, brush our teeth, dress in our BDU or ACU camouflage fatigues, lace up our boots, grab our rucksacks, and take them outside into the chill, pre-dawn Georgia air. We arrange our rucksacks and ourselves by squads of eighteen rangers on a small, gravel- and grass-strewn parking lot in front of the barracks and await the RI's 4:30 a.m. roll call.

The RI who greets us looks as pissed off and sleepy as we are. He conducts his count quickly. Everyone is present and accounted for, meaning no one has quit and run off during the night.

"Sit on your rucksacks, rangers." He tells us. "Don't go to sleep, don't put on any snivel gear, and don't go anywhere. Roger?"

We mutter our assent depressingly. It is the only guidance the RI provides before walking away.

He leaves us there to shiver in our thin-layered uniforms in sub-forty-degree temperatures. We have nothing to do but pray for the sun to rise. Newton and Leon embrace each other under a poncho liner.

"It's not gay if you're trying to stay warm." Newton retorts to the sniggers of his fellow bat boys.

"Hurry up and wait." After an hour of pointless waiting around, Fulton the green beret starts grumbling. "I hate this regular Army bullshit."

Addressing the bat boys in the squad, Fulton says, "I thought Ranger School was supposed to be high speed or something. This is just stupid. RIs are always saying we don't have enough time in the day and, here we are, just sitting around doing nothing. Let's get on with it for Christ's sake!"

I agree with him. I am from the regular Army, which can be absurd to the tenth degree, but even I think this is stupid.

But there is nothing for us to do but shiver and wait. Finally, after an hour-and-a-half in the cold, multiple RIs appear and march us a short distance away to the Malvesti Obstacle Course.

Obstacle courses are undoubtedly what most civilians and even many army folks imagine when they think of Ranger School. This one starts with six pullups before climbing up and over a high log fence without ropes. Then we enter and navigate the "worm pit," a muddy water obstacle covered by knee-high barbed wire, which we crawl through on our backs and bellies. Then we cross over another deep mud pit by going hand over hand on slippery, hard-to-grasp monkey bars. Then we climb a large cargo net and slide down a rope onto the ground on the other side. The course concludes as it started, with six more slow, underhand pullups.

No one in Charlie Company fails the obstacle course. Another task is completed, and we are one step closer to the Tab. The chill air, water, and exertion has me feeling invigorated and motivated, ready to take on whatever the day has to throw at me.

After breakfast and several hours of training and testing on basic infantry skills, the rangers who failed yesterday's land navigation course, about one third of the class, are separated from the rest of us and marched off for their second and last attempt at it, this time in broad daylight. They look nervous and glum. They know that if they fail again, they will recycle and be held over three weeks until the next phase can begin, if they are lucky.

I am happy, smug even, knowing that I will not be joining them, that is, until we are told by the RIs to change into tennis shoes and remove our belts, which can only mean one thing...

"Oh yeah! Hurry the fuck up, rangers!" An RI laughs at our misfortune. "Time for more Combatives in the Pit. Let's go!"

Oh wretched day! Four more hours in the Pit, we are less than thrilled. This time the RIs even pull-out stun guns to use on each other. "Simulated bladed weapon training," they call it, but I think they just like watching us shock each other.

Soon enough, after getting covered in splinters again and sporting a freshly bloodied lip, I am envious of the guys re-testing land nav.

Two hours later, the eighty rangers who re-tested land nav march past the Pit. They halt and split into two groups. Half of them join us in the Pit, the others are marched off to the Recycle barracks. Our class is now down to two-hundred-and-forty rangers.

Just like yesterday, we do not get to shower after Combatives. Instead, the splinters stay in our skin the rest of the evening while we pack and repeatedly lay out our rucksacks for tomorrow's twelve-mile road march, another major RAP Week event with a high failure rate.

It is after midnight by the time I get to wash the dread splinters down the drain. Liberated from my tormentors, I feel energized and content because I managed to survive yet another day of Ranger School. More than that, I feel like I am starting to figure this place out, how it's all supposed to work, and that maybe, just maybe, I actually belong here. I know it will undoubtedly be another long, strenuous day tomorrow, and the day after that, with no more than one to three hours of sleep each night, but that is all right with me. Somehow, I will make it work.

Everyone gets through the showers and into their bunks quickly tonight. The lights go out just before 1:00 a.m. I don't have a guard shift tonight and the promised three hours of uninterrupted sleep I am about to receive feels like a windfall.

As I settle into my bunk and begin to drift off into deep, dreamless slumber. I remind myself that all I must do tomorrow morning is walk a measly twelve miles with a thirty-five-pound rucksack in less than three-hours-and-fifteen minutes. This is something any infantryman worth his salt can do with his eyes closed.

Frankly, I yawn sleepily, I was expecting a little more suck out of Ranger School.

0740 Hours (7:40 a.m.)
Mile 10 ½ of the RAP Week Road March
Fort Benning, Georgia
Day 4 of Ranger School
Hours of Sleep in the last four days: 8 hours

Seven hours later, my feet are pulverized. Every step feels like I am walking barefoot on a jagged coral reef. My hot spots have hot spots, new blisters are being birthed by the mile, and every stride forward is increasingly becoming an effort of will. I must be close to ten miles into the ruck march by now, two miles from the finish line, but I cannot know for sure because I have not seen a mile marker or RI since the seventh mile.

With little more than forty-five minutes left to complete the march, my pace is rapidly dwindling. I do not have much energy, pain tolerance, or willpower left. Rangers I had confidently passed miles earlier are re-passing me now. They give me piteous and contemptuous looks as they leave me in the dust.

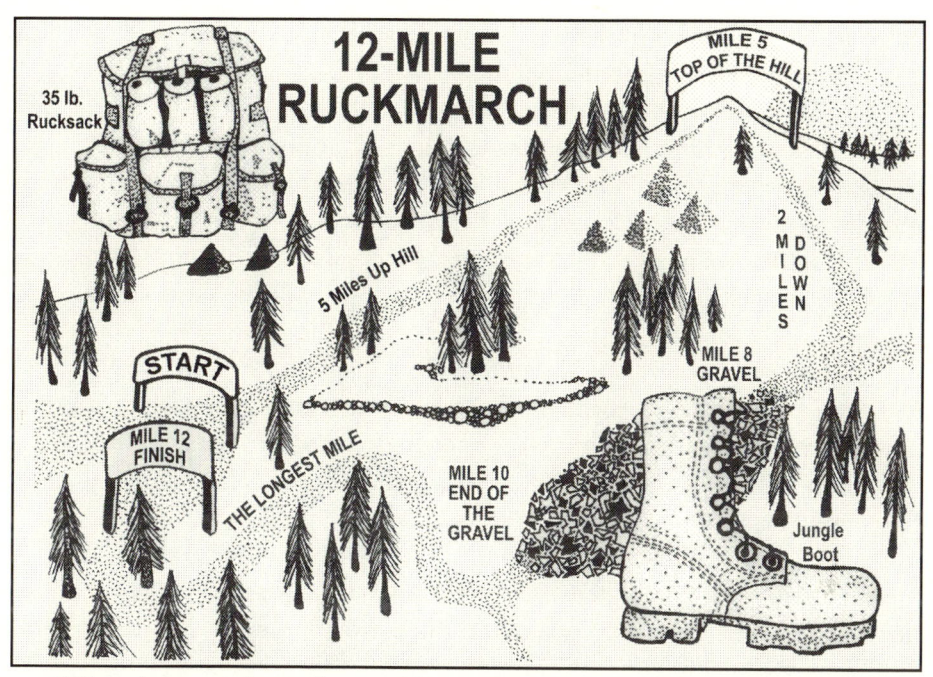

What happened? I ask myself dejectedly, remembering how high I was soaring mere hours ago. What did I do to my feet?

The loose, sharp-edged, granite gravel that covered the asphalt roadside for the last two miles delivered the coup de grace to the soles of my feet, but I made plenty of mistakes before that.

Mistake number one was wearing the same thin-soled, tan jungle boots I wore for a year in Iraq on this road march. The formerly padded boot inserts are now compressed as flat as a nickel, providing neither cushion nor comfort to my feet. While those boots were fine for walking an occasional klick or two, I never conditioned my feet to wearing them on a long ruck march in the weeks prior to coming to Ranger School.

Mistake number two was not doing enough ruck marching prior to coming here. I am a little ashamed to admit that, as a mechanized infantryman, I rarely ruck march at my unit back home. In fact, in sharp contrast to my bat boy, green beret, and light infantry peers, I can count the number of twelve-mile ruck marches I have performed on one hand.

But instead of shoring up a weakness, I ignored it, opting to focus on the five-mile run, done in sneakers, at the expense of walking long distances under a heavy pack, the heart and soul of Ranger School. Foolishly, I showed up to Ranger School with tender, baby feet, unconditioned for the rigors of good, old-fashioned light infantry ruck marching.

And I was going to pay for it.

Mistake number three was power marching confidently out of the gate and striving to get a place at the front of the pack of two-hundred-and-forty other ranger students. My lungs and leg muscles burned fiercely as I made rapid, lengthy, heavy strides up the long, steady incline that constituted the first five miles of the march. Here, I was making great time, on target to pass the event, perhaps even on track to earn a minor-plus from the RIs.

Mistake number four, another big one, was running downhill for the entirety of mile six. It was hard to resist. After walking uphill for over an hour, I greeted the long, gentle downslope on the other side as a reward, an easy "free mile," a good chance to stretch out my legs and log some good time.

So, I did what my basic training drill sergeants and multiple RIs told me adamantly not to do. I ran, hard and fast, wearing worn-out boots and a heavy pack on hard asphalt, and damn the consequences.

Thump! Thump! Thump! Thump!

While the thirty-five-pound packs we are wearing are relatively light, that weight combined with my two-hundred-and-ten-pound bodyweight means that over two-hundred-and-forty pounds of pressure are bearing down solely on the bottoms of my two feet.

Thump! Thump! Thump! Thump!

"Don't run, ranger." An RI posted at the roadside told me.

But I am making great time. I told myself, so I ignored him.

Thump! Thump! Thump! Thump!

"I wouldn't run if I were you, ranger." Another RI told me a short time later.

But I did not listen to that one either, rather, I just ran faster.

Thump! Thump! Thump! Thump!

I messed up because I wore the wrong boots, I did not train properly, I maintained a poor pace, I ran when I should not have, but most of all, the meta-mistake, was underestimating Ranger School, for entertaining the foolish dream that I actually belong here.

And that is how I find myself here now, limping and sliding over copious amounts of loose, pebble-sized, gray, black, and white granite road gravel, tearing up my feet and falling rapidly behind. With each step, I can feel the sharp, slippery gravel through my thin-soled boots on my raw and increasingly blistered feet. I am only two miles from the finish line, but close to the point of collapse.

Two more rangers pass me. They look back at my sorry, hobbling figure and exchange a quick chuckle between them.

In underestimating this road march, I overestimated myself. I even entertained false hopes of earning a minor-plus for completing the course early. Ha, what hubris! What in the world made me think I could get through RAP Week, let alone the entirety of Ranger School? This is what I get for violating what should be the first rule of this course: stay mediocre, do the bare minimum to pass and no more.

For the first time, I am facing a genuine challenge at Ranger School. For the first time, I must ask myself if I truly want the Tab.

Keep moving, Goldsmith, keep moving. I start chanting like a mantra. Each time I say it, I move forward another five steps.

And not only do I need to move forward, but I need to do it quickly, because the "Fall Out Truck," an Army five-ton picking up those rangers who cannot or will not complete the march and who are destined to recycle, is relentlessly rolling up behind me.

Finally, somewhere in the tenth mile and after more than two miles of seemingly walking on broken glass, the gravel peters out and eventually disappears from the roadway. It is a happy sight, but it is already too late, the damage has been done.

In the next half mile, many more rangers pass me up, including my ranger buddy Tobiri, who looks equally as haggard as me. Unlike everyone else, he offers some words of encouragement as he passes by.

"Don't..." Tobiri pauses to wheeze and cough, "give up... Goldsmith. You..." he coughs again, "can do it!"

Seeing Tobiri pass me by sets my heart into panic. My watch confirms that at the slow pace I am moving, with only half an hour left, there is very little chance I will be able to complete the ruck march on time.

I stare down at my battered feet, the source of all my misery. I am not having fun any longer.

What a pathetic wretch! I admonish myself while dragging my feet slowly forward. How could a simple twelve-mile road march be doing me in? What is wrong with me? What kind of infantryman am I?

"Are you alright? Goldsmith, isn't it?"

I must be muttering aloud because another ranger walking parallel to me on the far side of the road turns his head and hails me.

"Oh, hell yeah." I respond sarcastically. "Just, you know, living the dream."

"Ain't that the truth!" Banks, a light infantryman from the storied Tenth Mountain Division chuckles before asking me, "Mind if I join you over there, buddy?"

I grunt affirmatively and he limps over painfully to my side of the road. Banks is also in Charlie Company, but not in my squad, so we have not spoken much.

"Are your feet as fucked as mine?" I ask him.

"Ha!" Banks laughs, "Worse. That fucking gravel man... I was doing great until then."

"You and me both, brother." I sigh meekly. "I wish I had done more road marching at Fort Carson before coming here. I'm a mess right now."

"Fort Carson? Aren't you guys some kind of mechanized unit?"

"Yeah. That's right."

"I thought you all usually rode around in Bradleys?" Banks looks genuinely puzzled. "What are you doing here, in Ranger School?"

"Banks," I laugh for the first time in hours. "I am wondering that myself right about now."

"Well, hell..." Banks has a mischievous look in his eye. "What do you say, Goldsmith? There can't be much more than a mile, mile-and-a-half left. Does your sorry mechanized ass want to race me to the finish?"

I am smiling now too, the pain in my feet momentarily forgotten. "I can beat a cripple like you any day of the week, Banks."

We pick up our pace, together, stretching out our legs, increasing the pace of our strides, making each hard impact on asphalt, every painful step, worth it. We swap stories about where we grew up, our service in the Army, our tours in Iraq, and how we managed to find ourselves here at this crazy school.

For a few minutes at least, I am not alone. I have a comrade in the suck and that makes it bearable.

Because if Banks can keep going, so can I.

We make a poor but inspiring sight as we limp in across the finish line together, with eight minutes to spare. We even manage to re-pass Tobiri, his small frame bowed over under the weight of his rucksack.

Me and Banks embrace and slap each other heartily on the backs in celebration. It is my slowest time yet for a twelve-mile ruck march, over three hours, but it does not matter.

"We did it, buddy!" Banks says as he hobbles away towards the large pack of rangers who have already completed the march.

I grunt positively in response. I am too tired and beaten down to say anything.

Tobiri and a handful of other stragglers limp across the finish line just before time is called. They are immediately followed by the Fall Out Truck, which rumbles in with thirty-something of RAP Week's latest victims. Some of them were simply too slow, others twisted or broke ankles, sprained knees, or suffered from dehydration, cramps, or heat exhaustion. Others just wanted out. Whatever the reason, they are all recycling.

The two-hundred-and-ten rangers that remain in the class, down from three-hundred-and-forty only four days ago, are a mixed bag after the twelve-mile road march. Many of the bat boys and the green berets are comparatively fresh, capable of marching even further without complaint. Others are tired and a bit sore but have suffered no real or lasting injury. Then of course, there are rangers like me, Banks, and Tobiri. Worn-out, beaten down, and forlorn, we nurse our blistered feet, sprained ankles, and humbled egos as best we can.

But undoubtedly, there is always someone that has it worse. In this case, it is the spectacle-wearing engineer sergeant who managed to fracture his ankle during the march. I watch him limp past me in extreme and obvious pain, yet with a beaming smile on his face. He is going forward, but with a fractured ankle, I do not see how he can make it another day, let alone through the rest of this course.

Quite frankly, the way my feet feel right now, I am not sure I will be able to make it through another day either.

The fact of the matter is, everything until this moment has been prologue, only now has my personal Ranger School journey truly begun. Four hours ago, I was crushing RAP Week, kicking ass, and taking names, but no longer. Now I am in a world of trouble. Now I will have to earn my Tab, the hard way.

An infantryman, and a ranger no less, lives and dies on his feet. "Take care of your feet," the saying goes, "and they will take care of you."

Well, I have taken care of my feet all right. Through ineptitude and neglect, they are now covered in a dozen or more blisters and sores. Practically useless for walking, simply standing on them is painful agony.

My feet are going to take care of me all right, and I deserve it.

I am fucked.

0641 Hours (06:41 a.m.)
Buddy Run Course, Camp Rogers
Fort Benning, Georgia
Day 5 of Ranger School
Hours of Sleep in Last Five Days: 10 hours

Last night, while I got "treated" by the sadistic, quack medics for my blisters, Banks, my road march buddy, talked a fellow Tenth Mountain infantryman into quitting with him. They simply packed up their duffle bags and disappeared into the night.

Maybe he is the smart one... I muse to myself as Tobiri and I await our turn to do the Buddy Run course, the last pass-fail event in RAP Week. I shift my weight from one foot to the other in a futile attempt to lessen the pain caused by over a dozen nickel- and dime-sized blisters covering my feet.

"Get ready, rangers." A stern-faced RI tells us. "You're up next."

Me and Tobiri wobble and limp over to the starting line of the Buddy Run course. We are easily the saddest looking buddy team in Charlie Company. I can overhear some bat boys sniggering at us.

While I suffer primarily from bruised and blistered feet, Tobiri is weak generally, exhausted and overwhelmed by the last few days, easily the most brutalizing of his life. He is a brand-new, thirty-year-old engineer officer with no real Army experience. For him, Ranger School is a baptism by fire.

The RI motions us to wait a moment longer.

"How are you feeling today, Tobiri?"

"Pretty terrible," Tobiri says honestly, "but I'll make it through the course, ranger buddy, don't worry about me. How are your feet doing, Goldsmith?"

"They're devastated, but I'll make it through, too."

"We will help each other through it, OK?" Tobiri says with a hopeful note in his voice.

"Enough soap opera shit, rangers." The RI tells us as he motions us to go down the trail with two fingers. "Move out."

Me and Tobiri jog off together down the dirt trail. There is no time to pay any attention to the pain in my feet now, there is a task, a mission to accomplish. With every pounding step, each heavy inhale, the sensation of pain lessens, my mind clears, and I feel more like myself again.

And Tobiri, to his credit, is keeping pace with me. We purposefully and calmly approach each obstacle, navigate it together, and then move onto the next. While we wait patiently for the other to complete his leg of the course, we jog in place and cheer our partner on.

Until this moment, I have not bonded with or even enjoyed the company of Tobiri, my designated ranger buddy. I have no reason to dislike the man, we just don't have much in common. Tobiri is a decade older than me and new to the Army. He is from the Northeast; I am from Southern California. He is married and hoping to have kids soon. I am young, dumb, and single, free of attachment to anyone but the boys back home at the unit.

But I am impressed with my ranger buddy now. Even in his state of weakness he is climbing ropes, balancing over logs, jumping, and leaping with the best of them. I know he is in pain, but he sucks it up and pulls his weight to help us both get through the course.

We complete the buddy run together, well under time, coursing with pain-killing endorphins and, for the moment, happy.

"Looks like you two sorry rangers have successfully completed RAP Week." The RI at the finish line gives us a disdainful look. "Congratulations, you are going to Camp Darby."

"Roger, Sergeant!" I exclaim joyously.

"Hrrmph..." He snorts in response. "Good luck. You are going to need it."

Tobiri and I give each other high fives. We have made it through what is arguably the hardest part of Ranger School, RAP Week, where we went from three-hundred-and-forty to two-hundred rangers, during five long, relentless, sleepless days. Now we have earned the right to enter the first phase of Ranger School, Camp Darby, where the real training and evaluation will begin.

Every ranger in the class is exhausted, many of us are injured, and nearly everyone has lost friends along the way. Dozens of men who at first glance appeared stronger, tougher, and more capable than me have recycled or are already on their way home, tab-less.

But me and Tobiri are still here, just barely.

And I am proud of us. Two of the sorriest souls in the Ranger Class have made it past RAP Week. Deep down I know that I do not really belong here, but somehow, mostly through dumb luck, I keep making it through. Some small part of me even entertains the hope that my feet will slowly improve and that I will be able to complete Ranger School without being in constant agony. Maybe, just maybe, I will be able to earn my Tab.

If my feet can fix themselves, that is, because if they do not, I am screwed. If they don't heal, I won't last another two or three days, let alone fifty-five, in this incredible suck festival.

I may have made it through RAP Week, but my journey is just beginning, and I have no idea what lays in store for me.

So naturally, as the adrenaline wears off, the pain and nagging doubts return, and I find myself asking the same basic question:

Why did I get into this mess?

Chapter 3: "Darby"

Rule #6: Never volunteer for anything.
Rule #7: Follow the Five Principles of Patrolling.
Rule #8: Ranger School is fucking stupid.

1235 Hours (12:35 p.m.)
Camp Darby Training Area
Fort Benning, Georgia
Day 8 of Ranger School
Hours of Sleep in Last Eight Days: Unknown

"Hey! Hey, everyone! I got cheese over here, for anyone who wants it. Who wants to trade?"

Is this guy fucking serious right now?! I scream inside my own head. Again, with this bullshit?

"I got cheese, looking for peanut butter... who wants it? Hey... I know someone wants to trade peanut butter for my cheese, it's uh, hala-peno cheese."

I want to strangle Roberts, the cook from Ranger Battalion, as do several other members of the squad. Every day, without fail, he offers the same tired proposition: trading a packet of cheese for peanut butter, a sucker's trade that some fool might have made in the early days of RAP Week, when we were still careless, even reckless with our food, but not now. With hunger increasingly settling in, peanut butter is ranger gold.

In fact, it should be a rule: No one is going to trade you peanut butter for your tired-ass, lumpy MRE cheese.

"C'mon guys, I know one of you wants some cheese."

Roberts is met with a wall of silence from the rest of the squad. We are too busy devouring one of our only two MRE meals of the day. The RI only gave us fifteen minutes to do so, so there is little time to waste on foolish banter.

But Roberts does not seem to realize or care that no one will ever take him up on his sucker's trade. Like me, he is an odd man out in the squad, a cook of all people, a non-combat "support" job. This is a true rarity and severe handicap in Ranger School, and many wonder how he even got here. He is assigned to the Ranger Regiment, but he is not a bat boy, not an infantryman even, so, of course, the bat boys want nothing to do with him. He has no rank, combat experience, or much tactical knowledge and ability, so frankly, neither does anyone else.

"This is your last chance guys, your last chance for some delicious cheese before I dive in myself." Roberts is oblivious and does not quit. "All I am asking for is some peanut butter... c'mon..."

No one wants your fucking cheese, bro! I can barely contain my fury at this point. Hell, half of us already have cheese in our MRE. The heavily processed, green-tinged, Cheese-Whiz-like substance goes well with crackers and adds flavor to a main meal, that is without question, but it just cannot compare to the smooth, hearty, fatty, creamy, nutty taste of peanut butter, which even in a vacuum-packaged, heavily-preserved MRE tastes approximately how peanut butter should taste to an increasingly starving ranger student: delightful.

By a basic calorie count alone, peanut butter blows cheese out of the water, coming in at two-hundred-fifty calories per serving versus a mere one-hundred-eighty. Peanut butter, whether in packets at the chow hall or inside an MRE, is a valuable commodity here, much desired by all of us. At this point in time, seven days into Ranger School, we all know that only a fool would trade peanut butter for cheese.

Roberts, you are either a fucking clown or trying to cheat us. Either way, you should shut your goddamn mouth!

I want to scream it at his big, dumb cook face, but I do not dare. For many reasons, it is in my best interest to be civil with everyone, to make friends, and not enemies. I need their cooperation on patrols, good Peers marks, and for everyone to generally think of me fondly. It's better to just bite my tongue and keep quiet.

Ultimately, Roberts is an idiot, most certainly, or a cheat, probably, and he should just shut his mouth and eat his MRE like the rest of us, yes, but I am thoughtful enough to know that the real source of my anger comes from inside me. It is caused by extreme sleep deprivation, hunger, and most of all, regret for being a complete and utter idiot by voluntarily subjecting myself to this stupid school in the first place.

And I really mean "stupid," ridiculously stupid, because Darby is the "crawl phase" of Ranger School, as in "first you crawl, then you walk, then you run." Here is where we go back to basics, get treated like children, and have everything dictated to us by the RIs.

Indeed, Camp Darby takes regular Army stupidity to new heights of folly. As a regular infantry grunt, I figured I could eat shit and do dumb things better than most, but the ceaseless layouts, tying everything down to ourselves with cord so that we look like spiderman, getting smoked, freezing on the cold, hard ground, trying desperately to stay awake during the most basic doctrinal classes, hobbling around the woods on blistered feet under a heavy rucksack, having every spare moment filled with some inane detail or senseless RI demand, is steadily driving me crazy.

Guess it serves me right for violating a cardinal military rule: never volunteer for anything, especially Ranger School.

The glamour and romance of the course has worn off in the harsh reality of camp life at Darby, even for the bat boys, who no longer play grab ass and sing Airborne Ranger cadences. There are no more high-speed obstacle courses or motivational speeches from colonels. Now, we live like hobos, exposed to the elements, nursing various injuries and ailments, humping our possessions on our backs, ferrying them around the woods all day with no tangible result. Twenty-one hours a day I am cold, in pain, and struggling desperately to stay awake. I am alone, have no friends, and most of my mental energy is spent feeling sorry for myself and persuading myself not to quit.

It is not just me though, everyone is tired, slow, irritable, and easily rattled by even small slights and inconveniences. We are reduced to our most basic and selfish needs; all we want is food and sleep. The bat boys especially, many of whom are still in their teens, are increasingly having trouble staying awake, and have earned a reputation as the squad's "sleepy rangers." Newton

Ranger Rifle Squad

Alpha Team Leader (M4 Carbine)

Squad Leader "The Boss" (M4 Carbine)

Bravo Team Leader (M4 Carbine)

Plus, in Darby Phase:
- Radiotelephone Operator (RTO)
- M240B Machine Gunner
- Assistant Machine Gunner

Alpha Team

Rifleman (M16/M4/M14 Rifle/Carbine)

Bravo Team

Rifleman (M16/M4/M14 Rifle/Carbine)

Grenadier (M16/M4+M203 Grenade Launcher)

Automatic Riflemen (SAW Machine Guns)

Grenadier (M16/M4+M203 Grenade Launcher)

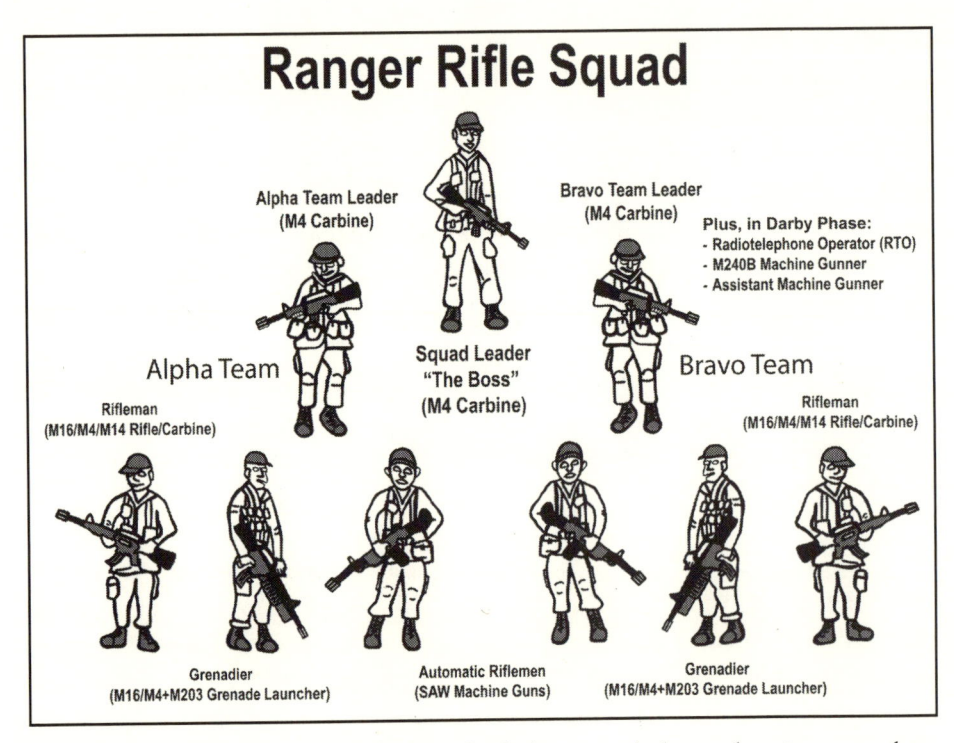

and Leon are the worst. We often find them curled up sleeping together, nestled up close to each other for warmth.

I no longer keep track of how much sleep I am getting in the course, mostly because I have become reconciled to the fact that the RIs will in fact prevent us from sleeping more than two or three hours a night for as long as they can, perhaps forever. Already, I am amazed at how little sleep a human body can function on. I want to sleep so bad it hurts, but somehow, although my thinking is a little hazy and labored, my brain is still working. I can walk, I can talk, I can do infantry things, but I do not know how.

Each member of the squad is lost in their own individualized suffering. Everyone, green beret to lieutenant, bat boy to cook, is suffering in many ways, but some more than others. With my savagely blistered feet, I am among the most visibly far-gone rangers in the squad, the new odds-on favorite to be the next Recycle. I have no true friends or allies in the squad. Even Tobiri, my ranger buddy, is distant from me. Mostly this is because he is only doing marginally better than I am, but also because we have nothing in common. He has taken to hanging out with the other officers in the squad. I keep to myself.

48 | THE MEDIOCRE INFANTRYMAN'S GUIDE TO RANGER SCHOOL

However, through it all, inertia carries me forward. I still want my Tab bad enough to stay here, to endure the endless stupidity of Ranger School, to be hungry, to be cold, to be exhausted, to be miserable, to be a ranger.

Most of the first two Darby mornings were spent in the cold, hard bleachers of the planning bays. There we sat through hours and hours of classes given by the RIs. Fully exposed to the increasingly chilly, fall wind, the squad shivered and struggled mightily to stay awake during blocks of instruction on the most basic infantry tasks like how to move through the woods, communicate with hand and arm signals, and react to enemy contact. The RIs lectured at us without asking for any feedback or taking any questions, pausing only to yell at us or to make us stand up if too many of us were falling asleep. They teach us the same things, basic things, repeatedly, until we can do it all in our sleep.

Although the classes allow my battered feet to rest, in many ways the long classes are worse than walking under a heavy rucksack, where staying awake is not so much of a struggle. I am not learning anything new; this is all basic infantry stuff I learned long ago in boot camp and at my unit. There is nothing "ranger" about any of this stuff. Everyone is bored, even guys like Roberts who know next to nothing about infantry tactics. Everyone has taken to openly griping and calling the course stupid, especially Newton and Leon.

What ties everything together is the concept of patrolling, walking around in contested or enemy territory with a dozen (or forty) of your best buddies, armed to the teeth, looking for someone to kill, without getting killed yourself. Patrolling is the essence of Ranger School: its device for teaching and evaluating leadership. Patrolling is simple and timeless. Chimpanzees, cavemen, and bands of tribal humans patrol. Yet, it can also be endlessly complex, an art and a science, as we will all learn in the months to come.

It can be immensely difficult to lead a band of young, hungry, exhausted, and cantankerous cutthroats on a combat patrol. Fortunately, Ranger School has devised a methodology to guide aspiring rangers, The Five Principles of Patrolling: Planning, Reconnaissance, Security, Control, and Common sense, five considerations to constantly bear in mind, for any mission. Violate any of these principles, fail to plan, forgo reconnaissance, drop security, lose control, or abandon common sense, and you risk mission failure and the deaths of your men.

The five principles guide us generally, but for the specific tactics, techniques,

The 5 Principles of Patrolling

All patrols are governed by five principles: planning, reconnaissance, security, control, and common sense. In brief, each principle involves—

- **Planning:** quickly make a simple plan and effectively communicate it to the lowest level. A great plan that takes forever to complete and is poorly disseminated is not a great plan. Plan and prepare to a realistic standard and rehearse everything.
- **Reconnaissance:** your responsibility as a Ranger leader is to confirm what you think you know, and to learn that which you do not already know.
- **Security:** preserve your force as a whole. Every Ranger and every rifle counts, either one could be the difference between victory and defeat.
- **Control:** clarify the concept of the operation and commander's intent, coupled with disciplined communications, to bring every Soldier and weapon available to overwhelm the enemy at the decisive point.
- **Common sense:** use all available information and good judgment to make sound, timely decisions.

battle drills, explanations, and doctrine we need to know to succeed in and pass this course, we consult the Ranger Handbook, the Ranger School bible and perhaps the infantry at large. The Ranger Handbook is an Army manual that has been published for decades. It is renowned throughout the Army as the doctrinal guide for light infantry operations.

The Author's Actual Ranger Handbook

Want to know more about Ranger tactics, history, and doctrine? Then check out The Mediocre Infantryman's Annotated Ranger Handbook. Available now!

The Mediocre Infantryman's Annotated Ranger Handbook

TC 3-21.76

RANGER

HANDBOOK

Not for the weak or fainthearted — *Ain't that the truth!*

"Let the enemy come till he's almost close enough to touch. Then let him have it and jump out and finish him with your hatchet."
Major Robert Rogers, 1759.

APRIL 2017

DISTRIBUTION RESTRICTION: Approved for public release; distribution is unlimited.

Headquarters, Department of the Army

Ranger Andrew Goldsmith, Roster # 185
Ranger Class 01-08 and 02-08

"Rangers," an RI tells us, "not only do your Ranger Handbooks contain everything you need to know to pass this course, they also contain all you need to know to succeed in life generally."

The RAP Week and Darby RIs both made it abundantly clear that they expect our Ranger Handbooks never to be far from hand. We keep them in our cargo pants pockets or in the top flaps of our rucksacks. The Handbook is so important and full of information there is even a standing rule that it is okay to pull out and consult your Ranger Handbook at any time, during a break at the patrol base, rucking to the objective, or in the middle of a firefight on the objective. Ranger School is an open book test.

"Whenever you are in doubt, but you need to make a decision," the RI continues, "consult the Ranger Handbook. If you have a question, the answer is in there, and if it's not, just apply the Five Principles of Patrolling. There's no secret, that's all there is to this."

And appropriately enough for the "crawl" phase of Ranger School, a principle they like to stress hard here at Darby is the first one, planning. A few days ago, the RIs started heavily training us on how to prepare and issue an operation order or "op order," the Army's handy template for planning any mission. Now, we spend the bulk of our mornings doing "Bay Planning," where, under the close supervision of an RI, the day's designated leader prepares and then issues an op order, before the squad heads out for the day to conduct the practice mission.

Preparing the order is not so bad. As a regular infantry guy, I rarely get assigned to do anything important, and usually just help construct the terrain table, a 3-D model of the route to the objective and the objective itself. But listening to the order, which can take up to two or three mind-numbing

---

5 Paragraph Operations Order

"Op Order" – remembered with the Aid of a pneumonic, "Sergeant Major Eats Sugar Cookies."

1) **S**ituation: what is going on - enemy forces, friendly forces, attachments/detachments;

2) **M**ission: a clear and concise statement of **what needs to get done** - who, what, when, where, and why, **what and why (task and purpose) being the most important**;

3) **E**xecution: **how you are going to do it** – concept of the operation, maneuver and fires, casualty evacuation, and a whole lot else;

4) **S**ervice Support: **what you have to accomplish the mission** – food, gas, and ammo; transportation; maintenance;

5) **C**ommand and Signal: **who is in charge and where you can find them.**

hours, is unimaginably terrible, and easily the worst part of my day.

Especially today, because Bailey, the squad's newly arrived recycled bat boy, is the squad leader. He will be issuing the op order.

And that is unfortunate for all of us, because Bailey is an idiot.

Bailey does not look or act like an Airborne Ranger. He is short and lightly built, with reddish-brown hair stubble, freckles, and thick basic training goggle eyeglasses. He is not particularly bright or motivated. He stutters, has no swagger, and tends to look down at his feet and mumble when he talks. Most of all he is not arrogant, devoid of sexual bravado, and does not talk about muzzle thumping or killing people all the time. He is unlike any other bat boy I have met.

Bailey recycled Darby Phase in the class before us because he failed both his patrols. Lucky for him, he did not have to re-do RAP Week, but spent the last week eating well, doing physical training, pushing a broom, picking up cigarette butts, and re-arranging rocks with the other Darby Recycles.

Bailey has inside information about what we will face in the next two weeks, wears a Ranger Scroll, and has even served with the Ranger Regiment in Iraq, but to an even greater extent than me or Roberts, he is a friendless outcast. A born nerd, the other bat boys, especially Jenson, torment and abuse him. They are embarrassed that someone like Bailey is a member of their elite fraternity. They make it readily clear to the rest of us that they do not vouch for Bailey and shun him in every conceivable way.

While comparatively well-fed and rested, Bailey has an uphill battle to gain the trust of the squad and pass his patrols his second time through Darby Phase. If he fails again, he will be kicked out of both Ranger School and his Ranger Battalion.

And today he has a tough task in front of him.

"That's the platoon op order, ranger Bailey." The day's RI briefs Bailey while Dale hangs out within earshot, feverishly taking notes. "Now go ahead and prepare your squad order. At ten o'clock you will issue it. Any questions?"

Bailey looks sick to his stomach but meekly mumbles, "No, sergeant."

Four hours is not a lot of time to prepare a Ranger School op order and preparing one to the Camp Darby standard can be a challenge for any ranger. Bailey, due to his poor reputation and lack of skills, faces even more of a challenge. Fortunately for him, he has the squad to help prop him up. The four lieutenants in the squad, to their credit, are more than eager to take on most of the planning burden, none more so than Dale.

The RI barely walks out of earshot back towards camp headquarters before young lieutenant Dale begins issuing orders to the squad. Bailey looks over his shoulder and nods approvingly.

"McCormick, Fulton, can you two work on the movement plan and pre-designated fires, okay? I assume you'll be taking point again today, Fulton, okay? Good, good... Tobiri, Sven... you two work on actions on the objective, okay? I'll start drafting the overall plan and preparing the annexes, okay? We're also going to want to..."

"Ahem!" Newton clears his throat loudly and stares squarely at Dale, "What do you want the rest of us to do, Bailey?"

"Hmmm... well, we kind of got this covered, okay," Dale hems and haws, "and, uh, we are going to need to work fast to prepare this thing, okay, and have time to brief and prepare Bailey, okay? That's like a mission in itself."

"Ain't that the truth." Newton acknowledges. "But I'm not just going to sit around here and twiddle my thumbs like Bailey. The RIs are watching us."

Both keep talking as if Bailey was not five feet away from them.

"Well, why don't you guys," Dale motions his hands towards me, Roberts, and the bat boys, "work on the terrain model, okay, cross-load everyone's rucksacks, and, uh... redistribute ammo, okay? Can you guys do that, okay?"

"Sure thing, boss." Newton mock salutes Dale as he walks away. Bailey follows lamely behind Dale and says nothing.

I join Newton and Leon in building the terrain model, a three-dimensional representation of our planned movement and the objective, where we are going to perform an ambush. We use dirt, sticks, moss, bits of string, and bits of paper to construct it. The squad leader will use it during the op order briefing to describe our movement and actions on the objective, so it is important. However, it is basically ranger arts and crafts, an easy and mindless job, a good opportunity to rest. Naturally, Newton and Leon have monopolized it, but fortunately, for today at least, they let me join them.

Already, many members of the squad have carved out specialized roles for themselves. Naturally, Fulton, the green beret, is the point man and expert land navigator. Dale, along with the other officers, takes charge of planning. Meanwhile, the bat boys self-appoint themselves the best tacticians and take charge as team leaders on each day's foot movements through the forest. Me however, other than preparing the fireguard roster, being the "rasta-man," I have yet to carve out a formal niche for myself.

The next few hours are fairly pleasant. I play in the dirt with Leon and

Newton and listen to them tell war stories about garrison life in Ranger Regiment and Leon muzzle thumping people in Iraq. I am off my blistered feet, not wearing a heavy rucksack, and the warming sun is rising higher into the sky. Other than MRE breakfast at 5:00 a.m. and MRE dinner at midnight, this is the best part of the day.

But the two- or three-hour presentation of the op order itself is pure misery, like attending the most boring college class of your life after not sleeping for a week with a professor who will physically and mentally crush you and your classmates if they catch you sleeping. We sit through one every morning now, but this one, we fear, stands to be the worst one yet.

By ten o'clock the squad is sitting in folding chairs under the semi-roofed, wooden squad planning bay. Dale shoves some last-minute notes into Bailey's hands and takes a seat in the front row.

Bailey clears his throat, looks at his notes, and begins.

"Good morning, uh, men. Grab your, uh, pens and, uh, paper," Bailey awkwardly stumbles his way through Dale script, "and, uh, please, uh, hold your, uh, questions, until the end…"

Poor Bailey. I cannot help but feel pity for such a sad figure. It is going to happen to all of us, but today, he happens to be in the RI's spotlight, and there is no way this is going to end well. The Darby RIs are particularly demanding about the op order process. They do not let us take shortcuts and do not tolerate any "finger-drilling," or going through the motions. They are going to make Bailey present this thing from start to finish, no longer how long it takes, no matter how painful it is.

"Today, uh, we are going to, uh, move five, uh, klicks, uh, to the objective, uh, to conduct, uh, ambush on, uh, enemy forces."

Two minutes in and I already want to shoot myself.

Today, like every day now, we are going to conduct a non-graded, practice patrol to help prepare us for next week's graded Field Training Exercise, or "FTX." Although it is going to take Bailey several hours to describe it we are going to walk three miles, set up a squad ambush on a trail, "kill" anyone who walks down it with our blank ammunition, and then run and hide a mile or so away in an overnight patrol base. Sounds simple enough, but there are a hundred tasks and a thousand things that must go right for the patrol to be successful. That is why the RIs make us break down the op order into such detail and why the issuance of the order takes so long.

"… and if we are, uh, engaged by the, uh, enemy along the, uh, uh, way, we will conduct, uh, React to Contact, uh, which, if you will look at this graphic, uh, here means that Alpha Team will, uh, hold on for a moment here..."

At first, I was flinching involuntarily at every "uh," but an hour into the op order, my mind has become accustomed to Bailey's almost hypnotic sputtering. For an hour now, Baily has stood at the podium speaking, a near-incoherent, rambling fool, parroting words and concepts that he only half understands. Dale can barely contain himself as Bailey breezes through important topics and mangles the transmission of the order he so diligently prepared. Jenson just stares at him with murderous hatred. The rest of us are near catatonic with boredom, fighting a losing battle with our eyelids.

"... then we will, uh, establish the, uh, the uh, the ORP... leaders, uh, leaders, uh, recon will head off after, uh, uh, the five, uh, point contingency, uh, plan..."

Another hour passes. Never in my life have I been so bored hearing about inflicting major carnage on a helpless enemy. I cannot believe Bailey, this turd of a human being, is a soldier, let alone an infantryman, let alone an Airborne Ranger on a quest for the Tab. I understand why Jenson and the other bat boys hate this guy so much, I desperately want to strangle the mumbling, "uh"-ing moron myself.

The worst part is, none of this matters, this is all just practice for next week. We have days and days of this to look forward to, and with our increasing exhaustion, each day is worse than the last.

Did I mention Ranger School was stupid?

"... back at the, uh, the ORP, we, uh, will, uh, retrieve our, uh, rucksacks and proceed to the, uh, the, uh, patrol base... order of, uh, march, will be, uh..."

My stomach snarls at me, momentarily waking me up just as I am drifting off to sleep again. The squad has been eating nothing but two MREs a day since we arrived at Camp Darby. While this might be enough calories for the average human being, we are grubby, cold-shivering, injured, angry, exhausted rangers, running on all cylinders, non-stop, and it is not enough. I have never been this hungry before in my life. With each passing day, our hunger grows and our waistlines shrink. Food becomes an obsession for all of us, but none more so than me and Newton, the squad's "food hounds."

Life is indeed miserable, yet it could always be worse. This is something Ranger School has already taught me a dozen times over. I unwrap one of my last remaining pieces of chewing gum and place it tenderly in my mouth. The chewing motion helps keep me awake while the sweet juices slightly alleviate my hunger. Life becomes bearable again, if only for a few short moments.

"... and once, uh, once, uh, priorities of work are, uh, completed, the squad can, uh, sleep at, uh, fifty percent, uh, strength until, uh, first light."

Bailey drones on and on and on until, finally, three hours into the presentation, he says the sweetest words he has ever spoken.

"And, uh, that's about it. Any, uh, questions?"

The RI's head lifts with a jolt. He too might have been sleeping.

"Well, that was something, wasn't it, rangers? Are you finished with your op order, ranger Bailey?"

Bailey dumbly nods his head up and down.

"Thank... fucking... God!" The RI growls, eliciting laughter from the squad. "Time to head out for the day, rangers. You have twenty minutes to conduct any rehearsals, fill your canteens, and get your rucksacks on your back. Get it done and get it done quick, something tells me, it's going to be a long day."

In Ranger School, that is something you can count on.

"One more thing, rangers." The RI adds. "Your MRE resupply just arrived. Ranger Bailey, make sure you task some rangers to distribute the meals and break up the boxes."

Jenson volunteers to distribute MREs. Everyone else starts packing up their rucksacks, making last minute preparations before we get ready to head out into the woods.

While I am overjoyed that Bailey's op order is over, the physically demanding part of my day is just beginning. Now, I swap boredom for pain as I rise to my feet unsteadily. Time to put on a heavy rucksack and walk around the woods for the next ten or twelve hours. Time to do repeated walkthroughs of ambushes, recons, and react to enemy contact drills. Time to punish my poor feet again.

Four days after the road march the bottoms of my feet are still mincemeat, with new blisters popping up every day. The bottoms and now the sides of my feet are covered with them, at least two dozen of assorted sizes and in varying states of infection. Every single step I take, whether wearing a fifty-pound rucksack or simply limping to the wood line at night to take a piss, causes me sharp and constant pain. Tasks that are easy and routine for non-blistered rangers cause me agony. My performance suffers as a result, endangering my reputation in the squad. Slowly, but steadily, the unending pain and inconvenience chips away at my will to endure the endless suck fest that is Ranger School.

The first ten steps are always the worst. That is when the pain is most acute, before the body and mind inure itself to the sensations. I seethe in agony, breathe out heavily, and moan involuntarily until I fall into rhythm. Clenching my teeth, I limp off to join my fire team in conducting rehearsals. Today I will be carrying a SAW light machine gun, the second heaviest weapon in the squad.

"Psst! Hey, Goldsmith. Get over here!"

It's Jenson, calling me over to him. I must listen to him today because he is my team leader.

I sigh, change direction and limp over to him and Salvador. They are standing by two unopened boxes of MREs.

"What do you need, Jenson?"

"Help me and Salvador issue the squad's MREs. Go ahead and open those boxes."

Jenson and Salvador are from different Ranger Battalions, but they have been thick as thieves since they both recycled RAP Week together in the previous class for playing with a snake. The class before that, unbelievably, Salvador also recycled RAP week, this time for killing a snake. Salvador has already been at Ranger School almost three months, Jenson for two, but almost all that time has been spent in the Recycle barracks.

"You guys must like it here." Fulton joked when he heard the snake stories.

"Anything to get a break from Ranger Battalion." Salvador chuckled.

Jenson is tall and lean, Salvador is short and stocky. Jenson is from the deep south, Salvador is from New York City. Jenson is disrespectful to everyone other than his fellow Airborne Rangers. Salvador, in contrast, is friendly with everyone in the squad, looking to earn their trust and confidence.

For the moment, I do not trust either one of them.

I pull out my Gerber folding knife and slice open the tops of the two 12-count boxes of Meals Ready to Eat, the squad's sole sustenance for the next 24 hours. Jenson and Salvador reach over me and start pulling out vacuum-sealed pouches of food.

Against one of the most sacred rules in Ranger School, they immediately start sorting the good ones from the bad.

"Chicken with Salsa... Vegetable Manicotti... Chili-Mac..." Salvador reads them off.

"Oh, give me that Chili Mac!" Jenson greedily grabs what is widely considered to be the best MRE of all. "Also, let me know if you see a beef patty. I want that one, too. Make sure Newton and Leon get something good, too, will ya?"

This is a serious breach of ranger ethics. MREs are supposed to be distributed blindly, without favor to anyone, yet Jenson and Salvador are cherry-picking the best MREs for themselves and their bat boy buddies. Worst of all, they ask me to be complicit in their crime.

"Don't be shy, Goldsmith." Jenson, with the instincts of a born criminal, knows what I'm thinking. "Pick out any two meals you want, so long as they're not beef patties. Those are mine."

I steal a glance over my shoulder to make sure no one is watching. The rest of the squad is busy, off doing rehearsals or making last-minute adjustments to their gear. I do not know where the RI is. I quickly grab two halfway decent MREs from the top of the pile, Chicken Breast and Beef Ravioli, and throw them on my rucksack.

Jenson looks pleased enough and continues to rummage through the MREs like a kid on Christmas.

I do not like what Jenson and Salvador are doing, but I am not going to confront them about it either. The last thing I need right now are unnecessary enemies. A ranger must pick his battles, and this one is not worth dying for.

"You see any beef patties, Salvador?"

"Nah, bro, not in these boxes, but oh, here's a Vegetable Omelet..." Salvador laughs as he mentions the most universally hated MRE, "and look, here's another one."

"Grossssss..." Jenson laughs as he punches Salvador in the shoulder. "Give 'em both to fucking Bailey."

Poor Bailey. No respect, especially from his fellow bat boys.

After separating their favorites, Jenson and Salvador divvy up the remainder of the MREs to the squad and have me place them on their rucksacks. We are finishing up when Dale, today's Alpha Team Leader strides up to where we are standing.

"Time to wrap this up, Jenson. The RI wants us ready to move out in five mikes."

Ranger Load Bearing Equipment and Rucksack

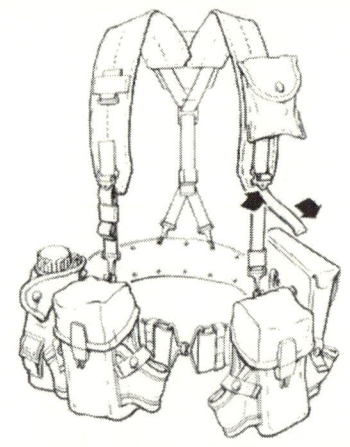

Load Bearing Equipment or "LBE"

A Compact, Tightly Packed Alice Pack Rucksack or "Ruck"

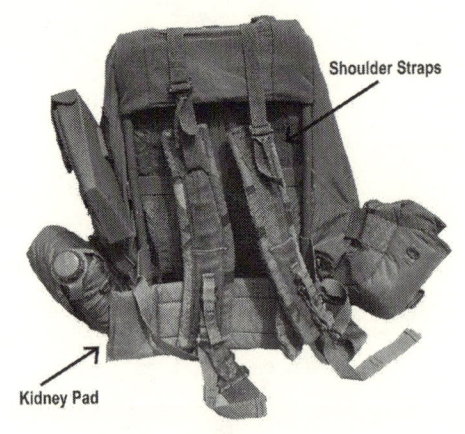

Ranger Rucksack (from the Rear)

Shoulder Straps

Kidney Pad

"Roger, that!" Jenson says sarcastically, before turning to me and Salvador, "Go tell the rest of the team to stop rehearsing and to get their rucks on. We're moving out."

For the first, but certainly not the last time today, I heave my fifty-pound rucksack onto my back, grab my twenty-year old SAW machine gun, and stand up shakily. The rucksack's Vietnam-era shoulder straps pull back and downwards on sore shoulders while the barely cushioned, metal kidney pad

60 | THE MEDIOCRE INFANTRYMAN'S GUIDE TO RANGER SCHOOL

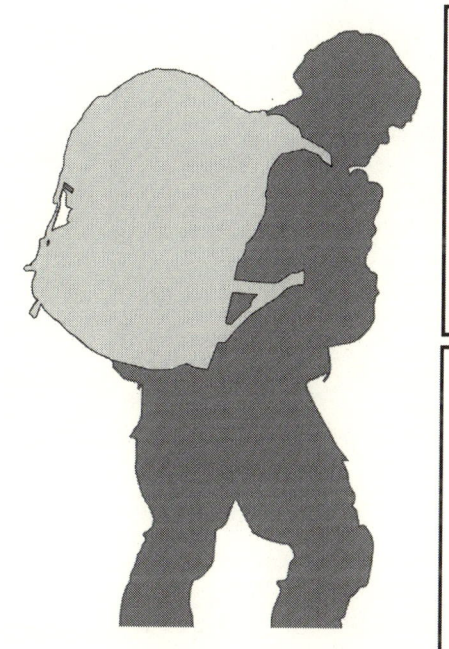

Some of the Things you Carry in Your Rucksack

Extra pair of combat boots	Hygiene kit
Cold weather undershirt and pants	Tape (duck and electrical)
Camelback hydration system	Wet weather pants
Camouflage pants	Wet weather jacket
Camouflage coats	Poncho
Neck gaiter	Poncho liner
Watch cap	Patrol sack sleeping bag
Socks (several pairs)	Bivouac cover sleeping bag
T-shirts (several)	MREs
Weapons cleaning kit	Extra ammunition
Compass	6-8 quarts of water
Flashlight/headlamp	Wet weather bag
Spare batteries	Ranger Handbook
550 nylon cord	Field jacket liner
Sewing kit	And more . . .

Ways to (Attempt to) Alleviate Rucksack Pain

- Shifting your rucksack around your back, alternately tightening and loosening the rucksack straps, transferring the weight from the shoulders to different regions of the back, and then back again;
- Lean against trees during short halts, allowing them to bear the weight;
- Run from mortars; the pain in your lungs and legs will temporarily distract from your back and shoulder pain;
- Think about all the pain in other parts of your body, your feet, your knees, your neck; the hunger in your belly; or your homesickness;
- Distract your mind by daydreaming about foods you are going to eat, women you should have asked out, things you are going to do with the boys back at the unit, etc.;
- But in the end, all you can really do is, embrace the suck, patrol like a ranger, and get lost in the work of the mission. Pain is temporary, a Tab is forever.

presses deeply into my hips and lower back.

We carry our homes and all our worldly possessions in giant green Army rucksacks on perpetually sore and beaten backs. Our twenty x twenty-two x nineteen-inch large Alice pack rucksacks carry all the clothing, water, food, mission essential equipment, ammunition, weapons, radios, and mines that we need to survive and operate as rangers deep inside hostile territory. I am so familiar with my rucksack, so reliant on its contents, so used to quickly grabbing things and stowing them back inside that it has truly become an extra limb, an extension of myself.

The extra weight of the rucksack makes my feet feel like they are on fire, and I have not taken a step. The next dozen hours of walking through the woods are going to be miserable, just like yesterday, and the day before, and the day before that. I do not know how I am going to walk one hundred meters, let alone five or more klicks.

The squad moves off into the woods. Dale, Alpha Team Leader, carries an M4 carbine and walks in the point position, with the rest of the squad following. Fulton walks immediately behind him and to the left, ready to advise him to change course if Dale starts veering us off in the wrong

M4 5.56mm Carbine

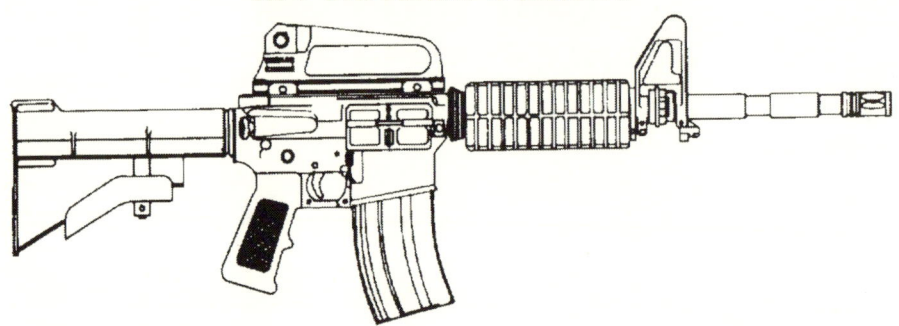

direction. I walk immediately to Dale's right. I am his right-hand man, his machine gunner. Leon, the grenadier, carries an M16 rifle with an M203 grenade launcher attached to its underside. He walks to the left and behind Fulton. Keeping our formation, and the distances between us, we move slowly, ponderously towards the day's objective.

We walk for hours and hours under our heavy rucksacks, practicing our "movement techniques," or walking as a squad. This is about as basic as it gets, yet, even something as simple as walking under a heavy pack has a science to it, especially when it is you and eleven of your buddies strolling through enemy territory.

During the day we walk in "file," a straight line, or better yet, in the "fire team wedge," the preferred formation, where two fire teams walk in "V"s with the squad leader and machine gun team in the middle. The wedge formation offers the best overall combination of control, speed, and security. At night, we walk in file if the terrain is especially difficult, or, more commonly, in a

M203 40mm Grenade Launcher Mounted on M16A2 Rifle

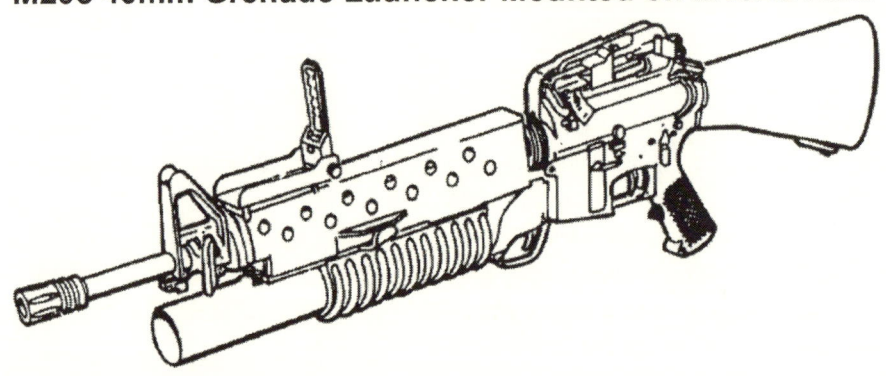

modified fire team wedge, a more collapsed and linear version of the fire team wedge.

There are many other things to consider when moving as a ranger. Every man must stay at least five meters away from his comrades, so that a single hand grenade cannot kill more than one person. At the same time, we cannot be too far apart, or we will not be able to see each other and communicate, especially at night. The squad leader needs to make sure that the integrity of the formation is always maintained so that effective gunfire can be directed against the enemy at all times, regardless of their approach. He also needs to continuously evaluate the terrain to determine how best to move the squad based on the likelihood of enemy contact.

Fortunately, I am a seasoned infantryman, and I already know how to walk tactically, as both leader and follower. In fact, this stuff would be downright easy for me, if it were not for my devastated feet, which make every step a struggle.

I am not the only one suffering. Some of the lieutenants, like Tobiri and Sven, and Roberts, the cook, trip and stumble mightily as they make their way through the rough ground and twisting vines of the Camp Darby forest. The bat boys get angry at their clumsy movements and curse them for being incompetent in the woods. Apparently, the RIs are teaching us the basics for a reason, this stuff is difficult and many of us need practice.

A mere hour into the day's walk we are confronted with a steep and muddy ridge to climb up and over. There is nothing even resembling a goat path, let alone a trail on this difficult terrain. Dale leads us up the face. My soles slip and slide ceaselessly inside my boots as I sidestep my way up the slick slope. The blistered flesh on my feet re-tears anew, leaking blood, pus, and fluid into sweat-dampened socks.

Nearing the top, on the verge of tears and while begging for divine assistance, I lose my footing completely and fall face forward towards muddy, rocky ground. My right knee bangs itself hard on a tree root but manages to save me from face planting into the earth. The barrel of my machine gun pierces the ground and is plugged up with muck. Needing a moment to rest, I pant for breath and stifle a heavy sob, on my knees, in the mud.

The squad's RI is close by. He simply shakes his head in disgust as he walks past me. Leon and Newton also stumble past me. Semi-lost in their own suffering, Newton is contemptuous enough of the weak, oafish, second-rate infantryman in his midst to hiss, "Pathetic" as he walks past me.

I violently suppress another urge to sob. I cannot lose it now, not in front of the squad. I desperately want to cry out for help, to seek some solace and support, but I know that it is no use. I am in Ranger School, where no one can or even should help me. My squad mates have enough to worry about just taking care of themselves. How could I ask them to help me, a weak and friendless outsider, someone who should not even be here in the first place?

Yes, Goldsmith, the sooner you are gone, the easier it will be for everyone else.

I sit there for several seconds, lost in despair, feeling sorry for myself. But I cannot sit in the mud forever. At some point, I must get back up and keep moving. After all, no one is coming to get me, no one is going to carry me home. I either walk out of these woods or I stay here and die in these woods, this is my reality.

And besides, you look like a baby right now.

I sigh and grunt as I climb back to my feet and adjust the rucksack on my aching back. I just have to endure six or eight or ten more hours of walking like this, a few more hours of silent, solitary self-torture, and then, and then...

And then what, Goldsmith? Another week, another month, another two months or three, of this? There's no way you can do it. Just make it easy on yourself. You should quit. Now.

No, not now, I tell myself, not yet. I just have to make it through the day. Tomorrow is when I give myself permission to weigh the decision to quit, but not today.

You can quit tomorrow, but not today.

I must confess it has become a mantra for me the last few days. A pitiful motto that sums up my wretched state. By repeating it, by really believing in it, I get short-term relief from my endless suffering.

You can quit tomorrow, but not today.

But these negative thoughts, though I have yet to act on them, are acting like a drug and slowly but steadily degrading me. Until four days ago, I did not think I would ever quit this course, but now there is a sinister, weak-willed, and indulgent voice that increasingly speaks to me, especially during these long, lonely hours on the march.

Throw yourself off that ridgeline! That one, right there! It screams at me impulsively from out of nowhere. Maybe you'll break an ankle, a rib, or better yet, something worse could happen.

The mere thought of throwing myself down the cliffside both nauseates and exhilarates me. I cannot help but peer over the edge of the slippery ridge we have just struggled so hard to summit.

Just think about it, with an injury, especially a severe one, you wouldn't be leaving Ranger School as a quitter, rather, you'd be a medical case, a tragic hero, someone with his dignity and honor intact.

Fear of heights drives me backwards from the edge but, at the same time, I ponder the suggestion. It would be remarkably easy to just take a leap of faith and let gravity do the rest.

Or maybe, the voice continues, you could place your ankle at a forty-five-degree angle and just stomp down on it with all your weight. Surely that would break it. What do you say?

That should be a sure ticket out of this place. I conclude in one moment before remembering that it is not working out so well for that engineer sergeant with the broken ankle. He is still here, after all, everyone can see his unmistakably tragic figure limping back to camp every night.

When I am walking, I am in pain, and I want to quit. When we stop in the short halt, I am cold, all I want to do is sleep, and I want to quit. When the RI teaches us something, I want to walk up to him, tell him how stupid this course is, and then quit. When I am defecating in the communal outhouse after midnight and Fulton and Newton sit next to me and talk about mundane matters, I am shocked at their lack of shame, and my own, and I want to quit. When I wake up at 4:00 in the morning two hours before the sunrise, after sleeping two-and-a-half hours or less, for the eighth day in a row, all I want to do, with all my heart and soul, is quit.

I am consumed with thoughts of quitting. Only inertia and some small shred of residual pride keeps me moving forward. The longer we walk, the weaker I get. As my senses start blurring together, it becomes harder to make sense of what people are saying to me, if what I am seeing and hearing is even real. I grow increasingly deranged in my exhausted and isolated state, concerned that I am slowly losing my mind. It takes all my effort and will to just blindly follow the rangers in front of me. If only we could stop and rest for a little while.

"Pick it up, Goldie!" Jenson snaps at me for the dozenth time as he marches up on my heels. "We're still three klicks away from the objective, keep moving!"

Everyone else, especially the bat boys, seem to know a lot more about what is going on here. This knowledge brings them a measure of comfort and control in the chaos, whereas I am just lost, bouncing along from struggle to struggle. I do not know rest, I have no networks or friends to rely on, and I increasingly find myself muttering to no one, like Bailey.

I am completely and utterly alone and always, always, my feet are hurting.

As should be abundantly clear by now, more than anything else in the world, I would like to quit Ranger School, if only to get a few hours of sleep and a day or two off my feet.

But the sad truth is, I don't even know how to quit, assuming I had the time to do so, even if I became dead set on it, because I am so damn lost in Ranger School.

So, for now, there is nothing to do but keep walking, and repeat my mantra.

Just one more day, I tell myself, and then you can quit... tomorrow.

The squad walks all day, slowly through the forest, under heavy packs. We react to enemy small arms fire, then enemy mortars, we identify rally points, then there's more enemy mortars, we establish the objective rally point, conduct an ambush at the objective, do a layout, pause in the short halt, cross a linear danger area, react to enemy small arms again, and always, always, we are walking.

The sun goes down, but that does not stop anything. A huge part of being a ranger is operating proficiently in the night: moving, shooting, and communicating expertly to dispatch the enemy when they least expect it and are the least prepared. We march and fight at night using night optical devices or "NODs," for short, which are mounted to our Kevlar paratrooper helmets. They allow us to imperfectly see the nighttime world in various shades of green. Their expert use takes a little bit of practice.

The low light and heavy NODs hanging off the front of our faces compound all the difficulties of the day. Everything is harder at night. It is harder to see, colder, more injuries, more lost rangers, communications break down, and everyone moves slower, oftentimes at a crawl. It is easily the hardest part of the day.

The RIs keep us out in the woods until close to midnight, after being up for twenty hours and not eating since five in the morning. Only then do they walk us back to Camp Darby where the entire ranger class, one-hundred-

Good Preparation for Ranger School Versus What I Did

Good Ways to Prepare for Ranger School	The Wrong Way to Prepare (My Training)
Confidently run five miles in less than forty minutes, but otherwise don't spend too much time on running (which you do little of in Ranger School);	Run five miles nearly every day (to the exclusion of almost all other training);
Be able to do 50 perfect pushups with ease, same for 60 sit-ups, and ten or more pull ups, maybe some rope climbing, but otherwise, do little to no extra calisthenics or weight training;	Do regular army physical training and lift heavy weights;
Ruck march varying distances (two- to twelve-miles) with a moderately-heavy pack (35-50 pounds) to condition your back and feet for Ranger School's inevitably constant ruck marching;	Perform one or two short 2-3 mile ruck marches and call it good;
Break-in new and comfortable boots that you know will be authorized for wear at Ranger School;	Bring an old pair of jungle boots you wore for a year in Iraq without any thought for your poor feet;
Practice and be confident in your land navigation skills, be able to navigate with a compass and map, during daylight and nighttime hours;	Rely on your basic infantry training, two prior land navigation courses in as many years, and "winging it," to get you through the second highest failure rate event in Ranger School;
Concentrate on the basics: passing the PT test, ruck marching, conditioning your back and feet, and land navigation, and avoid gimmicks and complex preparation regimens; consume your regular diet and even consider coming in a few pounds heavy to compensate for the lean times to come;	Force yourself to take cold showers, lower your caloric intake to reduce your body weight, and otherwise do stupid and useless things to prepare for "the suck," which you can't really prepare for anyway;
Consider attending a Pre-Ranger Course (for most units/people this is mandatory, anyway);	Never even know about a Pre-Ranger Course because your unit never sends anyone to Ranger School and you are a corporal, so you don't have to go;
Have several weeks, or better yet, months to prepare and train for the course (but not too long, otherwise you will psych yourself out); request some time off your daily work regimen to give you time and energy to train;	Have less than three weeks to give yourself a crash training course, pack up all your gear for an upcoming deployment, and work your regular 10-16 hour a day job as an infantry team leader;
Show up to Ranger School well prepared, well-rested, and preferably, with some comrades to share in the struggle and give you yet another reason to keep going.	Show up to Ranger School two days' prior to the course start date, little-rested, hungry, alone, and utterly clueless about what is to come.

and-eighty of us now, assemble nightly for the release formation. We must wait for every squad-sized patrol to walk in before we are released for the night to shower, eat, and sleep.

Sometimes it takes until 1:00 a.m. for everyone to arrive. While we wait, we sit down or stand on cold, hard asphalt and shiver in our bare, sweat-drenched uniforms. The RIs refuse to let us put on any additional, warm clothing. Only minutes before dismissal do the RIs allow us to put on a single piece of "snivel gear," usually our wool cap or smoking jackets, never both. Inevitably, there is some final work detail that must be performed, like emptying out a shipping container of duffel bags to pull out one single item before stowing all the bags away again.

Tonight, we are lucky, and we make it back to our squad planning bay at half-past midnight. I feel immense joy when we come home to the half-roofed, large wooden shack we call home. Everyone is exhausted, but there is still lots to do before we can rest. This includes eating MRE dinner, fixing any broken gear, shaving, emptying our bowels, cutting our toenails, and self-treating our injuries.

Like everyone else, at the end of a long, thankless day, even chronically sleep-deprived rangers like to unwind a little bit before surrendering to sleep. Jenson, Newton, and Leon, as usual, opt to play grab ass with each other, Tobiri and Sven write letters to their wives, while Dale reviews the day's notes in his Ranger Handbook.

After today's crucible, my feet are devastated and my spirit nearly broken. I need a little help, some medical attention. Humbly, with head bowed, I approach Fulton.

"Hey, uh, Fulton. How's it going?" I ask the squad's green beret awkwardly. "About to rack out, I see."

Fulton is in fact crawling into his sleeping bag and eyes me suspiciously.

"I'm well enough, Goldsmith. What's going on with you?"

"Honestly, man, I was hoping you could help me out." My voice cracks a little bit as I am hit with a sudden surge of emotion. "I'm in bad shape man, real bad shape, in so much pain, you wouldn't believe it... I know you don't have to, but maybe, maybe you could help me..."

"Just tell me what you want, Goldsmith."

"Can you help me pop some of my blisters? Just the largest ones? I just need to ease some of the pressure, there's so much blood and pus building up, they..."

"No." Fulton's answer is simple and direct.

"No?" It takes me aback. "I mean, c'mon... please? I heard you're a medic with Special Forces, this should be easy for you, can't you just help me with two or three of the biggest ones? It'll make walking so much easier, maybe they will finally heal, and I don't want to screw myself up even worse."

"Go see the medics at the Aid Station. I don't want to get involved."

Those butchers! The medics are partly responsible for the terrible condition of my feet right now. Had they treated me properly, I might not now be in this mess. I would sooner dance on hot coals than submit to the hotshot treatment again, no thank you.

"Please, Fulton, please." I plead with him. "It won't take long. I have the sewing needle and lighter all ready to go... and look here! A wet wipe to clean up afterwards. You can just watch, and I'll go ahead and puncture the..."

"Let me stop you right there, Goldsmith. It's late and I'm tired. There's no way I am going to help you tonight. I just can't do it. How about... tomorrow, we can do it tomorrow. How's that sound, buddy?"

Tomorrow? Tomorrow! Who knows what tomorrow will bring? Hell, even if you will not fix me, Fulton, at least remind me that I am still human, that I still matter, that my pain and sorrow are not going unnoticed.

But I do not say any of this. Instead, I mutter "Okay," lamely in response. Fulton simply rolls over in his sleeping bag and falls instantly asleep. I crawl back to my sleeping position on my hands and knees and on the verge of tears.

If you want something done, I sigh deeply, guess you've got to do it yourself. I pull out my largest sewing needle, a lighter, and a few sheets of MRE toilet paper. I remove the sock from my left foot, lay it in the dirt, and rest my heel upon it. I place the needle tip in the lighter's flame for fifteen seconds until it starts glowing red to sterilize it.

Dr. Goldsmith, the patient is ready for his operation.

I use the sewing needle to lance and squeeze out fluid from three of the largest blisters on my left foot. I re-sanitize the needle in the flame before I lance two more giant blisters on my right foot. At this point, I give up because my hands are shaking so bad. I am also worried that if I lance too many blisters, one of them is liable to get infected. I use toilet paper to wipe up the mess and smear hand sanitizer over the wounds. It burns a little bit, but nothing like the tincture of benzoin.

No one else in the squad helps me or even acknowledges my presence during the twenty-minute operation. They do not even want to look at me. I am like a wounded animal, marked for death.

Rather, one by one, they settle into their sleeping bags and fall asleep except for Newton, who has the first guard shift.

Even in my weakened state, I cannot rely on anyone else for support. This is totally understandable, this being Ranger School, after all. Everyone else is suffering too and has already seen so many friends and comrades pass by the wayside. How could I expect them to care about me, a mediocre infantryman, a stranger, a nobody? I am just deadweight, a liability, not an asset, a loser. I am in even worse shape than Bailey and Tobiri, and they themselves are hard to look at.

You ought to quit Goldsmith.

The voice returns, and this time, I know it speaks the truth. I have given it my all, but it just is not enough. Now, the only sensible thing to do is cut my losses and get the hell out of here. This level of stupidity is too much, the suffering just not worth it. The RIs can take their fucking Tabs and shove them right up their uptight asses.

"I am quitting tomorrow." I say it out loud, confidently in the darkness, but no one hears me because they are already sleeping. "Tomorrow is the day I quit Ranger School."

I settle into my sleeping bag and within seconds, I am sound asleep, a huge smile on my face.

Chapter 4: "Rock Bottom"

"In some way, suffering ceases to be suffering at the moment it finds a meaning…"
— Victor Frankl, Man's Search for Meaning

Rule #9: Have a purpose.

2338 Hours (11:48 p.m.)
Squad Planning Bay, Camp Darby
Fort Benning, Georgia
Day 9 of Ranger School

"Ahem," I take a deep breath and clear my throat as I approach the day's RI after another long, twenty-hour day of Ranger School, "Excuse me, Sergeant."

"What the fuck do you want, ranger?"

"Sergeant… I, uh… "

It is now or never, Goldsmith. Do it!

"I'm done. I can't do this anymore, my feet… my feet are so chewed up… I want out. I want to quit." It was very tough to get out, but it feels good to finally say it.

"Did I hear you right?" The RI is calmer than I was expecting. "You want to quit, ranger? Are you sure about that?"

My short life as a ranger student, all nine days of it, flashes before my eyes: that first sleepless night, the land nav course, Combatives in the Pit, the accursed road march and all the subsequent pain, misery, cold, boredom, solitude, and stupidity. Above all, I think about the endless throbbing, searing pain in my feet. Suddenly, I can think of a great many things I want more than a Ranger Tab, like a hot shower, a cold beer, sleeping in on the weekend, and a steak dinner with the boys back home.

The truth is, I do not belong here, and no one will be sad to see me go. Today was just as bad as yesterday and there is no reason tomorrow will not be even worse.

Enough is enough.

"That's right, Sergeant. I'm done. I want to quit." And to put the nail in the coffin, I add, "And there isn't anything that would change my mind."

"Hmmph," the RI still seems more bewildered than angry. "I heard you, ranger, but it is too late to do anything tonight. This will have to wait until the morning."

This is bad news. I would prefer to get this all over with tonight, but there is nothing I can do, so I say, "Roger, Sergeant."

"I want you to think overnight on this," the RI tells me. "Really think about this, and if you still want to quit in the morning," he looks me dead in the eyes for the first time, "then come find me."

"Roger, Sergeant." I nod my head up and down like a sycophant, bowing all the while. "I will, Sergeant, thank you, thank you."

"Now, get the fuck away from me!" Notably, he doesn't call me "ranger."

I limp-run away from the RI as fast as my bruised and battered feet will carry me towards the squad rucksacks, only a short distance away. Salvador is right there, waiting for me. He was close by and must have heard what me and the RI were saying.

I avoid meeting his eyes as I unpack my sleeping bag and prepare to bed down for the night, my last night in Ranger School. Salvador says nothing to me, but I can feel his eyes watching me.

Any shame I should be feeling right now, any worry that Salvador is going to tell the other bat boys what I am about to do, is checked by sheer exhaustion and the knowledge that my struggles will soon be over. Soon, I will be going home.

You are making the right decision. The voice tells me before I nod off to a deep and dreamless slumber.

Your suffering will soon be over, Goldsmith, a life of ease awaits...

0400 Hours (04:00 a.m.)
Squad Planning Bay, Camp Darby
Fort Benning, Georgia
Day 10 of Ranger School

We wake up two hours before the first light of dawn, just like any other day. I crawl out of my dew-soaked sleeping bag into the frigid morning air, rubbing my eyelids and stretching my legs. I pack up all my sleep gear into my rucksack in near-total darkness by red-lens flashlight. I shave eagerly, dress quickly, and lace up my boots with a purpose on this, my last morning of Ranger School.

Yesterday's RI shows up at the squad's planning bay at 5:00 a.m. The squad starts tearing into their MRE breakfasts while the medics conduct their foot checks. The RI beckons me towards him with his finger.

"You still want to quit, ranger?" He asks me as I approach him. The way he says "ranger" feels like a knife twisting in my coward's heart.

"Yes, Sergeant." I stare meekly at my own feet. "I do."

"Then grab your rucksack and duffle bags and follow me."

Other than Salvador, no one in the squad had any inkling I was going to quit this morning. I choose to confide in no one, to hide my weakness and shame. We have not had anyone leave the squad since we came to Camp Darby, so I imagine my quitting will cause quite a stir.

Yet, as I throw my rucksack on my shoulders and front-load a duffle bag, I am surprised to see that, in fact, no one bats an eye. Half of the squad are too absorbed in their MREs to even notice, the others do not seem to care. No one meets my gaze or waves goodbye. Indeed, other than Newton who mutters something that causes Jenson to snort, the squad is silent.

Needless to say, no one tries to stop me. Each ranger is an island. My squad mates either lack the capacity or energy for empathy or know that my leaving is for the best.

Loaded with gear, walking as gingerly as I can on my wound-encrusted soles, I follow the RI up the short, inclined path to Camp Headquarters. As we get closer to the top, reality starts to set in. From this moment forward, I am officially going to be a Ranger School failure, worse than that, a quitter, someone who could not hack it, a decidedly non-elite and substandard soldier.

My soldiers, peers, and bosses back home will surely take me back, that I know almost for certain. But will they still respect me the way they did before? Or, rather, will they have contempt for me, laugh behind my back, and derive no small satisfaction from my abject failure after soaring too close to the sun?

I know already that this day will forever haunt me and define my future, but I do not care. Any doubts that assail me are temporary. Due to my wretched condition, exhaustion, loneliness, but mostly, because of my poor, blistered feet, I am desperate and past caring. I have hit rock bottom. I am prepared to betray myself in every way, ready to grovel and beg if I must, just to get out of here, to relieve the constant pain in my feet, to make the voices in my head stop, to get some sleep.

But first, I have to face the music, I will have to tell the RI chain of command that I want to quit. This is going to be more painful than anything I have ever done in my life. If I could sacrifice an innocent to spare myself the indignity, someone like Tobiri or Bailey, I would do so in a heartbeat. Unfortunately, that is an impossibility. I must walk the road to the gallows alone.

The tight-quartered Camp Darby Headquarters building is crawling with RIs at this early hour of the morning. At least eight of them mill about, drinking coffee and dipping tobacco. All of them look at me with a strange mixture of indifference and disgust. The RI who walked with me up the hill motions me to stand by a table where five RIs are gathered together.

Almost immediately, they stand and swarm around me as I stand nervously at the position of parade rest, hands behind my back and legs apart, completely exposed to my tormentors.

"Are you serious, ranger?" A tall, Sergeant First Class wearing glasses who I have never seen before leads the interrogation. "You really want to do this?"

"Yes, I mean, no, I mean..."

"Nobody quits now, just out of the blue, right in the middle of Techniques Week. Why, for Christ's sake, are you quitting? Why?!"

The abrupt questioning sets me aback. I struggle for a moment to gather my thoughts.

"Well? You must have a good reason, high-speed, so what is it?"

"It's my feet, my poor feet..." I launch into my tale of woe, "so blistered up they will never heal. Every step I'm in pain. Ever since the road march… and those blasted medics, I've been in so much pain and I…"

"Feet! Your fucking feet! Everyone's feet hurt! Why I…"

"Hold on a minute, Sergeant." A lean, older-looking RI with a fresh haircut and Captain's bars interrupts the RI with glasses before he can really get started on his tirade. Because of his superior rank, the sergeant first class has no choice but to bite his tongue. "Come outside with me, ranger. I want to talk to you."

I follow him outside the building, leaving the other RIs behind. I notice that the sun is just beginning to rise over the horizon. The dew-covered pine forest, illuminated by the morning light, is serene and intensely beautiful.

"I hear you're from a mechanized infantry unit, ranger." The Captain says. "The Fourth Infantry Division, is that right?"

"Yes, Sir. From Fort Carson." And then I add sheepishly, looking down at my feet. "I'm just a regular old infantry guy."

"Not a lot of mech guys in Ranger School, that's for sure. This course is hard for them, extremely hard. Hard to get a slot, hard to get the time to properly train for it, hard to finish it."

"Yes, it is, sir." This RI is speaking to me like a real human being. It feels nice.

"You know, ranger," He pauses meaningfully and stays silent, forcing me to meet his gaze. "When I came through here as an enlisted soldier, a long time ago, I was in a mech unit."

"Really?" I say lamely. At this point, I don't really care about this Captain's service history. I just want to get this whole painful episode over with, but I have to say something in response. He still stands there silently, staring at me.

"That's… really interesting, sir." I do not know what else to say.

"That's all, ranger." The Captain says calmly. "Just wanted to let you know. You can go back inside now."

"Yes, sir."

I go back inside the headquarters building. The stern assembly of RIs is waiting for me. The one with glasses resumes his harangue.

"I mean, you made it past RAP week, halfway through Darby. Do you know what you're doing? What your unit is going to do to you when you go back?"

"I don't know what I'm doing, and they're not going to be happy with me back at my unit, but I'm done, Sergeant. I can't go on any longer, not with my feet, not alone, not with all this stupidity. I want out of here."

"Fine. Have it your way, ranger." The RI with glasses voice is filled with anger after my 'stupidity' remark. "You want out of here? Go right ahead. Give him the Lack of Motivation statement!"

The RI with glasses flicks his hand away distastefully while another RI whips out what looks like a single-paged legal document and slaps it down on the table in front of me.

"Read it and sign!"

The Lack of Motivation statement, or LOM, is the formal acknowledgement of my self-willed failure, my unconditional surrender, a one-page contract that will forever brand me as a quitter. As part of its terms, I forfeit the right to ever return to Ranger School and I will never earn the Tab. Signing an LOM is shameful and devoid of honor, worse than being medically or peer recycled, worse than failing patrols, worse than having an accidental discharge, worse than any other offense in Ranger School.

After all, a ranger never quits. It's part of The Creed, and here I am, quitting.

I skim the document quickly, rapidly print my name, and scribble my signature at the bottom. I push it across the table to the waiting RIs, but strangely, no one reaches for it.

Everyone is silent for a moment as the RI with glasses stares intently at my name tape, then my face, and then my name tape again.

"Goldsmith... Goldsmith... Now where have I heard that name before...?"

"Wait a second, ranger," suddenly a realization dawns on him, "you're not Castle's guy, are you?" It is as if he is really looking at me for the first time.

"Yes." I tell him. "He's my First Sergeant."

"Ha! Of all people." He shakes his head and addresses the other RIs in the room, "You all remember Castle, right?" Several heads nod and murmur in agreement.

"You know," the RI with glasses has a stern look on his face again, "he called here asking about you last night. I had to pull up your file. I told him you were doing good, flying beneath the radar. What the hell happened?"

I can only stare morosely at the ground. I want to cry.

"He said you were a good kid, and now, here you are..." The RI with glasses lets his thought trail off. "You know, First Sergeant Castle worked here a long time, ranger? I consider him a good friend and a mentor."

"Yes," I sigh. Back at the company, we all know that First Sergeant is a proud former RI. "I know."

This quitting business is taking too long and growing more painful by the second. I know now that no matter how painful this immediate quitting process is going to be, the worst part will be facing First Sergeant Castle back at home and telling him I signed an LOM. He vouched for my readiness, eased my paperwork's passage through the chain of command, helped me train, and even gave me a "drive-on Tab" that he cut off an old uniform. Hell, what am I supposed to do with that now? Give it back to him? Throw it away?

The truth is, I will never interact with him, or any of the other men back at the company, the same again. There will always be excuses, judgment, residual shame. They will know and, more importantly, I will know, that I came up short, that I was a quitter, someone who cannot be counted on to hold it together during the inevitable tough times ahead. How am I supposed to lead my men now, in Iraq, in combat? What a hypocrite and a fraud I will be.

I dread all of this more than anything else in my life, but it doesn't matter any longer – I am finished. I have already signed the LOM; the damage has been done.

Still, none of the five RIs make a move for my LOM statement. My confession of weakness just lies on the table motionless, taunting me.

Why are they keeping me here like this? I ask myself. To twist the knife in my heart? What else do they want me to say?

"Now that I know who you are," the RI with glasses breaks the silence, "I really want to know: why are you quitting, ranger?"

Until this point, mostly out of shame, I have been speaking as little as possible. But now, the dam bursts and emotions overwhelm me.

"My feet are devastated... thin, thin-soled boots... no time for this school... I need to be with my men, training for Iraq..." I verbally spew every rationalization, excuse, and complaint I can think of, "layouts... tie-downs... stupid, oh so stupid... all we do is freeze in the bleachers... my feet, my feet... haven't learned anything... so, so alone... my feet... my poor, poor feet..."

And then I fall silent.

The RIs have had their fun. Now that I have completely broken down, they are indifferent and disgusted by the whining of a miserable wretch. Two RIs blade their shoulders away from me, another spits a fat wad of dip disgustedly into an empty styrofoam coffee cup.

But the RI with glasses is not done with me yet. "Like I said ranger, Castle's a good friend of mine. Before we wrap this up, I think we should call him. You can tell him yourself that you're quitting."

Call him? No! This is worse than death itself. There is nothing on earth I would rather do less than talk to First Sergeant Castle right now. I could face him in a week, two days from now, tomorrow even, but not now.

"No-oh." I snivel. "No, Sergeant, please! You don't need to call him. It's uh, it's uh..." in desperation I scramble for an excuse, "It's too early! It's not even four in the morning yet in Colorado."

"No, no, ranger, I insist," The RI holds up his left palm as if to stop me as his right hand whips out his cellphone. "He's going to want to talk to you and hear the good news straight from the source. You owe him that, at the very least."

The spectacled RI punches in a few numbers and walks a few paces away. The other RIs look interested again.

"Hey, Castle... yeah, yeah, it's me... well hell, I'm sorry to call you so damn early in the morning, but I got your boy here... uh-huh, that's right, Goldsmith... uh-huh, uh-huh, well, he was doing fine, but now, he's trying to quit... I know, I know... I told him... You want to talk to him?"

No! I raise my right hand in front of my face and start shaking it, silently, back, and forth, mouthing the words, No. No.

"Hold on now, he's right here." The RI with glasses is smiling from ear-to-ear as he hands me his cell phone.

"... First Sergeant... ?"

"What's this nonsense about quitting, Goldsmith?" First Sergeant is right to business, as usual, his voice amazingly clear considering it is 3:52 in the morning in Colorado.

"I'm done, First Sergeant. I, I, I can't... honestly, I just can't go on anymore." Again, a flood of powerful emotions turns my speech into a confused blather. "I'm all alone, none of this makes sense, and my feet... you can't understand, my feet are so blistered up, never in my life—"

"You made it through RAP Week, Goldsmith," First Sergeant cuts me off, "through the hardest part. The rest is just a slow grind. You can't quit now! No one quits where you're at right now in Ranger School."

"I can't do it, First Sergeant. My feet are so jacked up. Every step I take... you can't even imagine... I'll quit complaining, it's just... I need to be back with you guys, with the platoon, with the squad, with my men, getting ready for the deployment."

"But we're not doing anything. We're just sitting around, with all our gear packed up, waiting to fly out, bullshitting."

"But that's why I need to be back there—to get ready to go back to Iraq, with you, with Alpha Company!"

"What you need to do is finish this goddamn school, Goldsmith!"

"But, but... I need to be back...with the guys." I whimper one final time, broken and beaten down.

But First Sergeant does not care one iota for my excuses and rationalizations, not now, not ever. How can I make him understand that I gave Ranger School my best, one-hundred-and-ten percent, but that I just have nothing left, no shame, no sense of humor, no body fat, no relief from pain, no one who cares whether I live or die, nothing to keep me moving forward on this grueling, ascetic path.

"I just want to come home, First Sergeant." I am on the edge of tears. "I just want to come back to Alpha Company."

"Look, Goldsmith, I'll make this easy for you," he says calmly. "If you don't finish Ranger School, you won't come back to us. I'll send you to Bravo Company, maybe trade you for someone at Battalion or Brigade. I don't really care either way, but I'm not having you back at Alpha Company, not without a Tab."

"Not coming back..." My voice trails off for a moment.

Not coming back? Not coming back to Alpha Company?

I never thought banishment from my tribe was a possibility. For the bat boys, sure, but not for me, a regular infantryman. I took it for granted that I would always have a home in Alpha Company and especially with my beloved First Platoon. I have spent nearly every waking moment for the past three years with them, training together, partying together, serving in Iraq for a year together with most of them, readying the new guys. They are dearer to me than family, they are my brothers.

"Hello, hello? You still there, Goldsmith?"

"Not coming back, First Sergeant?" I say it one more time, still in stunned disbelief. "But that can't happen. That's just... that's just not a possibility."

The Truth suddenly hits me hard, like Zen enlightenment. The mind sickness that has poisoned my thoughts and clouded my judgment lifts in an instant. I feel healthy again, strong, sharp, filled with... PURPOSE. I know what needs to be done now if I ever want to go home again, even if it seemed impossible only seconds ago. I have conviction now, a new religion, like everyone else here, a deep-hearted and genuine reason to earn the Tab.

First Sergeant has certainly made it easy for me, bless the man. Earn the Tab or do not come back. Well, not going to Iraq with my men and my friends is not a possibility. Nothing is going to hold me back, not family, love, health, wealth, fame, or anything else, and certainly, not Ranger School.

I must earn my Tab, there is no other way.

So, let's fucking do it then, Goldsmith!

"Hello? Hello? Goddamnit!" First Sergeant sounds pissed "Goldsmith, are you still there?"

Yes, First Segeant, I am. I am me again, though for a while there, I was lost. Already, I am disgusted with my former self and will likely remain so the rest of my life. How could I have gotten so wretchedly low?

It was a taste of rock bottom, something I was fortunate never to have experienced before. Until now, I have always had family, friends, ability, and even lady luck to aid me when I needed them in a tight spot. Even in Iraq, during the worst days, I had friends and leaders to rely on, to share in the adversity, so it was never that bad. Never before in life had I been abandoned, never had I lost the will to keep moving forward, never had I so thoroughly surrendered to my troubles, bad habits, and weakness.

I hit rock bottom, and all it took was nine days of Ranger School, but the good news is, there is only one way to go from here.

Up.

"I'm here, First Sergeant and you don't have to worry about me any longer. I'm going to finish this thing. I am going to earn the Tab. I'm sorry to make you deal with this so early in the morning."

"No more nonsense about quitting, Goldsmith." First Sergeant just sounds tired now, no longer angry. "Understand?"

"Yes, First Sergeant!" And without waiting for further orders, I flip the cellphone shut.

The roomful of RIs is silent. In these cramped quarters, they all heard the entire conversation. Nobody moves. The RI with glasses locks eyes with me, then his pupils look down toward the LOM statement, before shifting rapidly back to me.

Before he can blink, I lunge over the table, snatch up the single-paged LOM statement, and rip it to shreds.

"What the fuck do you think you're doing, ranger?!" Several RIs shout at me. One of them crouches down, as if ready to tackle me. The Captain RI pats him on the shoulder and lets him know that it's okay to ease off. The uproar settles down.

"Ahem," the RI with the glasses captures the room's attention. "You must have a guardian angel or something, ranger, because you are damn lucky. Anyone else, and I mean anyone else, would already be long gone, on his way out the fucking door, a certified tab-less wonder for life, but you, you're Castle's boy... and that means something to me. Consider this a rare second chance. Don't waste it."

"I understand. Thank you, Sergeant." Apparently, I am going to get away with my destruction of the physical evidence. "Really, thank you!"

He dismisses me with a wave of his hand, turns his back on me, and goes back to his morning's work.

"You really screwed yourself, ranger," the Captain RI tells me. "Until twenty minutes ago, we didn't even know who you were. Now, the spotlight is on you. You better shine out there during your graded patrols, really bust your ass and help your squad mates, because all of us here are going to hold you to the highest standard and will not cut you any slack. You're going to have to prove to us that you want the Tab."

"More than anything, sir. I want the Tab more than anything." And for the first time, I truly mean it.

"Then pick up your bags, get the fuck out of here, and rejoin your squad, ranger! They're waiting on you down there!"

"Yes, sir!"

Despite my bruised, battered, and bloodied feet, whose physical condition remains unchanged from half-an-hour ago, despite the hundred pounds of gear I hump awkwardly on my back and neck, I run as fast as I can, yelling like a maniac down the trail back to the squad planning bay.

Rock bottom is not so bad, I realize. Not only has it allowed me to see with real clarity for the first time, but it is the best place, maybe the only place, to truly start life anew.

As I dash and scramble down the trail, I run away from weakness and despair, away from the cheap and easy luxuries of the outside, non-ranger world, and towards my true purpose and destiny. The way forward will be long and arduous, but I have a reason now, meaning and a purpose, for enduring the pain, the cold, solitude, and hunger.

I have just learned an important lesson today, the most important rule of Ranger School, and perhaps life itself. That rule is: you better have a purpose, a damn good reason, to get you through Ranger School, or whatever challenging, heart-rending, brutalizing circumstances you may be facing. In the toughest of times, unless you are inspired with a sense of purpose, you will not be able to endure the suffering necessary to endure, to live, to win.

Without a deep sense of purpose, you will never earn the Tab.

I keep running down the trail, as fast as I can, ignoring the pain in my feet, just happy, so unbelievably happy, that I will be rejoining my ranger squad again. I want to get as far away from those RIs as possible before they change their mind. I also want to get back to the business of the day, without skipping a beat, so that I can start to repair the reputational harm I have just inflicted on myself.

I need to get my head in the game again. I need to quit feeling sorry for myself. I need to suck it up, bear the suffering, and earn my Tab. It is my only way back home.

So, damn the pain in my feet. It is not going to kill me or cause me to lose a limb, I just have to bear it. Damn the sleepless exhaustion, I'll sleep when I am dead. Ranger School can be pretty stupid, but so what? Embrace it, be even stupider. Lots of things are stupid. The infantry is stupid, the Army is stupid, life is inherently stupid, just grow up, stop acting like a child, and deal with it.

And as to feasting, drinking, and wild nights with the boys back home? There will be plenty of time for that, after Ranger School, after Iraq, and just think how much sweeter those good times will be, when we return together as conquering heroes.

It does not take long before I find myself back at the squad planning bay. There I re-gaze upon eleven faces I thought I would never see again. They crouch in a semi-circle around the new day's RI as he issues the day's operations order. I drop my rucksack and duffle bags next to my squad mates and limp-jog over to them to join the briefing.

My sudden reappearance barely registers with most of my squad mates, who are lost in their own suffering. Only Jenson, Newton, and Fulton laugh and make sly remarks under their breath. Tobiri claps me on the back and whispers, "Welcome back, Goldsmith." Bailey mumbles something undecipherable. Salvador says nothing yet looks pleased to see me again.

The RI finishes issuing his order and releases us to plan the squad op order. The day proceeds like any other day at Darby, we plan, listen to an excruciatingly long order, and then head into the woods to conduct practice patrols and drills all day, then late into the night.

This is my life now, the raw and miserable existence of a ranger, and I am okay with it, all of it: the cold, the hunger, sleep deprivation, solitude, injury, pain, madness, stupidity, all of it, for as long as it takes.

What choice do I have?

I may not always be running, but, at the very least, I will be limping forward. On the path to earn my Tab.

Chapter 5: "FTX"

Rule #10: Moving forward is better than sitting still.

0550 Hours (05:50 a.m.)
Camp Darby Training Area
Fort Benning, Georgia
Day 13 of Ranger School
Day 3 of the Darby FTX

"Good morning, little fella. How's your morning going?"
"He is a handsome little guy, isn't he?"
"Strong, too."
"And fast. Look at him go!"
Fulton and I lie belly down in the dirt and admire the shiny, jet-black exoskeleton, deft movements, and multi-jointed fine limbs of a beetle as he scrambles over leaves and small twigs.
"Oh no!" Fulton exclaims in a whisper. "Look, look where he's going, Goldsmith."
Our beetle friend is walking right into a small stream of fierce-looking black ants. Fulton starts nudging him away from the hazard with a twig, hoping he will alter his course.
"Don't do it friend," Fulton coaxes him. "There's just too many of them."

But the little beetle seems dead set on his course and cannot be stopped. He crosses right over the ants, stops in their midst, either ready for battle or reconciled to his own death.

"Here we go, Goldsmith," Fulton says with a little sadness in his voice. "This is going to be something."

Fortunately, the two parties do not seem to mind the other. The beetle passes unmolested through the ant battalion, and we keep watching him as he slowly crawls away from us.

We are lying face down in the dirt, pulling security at the squad patrol base, weapons facing outwards, and bored out of our minds. We desperately try to stay awake by playing with insects while we stare endlessly into trees, bushes, and more trees. Thus far, the Darby FTX has consisted of a lot of staring at trees. Walking through trees, stopping, and staring outward at trees, sleeping under trees, hallucinating, and seeing twisted and terrible faces in the trees. Under these conditions, watching a beetle is captivating.

"Say, Goldsmith," Fulton whispers to me as the beetle walks out of sight, "what do you think about loaning me something from one of your MREs?"

The hairs on the back of my neck stand up straight and I shoot Fulton a sideways glance as he continues.

"I didn't eat my breakfast MRE an hour ago because I wanted to save it for later, but man, am I hungry now. Probably shouldn't have done that. Foolish move, huh?" He chuckles and slaps me on the back. I continue to say nothing.

"I'll get you back with something good next time we stop and eat. Something really good. What do you say, pal?"

I am extremely suspicious about this unorthodox (and prohibited) food trade. I mull it over long and hard despite my general desire to please Fulton, the squad's green beret and my secret hero. During RAP Week or even in the early days of Darby, this would have been no big deal, but now, this deep into the FTX, things are different.

I am hungry.

It is thirteen days into Ranger School, three days into the Darby FTX, and real, deep hunger has grown in all of us. Every man in the squad is burning through calories and losing weight, even the skinny guys like Leon and Tobiri who can ill afford it. Walking in the woods all day and night, keeping our half-exposed bodies warm, and powering our perpetually sleep-deprived brains requires a lot of energy, a lot of food, every morsel of which has become precious and dear.

So, no. This is not an easy decision. Right now, I would just as soon sell my sister as I would loan out a two-hundred-calorie snack. Unless there is a damn good reason, I am not feeding anyone on credit.

"I don't know..." Fulton just sits there silently and pleasantly smiling at me, waiting for an answer. I scramble for a good excuse but cannot think of anything not based on greed.

"You're going to get me back with something good, right?" I reluctantly answer.

"Of course, Goldsmith, of course! I'll hook you up with something great." Fulton's eyes positively gleam with the thought of his impending snack, "So, what do you got in your MRE?"

I am already filled with regret as I take a 360-degree scan of the patrol base to make sure no RIs are watching us. I quickly loosen the straps on my rucksack, open the top flap, and grab an unopened MRE, tonight's dinner, which according to the rules of Ranger School, should not be opened or anything consumed until security is established at the new patrol base. Eating food when we are not supposed to is called "grazing" and strictly forbidden in Ranger School.

I am taking a significant risk by doing this favor for Fulton. He better pay me back.

"I've got Beef Patty." I whisper to Fulton as I take out my knife and slice open the top of the vacuum sealed meal. "Comes with... macaroni and cheese, cheese pretzels, wheat snack bread..."

"That's good. I'll take the wheat snack bread."

"The wheat snack bread?"

"Yeah, c'mon. Quick! While the RI isn't looking."

I hand over my precious wheat snack bread, all two hundred calories of it, to Fulton.

"Thanks, pal. I owe you one."

My stomach grumbles audibly in response. Yeah, you do. I think to myself. Green beret or not, better believe I am going to collect on this.

The new day's RI, the young, acne-scarred, no-nonsense Darby RI, walks into our patrol base at precisely 6:00 a.m. and gets right down to business.

"Assumption of command time, rangers." He announces aloud in the middle of the squad's cigar-shaped base. "Your new leadership will be as follows: Ranger Dale, squad leader; Ranger Goldsmith, Alpha Team Leader;

Ranger Salvador, Bravo Team Leader."

Here we go! Three days into the FTX and now, it is my turn to take charge, my first graded patrol, my chance to show the RIs that I have what it takes to lead. I really hope I can do this.

"Ranger Dale, come over here to receive the order," the RI commands. "Let's go, ranger!"

Passing at least one graded patrol is the only way for a ranger to move forward in each of the phases of Ranger School. To do so, a ranger must lead either a fire team or the entire squad to the RI's satisfaction, meaning the mission gets accomplished, the squad performs all its required tasks, and everyone works smoothly together as a team.

This is a difficult task when one is leading a dozen ornery, hungry, sleepy, lazy rangers, some of which may be out of their minds with sleeplessness and totally incapable of comprehending a single word you say. A ranger leader has no real rank or authority and must rely on his personality and presence to get debased men, some of whom may be having the worst day of their lives, to follow him. No easy task.

If a graded leader cannot make the men follow and accomplish the mission, he will fail his patrol, but there are many other ways to fail. A ranger won't pass his patrol if he gets the squad lost or if he doesn't know where he is on the map when the RI quizzes him. Any of your soldiers losing a piece of equipment, getting caught burying ammo, or even sleeping on the line could be grounds for an instant "no-go" for the leader, as is failing to conduct rehearsals, losing control of the patrol base at night, arriving late to the objective, taking too long to plan the mission or, alternatively, taking too little time to plan for the mission.

Everything must go smoothly, and the men must respect and follow the patrol leaders for the RIs to bless them with the coveted "go." Failure means a recycling of the phase at best and getting kicked out of the course at its worst, a fate no one wants to endure. Naturally, the graded patrol experience is nerve-wracking and a huge source of anxiety for many rangers, especially, it seems, for the bat boys.

But I consider myself fortunate to be graded today. I have the good luck of being graded on the third day, as opposed to the fifth or sixth day of the FTX. Good luck because the longer this thing goes on, the worse for wear we become. I have also been assigned the Alpha Team Leader position, which is not only easier than being the squad leader, but also happens to be the position I hold back at my unit. Provided the men listen to me, I am confident I can do the job in my sleep, which, in Ranger School, is almost a requirement.

I am even grateful to have Dale as the squad leader. Although I dislike the young lieutenant for his youth, eagerness, smug sense of superiority, and habit of talking down to the enlisted guys, I am sure he will perform well in the role. Dale is smart, knows tactics well enough, and his body and mind have held up well under the stresses of Ranger School. Most importantly of all, he is confident, motivated, and eager to demonstrate his worth.

So overall, it is a good day to be assigned a graded patrol. Assuming the men follow us today, we all stand a good chance of getting "go's."

Salvador, however, does not share my confidence. Upon hearing the news of his appointment as Bravo Team Leader his skin has grown pale and his eyes downcast.

After a few minutes, the RI wraps up his op order briefing and Dale is let loose to prepare the squad op order. He walks over to brief me and Salvador.

"Salvador, Goldsmith."

"What's up, Dale?" Salvador replies.

"We have to prepare the op order now, okay." Dale's tone is all business.

"Roger that," I respond.

"Now, usually the team leaders would help me prepare the order, okay? But in this case, okay, I think it would be better if you guys walked the line, okay, supervise hygiene and weapons maintenance, okay, and just watch the men and keep them awake." Dale pauses and cocks his head at Leon and Newton's fighting position before concluding, "Can you do that for me, okay?"

I nod affirmatively in response while Salvador replies with a crisp, sarcastic, "Yes, boss!"

We both understand that Dale wants to take charge of all the planning himself, with a little help from his officer friends and maybe Fulton. We know that he doesn't trust dumb enlisted guys like Salvador and I to do the job well enough.

Well, young Dale, besides being an asshole, you are probably right, and you certainly will not get any objection from this mediocre infantryman. I hate preparing op orders.

"Great, okay," Dale says in his dry monotone. "You two can help me right now by rounding up McCormick, Sven, Tobiri, and Fulton and telling them to report to my position, okay?"

As usual, while every LT in the squad and Fulton work on preparing the operations order, the bat boys and I are left pulling security around the patrol base. Me and Salvador walk and crawl around the perimeter, talking to the men, making them shave, clean their weapons, and kicking them awake as needed.

As the LTs keep planning, a light, misty rain starts falling out of the sky around 8:30 a.m. Naturally, the RIs forbid any of us from putting on the rain jackets we have stowed away in our rucks. This is the first rain we have seen in Ranger School and the bat boys take it as a bad omen.

Thirty minutes later, everyone's uniform and rucksacks are thoroughly dampened from the rain, and Dale is ready to issue the op order. Since we are out in the field, me, Salvador, and a single RI will be the only ones in attendance. Everyone else, the regular Joes, will keep pulling security on the perimeter of the base.

The rain is coming down harder now, in big, steady droplets, and the RI instructs Leon and Newton to cover the four of us with a poncho liner and a waterproof poncho to keep us, our maps, and our notebooks dry during the briefing. I cannot help but feel a little ridiculous, all of us assembled under a makeshift poncho fort. Salvador illuminates the darkness with a red-lens flashlight while Dale holds court. Outside, the rest of the squad shivers in the rain.

"Welcome to the operations order, gentlemen, okay. My name is Ranger Dale, and this is Op Order #5467, okay. Today, we will be conducting an ambush in order to destroy enemy personnel and equipment, okay?"

Everyone is packed so close together inside our poncho fort that our knees touch. I can feel the heat of Dale's warm breath on my face, and I can see small torrents of steam rising visibly from everyone's damp uniform as the layers of quilted nylon and polyester trap our body heat. After only a minute inside, it already feels like a wet sauna. For the first time in days, I am pleasantly warm, and therefore, happy.

"Weather reports indicate a high chance of precipitation today, okay?" Indeed, outside our warm shelter, the wind howls and the rain falls even harder on our squad mates. "Nighttime illumination will be 60%, okay?"

An outsider might be fooled by Dale's dull monotone, flawless enunciation, and deadpan delivery, but the young lieutenant has been waiting eagerly for this moment for years and could not be more excited. As the first of two squad leaders for the day, he knows that his "go" or "no-go" will largely depend on his delivery of the op order. Salvador and I know he is nervous because he says "okay," his filler word, even more than usual.

"We will approach the objective from the southwest, okay, and generally skirt this ridgeline here, okay?" Dale traces the route of the march on his map with a small twig as droplets of sweat from his forehead drip steadily onto the laminated paper. "We will move in squad column, fire team wedge, okay, per the standard operating procedure, okay, and if engaged by the enemy, okay, will conduct react to contact in accordance with standard operating procedures, okay, wherein the team that is engaged will…"

Our shelter is a steam bath, Dale is the most boring orator I have ever heard, and I have never been more tired in my life. It is barely ten minutes into what will surely be a marathon op order and already it is a monumental effort just to keep my eyelids open. I would trade anything in the world right now just to lie down and sleep for an hour, even in the rain.

All my powers and energy are invested in one critical mission: keeping myself from falling soundly off into a deep, dark sleep. This is extremely difficult, despite the fact the RI is literally breathing down my neck. Through it all, I increasingly lose the mental capacity to process anything Dale is saying.

Salvador is engaged in the same struggle. Twice already he has nearly dropped the flashlight illuminating our briefing before shaking himself awake and regaining consciousness. The RI looks annoyed and shakes his head each time.

"… and then we will cross this stream here before establishing the ORP at the following coordinates, okay? Make sure to write this down, okay? Zero-One-Eight-Four-Five-Two-Five-Five, okay?"

I do not write anything down. I am too tired. Tired of this op order, tired of Dale and his arrogant way of saying "okay" after everything, tired of Ranger School, just so tired of everything.

"… now Goldsmith, I want you to take special note of this, okay, before we set out on the leader's recon, okay…"

How about I rip your Adam's apple out of your goddamn throat, okay? A surge of intense, repressed anger washes over me. Is that OKAY with you, Dale, you schoolhouse motherfucker, OKAY?

I welcome the anger and the accompanying surge of adrenaline. For the briefest of moments, I am wide awake, able to keep my eyelids open again, with little effort.

But it does not last. One minute later I find myself head-bobbing along with Salvador, on the razor's edge of sleep oblivion. I hope the RI does not notice. It is a good thing it is dark under here, which makes it hard to see our eyes in the glow of a red-lens flashlight. Besides, it is just so pleasantly warm under here, anyone could be forgiven for closing their eyelids just a little bit...

"WAKE THE FUCK UP, RANGERS!"

The RI's shout jolts both me and Salvador awake, for at least another minute or two.

"Now listen up, Salvador, okay?" Dale, unperturbed, resumes his op order. "You are going to take your team, okay, and set them up on the assault line here, okay?"

Salvador nods his head up and down as if he understands, but I cannot comprehend anything Dale is saying. In one ear, and out the other, but that is okay, no pun intended, because not only have I sat through the same exhaustive lectures Dale has but, after three years in the infantry, I know basic infantry tactics and doctrine better than almost anyone here. Moreover, knowing Dale, he will micromanage the patrol all day anyway, giving way more direction than necessary. So long as he points me in the right direction, me and my teammates, Leon, Newton, and Fulton, should be able to get the job done.

After what feels like ten hours, Dale finally wraps up his op order.

"Any questions?" He asks us.

"Nope," says Salvador.

"Negative," I say, even though I have no idea what the mission is about other than walking five or six klicks through the woods and conducting an ambush before sundown.

"Then go ahead, team leaders, okay? Brief your men about the mission and conduct rehearsals, okay? We move out in twenty mikes, okay."

The RI whips the poncho and poncho liner from our heads, exposing the four of us to the cold, damp, early morning daylight again. Rain is still trickling down, but the clouds are clearing, and it looks like it might shape up to be a somewhat pleasant, even beautiful day in the forest.

Salvador and I "brief" the men about the mission, which naturally does not take long, as we know virtually nothing about it. We then have the men retrieve the claymore mines, breakdown the patrol base, and pack up their rucks.

Five minutes before we are set to move out, I throw my heavy, awkwardly weighted rucksack over my head and onto my back. I wince at the familiar pain in my neck and upper back muscles that greets me. Meanwhile, my feet are still as torn up as they always are, covered in blisters and bruises, every step just as brutal as the last, but somehow, I have learned to live with the constant pain.

I still have lingering temptations of throwing myself off a ridgeline or hillside to purposefully break an ankle, but hey, what ranger student doesn't?

And thus far, I have successfully resisted the urge.

Dale makes some hand motions, and the squad forms up into three triangular wedge formations. With myself at the tip of the spear, Alpha Team Leader, at 11:32 a.m. we move off into the woods to start the graded patrol.

We march, or walk tactically, that is, slowly and ponderously, under the weight of our heavy sixty- to seventy-pound rucksacks for the entire rest of the day and long into the night. The whole time, we "scan our sectors," constantly searching around us for our enemy, the Opfor, who are always out there somewhere, waiting to ambush us in the woods. We want to avoid running into the Opfor, if possible, so we exercise "noise and light discipline" — moving quietly without speaking and without light at night. We also maintain our fire team wedge formations, keeping the appropriate distance between us, and communicate solely using hand and arm signals. We take minor injuries such as falls, twisted ankles, and tree branches to the eye, in stride and, ideally, without uttering a single audible whimper.

Frequently we will stop, get down on one knee, listen, and look outwards, pulling security against any unseen threats, but it is only a brief respite from the constant walking. Soon enough, we are up and marching forward again.

Why do we walk all day? What is the purpose of the patrol? A patrol is timeless, it entails heading out into enemy territory to sneak around, lay traps, kill bad guys, plunder his goods, take his women, and slip back unseen into the bush. It is a painful, solitary, boring, at times fearful, existence. It means walking endlessly through woods and swamps, up and down hills, rain or shine, day and night, humping all one's possessions on his back, in order to spy on, raid, or ambush the enemy. This is patrolling, this is the ranger way.

As a team leader, my primary job on the patrol is to make sure the individual men are following the rules on the march. Today, Leon, with the SAW machine gun, is my right-hand man, placed about five meters to my

5.56mm Blank Cartridge

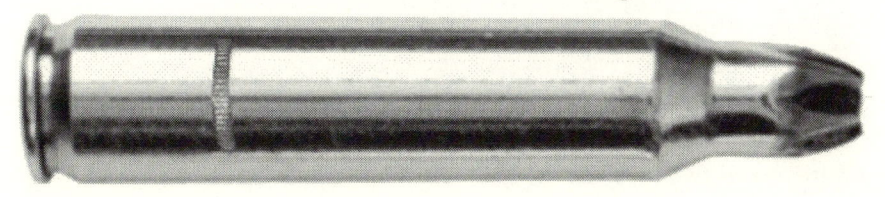

right and back a few paces. Fulton, a grenadier and the squad's perpetual navigator, is similarly arrayed off to my left. Off to his left in turn and back a few paces, is Newton, who carries an M16 rifle and an AT-4 rocket tube. As usual, he is chewing gum and quietly humming Journey songs.

After RAP Week, Techniques Week, and now several days into the FTX, we look lean, dirty, and ragged. Numb and inured to the constant hardships of the march, if we do not quite look like a hardened guerrilla band, at the very least we look like impoverished, heavily armed vagrants.

This is not an easy life. We do not eat enough, we do not sleep, we barely speak, we are constantly exposed to the elements, but most of all, we carry heavy rucksacks that rarely leave our backs. Everything we need to accomplish the mission, to live and survive, we "hump" or carry with us: extra boots, pants, shirt tops, t-shirts, socks, rain jacket, rain pants, sleeping bags, poncho, poncho liner, Ranger Handbook, MREs, six quarts of water, ammunition,

7.62mm Blank Cartridges in Metallic Belt

and various assorted pieces of squad equipment including claymore mines, radios, medical supplies, and AT-4 anti-tank rockets. The three men of the M240B machine gun team have it worst of all. Among them, they must hump the standard ranger load plus the big gun, its unwieldy, heavy tripod, and nearly a thousand rounds of 7.62 blank ammunition.

All of us must utilize various tricks, twists, and contortions to just get our heavy packs onto our backs in the first place. In the process, we strain and tweak our knees, hips, backs, and shoulders. Leon and Tobiri, the smallest guys in the squad, can barely put their rucksacks on by themselves and have to sit down, place the straps on their shoulders, and roll over on all fours to stand up.

But as bad as it is to put the rucksack on, the real pain of the march only grows with each passing hour. The shoulder straps increasingly grind into my shoulders, causing dull, but steadily increasing pain to my upper back, neck, and shoulders. The kidney pads, cushions worn thin through long years of use, slide and grind along the skin of my hips and lower back, causing rashes and bruising. Periodically, the pinched nerve in my upper back sends paroxysms of pain up and down my spinal column.

And the longer the ruck is on my back, the worse it all gets.

Unfortunately, there is no real way to reduce the suffering entailed by long marching under a heavy pack, not now at least, not in the middle of Ranger School. One has no choice but to keep walking, you just have to grin and bear it, find some way to ignore the pain or block it out of your consciousness.

In a way, it is fortunate that I am a team leader today. I am too busy monitoring the men and navigating through the woods to focus on my own suffering. My attention is consumed by the hundred odd tasks that go into patrolling. When one is a regular "Joe" for the day, responsible only for oneself and one's load, it is far easier to get lost in your own suffering.

And at least while we are walking, we are moving steadily closer to the objective, to the patrol base, to a blessed meal and maybe two or three hours of sleep. If we hurry, that is.

The only thing worse than marching in Ranger School is sitting still.

Dale thrusts his left fist into the air. Within seconds the halt signal is passed amongst the entire squad, and we all stop walking. Dale levels his forearm and makes a subtle patting motion, telling us to "take a knee," or assume the short halt.

Per our standard operating procedure, Salvador and I dash over to the squad leader's position for guidance. Slowly, painfully, I drop my right knee to the ground, rucksack still on my back, to listen to what he has to say.

"Let's do a map check, guys, okay? Just to make sure we are on the right track, okay?"

"Sure thing, Dale." I respond, happy to take note of where Dale believes we are on the map, just in case the RI quizzes me on it later.

"We need to stop less and keep moving." Salvador grumbles. "At this rate, we are going to miss the hit time."

"Let's see here... okay..." Dale ignores Salvador's advice. "We are here, okay, the objective is here, okay, which means we really should be moving a little more to the northwest, okay..."

As Dale muses over the map, the rest of us crouch on one knee in the short halt, sixty-pound rucksacks still on our backs, their straps pulling on our back muscles and shoulders at a new and different angle. The short halt would be restful if only we could take these damn packs off our aching backs, but only the machine gunner and his assistant have this privilege. The rest of us must keep them on.

"... perhaps, okay, if we went this way here, we could avoid these two streams, okay, at the expense of a greater distance, okay..."

Dale is lost in his map, second guessing himself, while the rest of the squad stays crouched in the short halt. Get a move on! We want to scream at him, sweat dripping into our eyes, backs howling with pain.

I see Newton and Fulton supporting some of the weight of their rucksacks by leaning against trees. Leon simply plops down on his backside, damning anyone who would try to stop him. As the minutes wear on, our sweat starts drying, and we get colder and colder.

When you stop moving, all your attention is focused on the pain. With no distractions, with nothing to do but peer out in the trees, into nothingness, it is difficult to focus on anything but the pain. Your back screams at you, your head drops low into your chest, you experience feelings of homesickness and regret, you feel sorry for yourself. All you want, in the entire world, is to start moving again.

So, despite the pains of the march, it is always better to be moving than sitting still.

Dale finally mutters something to himself, places his map in his back pocket, and stands up. After almost ten minutes in the short halt, he is ready to move again.

"About goddamn time," Salvador grumbles again.

We start walking again.

After making sure my whole team is up, moving, and spaced out appropriately, my mind inevitably fixates on its favorite subject: food. But I do not just think about food, I crave it, I yearn and ache for it, I am obsessed by it. I have both waking and sleeping dreams about steak, sushi feasts, blooming onions, beer, milkshakes, cheeseburgers, french fries, chocolate, and most of all, peanut butter, endless gobs of rich, gooey, creamy peanut butter.

All I am going to do when I get out of this wretched school, I tell myself for the hundredth time today, is eat and sleep, and eat and sleep, and eat and sleep, all day.

Not only am I half-starved but, after living in the bush and not seeing a shower or a mirror for several days, I am filthy. I am covered in dirt and mud, reek of stale sweat, and wear soiled, disheveled, and torn clothing. I also have a budding bacterial infection called cellulitis just underneath the surface of the skin in my right knee.

I am leading three men today, two bat boys and a green beret, and the second most important man in the squad, but the stability and quality of my own mental state is questionable. I am half-crazed due to sleep deprivation and the never-ending silence and solitude of the march. Every single step I take is accompanied by pain shooting up from the forever blistered soles of my feet, my back and shoulders are sore, tweaked, and strained by my rucksack, and I walk with a minor limp because I twisted my ankle falling over a tree root yesterday.

I must look pathetic, more like a wretched street urchin than an elite ranger, but I am not the only one, everyone in the squad looks ragged.

We do not appreciate it, but this deprivation, hardship, and want is useful and valuable to our ranger training. The life of a real ranger is a simple one, full of austere suffering, and endless toil. This kind of existence, that of the bedraggled guerrilla warrior band, is timeless, and only requires restricted rations, a heavy rucksack, impossible deadlines to meet, and simulated enemy assaults to recreate.

Dale halts us for his fourth map check in an hour when we hear a familiar sound.

Wheeeeeeeeeeeeee-ooooooooooooooooooooo!

"Incoming!" Salvador yells out loud, breaking our silence. There is no need to be quiet any longer, the Opfor are dropping mortar rounds on us.

"Get down!" Dale yells out as the squad drop to their faces, rucksacks still on, to wait for the impact and explosions to pass.

BOOOOOOOM!

The artillery simulator or "arty sim" goes off somewhere behind us. They are like large firecrackers designed to mimic the noise of an artillery or mortar round during training. The RIs use them for several purposes, primarily to evaluate our squad on our "React to Indirect Fire" battle drill, when the enemy starts lobbing artillery at us, but also, to get us moving with a purpose when we are walking too slow.

Wheeeeeeeeeeeee-ooooooooooooooooooooo! Booooom!
Wheeeeeeeeeeeee-ooooooooooooooooooooo! Booooom!

Two more whistles and explosions, and then for one, two, then three seconds, nothing but silence.

Dale needs to get the squad out of the kill zone during this momentary lull, and fast, before the enemy can adjust his fire and send more rounds right on top of us. Everyone in the squad knows what to do. Our muscles are tensed as we prepare to spring to our feet and run. We simply await the order.

At this point, the squad leader needs to provide a direction and a distance to run, somewhere safe, away from the mortar fire, and preferably with some cover and concealment. And while technically a squad leader could yell out any cardinal direction and distance to run, the standard procedure has always been to yell "twelve o'clock, three hundred meters" so that we can continue at the present line of march and run the bare minimum distance.

But of course, Dale has to be different.

"THREE O' CLOCK! FOUR HUNDRED METERS!"

The squad winces at the command. Jenson, the M240B machine gunner for the day, stands up with a blank expression, and says, "3 o'clock? Really?"

But Dale has made his decision and sticks with it. "Go! Go! Get out of here, okay!" He hollers at all of us before dashing off into the tree line to the right.

Time to run.

Thwack! Thwack! Thwack! Thwack! The soles of my boots slap down on the ground, over and over again. Two-hundred-and-eighty pounds plus, jack hammering my poor little feet.

There is no order of march, no method to the madness, just twelve

ANDREW GOLDSMITH | 97

individual rangers running for their lives as simulated mortars resume landing behind us. The faster rangers are in the front while the slower, more heavily weighed down, and injured rangers are in the back. I do not know where my team members are, other than little Leon, who struggles with his SAW machine gun beside me.

Thwack! Thwack! Thwack! Thwack!

In a way, it is nice to step out our strides and cover some serious ground, close to half-a-klick, so quickly. While running, the steady, numbing pain in my upper back and shoulders is temporarily eased while other body parts bear the pain. It is almost worth the damage being done to my feet, even at the risk of twisting a knee or an ankle.

The running would be worth it, that is, if we were actually getting closer to the objective. But not this time, this time we are heading off somewhere unknown to our right, farther away from the objective.

Thwack! Thwack! Thwack! Thwack!

After several minutes of running, Leon and I catch up with half of our squad in a small clearing surrounded by tall trees. Everyone is panting hard and catching their breath.

"Form a perimeter... men... okay..." Dale, who came in right before us, takes a moment to catch his breath. "Team leaders... on me... okay."

Salvador and I walk over to Dale. The RI is already there waiting for us. The rest of the squad forms up in a rough, cigar-shaped perimeter, takes a knee, and looks outwards.

Jenson, with the big 240B machine gun, is the last to run up. He throws his rucksack down angrily. "Three o'clock? Three o'clock! Who in their right mind says three o'clock. Fucking lieutenants, that's who!"

"Goldsmith, Salvador, pull out your maps, okay?" Dale either does not hear Jenson or pretends not to. "We were here, okay... but now, I think, um, okay, I believe we are... here... okay?" Dale points a twig at our alleged location on the map and looks up at Salvador and I for confirmation.

"You sure about that, ranger?"

"I... um... I..." The RI's pointed question stupefies Dale for a moment before his confidence returns. "Why, yes, I am, Sergeant."

"Hmmph," the RI's eyes scan quickly over Salvador before finally resting on me, "what do you say, team leader, where are we?"

I am screwed. Even though I have been walking point all day, at the very front of the formation, I have been taking my marching orders from

Dale, today's micro-managing squad leader, and Fulton, the squad's land navigation guru. I have little idea where we actually are on the map right now, especially after Dale's deviation from our route of march, and that is unfortunate, because not knowing the squad's position on the map can be instant grounds for failing a graded patrol.

The RI is still looking at me, expecting an answer. Should I just guess where we are? Tell the RI the ugly truth, that I don't know?

"Actually, Sergeant," Salvador declares, "based on that ridgeline over... there... and the stream we crossed one hundred meters ago, I believe we are closer to... here." Salvador points a blade of grass at a spot on Dale's map two grid squares diagonally from the spot Dale selected.

"Okay, ranger, okay..." The RI seems pleased with Salvador's answer, then his eyes dart back to me. "What do you think, ranger?"

I point confidently to the same spot as Salvador.

And thank the ranger gods, the RI nods and seems happy with my answer. I breathe a huge sigh of relief. Salvador may have just saved me from a no-go.

"Well, squad leader," the RI re-focuses his ire on Dale, "why don't you figure out where we actually are, and then get this squad moving out to the goddamned objective... OKAY? You think you can do that? Otherwise, you are all going to start taking casualties and will have to buddy carry each other through these woods."

"I can do that, Sergeant, okay." Dale declares confidently as always, ready to assume command of the patrol again.

"Good. Then move out, rangers!"

Two hours later, the soles of my feet are howling, my back is in agony, and my lungs are burning after summiting another ridgeline. My rucksack feels heavier than ever and spares me no relief from pain. Dale keeps halting the squad and consulting with Salvador and I as to what direction to head.

The men grow increasingly surly. They know we are lost.

"Who the hell says, 'three o'clock?'" Leon whines off to my right.

"A fucking idiot, that's who," Newton responds somewhere far off to my left.

"Shhh! Keep your gripes to yourselves," I scold the two bat boys.

Leon gives me his trademark hollow-eyed death stare, the really disconcerting one, for several seconds before breaking the silence one last time. "Fucking officers, that's who... can't walk quietly neither."

Dale is about to halt the patrol for his third map check in half-an-hour when the RI calls a pause to the exercise.

"All right, squad leader, that's good enough." The RI continues. "Let's see if the next squad leader can unfuck this patrol. It is assumption of command time, rangers!"

The typical twenty-four hour graded patrol is composed of four stages: planning, movement to the objective, actions on the objective, and establishment of the patrol base. Dale led the squad during planning and the start of the movement to the objective but now, it is time for a second squad leader to step up and take command. Salvador and I, however, stay in place. Team leaders occupy their positions for twenty-four hours.

Dale, who looks relieved to no longer be in command, executes his last order as squad leader by motioning the squad to assume the short halt and take a knee, guns facing out.

"Let's see, here..." The RI flips some pages in his notebook, everyone in the squad other than Salvador, Dale, and me are on edge. "Tobiri, ranger Tobiri, step right up. You are the new squad leader."

Tobiri gulps as he rises to his feet and processes the hard reality that he is in charge. Tobiri, the frail and pale, unassuming, mild-mannered, freshly minted engineer lieutenant is getting his first real opportunity in his Army career to lead grizzled, exhausted, rough men, many of them combat veterans and elite special operators, in a realistic training scenario.

Up until now, Tobiri, though just barely hanging on, has been a "gray man" to the RIs, someone they do not think about much or concern themselves with. Tobiri is just there, neither shining nor visibly failing, which is generally a good thing in a school like this.

But now, Tobiri is the leader. He will be under the microscope and will be forced to shine.

I really hope he can, but I am not too optimistic.

"Ranger," the RI advises, "change over your equipment, get briefed by the outgoing squad leader, confirm your location on the map, and get this squad ready to move out. You have ten minutes. Understand, ranger?"

"Ten minutes, but, sir, I mean, Sergeant, I..." Tobiri starts rambling.

"You have ten minutes to get your shit in order and get moving towards the objective with a goddamn sense of purpose. Do... you... understand... ranger?"

"I do. I do, Sergeant."

Tobiri and Dale get busy un-tying and exchanging weapons, night vision devices, maps, and other equipment while Dale hurriedly briefs Tobiri about the mission. Dale is about to assume Tobiri's former place as a grenadier for the day and has a steadily growing grin on his formerly serious face. All Dale has to do now is stay awake and march all day and night, a cake walk when compared to being the squad leader. Whether or not he passed his patrol, he is undeniably glad to be a regular Joe again.

After getting us lost for the last two hours, the rest of the squad is happy to see Dale go, too.

But his successor, Tobiri, does not inspire much confidence. Whereas Dale, for his faults, possesses a natural air of authority and command, Tobiri is soft-spoken, slightly built, and a decade older than most of us. He has no combat experience, is not particularly skilled in tactics or fieldcraft, and just does not look like a warrior. To his credit, he has weathered the severe beatdowns of RAP Week and Darby Phase silently and stoically. He is humble, intelligent, and an asset during the squad planning process. More importantly, he has never screwed anyone in the squad over in any meaningful way, so no one bears him any ill will.

But the bat boys remain skeptical.

"Another fucking LT?" Leon whines. "Ugghh!"

"This day just keeps getting better," Newton coolly states within earshot of Tobiri.

"Maybe this one can tell his ass from a hole in the ground," Jenson adds his two cents. "But I doubt it!"

Dale wraps up his briefing of Tobiri and takes his new spot with Bravo Team in the back of the squad formation. Fulton subtly shows Tobiri exactly where we are on the map.

"Your ten minutes are up, ranger!" The RI barks angrily. "Let's get this patrol back on track. Move out!" The RI suddenly barks.

Tobiri fumbles with his map for the briefest moment, looks out at the wood line, and then back at his map again.

"Jesus-fucking-Christ!" RIs hate indecisiveness. "Go that way, ranger!" The RI's rigid palm points off to the ten o'clock direction. He then turns to address all of us.

"It's going to be a long day, isn't it, rangers?"

Tobiri shoves his map into his cargo pocket and motions me to move the squad in the direction indicated by the RI. The squad rises shakily from their knees to continue the march.

After walking briskly for an hour, the sun is falling increasingly low on the horizon. We are closer than ever to the objective, but the terrain becomes more difficult to traverse. Small trees and ankle-tripping vines increasingly impede our rate of march and, most alarming of all, our boots start sinking deeper into the mud.

I make eye contact with Fulton who signals me to halt the squad. I tell everyone to get down and take a knee in the short halt before dashing back to Fulton.

"Goldsmith," Fulton says woefully, "tell Tobiri we're walking into a swamp, probably towards a stream. This wasn't on the map, I'm sorry. We're going to need to find another way to the objective."

I walk over to Tobiri and Salvador to tell them the bad news.

"Fulton says we're walking into a swamp or a stream. We need to find a way around it."

"Swamp?" Salvador says. "No way we're marching through a swamp! The men don't want to get wet again today."

"Well, damn it all to hell..." Tobiri weighs his options before deciding on a course of action. "I know the men don't want to get wet, but we are running short on time to hit the objective. If we can only keep this same bearing for another eight hundred meters or so, we can make it there on time, maybe even early."

"So..."

"So, Salvador," Tobiri tells the bat boy with no little anger in his voice, "if there is a stream, we're going through it."

Salvador gives Tobiri a silent, hard stare before shrugging his shoulders resignedly and turning back towards his team.

"Up to you, squad leader," he says over his shoulder, "your patrol."

It is a good thing Tobiri has made up his mind because the RI suddenly bursts in on our position.

"What are you doing, ranger?" He queries Tobiri rhetorically. "You're burning daylight. The sun sets in an hour. Get... this... squad... moving... now!"

"Roger that, Sergeant." Tobiri says snappily before turning in my direction.

"Goldsmith, Salvador, stay on the stragglers, make sure they keep up."

Tobiri motions in Leon's direction before pointing his knife hand to our front. "We're going forward, and we're moving fast. Let's go!"

So, it will be a frontal assault on the swamp then, Tobiri? Screw it, you're the boss. It already rained on us this morning, everything in my ruck is already damp, what's the harm in getting my boots wet, too?

I retake my spot at the apex of the formation, wave my squad mates forward, and take a step into the muck.

Five minutes later, we are trudging knee deep through brown, muddy swamp water, in single file, close together, our pace slowed to a crawl. Then, through the dense vines and trees I first see it, the watery chasm we will have to cross, a fifty-meter-wide stream, and the swampy bank on the other side.

No one knows how deep the water is and no one wants to cross. Fulton and Salvador start arguing with Tobiri to turn around.

But Tobiri is conscious of the RI breathing down his neck and the rapidly diminishing time we have left to hit the objective. He has made his decision, we are moving forward, and to demonstrate his resolve, he now pushes forward, past me, and plunges waist deep into the stream.

We have no choice but to follow him deeper and deeper into greenish-brown swamp water. The mud bottom is slippery, and it is hard to keep one's footing. First Bailey and then Leon slip and plunge face first into the stream, their SAW machine guns becoming completely submerged in water. Others barely catch themselves on trees or rocks before suffering the same fate.

As we wade deeper into the stream, the water rises to our hips, then up to our chests. Some of us look imploringly backwards to the RI, but although he looks annoyed at having to get wet with us, he makes no efforts to stop us or turn us around.

This is Tobiri's show now.

At the deepest point in our impromptu stream crossing, I find myself neck deep in water, my rucksack bobbing in the water behind me, somewhat helping to keep me afloat. I hold my M4 carbine precariously over my head to keep it dry. Unfortunately, no one waterproofed their rucks today, that is a skill we have yet to learn, so our ammunition, clothing, bedding, everything we own, is soaking in swamp water.

I am over six feet tall, and I barely manage to keep my head above water. This crossing must be quite the challenge for my squad mates that stand a head shorter than me, guys like Leon, Bailey, and Tobiri. Indeed, five feet in front of me, I see the crown of Tobiri's head emerging from the water after being completely submerged. Somehow, he manages to bob up and down and move forward towards the far stream bank.

When I look behind me to check on my team, I can barely make out Fulton, walking neck deep in the water like me. Leon and Newton are somewhere behind me, out of sight. There is nothing I can do to help them at this point. Sink or swim, literally.

Fortunately, our boots eventually find purchase on the raising bank on the other side and the squad emerges from the swamp. Tobiri has crossed the natural obstacle, placing us within striking distance of the objective, but it has cost us dry boots and uniforms, and created some angry, grumpy rangers.

Fulton merely chuckles to himself, but Newton and Leon are seething mad. I have a feeling many of us will remember this little incident when it comes time to do Peers assessments at the end of the field exercise.

But there is no time for Tobiri to worry about this now. The objective is just within reach, but there is little time left to traverse four-hundred meters of forested ground, travel up and over a hill, drop off our rucksacks at the objective rally point, recon and prepare to hit the objective, emplace the squad, and then finally, initiate the ambush.

The enemy is scheduled to die just before sunset, in thirty minutes. This is going to be a race against the sun, and it is going to be tough. Tobiri orders the squad to start running.

Ten minutes later, dripping sweat and swamp water, lungs aching, we stumble into a small clearing in the forest about a hundred meters away from the objective.

"This..." Tobiri pauses to catch his breath, "is the ORP." The ORP, or objective rally point, is where we will stage our rucksacks and prepare to execute the ambush. "Drop your rucks everyone... quickly...," Tobiri sucks in another deep breath, "and get ready to move out."

With joy and relief, we toss our rucksacks on the ground and pull out our Kevlar helmets, extra ammunition, claymore mines, AT-4 rocket tubes, and all the other equipment necessary to conduct a squad ambush. Usually, we would also be mounting our night vision devices to our helmets, oiling up our weapons, and adding foliage to our uniforms before moving to our final positions, but today there is no time.

"There's not enough time..." Tobiri tells Salvador and I between gasps for air, "to conduct a leader's recon... we need... to be set up in ten minutes or ...

we are going... to miss the hit time."

"The trail should be out there... about seventy-five to a hundred meters to our front..." Tobiri takes in one final breath, "we are going to have to emplace this ambush quickly."

On an ambush, Alpha Team is assigned to flank security. I split my team in two, Leon with me and Fulton with Newton, and we separately push out to where we believe the far ends of the trail should be.

Meanwhile, Tobiri, Bravo Team, and the machine gun team march towards the objective to locate the last covered and concealed position with an unobstructed view of the "kill zone," the area of the trail selected to be the focus of our destructive efforts. Tobiri and Salvador emplace Bravo Team, the assault element, on the ground in a rough line about thirty meters from the trail. The machine gun and his crew are set up just to their right on a slightly elevated mound. Jenson, the machine gunner, lays down behind the M240B, rests his hand and head on the buttstock, and peers down its iron sights. He stares intently at a slight bend in the trail.

"That's the kill zone." Salvador whispers to Jenson. "Get ready to light it up."

Pssshh. "Alpha Team," it's Tobiri, coming in on the squad Icom radios, "Bravo Team and the machine gun are in place. Are your guys ready?"

"Roger that, squad leader," I radio back, just as me and Leon settle down behind a large rock for cover as we watch the west end of the trail, "security teams are set."

And just in time, too, because a moment later Leon nudges me in the ribs.

"Here they come, Goldsmith. Call it in."

I see them now, too. Three Opfor guerrillas wearing a hodge-podge of camouflage uniforms marching casually down the trail, heading in our direction.

I key the radio and whisper into the mike. "Tobiri, enemy personnel coming your way."

Pssshh. "I see them."

Everything is quiet and serene for a few seconds.

Then, pop, pop, Tobiri fires his M4 carbine twice into the kill zone. It is the signal to initiate the ambush. The machine gun and Bravo Team join in a half-second later. The ragtag enemy band is suddenly caught in a deadly dilemma as two machine guns, five rifles, and a grenade launcher open up on them out of nowhere. Within seconds, all three drop to the ground, still and lifeless, simulating death, yet we keep firing.

Bailey's water-soaked SAW machine gun jams after the first twenty rounds and two of the rifles go down after their first magazines, but fortunately, Jenson kept the M240B relatively dry during the stream crossing, and the squad's main casualty producing weapon is spewing out hot fire. Jenson is good at his job. His trigger finger releases six-to-nine round bursts of 7.62 mm blank ammunition repeatedly into the Opfor's lifeless bodies. He and Roberts, his assistant gunner, yell and howl with glee.

Meanwhile, after providing advance warning of the enemy approach, my security element does not have much to do. We keep an eye out for additional enemy forces that may come upon our ambush, but other than that, we sit back detachedly and listen to the enfolding slaughter.

After thirty seconds of firing, no doubt overkill in this situation, Tobiri orders everyone to "Cease fire!" Jenson sends one final burst of machine gun fire into the kill zone before everything is quiet again.

"Bravo Team, assault!" Tobiri yells out to Salvador.

Bravo Team springs to their feet and starts bounding by buddy teams towards the kill zone. As they pass over the three-bullet riddled Opfor lying on their backs, they simulate kicking them in the groin to ensure they are in fact dead and not just faking. They move past the bodies, beyond the trail, and a bit into the surrounding woods, forming up in a semi-circle at the limit of advance, or LOA.

"LOA! LOA!" They shout.

The four rangers in Bravo Team crouch down on one knee and face out to repel any potential enemy counterattack. Salvador, the team leader, receives ammo, casualty, and equipment reports from each of his soldiers and tells them to drink water.

"EPW and search teams!" Tobiri calls out as he walks over to Bravo Team's perimeter. Dale and Sven break off from the formation to search the bodies of the enemy dead and the immediate area for any prisoners, useful papers, or intelligence. They also consolidate enemy weapons and equipment for a demolition charge.

The squad continues wrapping up actions on the objective. We managed to dispatch the Opfor without sustaining any casualties and, by the slimmest of margins, hit the objective on time. As far as Darby ambushes go, this one went off pretty well, especially considering our poor, water-soaked condition. Indeed, Tobiri looks pleased as the demo man rigs the small detonation cord explosive charge with a timed fuse and places it on the pile of enemy weapons and equipment. We cannot hump this stuff out of here and we do not want to leave anything useful behind for our enemies to use against us later, so we will blow it up.

Bravo Team finishes their search and Tobiri orders them to head back to the ORP. Their withdrawal is watched over by the machine gun team, who leave with Tobiri shortly thereafter. Last of all, my security teams pull off the far ends of the trail to reunite with the squad at the ORP. As we start walking back, we hear the "Boom!" of the demolition charge exploding behind us.

The sun sets, and the fun times are over. Now it is time to mount our night vision goggles, re-shoulder our rucksacks, and start the inevitably hours-long, soul-crushing movement to the patrol base, but first, the RI calls a brief halt to our exercise.

"Admin time, rangers! We're going admin." This means the exercise is temporarily paused; we can talk quietly, make some noise, and even use headlamps to see in the darkness. "Drop your rucks, pull out your lights. Let's start seeing those sensitive items!"

The RI has to systematically check and account for all our weapons, gear, and equipment before we can leave the objective. If everyone has everything, things go smoothly, and it is a good chance to rest for a few minutes. However, if we are missing anything, and I mean anything, the squad will have to go back to the objective and scour it until the missing item is found.

Fortunately, tonight, we have all our equipment.

"Tie everything back down again, rangers." The RI orders us. "We're going tactical again in two mikes. Get 'em ready to move out, squad leader."

Time to play ranger again.

As I pack up my rucksack, I notice a one-inch rip in the crotch of my ACU pants, a common enough occurrence with the army's new and "improved" battle uniform. I briefly consider changing them out for a sturdier pair of BDUs but there is not enough time. More than that, the thought of taking off and putting back on my soaking wet boots makes me cringe.

After not wearing the damn thing for an hour, I throw my sixty-pound rucksack onto my back and embrace the dozen familiar pains that greet me.

Time to march again, but this time, into the night.

Now begins what is easily the worst part of our day: the long, slow, dangerous march "home," to the patrol base, our armed hobo camp in the woods, where we will establish security, conduct maintenance, and lastly, rest. The distances we move are not that far, usually a mile or two, but even with Fulton taking point, the squad always seems to move at a crawl at night and it takes hours to reach the patrol base. There are several reasons our pace is so slow: it is hard to see in the woods with night vision, we stop frequently, but most of all, it is because of frayed, exhausted, and battered rangers tripping and stumbling in the darkness due to physical fatigue and mental delirium. Leaders must constantly count and corral the men, who if not watched closely, will stagger off alone into the woods or fall asleep under a bush.

That is why, four hours after sundown, we are still marching, single file, in the dark.

We wear night vision goggles to help us see at night. But it is not like the movies, it is pretty hard to see through them, especially the worn-down, beaten-up pieces of junk they issue here at Ranger School. I "see" the world through contrasting shades of green, everything around me blurred and obscured by static. It is hard to comprehend depth, and nothing is ever clearly in focus. Fortunately, we have the small glowing "cat-eyes," glo-vinyl luminous strips sewn onto our helmet bands, to help us follow the man in front of us. Without them, we would be truly lost.

There are countless hazards in the woods at night: holes in the ground, felled trees, low hanging tree branches that catch your NODs and yank your head violently to the side, sticks that poke you in the eye. No one is immune, even the most adept rangers struggle at night, when it seems as if the woods themselves are trying to consume us.

I hate marching at night, but things can always get worse.

First, as I am trudging along, a small tree branch catches on the small hole in the crotch of my pants. I hear it rip open a few more inches.

"Cheap ass ACUs." I mutter aloud.

Then, right after that, for the first time in Ranger School, it starts raining at night, and it starts coming down hard.

This is terrible. More than hunger, sleeplessness, the Opfor, more than the RIs even, nature is the true enemy of the ranger student, and few things nature can throw at us is worse than rain, mud-making, clothes soaking, sleeping bag drenching, morale destroying rain. Rangers can only pray they are not in a leadership position when the rain starts falling because, when it does, rangers stop listening to their leaders, they feel sorry for themselves, they retreat inwards, they seek warmth, shelter and, more than anything else, sleep, and good luck trying to stop them.

It should be a rule: Don't get wet and pray there won't be rain. Well today, our squad has been screwed on both accounts.

And I am lucky enough to be a team leader.

Raindrops stream down the outside lenses of my NODs while the inside lens is obscured by fog, further degrading my vision. This lack of visibility causes the squad to start bunching up even closer together. Now, I dare not let Fulton's cat-eyes get more than two-arms distance away from me, lest I lose him in the darkness.

Naturally, under these conditions, I start seeing little green goblins in bushes and evil-looking, shape-shifting faces in the trees. They do not bug me so much while we are moving, but when we stop and take a knee for five, ten minutes at a time, their hostile grins and laughter perturb me.

I have hallucinated once or twice already in Ranger School, but not like this. Now, I am seeing evil green faces everywhere. What are they? Forest spirits? The souls of people who lived in these woods hundreds and thousands of years ago? Surely, they cannot be pure figments of my imagination, they look so, so real…

I shake my head to wake myself. I am a team leader tonight, watched by the RIs, getting graded, I cannot just wallow in my own head like the rest of the men. I have responsibilities, especially in this miserable weather, I need to make sure everyone in my team is still here, in their proper place in line, and in their right minds, doing their jobs. I briefly touch base with Fulton before tripping and stumbling my way backwards down the formation to check on Leon and Newton.

Ten minutes pass before Tobiri has us rise to our feet again and resume marching. With all these stops, it is no wonder it is taking us all night to walk a measly two klicks, but unfortunately, the frequent stops are necessary.

That is because the rain worsens the "accordion effect" of marching at night. Alpha Team, at the front of the column, can set the pace and walk as slow or as fast as we want. This is not true for the rest of the column, who may be slowed down by the terrain, getting snagged by a tree branch, or slipping and falling. This dynamic inevitably causes our squad column to stretch increasingly further out with time, until the men start losing contact with each other, which causes the leadership to halt the column.

"Slow down." Newton grabs my shoulder and whispers in my ear for the hundredth time tonight. "We're losing Bravo Team again."

Goddamn them! Why can't they keep up! I decide not to halt the squad but tell Fulton to slow down the pace.

This is when the accordion contracts. Soon there is a traffic jam of halted, zoned-out, swaying rangers cursing the men in front of them for not moving fast enough.

Soon enough, Newton relays the inevitable, "Tobiri says to pick up the pace." He sighs, "Everyone is bunching up back there."

Fulton moves faster again, and, within fifty meters of walking, the accordion is drawn out again. Out and in, in and out, over and over again, thus our column moves like an inch worm through the dark, rain-soaked forest.

It is eleven o'clock and we have been walking in the rain for two hours now. The tear in my pants keeps growing larger. I drop to a knee during one of our innumerable short halts only to see and hear my pants rip fully all the way down from my crotch to my shin. Because I'm an infantryman, and I go "commando," meaning I don't wear underpants, my manhood, as cold and shriveled as it is, is now fully exposed to the elements.

Fortunately, not only is it pitch black and the only people within miles fellow miserable rangers or RIs, but by this point of the course, I have lost all sense of shame. So, what if I find myself lying with my literal dick in the mud, in the middle of a cold forest at night? Welcome to life as a ranger.

Finally, ten minutes before midnight and with the rain still steadily drizzling down on us, our squad stumbles into the patrol base. Tonight's hard march is over.

But the work is not done. First, we must occupy the patrol base, establish a security plan, and then tackle the priorities of work: weapons maintenance, equipment maintenance, and personal hygiene. If we hustle and get the patrol base set up quickly, we can look forward to eating an MRE and maybe getting one or two hours of sleep tonight.

Salvador and I quickly get to work laying our respective teams in battle buddy pairs back-to-back to each other in a cigar-shaped, oval perimeter, weapons facing outwards. Jenson and the rest of the machine gun team take their place at the tip of the base, facing the most likely route of enemy approach. Tobiri the squad leader, drops his ruck in the center of the formation and immediately starts supervising the placement of claymore mines outside our perimeter, the preparation of sector sketches, and a basic withdrawal plan in case the enemy finds us and we have to flee. It takes us an hour to fully

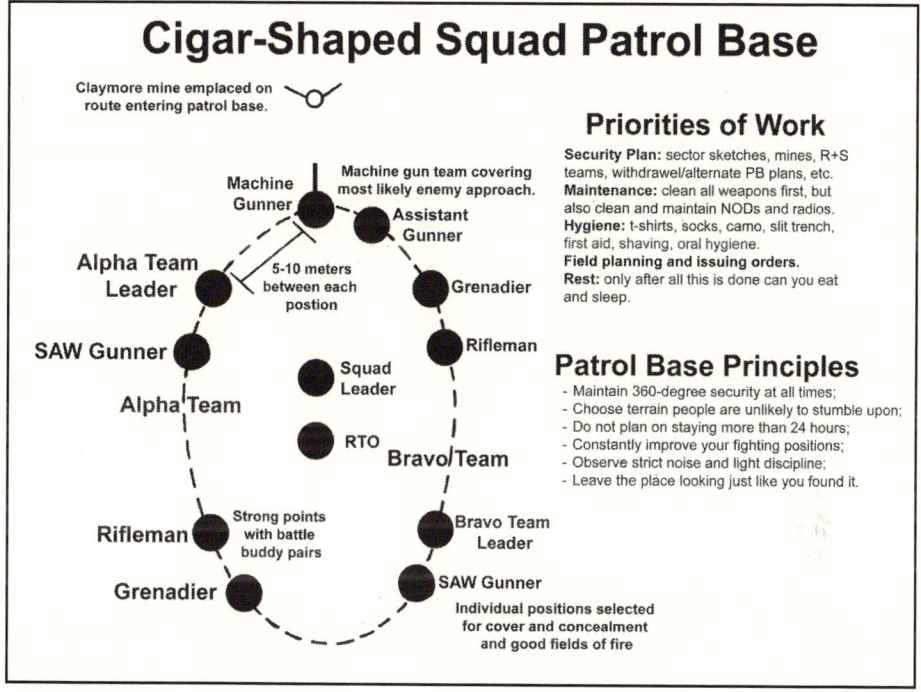

Cigar-Shaped Squad Patrol Base

Claymore mine emplaced on route entering patrol base.

Machine gun team covering most likely enemy approach.

- Machine Gunner
- Assistant Gunner
- Alpha Team Leader
- Grenadier
- 5-10 meters between each postion
- SAW Gunner
- Rifleman
- Alpha Team
- Squad Leader
- RTO
- Bravo Team
- Rifleman
- Strong points with battle buddy pairs
- Bravo Team Leader
- Grenadier
- SAW Gunner

Individual positions selected for cover and concealment and good fields of fire

Priorities of Work
Security Plan: sector sketches, mines, R+S teams, withdrawel/alternate PB plans, etc.
Maintenance: clean all weapons first, but also clean and maintain NODs and radios.
Hygiene: t-shirts, socks, camo, slit trench, first aid, shaving, oral hygiene.
Field planning and issuing orders.
Rest: only after all this is done can you eat and sleep.

Patrol Base Principles
- Maintain 360-degree security at all times;
- Choose terrain people are unlikely to stumble upon;
- Do not plan on staying more than 24 hours;
- Constantly improve your fighting positions;
- Observe strict noise and light discipline;
- Leave the place looking just like you found it.

establish patrol base security.

Next, the 240B machine gun is taken apart and quickly cleaned and oiled. This is especially important after today's dip in the stream and the continuing rainfall. While the big gun is non-operational, every other weapon in the squad must be up and facing out, everyone ready in case the enemy attacks. Once the machine gun is re-assembled and operational, the rest of the squad take turns lubricating and wiping down their machine guns and rifles, ensuring that at least every other man is pulling security. It takes thirty minutes to clean all the weapons.

Next in the priorities of work is personal hygiene which because we are squalid, rain-drenched, sleep-deprived, and hunger-crazed rangers, is a very low priority indeed. Most of us decide that shaving and brushing our teeth can wait until at least tomorrow, and gladly shrug off the task. Some of us build poncho shelters to stay out of the rain. Others, myself included, don't bother as it is only drizzling down now and everything I own is wet already anyway.

It is now 1:10 a.m. Only now can I finally eat my dinner MRE, my second and last meal of the day, and get some sleep. The RI orders us to maintain the usual fifty-percent security overnight, meaning every other man must be awake behind a gun while his battle buddy eats or sleeps.

This means that, at most, I will be getting an hour-and-a-fifteen minutes of sleep tonight, just like last night, and the one before. Yet, for the first time since being appointed a team leader this morning, after twenty hours of near-constant labor and stress, I can relax and breathe easy for a moment.

While I should be paired up with Leon, my SAW gunner, him and Newton are inseparable, so I find myself paired up for the second night in a row with Fulton. I am still the team leader, so he gets to eat first. I put on my poncho, pull security, and cover our sectors of fire through the slackening rain, which is now coming down in fine droplets, almost a mist.

It is convenient that we are paired up together, I have been looking forward to collecting on our little MRE deal all day. It was something to look forward to, something to savor on the march: the mystery snack I was owed for loaning out my wheat snack bread.

I feel like a little boy on Christmas. I cannot help but turn around expectantly and eagerly every time I hear Fulton opening another item in his MRE.

"What?" Fulton finally whispers to me after I turn around and look at him for the third time in as many minutes.

"I was hoping we could square up on our little deal from earlier today." I say sheepishly, almost ashamed that I have to bug a real-life green beret, a badass, over something as little as an MRE snack.

"Deal?" His eyes narrow quizzically.

"You know... the wheat snack bread. This morning, you remember." Fulton may have forgotten or pretended to have forgotten about the two-hundred calories he lifted off me earlier in the day, but I have not. "You were supposed to get me back with something good."

"That's right, that's right." Fulton nods his head up and down solemnly, but otherwise does not say or do anything. He just keeps chewing.

"So..." I am not going to let this go until I get what is mine. I do not care if Fulton is a green beret, a general's son, or the goddamn President of the United States, this is food we are talking about here, this is Ranger School, and I am not messing around.

"Okay, buddy. I gotcha, hold on." Fulton must sense my agitation, he reaches into his MRE pouch, digs around, and then plops a single toffee and walnut chew, one of a pack of four, into my outstretched hand. "Enjoy!"

I keep my hand outstretched and stare coldly at Fulton in the darkness. A single, measly toffee chew, barely forty calories! He must think I am a sucker. He has gotten a windfall of wheat snack bread, two hundred substantial, filling, whole grain carbohydrates, minerals, fat, even some protein, in exchange for a weak shot of high fructose corn syrup? I throttle the urge to throw it back in his face and to demand something more substantial. Slowly, painfully, I close my fist around the piece of candy.

Meanwhile, Fulton has already moved on. He gulps down a cold meatloaf and gravy entrée, takes a hearty swig of canteen water, and belches loudly.

What a fucking asshole! Somehow, this little swindle hurts worse than his refusal to pop my blisters one week ago. I will not soon forget this, Fulton, you can count on that.

Fulton finishes his meal and takes my place on the perimeter. I devour my dinner MRE in ten minutes, saving the toffee chew for the very end. It is small, but deliciously sweet. The caramel slowly melts in my mouth with an almost burning sensation, the walnut pieces are tender and chewy. I wish I had a bag full of them.

Fulton gets to bed down first, while I pull the first of two equal length guard shifts of one hour and ten minutes. I sit up Indian style, leaning up against a small tree, rain poncho over my shoulders for warmth, and patrol cap pulled down low over my eyes to keep out the misty rain. Screw wearing NODs tonight, I decide. My eyes need a break, I pull security by moonlight.

At 2:50 a.m. I shake Fulton awake for his guard shift, take off my wet boots and socks, and climb into my rain-dampened sleeping bag.

What a day! I think to myself as my deeply exhausted brain rapidly winds itself down. My first graded patrol in Ranger School… I hope I passed, is all I manage to think before, seconds later, I slip into the deepest of heavy slumbers.

It feels like only seconds have elapsed when I feel Fulton's hands on my shoulders, shaking me awake. I reluctantly crack one eyelid open. It is still pitch-black outside, but at least the rain has stopped falling.

"Rise and shine, buddy. It's four a.m., time to enjoy another glorious day in Ranger School."

I feel like death. My body does not want to wake. I must exert all my conscious will to force both weary eyelids open. Slowly, reluctantly, I crawl out of my dew-soaked sleeping bag and stand up in the brisk, chill morning air.

"And good morning to you too," Fulton glances below my waist, "little fella."

I glance downwards to see my exposed pasty-white thigh and genitalia. I realize now that I never changed out of my ripped trousers from last night.

I let out an involuntarily guffaw as I realize how ridiculous I must look, and Fulton starts laughing. Any residual anger from the MRE snub of the night before momentarily forgotten.

1101 Hours (11:01 a.m.)
Camp Darby Training Area
Fort Benning, Georgia
Day 18 of Ranger School
Last Day of the Darby FTX

According to the bat boys, who tend to know these things, today is the last day of the Darby FTX. Soon, it will be over and we will be heading back to camp.

Roberts, the Ranger Battalion cook, is today's squad leader. It is his third graded patrol, a sure sign that he failed his first two. It is obvious that he is stressed out and nervous about taking command of the entire squad. Roberts is just as hungry, exhausted, and injury plagued as the rest of us, but worse than all of that, he is alone and out of his depth. He has never been anything higher than a team leader in Ranger School and has no experience working in, let alone leading, an infantry rifle squad.

He may come from the Ranger Regiment, but he is a support soldier, a cook no less, without combat or infantry experience and definitively not an Airborne Ranger. Along with Bailey, he is easily the least popular member of the squad.

So far, he has physically borne the suffering of RAP Week and Darby well, but his leadership skills have proven to be subpar. If he could not pass the first two graded patrols as a team leader, he thinks to himself, what makes the RIs suppose he can do it as a squad leader? This task will be especially difficult given that he must lead tired, hungry, and pissed off rangers who are physically, mentally, and emotionally battered after a week in the field.

The squad knows that Roberts is going to have a tough time today.

An hour into the day's march Roberts halts the patrol in a small clearing and calmly announces, "Hey guys, I think I lost my squad radio."

"Hold the fuck on, ranger..." The day's RI's storms up to him, already red in the face. "What do you mean you lost your radio?"

"I lost the radio, Sergeant. I don't have it anymore." Roberts stares the RI calmly and directly in the eyes. He seems exceptionally serene, given the circumstances. Newton and Jenson start laughing.

"Was it tied down? To you, to your rucksack?" After all, this eventuality is why the RIs have us tie everything down to ourselves with cord.

"It was." Roberts shrugs. "The knot must have come undone or something, Sergeant."

"You are quite the fuck up, ranger! Goddamnit! Well, you know what this means, rangers," The RI addresses the whole squad, "Hands Across Fort Benning! That's right, drop your rucksacks, ground your weapons, get on-line, and let's comb these woods until we find that fucking radio."

The bat boys groan, the officers sigh, and Jenson and Salvador, both team leaders today worried about passing their own patrol, call Roberts a "fucking pog."

"We will be out here all day if we have to, rangers," the RI says. "We can hit the objective tonight, tomorrow morning even. It does not matter to me. We are not going back into camp until you find this radio. Get on-line, rangers!"

The squad lines up shoulder-to-shoulder, a double arms' distance between each man, and then we start scouring the woods of Fort Benning, looking for the radio.

Resigned to be searching for hours, it is a great relief when, within ten minutes, the squad hears Newton cry out. "I found it! I found it!"

The squad cheers Newton and several men clap him on the back. Roberts, however, is not among them and looks strangely disappointed.

"All right, squad leader," the RI is also relieved the radio has been found so quickly, "let's get the men formed up again and moving. You only have four more hours to make it to the objective and..."

BAAAAAAMM!

A single gunshot goes off in the middle of the RI's directive. Every man in the squad stops in his tracks, his eyes wide in astonishment. Some of us crouch down low and reflexively start looking for the presence of enemy Opfor, listening for the sounds of continuing gunfire, but we see and hear nothing.

Did someone just accidentally discharge a round? Many of us wonder. Did one of us commit the gravest sin of an infantryman, grounds for instant expulsion from this course? I have never had this actually happen before, whether in basic training, Ranger School, or Iraq.

Roberts the cook, for the first time today, is the only one truly in command of the situation. He props his rifle up on his shoulder, one-armed, an almost undetectable wisp of gun smoke rising from the barrel.

"It was me, Sergeant." Roberts calmly states. "I shot the round."

"What, what? Why?" The RI is uncharacteristically stunned, just as shocked as all of us. "Why did you shoot, ranger? What were you shooting at?"

"It was an accident." An involuntary smile starts to form at the corners of Roberts' mouth. "I accidentally pulled the trigger."

If Roberts was smart, if he wanted to cover his ass, he should have said, "I saw a bad guy," shot more blank rounds into the trees, and even ordered us all to execute an assault into the woods. After all, in Ranger School, hallucinating and shooting into the woods at an imaginary enemy is a pardonable offense, understandable, if not stupid. But a negligent discharge, that is an unforgivable crime, with no mercy given.

The squad is still shocked by the discharge, but the RI has regained his composure. He knows what is going on now, why Roberts is making no effort to protect himself, why he seems so serene and at peace with what just happened. The RI understands because he has seen other rangers make plays like this before, if not exactly like this one. The lost radio, the negligent discharge, it all makes sense to him now.

People should not live like this, Roberts thought to himself, how can they? No piece of fabric, no matter how much respect it endears, is worth this much suffering.

This place was just too much for a man like Roberts, the lonely cook, an outlier, an outcast, so he took the easy way out, he took the shot.

He committed Ranger School suicide.

Roberts has his ticket home now, weeks, even months, before the rest of us. Roberts is happy to be getting away from all the crazy bay boys, away from the sleep deprivation, the shitty quarters, and the endless hunger. He may not be going home with a Tab, but tonight, he will be going somewhere far, far away from here. For the moment, that makes him incredibly happy, and the rest of us, just a little bit jealous.

In a way, I have never had more respect for the man. Roberts' move was as sudden as it was effective, irreparably final, with no possibility of going back. Even when I was in my absolute lowest state, when I hit rock bottom, I never entertained the idea of purposefully discharging a round to get kicked out of Ranger School. It is genius, in a way, like shooting yourself in the foot or severing a toe. Sure, it is shameful, but it is also effective.

Roberts is smiling, ear-to-ear now, because he is going back to a magical land where we all used to dwell, where the peanut butter is free-flowing, where there is central heating, weekends, and more than three hours of sleep a night, a place with cheeseburgers, steaks, ice cold beer, and even women, a most wonderful place, a dream to a long suffering ranger student, a utopia.

The RI tells us to sit on our rucks and makes a call over the radio. Within minutes, a second RI pulls up close to our position in a soft-top Humvee. Roberts unties and hands over his squad items, weapon, and ammunition to Salvador and Jenson, packs up his rucksack for the last time, and loads it in the back of the Humvee.

Roberts takes a seat in the back of the Humvee. As the RI in the driver's seat backs up the vehicle to take him back to Camp Darby, he avoids making eye contact with the rest of us. No one in the squad waves or says goodbye.

"Ranger McCormick, where is McCormick?" The RI breaks the silence.

"Right here, Sergeant."

"You are now the new and improved squad leader for the rest of today. You think you can un-fuck this patrol and get us to the objective on time?"

"Roger, Sergeant," McCormick says confidently despite knowing that we will have to move fast to make up the hour of daylight we just lost. "I can get us there before the hit time."

"Good," is all the RI responds.

McCormick waves us forward and we step off into the bush once again.

Chapter 6: "Peers"

Rule #11: Don't be a buddy fucker.

2248 Hours (10:48 p.m.)
Classroom, Camp Darby
Fort Benning, Georgia
Day 18 of Ranger School

There is a rule, a law even, that says something to the effect of "what goes around, comes around," or "you get what you give." It requires us to treat others well or somehow, someway, we will be punished. Call it divine retribution, karma, the chickens coming home to roost, whatever you like, it is nice to think that those who do harm to others, who take shortcuts, who lie and steal, will not be rewarded in the end, that there is some cosmic justice in this world.

In Ranger School, the law can be summed up as: Don't fuck your buddy, or it will come back to bite you in the ass. Although it is a simple enough precept, in the crucible of Ranger School, where people are at their most vulnerable and their true natures laid bare, it is not always followed.

Fortunately, Ranger School has an enforcement mechanism, a way for each of us to hold our squad mates accountable for their virtues and their sins during the rigors of the last three weeks. Ranger School has peer evaluations or quite simply "Peers," at the end of each phase where everyone gets to individually rank every other member of the squad in sequential order, best to worst, and describe their strengths and deficiencies.

All of us have a lot to say about each other. Peers is our chance to punish those who have done us wrong and to give the squad heroes their due. What's more, unless someone recycles, and must repeat the phase in a new squad, each person's Peers sheet is fully anonymous. No one holds back.

You can be an absolute stud and blow away your graded patrols, but it doesn't mean you will go forward and pass the course. If you receive too many low rankings from the squad, in any phase, you can be recycled, or worse, kicked out of Ranger School entirely. Peers ensures rangers are team players who take others into consideration. It also makes sure that Tab wearers have the ability to earn the love and respect of their men, without the benefit of rank and hierarchy.

Peers is a subjective test, and there are many intangible, even instinctual factors at play in how others will rank you. They could score you low because you sucked as a leader, failed to make friends, did not carry your weight, were tactically incompetent, stole someone's food, or simply because you are a weirdo, a loser, someone who does not belong in the ranger fraternity.

If you want to peer well in Ranger School, you think of others. You do things you really do not want to do to help your squad mates. You share your chow, dig a foxhole for someone else, hump extra equipment, volunteer to carry the heavy machine gun, no matter how painful it is. You do this hoping, praying that they remember the good things you did for them, and more importantly, that they overlook the bad.

But mostly, if you want to pass Peers, remember this: don't fuck your buddy.

Because whatever wrong you did to them, large or small, a ranger in need does not forget and, more likely, he seethes with the urge to get revenge. It could have been that bad order you gave, the time you yelled at him during the patrol, that guard shift you slept through, or that stupid thing you did that got the whole platoon smoked, he does not forget. You may not even remember doing it, you may have even had a good reason for doing it, especially given the constant duress imposed by the course, but it does not matter. Your buddy blames you, he does not forgive you, and worst of all, he wants to pay you back, even if that means you will fail the course and go home tab-less.

Karma is a bitch.

"Hurry up, rangers!" The RI shouts at us as he corrals my squad into an empty classroom. "Lots to do tonight before you can sleep."

The RIs have brought us in here immediately after re-entering Camp Darby from the FTX. It is already almost eleven at night. I can feel the magnetic pull of my sleeping bag, calling to me, but first, we need to rank our comrades. Peers is done straight out of the field, while the wounds are still fresh, before memory fades, before hearts soften.

We take our seats behind long, plastic tabletops. Each man has at least two empty seats between him and anyone else so that we can't talk to each other or see what others are writing down. Two RIs walk along the tables and slap down two-page evaluation sheets in front of each of us.

"Fill out your Peers evaluations as completely and honestly as possible." An RI instructs. "Don't hold anything back, rangers. If you finish early, you can put your head down and go to sleep. You have thirty minutes, go!"

Even though I am dirt-encrusted and smell like a vagrant, have not slept more than three hours in a night for weeks, nurse a minor cellulitis infection in my knee, have a sprained ankle, a pinched nerve in my upper back, swollen knees, and I am still afflicted with blistered, battered feet, I am positively abuzz now that the time has come to peer my comrades.

After all, I have a lot to say. Thirty minutes is not long enough to get it all down.

I start at the top, numero uno, the best ranger in the squad. This one is easy. Hands down it goes to McCormick, the special forces support Captain, the oldest, wisest, most stoic member of the squad. He never complains, never raises his voice to anyone, and after Fulton, he is the second-best man at land navigation. In the last three weeks, he has earned everyone's respect, even the bat boys.

Position number two is more difficult. I waver between choosing Dale or Salvador, before ultimately awarding the silver medal to Dale. As much as I hate the guy for being a dull, boring, know-it-all, young pup of an officer who got us lost during that infamous "3 o'clock" mortar run, at the same time, I cannot remember a time when he truly screwed me or anyone else over. He was tactically sound, carried his weight, and we worked well enough together during my graded patrol. I dislike the guy personally and do not consider him a friend, but I respect him professionally. Overall, he deserves a spot near the top of the list.

Salvador, on the other hand, my dark horse, I give him spot number three because he needs some high Peers rankings. This is because many in the squad will rank him low, especially the officers. They did not like the fact that he slept through guard shifts, that he would cherry pick MREs with Jenson, that he has a visible neck tattoo, that he always tells it how it is, or that he is a brash, young Airborne Ranger, with all that entails.

Salvador is admittedly a little shady and close with miscreants like Jenson, but he isn't a thief, he's tough, an asset in the field, and his sleeping through guard shifts actually benefited the squad by collectively giving us more time to sleep. Unlike Jenson and Newton, Salvador does not actively disrespect anyone and he is one of the more humble and mature bat boys I have met at Ranger School. Finally, Salvador is funny and routinely brings out smiles from the rest of us with his self-deprecating jokes and epic bat boy bedroom tales.

But Salvador's buddy Jenson, on the other hand, fuck that guy! I am thinking about ranking that son of a bitch dead last. If Bailey was not such an idiot, it would not even be a contest.

Meanwhile, five minutes into Peers, Jenson subtly attracts Salvador's attention from across the room by clearing his throat several times. When their eyes meet, Jenson raises a single eyebrow while Salvador responds with a little head nod.

For both Salvador and Jenson, ranking the squad from best to worst is easy compared to my analytical method. For one, they have entered into a "reciprocal Peers agreement," explicitly banned in Ranger School, wherein they both agree to rank the other as number one on their respective Peers forms. A number one ranking carries a lot of weight in the Peers calculation and will help to offset the inevitable bottom rankings both are going to receive. Like many ways to game the Ranger School system, it is a good idea if you do not get caught and can trust the other fellow to live up to his end of the bargain.

Jenson, with his rat-like cunning, knows that in a straight up Peers contest he will be recycled. To prevent this from happening, he has entered into reciprocal Peers agreements not only with Jenson, but also with Newton, Leon, and even Bailey. He also approached me yesterday, in the patrol base, promising to rank me number one in exchange for the same. However, I didn't want to break the rules, I don't trust Jenson, and I know full well he could not possibly honor all the other Peers agreements he has made with everyone else. I politely declined.

Salvador had a little more class. "Please," he asked each member of the squad forlornly this morning "just don't rank me last. That's all I ask."

For Salvador, Jenson, and the other bat boys in the squad, other than the number one or two slots, the rest of the rankings are easy. Any other bat boys worth their salt, other than that idiot Bailey, will automatically get the highest Peers rankings just because they're Airborne Rangers. After them comes Fulton, naturally, because he is a green beret and thus also worthy of respect. Other people in the squad with some combat experience, like me, will get middling marks from the bat boys, along with McCormick because they all think he is a halfway cool old man.

The bat boys peer the lieutenants last, as a matter of course. To the bat boys, they are all just a bunch of "cherry LTs," college boys destined for boring commands in the regular army, and thus, no friend of theirs. This early in the course, caste lines are still recognized, and the bat boys hold fast to their tribe, with one notable exception.

The bat boys rank Bailey with the LTs, at the bottom, because they consider him an embarrassment to the Ranger Regiment. For Jenson, this is a clear violation of the reciprocal Peers agreement he made with Bailey yesterday.

"Fuck him," Jenson says to himself with a devilish smile as he ranks him dead last.

But the scales of justice balance out because Bailey also fails to live up to his end of the agreement. When the bargain was struck, Bailey was so weary and impaired from lack of sleep he was barely aware of even talking to Jenson, let alone what he was saying. Bailey merely mumbled in a positive tone to get the guy to leave him alone.

In the classroom now, Bailey is still weary and impaired from lack of sleep. Filling out the evaluations is proving to be difficult. The sheet asks for so many details, but he has enough trouble just remembering the names of everyone in the squad. He doesn't give coherent reasons for ranking the squad from best to worst, he relies instead on hazy flashes of memory of the petty kindnesses and cruelties inflicted on him by his squad mates, none of whom he considers a friend.

All Bailey knows for sure is that he is going to rank his fellow bat boys the lowest of all because they laugh and taunt him more than anyone else, especially that asshole Jenson.

Finished with the basic rankings, Bailey scribbles some illegible gibberish onto the page to fill up the Peers evaluation, places his head on his hands, and falls instantly asleep on the table.

Meanwhile, I am still working my way through the middling guys in the squad, those ranking neither high nor low. This includes Newton and Leon who score low for being immature, elitist bat boys who constantly fell asleep on patrol, yet high for being tactically sound, tough as nails, and knowledgeable about Ranger School. Then there is Tobiri, technically still my battle buddy, who, despite leading us neck deep through that swamp and having no particular talents, has borne his suffering patiently and bravely and wronged no one. After him comes Sven, the frail looking lieutenant with the quiet voice, the gray man of the squad, a brick in the wall that no one notices. No one has anything bad (or good) to say about the guy. For this, he gets a number seven ranking.

Now, with eight minutes to spare, I come upon the best part of the Peers rankings, the bottom tier, where I can single out those individuals who lack the leadership ability and morals to wear the sacred Tab, those who, I believe, should not be rangers.

This is my opportunity to punish those who have fucked me over in the last three weeks. I remember you. Rangers do not forget, nor do they forgive, those who shirked their duty in rough times, stabbed us in the back, or kicked us when we were down. Heed my words, and this should probably be rule number one of Ranger School, "Don't be a buddy fucker."

For this reason, I rank Fulton third from the bottom. To his credit, he was the best land navigator in the squad, and routinely guided us to the objective and the patrol base on time and as efficiently as possible. His tactical knowledge and fieldcraft were without peer and he was calm, detached, and level-headed when he led his graded patrols. But for all that, he was an asshole for not helping me pop my blisters and for scamming that wheat snack bread off me during the FTX. The man conned and extorted me out of calories in the field, knowing I would not have the balls to call him on it, which is almost worse than just stealing it outright.

Until my dying day, I will never forget nor forgive him for that wheat snack bread.

But Bailey, the nerdy, incompetent, mumbling, sleep zombie bat boy, is even worse, and I have no choice but to rank him second to last.

As the other bat boys are fond of saying, "Bailey is a fucking idiot." After knowing the guy for two weeks, after spending more than two hundred waking hours with the man, I am amazed he made it through infantry basic training, let alone the Ranger Regiment selection process. Bailey's Ranger School experience seems to be one of sure, steady degradation. He has no confidence, no friends, cannot communicate worth a damn, and has only the bare minimum of tactical skills to allow him to sleepwalk through his patrols.

Worst of all, only a few days into Darby Phase, he developed a terrible habit of muttering incomprehensibly to himself at all hours of the day and night. It is like having a crazy person or a dying man in our midst. It is eerie and unnerving.

Hell, peering Bailey low is practically doing him a favor. It is probably in the best interests of his health and sanity that he be kicked out of this school as soon as possible.

Yet, for all his faults, I cannot rank Bailey dead last. He tries hard, real hard to accomplish the tasks given to him in this course and there is no quit in the man, no matter how much he is droning. He may not always rise to the occasion, in fact, he rarely does so, but he is doing the best he can in a situation and environment that chews up harder men and spits them out. Moreover, Bailey has never intentionally screwed over anyone in the squad, despite being bullied, exploited, shunned, and ignored by everyone.

So, he gets peered low, but not lowest.

At this point, I have three, glorious minutes left for my Peers evaluation, and I get to spend it all on Jenson, arrogant, loud-mouthed, crude, shady, buck-toothed, backwoods, Private-First-Class, Airborne Ranger, Jenson. Take all the worst qualities of the typical bat boy, multiply them by ten, add a dash of deep south cracker and you get Jenson, someone who does not treat anyone who is not a fellow bat boy with even a modicum of respect, unless he happens to need something in that moment. From Day One he has been openly contemptuous of the young officers, regular infantry guys like me, and even Fulton, the green beret, who he finds singularly unimpressive.

My hatred of Jenson is instinctual. I have wanted to punch him in the mouth since the moment we met. Two weeks ago, it was even one of my better ideas for getting kicked out of this place, and maybe, I thought, I could even take the bastard out with me.

Of course, the man is no monster. Like everyone else, Jenson has positive traits. During his two graded patrols, probably because he wanted to keep us all happy and performing well, he was respectful and professional to the squad. He is tactically proficient and knows how to shoot, move, and communicate with the best of them. Like Leon and Salvador, he has a combat tour with the Ranger Regiment under his belt, and undoubtedly a few kills as well. This alone makes him worthy of some respect, no matter how much of a prick he may be.

Of all the men in the squad, Jenson needs another last place Peers ranking less than anyone. He is close with Leon, Newton, and especially Salvador, but he is extremely unpopular with the rest of the squad. Worst of all, he has already recycled once and, if he fails again, there is a very good chance he will be ejected from Ranger School entirely. Of course, if this happens, he will also be kicked out of his beloved Ranger Regiment, the core of his identity, and be forced to join a regular army unit as an infantry grunt. To an Airborne Ranger like him, this is a fate worse than death.

Unfortunately for Jenson, he is an asshole and the biggest buddy fucker in the squad, so I do not care about any of this. I rank Jenson dead last, and it feels damn good to do it.

With one minute to spare I put the finishing touches on my Peers evaluation sheet, lay my head down on the top of my hands, and fall asleep with a huge smile on my face.

Fuck that guy.

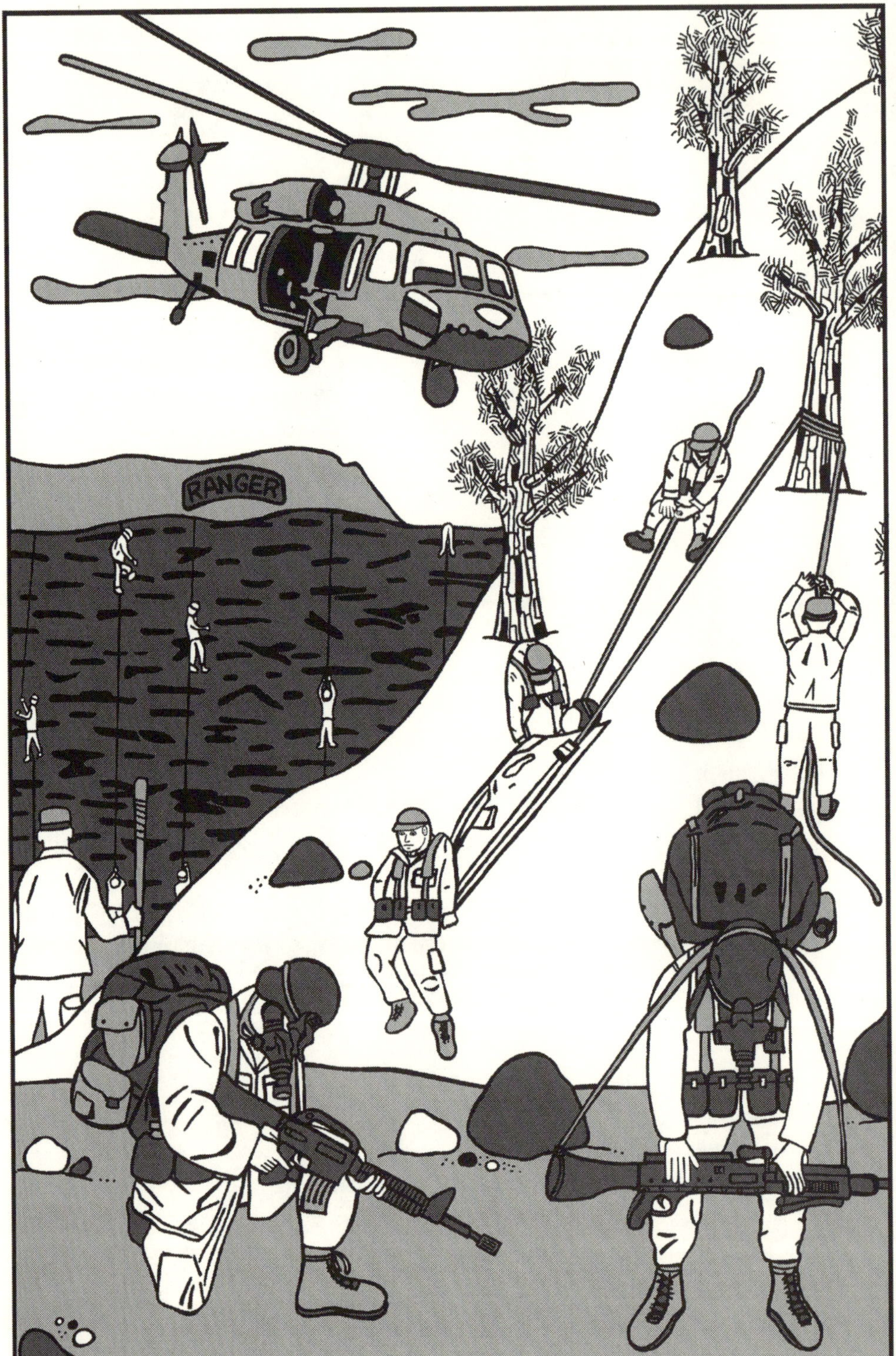
RANGER

Part II – "Walk"
Mountain Phase
Camp Merrill, Lumpkin County, Georgia
Days 21 - 40

"I woke up in a cold sweat, I had a nightmare that I was still in Ranger School. Thank God [] I was [only] in Vietnam."
                    Attributed to Colonel Robert "Tex" Turner.

Rule #12: Do not be afraid to step up and lead.

Chapter 7: "Mountain Men"

Rule #13: *You can endure anything for just one day.*

0429 Hours (04:29 a.m.)
Charlie Platoon Barracks, Camp Merrill
North Georgia Mountains
Day 28 of Ranger School

The barracks is dark, illuminated only by the glow of green-lit exit signs. The room is also silent, but for the snores of a dozen rangers and the soft footsteps of the two fireguards. One of them, Dale, glances at his watch before making his way briskly to the far end of the building.

Flick. Flick. Flick.

He turns on the light switches and strong fluorescent light instantly floods the room. My eyelids dart open as I simultaneously hear the sorrowful groans of the other rangers in Charlie Platoon reluctantly waking. Time to face the daunting reality of another long, miserable day of Techniques Week in Mountain Phase of Ranger School.

"Wake up, okay!" Dale shouts at some of the slower moving members of the platoon. "Hey everyone, it's time to get up out of your bunks, okay!"

Dale was lucky enough to have the last fireguard shift of the night, the best one to get if you must pull one, and has a head start on the rest of us. His

Mountain Phase of Ranger School

North Georgia

Chattahoochee National Forest

Chattahoochee National Forest

Hogback Mountain

Camp Frank D. Merrill

Mount Yonah

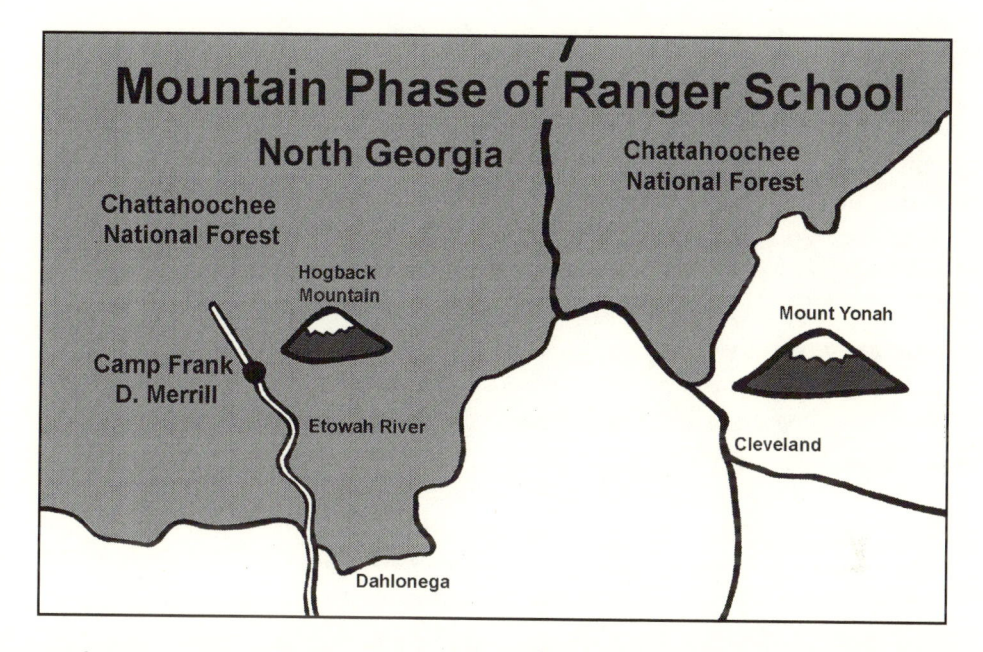

Etowah River

Cleveland

Dahlonega

uniform already on, boots tied, and face shaven, he has the time and energy to rouse the slow movers, like Newton, Leon, and Jenson, who are prone to snooze in their bunks long after wake up.

"You don't want the RIs to catch you in your bunks, okay," Dale reasons with them, "time to get up and get moving guys, okay..."

All three of them give him murderous stink eyes, but they too reluctantly rise.

I do not need any pestering to get out of my bunk. Three years in the infantry have taught me that it is always best to get up and move fast during the early morning wake ups demanded by the Army. I have to wake up anyway, there is no changing that basic fact; I might as well rip the band-aid off and seize the day. For practical reasons, it also makes sense to secure a spot at the limited number of bathroom sinks and toilets serving the needs of forty-five rangers before the lines back up.

Besides, the sooner I can brush my teeth, shave, piss, and put on my uniform and boots, the sooner I can catch a five- or ten-minute nap leaning up against my wall locker.

That does not mean it is easy to move with a sense of purpose. Scraping my razor-burned, weather-beaten face with my blunt, fifty-cent disposable razor is one of my least favorite parts of the day. I stare into the mirror, into yellowed, puffy, bloodshot, sleepless eyes, and can barely recognize myself in them.

After surviving RAP Week, limping through Darby, and passing the first FTX, they bused our ranger class to Camp Frank D. Merrill, nestled in the foothills of North Georgia's Chattahoochee National Forest, to begin Mountain Phase of Ranger School. The first four days were spent learning and being tested on mountaineering skills: tying knots, climbing, rappelling, moving things up and down vertical slopes. These were long and eventful days which saw us summiting Mount Yonah, training through our first snowfall, and freezing in the chill mountain air whenever we were not marching, climbing, or getting smoked. These were, by far, the easiest, most fun days of Ranger School.

Now, we are in the middle of Mountain Phase Techniques Week, the prelude to the Mountain FTX, a solid month into Ranger School now, and I am physically breaking down. Like many of my fellows, I suffer from over a half-dozen physical ailments, including a tweaked back, pinched nerve, chapped and bleeding lips, blistered feet, nerve damage and loss of sensation, a twisted ankle, and cracked and bleeding fingertips.

Others have it worse. Fulton and Salvador's neck muscles just stopped working one day, a condition called "rucksack palsy." They can't hold their own heads up any longer and must hold their chins up with one of their hands or tie the back of their helmets to their rucksacks. They look pathetic, and I feel sorry for them. I do not know how they are going to survive the FTX without working necks.

We get one or two more hours of sleep a night here, under a roof, but that is about the only improvement over Camp Darby. Four or five hours of sleep after what we are asked to do every day, after the sustained sleep deprivation of last phase, is nowhere near enough. Tobiri especially is rapidly deteriorating under the strain while Bailey is steadily losing his mind.

So yes, life is rough right now, up here in Mountains, but as I hack off the hardest part of my beard stubble, from the very tip of my chin, I take comfort in the Taoist mantra which lifts my spirits, if only briefly, for the darkest moments of the day:

I can endure anything for one day. For just one day, I can do and put up with anything.

This means that I do not get to worry about tomorrow, the FTX in a few days, the next phase after that, and especially, some unknown, impossibly distant future outside of Ranger School. If I want to survive this place, and one day earn my Tab, I need to focus solely on today, the next hour, now.

I quickly brush my teeth and relieve my bladder, put on my full uniform, pants, t-shirt, and BDU shirt, and finally tie my boots. While other rangers scramble to get ready, I slump down next to my wall locker, lay my head back on cold metal, and fall asleep for ten precious minutes.

At 5:10 a.m., the shuffling of dozens of boots on the cold tile floor wakes me from my sweet, brief slumber. I rise reluctantly to my feet, throw my patrol cap on top of my head, and follow the other rangers of Charlie Platoon out into the cold, foggy, damp mountain air for morning roll call.

Roll call will not actually be held for another twenty minutes but, this being Ranger School, the RIs insist on us being ten minutes early, to being ten minutes early. So, at this ungodly hour, well before it is necessary, the platoon assembles in rank and file to shiver and curse our fates in near-freezing temperatures. Some rangers crack jokes or chatter idly, but most stand around silently, feeling sorry for ourselves. We fall asleep standing up, waking as we wobble and start to fall towards the concrete.

Tobiri stands hunched over in a primitive protective posture next to me, shivering and moaning almost imperceptibly in the streetlight-illuminated semi-darkness. It might be because of his advanced age, he is close to thirty after all, or his inexperience with the tough, infantry field life, but whatever it is, this school is causing him to fall apart.

Several days into Mountains, Tobiri developed a chronic cough, has increasingly become short of breath, and finds himself with little appetite, despite the fact his already small frame is simply wasting away. Like the rest of us, his leg, back, and neck muscles are continuously under great strain, and he is so stiff upon waking in the morning that he can hardly get out of bed. What's more, his knee is badly sprained and every time he throws on his sixty- or seventy-pound rucksack, easily half his body weight, his body is bent and broken just a little bit more. Already a pale-skinned, Nordic-looking guy, Tobiri's pallor is now ghoulishly white and pasty.

Few of us believe Tobiri will even make it to the FTX. Newton, Leon, and Jenson have taken bets as to how many more days Tobiri will last before he collapses. I feel sorry for the guy, especially because he is still technically my battle buddy, though we barely talk now.

However, I remain impressed by Tobiri's ability to suffer in silence. The man rarely complains and never asks for help because he does not want to be a burden on the other members of the team, who are going through their own struggles. He may not be physically impressive, tactically adept, or a born leader, but Tobiri is still a hard guy, in his own way, worthy of admiration. It is going to be a sad day when he eventually washes out of Ranger School.

Finally, after a long, teeth-chattering twenty minutes, the day's new RIs show up punctually at 5:30 a.m. Today we have the privilege of getting the meanest, orneriest RI of them all, our good friend Sergeant First Class Rodriguez, the Crusty Mountain RI. He was the son of a bitch who smoked us for an hour when we first arrived at Camp Merrill because someone allegedly left orange peels on "his" bus. He is an intimidating man, standing six-feet-two inches tall, with dark features, a barrel chest, a booming voice, and a nasty disposition.

"Platoon guide! Get up here and bring these sad sacks of shit to attention. Report!"

"Roger, Sergeant!" Dale, the young and eager LT, has been the Charlie Platoon admin platoon sergeant or platoon guide for the last week. It is an inglorious administrative position which makes him responsible for bringing us to order and acting as a liaison between the platoon and the RIs while we train in Techniques Week.

"Pla-toon..." Dale issues the preparatory command as he dashes up to the front of our formation, "Atten-shun!"

Charlie Platoon's heels snap together, our hands go down by our sides stiffly, and our sore, hunched-over backs get just a little bit straighter.

"Squad leaders," Dale pauses for a moment, "issue the report!"

Each of the four squad leaders salutes Dale in turn and tells him the number of men present in their squad and whether anyone is going to sick call. Dale adds up the platoon's numbers and then reports back to the RI.

"Forty-five rangers present and accounted for, Sergeant." Dale tells him. "No one has left or gone AWOL, and five men are requesting to go to sick call."

At Darby we operated as a reinforced squad composed of twelve men. Now, we work as a platoon, a larger element composed of four squads: the security squad, two assault squads, and one heavy weapons squad with three machine guns. The squad is still the most integral unit, composed of the men I am the closest with, but now we do everything together as a forty-five-man team, Charlie Platoon.

Task Organization of a Ranger Platoon

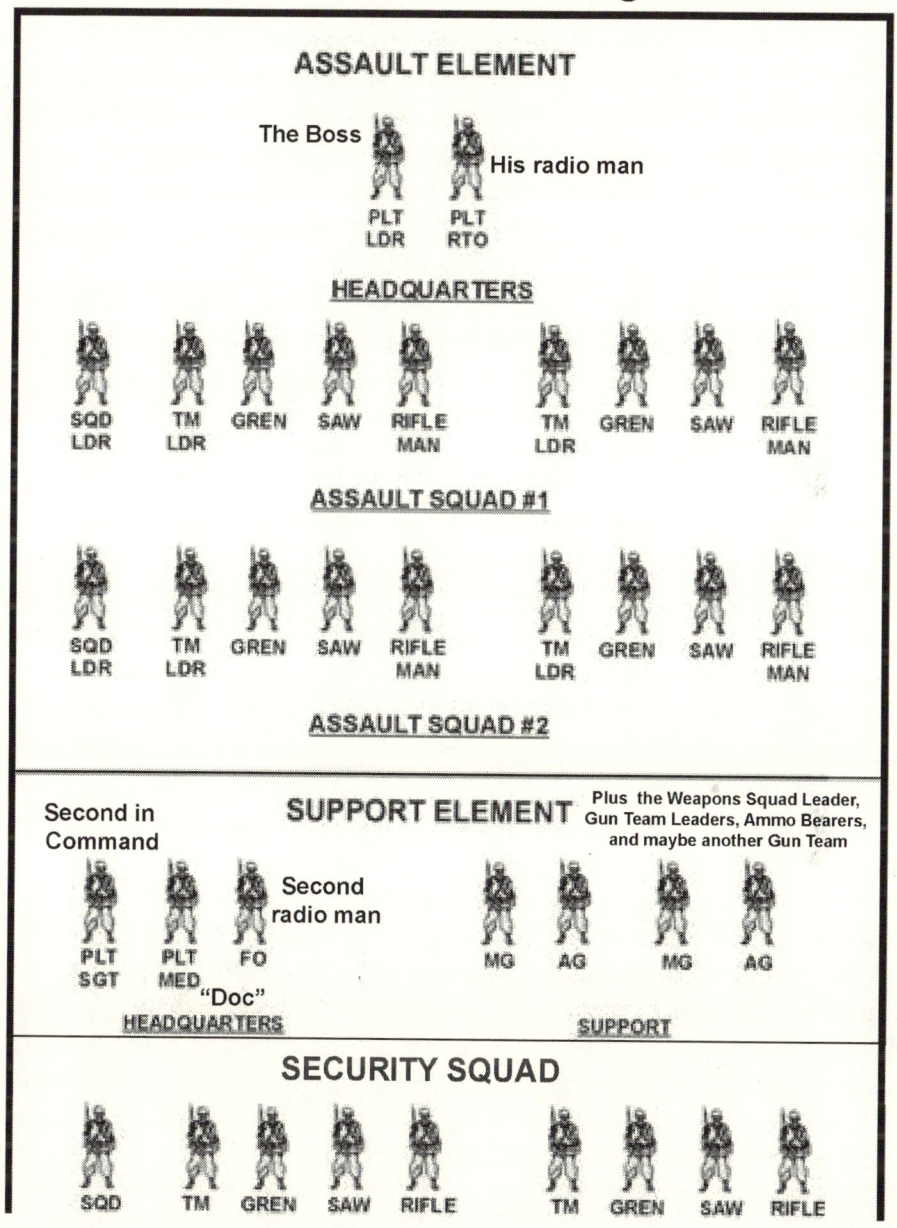

ASSAULT ELEMENT

The Boss — PLT LDR
His radio man — PLT RTO

HEADQUARTERS

SQD LDR | TM LDR | GREN | SAW | RIFLE MAN | TM LDR | GREN | SAW | RIFLE MAN

ASSAULT SQUAD #1

SQD LDR | TM LDR | GREN | SAW | RIFLE MAN | TM LDR | GREN | SAW | RIFLE MAN

ASSAULT SQUAD #2

SUPPORT ELEMENT

Second in Command — PLT SGT
PLT MED "Doc"
Second radio man — FO

Plus the Weapons Squad Leader, Gun Team Leaders, Ammo Bearers, and maybe another Gun Team

MG | AG | MG | AG

HEADQUARTERS — **SUPPORT**

SECURITY SQUAD

SQD | TM | GREN | SAW | RIFLE | TM | GREN | SAW | RIFLE

A platoon is led by a Platoon Leader, or "PL," who has ultimate responsibility for the execution of the mission and whatever happens or fails to happen during

ANDREW GOLDSMITH | 133

the patrol. In the real world, he is a first or second lieutenant, or more rarely, a sergeant first class, but here in Ranger School, it could be anyone, a bat boy like Leon or Bailey, or even a regular infantry corporal like me.

The Platoon Leader is assisted by the Platoon Sergeant, the platoon's senior non-commissioned officer and second in succession of command. He is responsible for the men's health and welfare, helps and advises the PL during all aspects of the patrol, and supervises the patrol's administration, logistics, and maintenance. In the real world, this position would be occupied by a sergeant first class or senior staff sergeant, but again, here it could be anyone.

The squad and team leaders of each respective squad are subordinate to the PL and the platoon sergeant and are the leaders directly responsible for managing the men who will conduct the patrol and execute the mission. In Darby, team leader was a graded position during the FTX, but now, it is a non-graded, yet still essential (and thankless) role.

These leaders are also joined by three new non-graded, but important positions in the platoon hierarchy: the radiotelephone operator or "RTO," forward observer or "FO," and a medic.

"Hmmmpph." The Crusty Mountain RI is satisfied enough with the report. "Platoon guide, get these rangers to chow," he tells Dale before executing an about face and walking away.

Chow, beloved food and sweet sustenance. Is there any sweeter sound to a ranger student? I don't think so. Charlie Platoon, to a man, starts silently salivating over thoughts of blueberry pancakes, biscuits and gravy, eggs, bacon, and peanut butter. Say what you will about Mountain Phase, but here, they feed us a good breakfast. What is soon coming to us is, by far, the best part of the day, worth standing out here in the cold, the main reason I was able to get out of bed this morning without openly weeping.

We march the short distance up the hill to the front of the chow hall where we form up again with the entire class, 180 rangers, to wait another twenty minutes before the chow hall opens. Again, we stand and wait, ten minutes early to being ten minutes early, shivering in the cold, whispering jokes and war stories, wracked with boredom, and falling asleep standing up.

Time passes slowly until, finally, it is 5:58 a.m.

Time to say The Creed.

"Recognizing that I volunteered as a ranger," one-hundred-and-fifty ranger students shout out in unison, "fully knowing the hazards of my chosen profession…"

RANGER CREED

Recognizing that I volunteered as a Ranger, fully knowing the hazards of my chosen profession, I will always endeavor to uphold the prestige, honor, and high esprit de corps of the Rangers.

Acknowledging the fact that a Ranger is a more elite Soldier who arrives at the cutting edge of battle by land, sea, or air, I accept the fact that as a Ranger my country expects me to move further, faster, and fight harder than any other Soldier.

Never shall I fail my comrades I will always keep myself mentally alert, physically strong, and morally straight and I will shoulder more than my share of the task whatever it may be, one hundred percent and then some.

Gallantly will I show the world that I am a specially selected and well trained Soldier. My courtesy to superior officers, neatness of dress, and care of equipment shall set the example for others to follow.

Energetically will I meet the enemies of my country. I shall defeat them on the field of battle for I am better trained and will fight with all my might. Surrender is not a Ranger word. I will never leave a fallen comrade to fall into the hands of the enemy and under no circumstances will I ever embarrass my country.

Readily will I display the intestinal fortitude required to fight on to the Ranger objective and complete the mission, though I be the lone survivor.

Yelling the Ranger Creed at the top of my lungs always feels good in the cold mountain air. I am suddenly a little more awake, a little warmer.

"I will always endeavor to uphold the prestige, honor, and high esprit de corps of..."

Most of us in the class finish this stanza with, "the rangers," but we are inevitably drowned out by, "my Ranger Regiment!" shouted proudly by sixty bat boys scattered throughout the platoons. This is "the proper version of the Creed," at least according to them as, they are fond of telling us, to be a real "Ranger" you also must wear a scroll from the 75th Ranger Regiment.

"Acknowledging the fact that a ranger is a more elite soldier," the class resumes shouting as one, "who arrives at the cutting edge of battle by land, sea, or air, I accept the fact that as a ranger, my county expects me to move further, faster, and fight harder than any other soldier."

Up here in the mountains, we operate a little differently. Here, walking a klick in broad daylight takes an hour. We move slower, hump more weight, and are collectively, more crippled and dispirited than ever before in our Army careers. Our legs are lamed, our backs are tweaked, we harbor numerous bacterial skin conditions, and it can take the shouts of an enraged RI to make us do even the simplest tasks. In many ways, we resemble a geriatric ward more than an elite band of soldiers.

"Never shall I fail my comrades!" We always emphasize the first word here. "I will always keep myself mentally alert, physically strong, and morally straight, and I will shoulder more than my share of the task, whatever it may be, one hundred percent and then some."

We could all use a little work on this stanza. After all, we fall asleep in the bleachers and on the ambush line. We avoid the harder tasks, like carrying the machine guns, their tripods, or the radios, like the plague. Many of us are willing to beg, lie, cheat, and steal for an extra morsel of food or a ten-minute nap.

"Gallantly will I show the world that I am a specially selected and well-trained soldier," the class continues to shout. "My courtesy to superior officers, neatness of dress, and care of equipment shall set the example for others to follow."

Neatness of dress? That's funny. I have not changed my raggedy uniform in days and my last shower is a distant memory. Up here in the mountains, who do I have to impress? Time spent showering is time not spent sleeping, a fool's trade, if you ask me.

"Energetically will I meet the enemies of my country." This stanza is my favorite and always gets my blood flowing. "I shall defeat them on the field of battle for I am better trained and will fight with all my might. Surrender is not a ranger word." We always hit this line hard. "I will never leave a fallen comrade to fall into the hands of the enemy and under no circumstances will I ever embarrass my country."

The Ranger Creed has to be the most badass military creed in existence and no Marine, or Navy Seal even, will ever be able to convince me otherwise. But let us be honest, at this point, halfway through Ranger School, the only thing we are looking forward to energetically is devouring a large breakfast, getting an honest night's sleep, and leaving these damn mountains.

"Readily will I display the intestinal fortitude required to fight on to the ranger objective and complete the mission, though I be the lone survivor."

No matter how wretched and jaded this school makes me, this conclusion to The Creed will always send chills down my infantry spine.

"RANGERS LEAD THE WAY!"

And with that, IT'S TIME TO EAT! The men of Charlie Platoon line up behind several rows of pullup bars to bust out six pullups to earn the right to enter the chow hall. For most of us, after several weeks in Ranger School, doing six pullups is a struggle.

After we complete our pullups, we take our place in one final single file line to silently await our chance to enter our happy place.

"Seven-five-three-eight, ma'am." A middle-aged civilian woman writes down the last four digits of our social security numbers into a ledger at the entrance to the chow hall. These four numbers are the only words we are authorized to speak during our dining experience. The chow hall is a place to eat, not fraternize or unwind, so we are silent. Everyone follows the rules because no one wants to get thrown out.

Finally, after waiting an hour in the cold, it is my turn for breakfast. I pick up my mess tray eagerly and grasp it firmly as I sidestep my way through each food station. Good-natured middle-aged and elderly women in hair nets serve us. These women are the only members of the fairer sex us rangers have seen in weeks, but I have never heard anyone speak lewdly about them. Not only are these matronly figures old enough to be our mothers and grandmothers, but they feed us, give us kind smiles, and sometimes even words of encouragement. It is a little comfort in a hard place, and it means a lot to us.

I find it difficult to not murmur a furtive "thank you, ma'am," as each chow hall angel successively piles my tray high and heavy with hot and steamy scrambled eggs, soft-cooked bacon, a generous hunk of ham, or the ever-coveted biscuits and gravy. For those who want it, which is everybody, there are bowls of oatmeal and grits, along with toast, and boxes of cereal. Best of all are the infamous Mountain blueberry pancakes which, drenched in slabs of butter and two packets of maple syrup, are truly a taste of heaven itself to a starving ranger student.

I ring the outer edges of my food tray with a banana, two packets of maple syrup, peanut butter, jelly, orange juice, regular milk for my cereal, and chocolate milk to wash everything down. Finally, to make sure I get my electrolytes, I fill up two plastic glasses with Powerade from the fountain dispenser.

My tray is heavy, piled awkwardly high with food and beverages, so I have to take great care not to spill anything as I make my way to my seat, directly next to the man in front of me in line. I gingerly place the tray on the table and take my seat. I pause and inhale deeply, savoring the moment before digging in.

This is my time, a glorious time, the only time of the day I can truly call my own, a time to fill my eternally ravenous stomach with delicious sustenance and, for a moment at least, quell the relentless hunger.

I move briskly and purposefully through my meal, following a Ranger School dining protocol I have sharpened to a fine edge over the last several days. First, I wolf down the mandatory piece of fruit, preferably a banana because I can devour it in seconds, before moving on to the heart of the meal which, today, is scrambled eggs, bacon, and blueberry pancakes. Once the last bites of pancake are gone, I scrape my leftover syrup and butter onto my grits and oatmeal and slurp it all down. Meanwhile, I spread peanut butter and jelly on one slice of toast while I use the other to wipe up the last remnants of syrup and egg grease on my now spotless plate. Ample swigs of Powerade and orange juice help to wash everything down and cereal with milk is great as a light, first dessert.

After I chug my chocolate milk and belch, I can honestly say that I have demolished every edible speck of food on my plate, and in record time. Anywhere else, I would be enormously, painfully full, but this is Mountain Phase of Ranger School, I am one of the platoon's food monsters, and I am still hungry.

Time to see if I can scavenge anything of value from my fellow rangers.

Newton sits immediately to my left, his thick neck and shoulders hunched protectively over his own tray of half-eaten food. There is no use trying to skim anything off him because, other than me, he is the biggest chow hound in Charlie Platoon. Fulton sits diagonally to my right, but the mean glare he gives me says it all, "Don't even try, Goldsmith!" Another dry hole.

Fortunately, both Bailey and Tobiri are also seated close by, and they are usually good for at least a packet of peanut butter or a half-drunk carton of milk.

Silently, slyly, communicating only with eyebrow raises and subtle finger gestures, I persuade them both to toss small items onto my tray. Bailey parts with a packet of peanut butter while Tobiri gives me half a syrup-sodden pancake, a real score. Newton eyes me jealously for getting the jump on him before convincing Bailey to give him a piece of toast.

The charity of my fellows exhausted, I push my chair back and stand up, tray in hand, and walk toward the trash cans with my food tray, plates, and cups. However, the meal is not over. It's time for trash can dessert.

My cheeks still chipmunked with food and chewing furiously, I line up behind a handful of other rangers awaiting their turn to dump their food scraps and trash into the garbage. Soon enough, it is my turn to dump my tray. Excitedly, like a kid on Christmas, I step up to the large, gray plastic trash cans, and peer over the edge.

Let's see what destiny has gifted us this morning...

While it is strictly forbidden, for many reasons, to eat out of the trash in Ranger School, this hungry ranger simply cannot help himself. It would be a sin to waste all these delectable scraps tossed by smaller framed, less voraciously hungry rangers. We are talking about quarter-full cartons of milk and orange juice, unopened packets of artificial butter substitute, toast crusts, pancake leavings, sometimes even a bite of biscuit and a healthy smear of gravy... um, um! Screw my dignity, screw any RIs who may catch me, screw anyone in polite, "normal," non-ranger society who would judge me for eating out of the garbage because they have never known hunger.

A hungry ranger has to eat.

And today continues to be a blessed day. I score two unopened packets of peanut butter and another decent-sized piece of syrup-soaked blueberry pancake. In between dumping my trash and busing my cups, dishes, and cutlery, I deftly open the peanut butter packets, scoop out the gooey insides with my finger and pancake scrap, and throw the whole mess into my mouth. I pray no RIs have seen me.

Fortunately, the only person who sees me is Dale, who stands immediately behind me in line with a disgusted look on his face.

I exit the chow hall satisfied and triumphant. For the moment, fueled by the massive influx of calories, the world is my oyster, and I am ready to seize the day. If I ever get out of here, I tell myself for the hundredth time in Ranger School, I will never take food for granted again.

The best part of the day continues. I walk back to the barracks knowing I have half an hour to do any last-minute preparations for the coming, long day of instruction and practice patrols, which officially begins at 7:00 a.m. As usual, I spend about fifteen minutes enjoying some precious solitude on the toilet before I check my equipment tie-downs, shoulder my fifty-pound rucksack, grab my M4 carbine, and march out of the barracks.

Today, Tobiri and I walk the short distance up a hill to our platoon's planning bay. It is only a five-minute walk, and our pre-FTX rucksacks probably weigh only fifty pounds, but it takes a great amount of will and effort from Tobiri to get up there. A chill wind which arose with the cloud-obscured sun blows steadily against us. Tobiri walks slowly, hunched over, dragging his feet, all while emitting low animal groans.

Along the way, several other battle buddy pairs from our platoon pass us. Some carry machine guns, others hump radios, others have spent AT-4 missile tubes attached to their rucks. Everyone has their burden to carry, and all wear an increasingly gloomy look on their face. The fun times are over. Time to go to work.

Two-by-two the rangers of Charlie Platoon summit the hill and trickle into the platoon training area, a small clearing near the top of the hill with a semi-roofed wooden planning bay, similar to but larger than the squad training bays we utilized in Darby. There is a set of chalkboards, a terrain table, and a set of bleachers just large enough to uncomfortably seat forty-five rangers. The bleachers, where we will spend many a miserable hour, sits near the edge of the structure, unroofed, its backing fully exposed to nature.

At the planning bay, we take off our rucksacks and arrange them by squads. My watch tells me it is 6:55 a.m. We have five minutes until the start of our day's instruction and there is not an RI in sight.

Near the middle of the small clearing, twenty feet from the bleachers, sits a 55-gallon steel drum with air circulation holes punched through it with an axe. Mercifully, some platoon heroes have taken it upon themselves to start a hobo fire and thirty rangers are crammed, "nut-to-butt," around it, sharing the warmth, and telling jokes and war stories to pass the time. Those of us with painfully cracked and bleeding fingertips, myself included, pass around a small vial of precious hand salve.

I feel very close with all these men as we jostle and twist, nestled close together in a human warming pile, trying vainly to shield ourselves from the wind. Green beret, bat boy, officer, paratrooper, infantry grunt, pog, if it ever mattered who we were before we came to this place, it certainly does not matter any longer. We are all equal in indignity and misery now, just a bunch of stinky, grimy, sleep-deprived, crippled, hungry, mountain rangers.

"Goddamnit! What is this clusterfuck, rangers?!" As we all figured based on his presence at morning roll call, it looks like the Crusty Mountain RI is going to be our walking RI today. "Who the fuck told you pussies that you could have a fire?"

All of us gathered by the fire barrel continue to stand there, meek and silent, doing all we can to soak up a few more precious seconds of warmth.

"You, you, and you," the booming voice of the Crusty Mountain RI shatters our dumb silence, "put out that fire. Everyone else, get behind your rucksacks, front leaning rest position, move! Time to work off those breakfasts, rangers!"

Other than the terrible layouts, there has been much less "smoking," and by that, I mean physical punishment by way of calisthenics, than I was anticipating in Ranger School. Even the most uptight Darby RIs rarely felt the need to drop us after RAP Week. But the Crusty Mountain RI is old school, he likes to start the day off with twenty minutes of push-ups, flutter kicks, and mountain climbers to get the blood moving. Better yet, is the long, invective-ridden monologue about how much harder Ranger School used to be, when he went through, and how weak and privileged we all are.

"... one MRE a day, record-breaking snowstorms, and no fucking snivel gear..."

Yeah, yeah, we know the story, old man. We all have it so easy. It certainly doesn't feel that way to us. Hell, Tobiri looks minutes away from death.

It is 7:22 a.m. by the time we all struggle to perform the last push-up.

"Weak, rangers, weak. I've seen enough." The RI says ruefully. "ON YOUR FEET! Let's go, get your asses in the bleachers!"

We limp and stumble our way into the bleachers. The only way we can all fit is crammed together tightly, shoulder to shoulder, knees touching knees.

"Today," the RI pauses suspensefully, "we are covering the Raid, and we have no time to waste."

Hurray! Raids! I scream sarcastically inside my own head. The same damn thing we have covered every other day for a week now. Raid, then ambush; raid, then ambush; then guess what? Another raid and ambush. Throw in an occasional movement to contact and you have Techniques Week of Mountain Phase in a nutshell.

Indeed, the next four hours just may be the worst part of the entire day. We can look forward to a long, unidirectional block of instruction on an infantry battle drill that I have practiced and trained on since the first days at my unit. I have also been on many raids in real-life operations during a year-long deployment to Iraq. By now, we have spent at least ten hours in the classroom covering the planning, tasks, and actions on the objective that go into a raid and at least twice that amount of time out in the woods doing raid rehearsals and walkthroughs. I can describe each step of the raid in intricate detail, tell you what each member of the platoon is tasked with doing from start to finish, and I could even lead one today if I had to.

In short, I know how to raid, and so does everyone else, even Bailey, but Ranger School hammers the same damn information into our tired and delirious brains over and over and over again, so that we can execute everything in our sleep.

Which will certainly come in handy in the days to come.

Within minutes of taking our seats in the bleachers our heads start bobbing and weaving as we fight vainly against the relentless urge to sleep.

It is unbelievably difficult to stay awake. Weeks of chronic sleep deprivation, twenty-hour workdays, the boredom of going over the same material repeatedly, and the cold all blend together into one potent sleep cocktail that leaves no ranger untouched.

"Hey, you! Yes, you, ranger, WAKE THE FUCK UP!"

Despite the jarring corrective yells of the Crusty Mountain RI, I catch myself slipping into unconsciousness several times during the first half-hour. First, my head starts to tilt forward, just a half-inch or so, then everything gets a little hazy, consciousness blurs, and I feel good, really good, then, realizing what is going on, I jolt awake, and my head slams back upright again.

I observe similar head-bobbing and jerking from other members of Charlie Platoon. Rangers in the back row must be careful that they do not tilt completely backwards and fall out of the bleachers. Many a sleepy ranger is saved by the arms of his comrades which keep him from plummeting to the ground. Newton and Leon, of course, are the worst. McCormick and Dale seat themselves next to them to prop them up, elbow them in the ribs, and otherwise do what is necessary to keep them awake through four hours of instruction.

Periodically, the RI will order all of us to stand while he continues the lecture. Ten or fifteen minutes after that, he will let us sit down again. Unfortunately, the head bobbing will resume almost immediately.

Frankly, we need more sleep, but we are not going to get it. There are no weekends here, just incredibly long days stacked upon incredibly long days. Days of nursing injuries, days of exposure to the elements, days of humping a heavy rucksack and running through the woods. Despite the lavish breakfasts, our waistlines continue to shrink, and our cheeks grow hollower.

So yes, other than the blueberry pancake breakfasts, everything about Mountain Phase of Ranger School does indeed suck, and staying awake during the morning lecture in the cold bleachers is probably the worst.

Fortunately, I have found a few ways to cope. Sucking on instant coffee crystals from our MREs gives a ranger a quick shot of caffeine. Newton and many others swear by chewing gum, which is becoming as precious as gold now that our supplies are dwindling. I have also had success pressing a ballpoint pen in between my thighs and squeezing, the pain helping somewhat to keep me awake, but not much.

But the best method of all is filling up every available space in my pocket-sized notebook with lists: list of things I will do, places to go, people to see, but mostly, long, detailed lists of all the luscious, hearty foods I will eat in the unimaginably happy future that awaits me outside of Ranger School. Lists of meat, candy, fast food, drinks, snacks, restaurant meals, baked goods, cheeseburgers, pizza, sandwiches, diner breakfasts, steak, Mexican food, sushi, barbeque, a dozen different pies, things to spread peanut butter on, things to spread chocolate peanut butter on, Mr. Pibb mixed with Sprite, KBR chow hall sweet tea to wash it all down, a thousand and one delectable treats.

For some reason, composing, endlessly revising, and annotating my lists helps keep me awake and, another plus, it makes me look attentive and alert, a studious ranger soaking up doctrine and tactics like a sponge. If only the RIs knew what I was really doing.

For hours, the inexorable struggle to stay awake grinds away at us all until, finally, just after eleven a.m., as the lukewarm, gray sun climbs high in the sky...

"And that wraps up the Raid, rangers," the RI says before asking rhetorically. "Any questions?"

Several rangers are shaken awake by their seatmates. Leon, elbowed in the ribs by Dale, says out loud, "What! What! Is it over?" Otherwise, the platoon is silent.

"No questions? Nothing at all, rangers?" The Mountain RI glares at us. "Fine. We will see if you really understand this stuff. We'll practice the rest of the day and night until I am satisfied you rangers can pull off a halfway decent raid, to the Mountain standard. That could take us until eight tonight, midnight, or three o'clock in the morning. It does not matter to me, it is all up to you, rangers."

Three in the morning, meaning one hour of sleep tonight? This guy cannot be serious.

Apparently, he is. The Crusty Mountain RI proceeds to just glare at us for several long seconds, a deep-set scowl on his face.

"It is now eleven-oh-six," he says looking down at his watch through cold, dark eyes. "You have until," he pauses for dramatic effect, "eleven-sixteen to eat your MREs, dispose of your trash, and have your rucksacks on your back, ready to go."

Ten minutes! Jesus fucking Christ, I hate this guy. Ten minutes is not enough time to consume our second and last meal of the day, the last time we will eat anything until breakfast tomorrow morning, eighteen hours from now.

"Understood, rangers?" The Crusty Mountain RI does not care. "Good. Go!"

The Mountain RIs give us even less time than the Darby RIs to eat our MRE meals, usually fifteen minutes, but sometimes less. They want to reinforce the lesson that food comes secondary to the ranger mission and that we eat to survive, not for pleasure. We cannot "graze" or hold food items for later consumption or we risk getting a major-minus or even recycled from the course. Whatever we cannot eat in the allotted time goes in the trash.

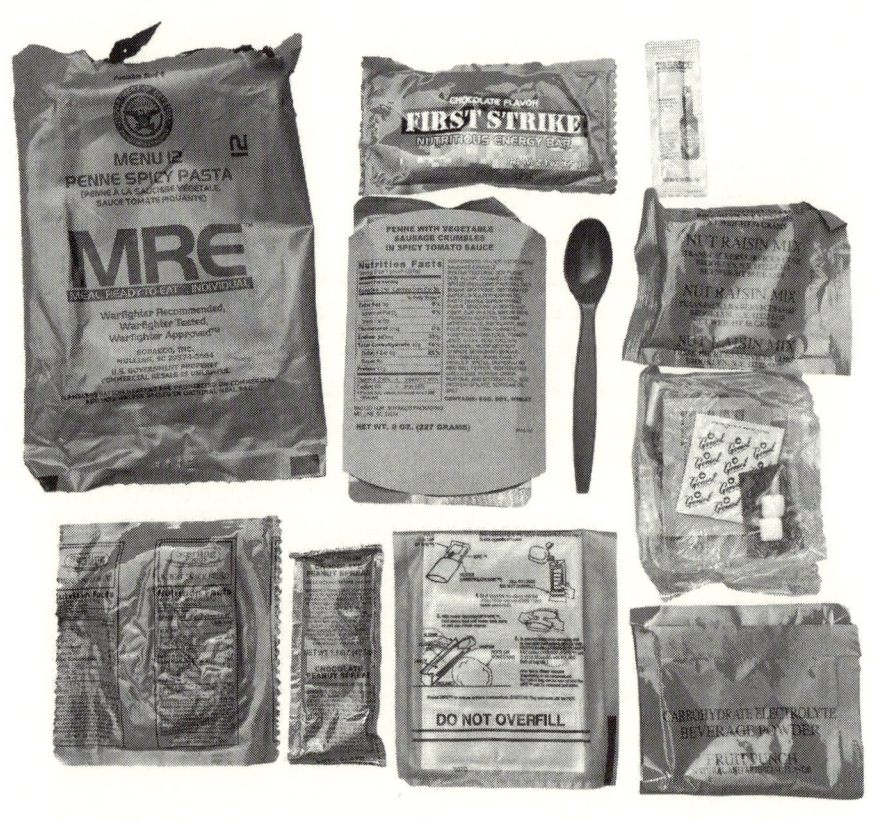

With such little time to eat, there is no time for trading, friendly banter, or ceremony. Many rangers, especially the green berets, opt to simply eat their entire meal cold, without taking the time to warm up their entrées or otherwise prepare and season their meals. But not me, I am not a savage. Food is my driving purpose right now, one of the few things I can look forward to in life, and I am not going to squander this gift.

Good thing my time at Ranger School has trained me for this, and good thing I have a plan, the plan, to eat an MRE in ten minutes or less. Here is how you do it:

> *Take out your trusty MRE opener (also known as a "knife") and slice open the top of the outside plastic MRE pouch to gain access to the contents of your meal. (0:05 seconds).*
>
> *Dump out all the contents of the pouch and locate the easiest to eat substantial snack, for example, pound cake or wheat snack bread. Open the pouch, shove as much of the snack as you can possibly fit into your mouth, and start chewing vigorously. (0:10 seconds).*
>
> *Continue to consume the snack while removing the main entrée pouch from its cardboard box. Place the entrée pouch into the empty green water-activated heater bag and add a splash of water from your canteen to the bag. Fold over the top of the heater bag and insert the heater bag with the entrée pouch inside into the entrée's cardboard packaging. Set this aside for at least ninety seconds, longer to ensure maximal and even heating. Optional: You can also insert any accessories, for example cheese, beans, or rice, into the heater bag with the entrée pouch, but this will increase heating time and decrease the heater's effectiveness. (0:30 seconds).*
>
> *While the entrée pouch is heating, open and rapidly consume every food item that will not be eaten with or mixed into the entrée. (2:30 minutes).*
>
> *Throughout the MRE consumption process, liberally drink water from your canteen to facilitate swallowing half-chewed chunks of food and avoid choking. This is especially important when consuming crackers. You can also dump any flavored drink packets into your canteen to improve the taste of the iodine-treated creek water.*
>
> *Once the entrée and any accessories are done heating, carefully remove the entrée pouch from the heater bag. Careful, the bag will be hot! (3:00 minutes).*
>
> *With your knife, slice open the entrée pouch lengthwise to ensure easy access to every last morsel of food. Utilizing your plastic MRE spoon, mix in any accessories, for example, hot sauce, cheese, or crackers, and then use your spoon to eat and enjoy the resulting warm*

slop. (4:00 minutes)

If all the above steps have been carefully and expeditiously followed, the ranger should have four or five minutes left to enjoy a hot, leisurely MRE entrée. (8:00 minutes).

After the entrée is consumed, finish eating anything that is edible, including candy, jam, or "ranger pudding," an improvised mixture of sugar, non-dairy creamer, and powdered cocoa mix. Save any gum or instant coffee crystals for later. (9:00 minutes).

Gather all the trash together and shove it back into the plastic MRE pouch in preparation for the RI announcing that...

"Your time is up, rangers! Don't even think about eating another fucking bite. If it isn't sliding down your throat, spit it up, it belongs to me now. Deposit your trash into the bags to my front and get ready to move out, rangers!"

That was fast, only nine minutes by my watch, but although my cheeks are still chipmunked with skittles and chicken with salsa, I have managed to eat every tangible speck of food in my MRE. I watch sorrowfully as some of the other rangers toss edible portions of food away into the trash. I debate fishing around for some tasty scraps, but the RI is watching too closely, so I decide against it.

Another dreaded moment has arrived. Time to throw our heavy rucksacks onto our aching backs, move out into the surrounding woods, and conduct rehearsal after rehearsal of the material covered in today's class. Movement techniques, react to contact, movement to contact, and most of all, raiding. For the next ten to twelve hours, maybe longer, we can look forward to slow marching, kneeling, laying down in the dirt, and more instruction on executing a raid from everyone's least favorite RI.

Thus is the life of a Mountain Man.

We struggle to stay warm as the nighttime temperatures fall into the low forties. The RIs forbid us from putting on any additional warming clothing, despite the fact we carry an entire rucksack full of it all day, every day. As always, there is the constant battle against sleep overtaking us, which is nearly impossible as we lie down and stare into green nothingness, for hours on end. Our backs ache, we are hungry, and if this RI catches us doing anything stupid, we will get written up or recycled for sure.

In short, it takes a lot of grit and will power just to make it through one long, boring, chilly, grueling fall day in Mountains, and it is not over yet.

Several Hours Later

"When is the RI going to call it a day and let us all get some sleep?" Newton mutters into my left ear. "It's eleven-thirty at night, already. I fucking hate this guy!"

"Maybe never. He likes to mess with us and keep us out in the cold." I shiver and gripe in response, before adding, "Crusty bastard!"

Newton chuckles a bit before we resume a mutual, sullen, angry-at-the-world silence. We lie next to each other, on our bellies, on the cold, hard ground. We peer down our NODs into a small open clearing below us surrounded by tall trees whose branches sway lightly in the breeze. We man an overwatch position while our platoon rehearses a raid for the sixth time today, the third time in darkness.

Five minutes later, Newton breaks the silence again.

"Goldsmith," he says through chattering teeth, "are you as cold as I am?"

"Yep. Probably colder." I tell him.

"Then get closer, you big oaf, and share some of that body heat."

I hesitate for a moment.

"Ah, c'mon Goldsmith!" Newton rebukes me. "Don't you know it's not gay if you're in Ranger School? This is a matter of survival."

Newton is right and, besides, who am I kidding? By now, Ranger School has robbed me of whatever shame or residual homophobia I may have left. I'm an infantryman, after all, and I would be lying to the reader if I told you this was the first time I snuggled up close to a battle buddy to make it through a freezing cold night.

So, I slide closer to Newton, our shoulders touching, legs mashed together and intertwined. We continue to shiver in the darkness, but Newton's additional body heat does help with the cold, if only a little.

A few minutes pass and I observe some shapes rustling around in the green darkness below. Either I am hallucinating again, or it is the two assault squads setting up at the last covered and concealed position before the objective. My Timex watch tells me it is now a quarter-to-midnight. Most RIs would have called it a night by now, but not the Crusty Mountain RI, five hours after sundown we are still training. Yet, I still have hope that this could be the last rehearsal run of the night before the RI lets us return to the barracks and get some sleep.

"C'mon!" Newton moans. "All we have to do is hit the objective one more time. What's the hold-up?"

Suddenly, we hear the platoon leader shout out "Bang, bang! Bang, bang!" somewhere in the darkness. This is followed one second later by the machine guns of the support by fire position on the small hill off to our right, who open up with their own staccato "Bang-bang-bang-bang! Bang-bang-bang-bang!" Finally, the eighteen rangers in the two assault squads join in on the "mad minute" of overwhelming firepower by adding their own "bang-bangs" to the mix.

"Bang, bang, motherfuckers." Newton adds dryly from our detached position. "Now, let's get this thing finished, pack up, and go home!"

The platoon leader stops the mad minute and has the machine gun teams shift their fire. The two assault squads pick themselves up, and they start moving, one battle buddy pair at a time, through the objective. Two fire teams separately clear two small "structures" consisting of imaginary huts outlined with strips of white engineer tape. Soon enough, the assault squads have pushed through the entire objective. They take a knee, face out in a semi-circle, and await an enemy counterattack as the PL calls for the search teams to sweep the objective.

It is now ten minutes to midnight. Every ranger in the platoon is desperately praying that the Crusty Mountain RI will be satisfied enough with this last performance to let us call it a night.

"END EX! END EX!" The RI suddenly shouts out loudly. "Bring it in, rangers. Bring it in. We're going admin, pull out those sensitive items."

The Crusty Mountain RI must be satisfied because he is calling an end to rehearsal before we even had the chance to execute our phased withdrawal plan. This administrative break and sensitive item check should be our last task of the night before we can return to camp. The platoon rapidly filters into the small clearing we just raided, the smiles on everyone's faces visible by the light of our red-lens headlamps.

Unfortunately for us, the headcount is one short. We are missing someone.

"LOST RANGER! LOST RANGER!"

Those nearest echo the dreaded cry. Stop doing whatever you are doing and look for your buddy, it commands us.

"Lost ranger! Lost ranger!" Soon, the whole platoon is shouting it. "Lost ranger! Lost ranger!" We cry out with anger, sadness, and resignation. "Lost ranger! Lost ranger!" Sleep was so close, but now, we can feel it slipping away.

"Use your white-lens headlamps, rangers, and keep shouting!" The RI says in a rage. "You better find your missing buddy and you better do it fast!"

Who are we missing? After a few minutes someone figures out that it is Fulton, of all people. Our squad's resident green beret and land navigation guru, he is out there, somewhere in the darkness.

"FUL-TON! FUL-TON!" We all shout as we fan out to beat the brush in search of the lost ranger. "Where are you!"

Ten, fifteen, then twenty minutes pass. Still, we cannot find him. Lost rangers are a serious safety hazard in Ranger School and a ranger can only be separated from his platoon for thirty minutes before he becomes an automatic Recycle. We must find Fulton fast, in case he is injured or, even worse, has to repeat this phase all over again.

"You're not going in tonight until you find him, goddamnit!" The Crusty Mountain RI is growing increasingly irate. "Yell louder, rangers! Find him! NOW!"

The minutes tick away on Fulton's recycle clock, but more importantly, on our precious sleep time. Knowing this, half the platoon gives up early in the search and instead sit down dejectedly on rocks and fallen trees, resigned to getting zero sleep tonight.

The rest of us keep hollering for him, "FULTON! FUL-TON!" but he is nowhere to be found.

It is 12:23 a.m. when the RI yells out in a great rage. "Rangers, you have one minute to find this shitbag! One minute before he's out of the course and you're all doing mountain climbers for the rest of the night. You think I get tired? Oh, hell no! I got no problem keeping you all up all night!"

"Fulton! FULTON! FUL-TON!" The platoon yells out in unison, scattered in a dozen different directions. "Where are you?"

"Here I am!" Fulton suddenly emerges out of the darkness. He strolls casually into the center of the clearing, looking innocent, if not a little pathetic, with his palsied neck causing his jaw to slump pathetically forward on his chest. He has to use his left hand to hold up his head to address us.

"Sorry guys. I don't know what happened. I must have lost track of time out there on the security position." He shrugs one shoulder. "Geez, I hope you weren't out there looking for me long." He releases his grip and lets his floppy head slump forward on his chest again.

By the light of the night's half-moon, I can see the RIs beet-red face and shaky hands.

"Lost track of time? Lost track of time? I'm, I'm..." For the first time, I am seeing the Crusty Mountain RI literally speechless. I cannot tell if he wants to throttle Fulton or burst out laughing. Abruptly, the RI turns his back to him, thrusts his hands in the air, and emits a frustrated beast-like shriek.

"I'm done with you, rangers, I'm fucking done." He shakes his head ruefully for a moment before continuing again. "Platoon leader, get everyone's packs on their backs and get ready to move back to the barracks. Platoon sergeant, I want another headcount. NOW!"

With mere seconds to spare, purposefully or not, Fulton has reemerged, the lost ranger found. We have lost out on at least forty-five minutes of sleep and any lingering illusions about the invincibility of green berets, but at least our long, grueling day is almost at an end. We will get at least some sleep tonight, and for that, I am happy.

It is 12:45 a.m. by the time we make it back to the barracks. There is no question of showering or changing into a clean uniform before bed. Who do I have to impress, anyway? A bunch of mountain men? We are used to living rough up here, and sleep is far too precious.

Even though I have the good luck of not pulling a twenty-minute guard shift, I still stand to get less than three hours of sleep tonight, less than usual, even for Mountains. Tomorrow morning's four a.m. wake up, like every morning's, is going to be rough.

I am still chewing my last piece of Juicy Fruit gum and the overhead lights are still on, but I manage to fall asleep the second my head hits my camping pillow.

It feels like only a few minutes have passed when my eyelids snap open to the shouts of "Wake up! Everyone, wake up!" and piercing bright, overhead lights. I resume chewing my stale piece of gum, shakily grab my toothbrush and razor, jump off the top bunk, and steer myself towards the bathroom sinks.

Another fucking day in Ranger School. I contemplate woefully as I stare into my reflection, into vacant, hollow, and bloodshot eyes. How will I get through this one?

"You can do anything," a voice somewhere deep inside reminds me, "anything for just one day."

I scrape a dull razor across my chin before rinsing my face with cold water and hopping into a short line for the bathroom stalls. I am only five minutes into what promises to be another epically long and tragic day, but after getting up and moving, I already feel better.

Waking up is oftentimes the hardest part and, as Ranger School has proven to me, I can put up with practically anything.

Anything for just one day.

Chapter 8:
DELTA DAN!
YOU OKAY, BATTLE BUDDY? YOU DON'T LOOK SO GOOD.
GOOD ENOUGH . . . I'LL MAKE IT THROUGH THE DAY.
"GOOD . . . BECAUSE WE ARE DOING AN AIR ASSAULT TODAY . . ."
". . . AND IT SHOULD BE FUN FOR A CHANGE."
ZZZ
SOMETIMES . . . RANGER SCHOOL CAN BE BADASS!
I THINK I'M GOING TO PUKE.
ZZZ

ANDREW GOLDSMITH | 153

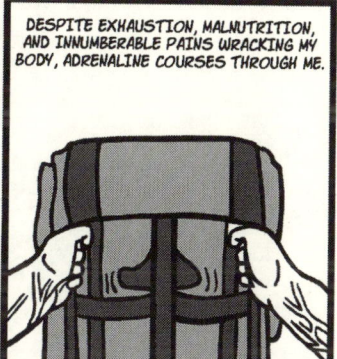

. . . AND LANDS A SHORT DISTANCE AWAY.
WHAT THE HELL DID I JUST DO?!
GOTTA GET MY RUCK! GOTTA GET MY RUCK!
ARRRGH!
I HOPE THE RI DIDN'T SEE ME!
BUT THE RI SAW.

ANDREW GOLDSMITH | 155

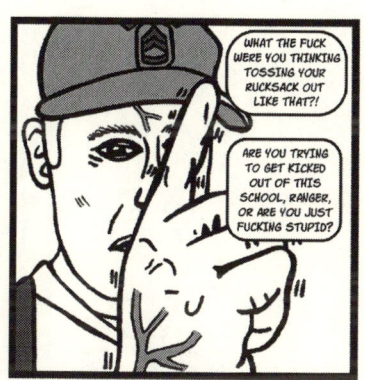

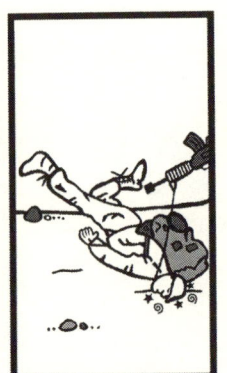

156 | THE MEDIOCRE INFANTRYMAN'S GUIDE TO RANGER SCHOOL

Chapter 9: "Just Another Day in Mountains"

"Textbooks tell lies!" Somewhere it is said that man cannot exist without sleep for more than a stated number of hours. Quite wrong!"
                                      Victor Frankl, Man's Search for Meaning

Rule #14: Always top off your canteens.
Rule #15: Never trust a sleepy ranger.
Rule #16: Pray there won't be rain.

0402 Hours (04:02 a.m.)
Camp Merrill Training Area
North Georgia Mountains
Day 6 of the Mountain FTX
Hours of Sleep in the Last 24 Hours: 2¼ Hours

The sounds of zippers and men rustling around in their rucksacks causes my eyelids to slide reluctantly open. I slip my rain poncho off my head slightly to see Newton packing away his sleeping bag in the predawn darkness.

"Rise and shine, Goldsmith," he says as I yawn, check my watch, and rise to my feet. I feel surprisingly rested and consider myself lucky. No one woke me for a guard shift last night so I was able to get more than two hours of uninterrupted sleep.

Health Problems of a Ranger Student

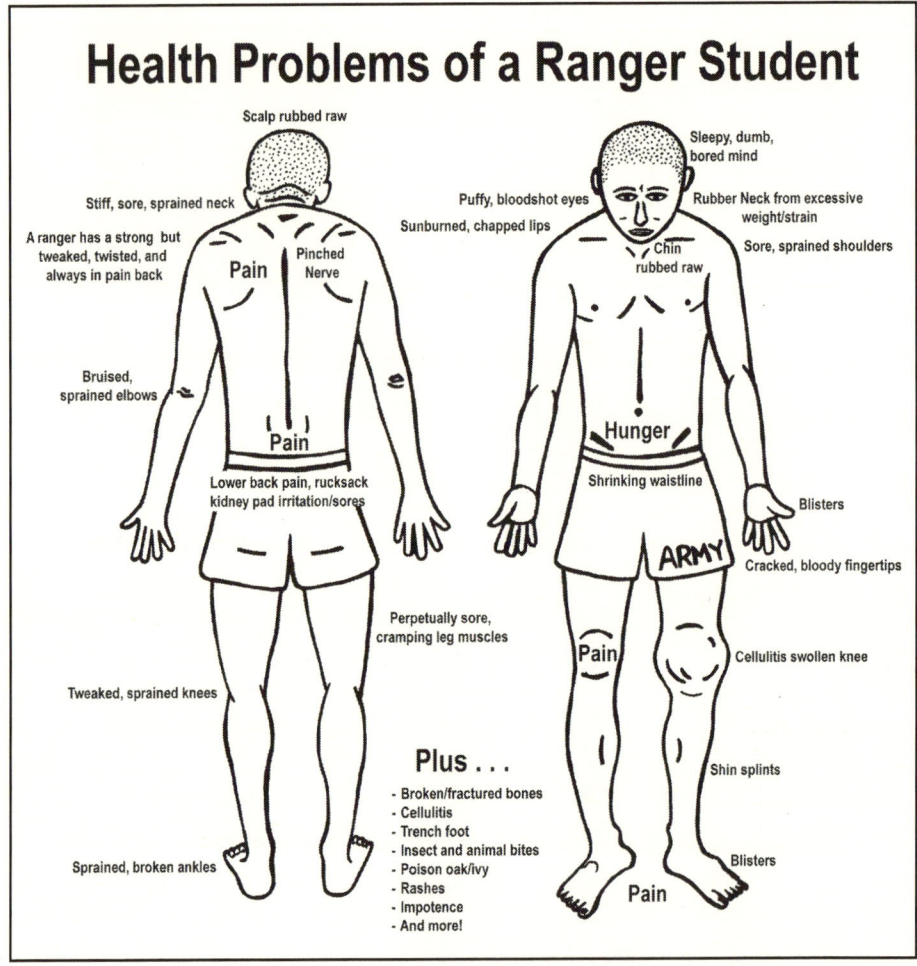

- Scalp rubbed raw
- Stiff, sore, sprained neck
- A ranger has a strong but tweaked, twisted, and always in pain back
- Pain
- Pinched Nerve
- Bruised, sprained elbows
- Pain
- Lower back pain, rucksack kidney pad irritation/sores
- Perpetually sore, cramping leg muscles
- Tweaked, sprained knees
- Sprained, broken ankles

- Sleepy, dumb, bored mind
- Puffy, bloodshot eyes
- Sunburned, chapped lips
- Rubber Neck from excessive weight/strain
- Chin rubbed raw
- Sore, sprained shoulders
- Hunger
- Shrinking waistline
- Blisters
- Cracked, bloody fingertips
- Pain
- Cellulitis swollen knee
- Shin splints
- Blisters
- Pain

Plus . . .
- Broken/fractured bones
- Cellulitis
- Trench foot
- Insect and animal bites
- Poison oak/ivy
- Rashes
- Impotence
- And more!

But as the numbing effects of the deep slumber wear off and I am forced to move, I quickly come to my senses. Like many of the rangers in the platoon, my twenty-two-year-old body is bent, broken, and beaten down. Starting from the ground up, I sprained my left ankle tripping over a tree branch four days ago. I re-tweak it painfully several times a day now, with no option but to simply keep marching on it until the pain gradually subsides. The soles and even the sides of both of my feet are once again covered in a dozen-odd blisters reminding me of a familiar, maddening pain that nearly drove me to quit in Darby. My right knee is stiff and inflamed; the deep, core muscles in my quadriceps and hamstrings are perpetually sore and broken down; and my legs cramp frequently due to dehydration and exertion.

My legs must move me forward, but my back has to carry my seventy- or eighty-pound rucksack. Everything that touches the rucksack hurts. The flesh on my hips is rubbed red and raw from the thinly padded, half-exposed metal of the rucksack's kidney pad. Unlike many other rangers, especially the old guys, I do not suffer from much lower-back pain. However, I do have a pinched nerve in my upper-back that sends a painful but familiar jolt of pain down my spine every time I put on or remove my rucksack, dozens of times a day. Individual bands of muscles in my back, shoulders, and traps are torn, tweaked, and forever sore from constantly humping such a heavy load. Our backs are perpetually crushed under the weight, never given the opportunity to heal.

Moving on up, my neck is sore and perpetually stiff, largely due to the strain of supporting heavy night vision devices during long night movements. But again, I am lucky, at least mine still works. Salvador and Fulton's necks can't even lift their own heads up. It's a miracle they are still in the course.

Coming back to my problems, my lower lip is chapped so badly it has developed a half-inch split in the middle that bleeds every time I eat or take a sip of water from my canteen. My face is scratched from tree branches and my chin irritated and razor-burned from dry shaving without cream or running water.

Worst of all, my fingertips are deeply cracked and bleeding from exposure and dehydration. This causes me unusually intense pain and is a great challenge whenever I must perform any fine motor skill. To adapt, I have learned to tie my bootlaces with only the side of my thumbs and my ring fingers, the least cracked portions of my fingers. The other digits are practically unusable. A dozen or more other rangers in the platoon share this painful affliction and, unfortunately, we ran out of the soothing hand salve two days ago and we have yet to be resupplied.

But as bad as I have it, others have it worse. After all, my neck still works, and I have yet to suffer a complete physical collapse like my former ranger buddy Tobiri. He walked sixty feet off the Blackhawk helicopters before falling face first into the dirt a week ago. He could not get up under his own power, so they recycled him, or worse. Then there is always the engineer sergeant who broke his foot in RAP Week. Somehow, he is still here, limping through the course, a perpetual cripple.

Moreover, while I have lost twenty pounds and inches off my waistline, let us just say, at two hundred and twenty pounds, I started this course with a lot more to spare than most rangers. Little Leon is different. He must weigh no more than one hundred pounds now. He looks paper thin and frail, his formerly tanned, Cuban skin sallow and ashen. It hurts to watch him put his massive ruck on. He is impossibly, ceaselessly tired and falls asleep like clockwork whenever we stop on the march. His mouth hangs open in a perpetual "o" shape and sometimes he is drooling.

Meanwhile, Bailey has lost possession of his mind and has not uttered a comprehensible syllable to anyone in days. Bailey stumbles through the woods clumsily, following other squad member's pointed fingers, frustrated growls, and angry shouts. We worry that he may wander off into the woods one night and never return.

All of us are hurting, fighting a losing battle with the Mountains. Everything here is just like Darby, but worse. The terrain is steeper, the nights longer, the weather colder, the woods denser, the movements longer, the RIs more bad-tempered, our bodies are more broken, we are getting even less sleep, if that is even possible, and we are hungrier than ever. We look like vagrants and move and think like geriatric hospital patients.

Welcome to Mountains FTX, where every day feels like a lifetime of struggle.

MRE breakfast is at 5:00 a.m. which we eat while the medics come by to check out and nominally treat our unshod feet for blisters, trench foot, frostbite, cellulitis, and insect bites. By far, this is the best part of the day, my only chance to eat a leisurely meal and chat a bit with the squad. The frigid air feels good on tender and brutalized feet which will be smashed into boots for the next twenty-one hours.

The new day's RIs show up at 6:00 a.m. as the sky near the horizon begins to lighten. They designate the day's leaders and brief the new platoon leader on the mission. The good news is, I have not been selected to be a graded leader today; the bad news is, after giving up my radio to the new RTO, the only unclaimed weapon in the squad is a SAW machine gun.

Now, don't get me wrong. I love the SAW, the M249 Squad Automatic Weapon, an individually portable, air-cooled, gas-operated, belt-fed, light machine that fires the NATO standard 5.56 mm cartridge and forms the basis of firepower for an infantry fire team. I carried one with pride for almost two years back at my unit, but trust me, you do not want to hump a SAW in Ranger School, and it should be avoided whenever possible.

In many ways, the SAW is an even worse weapon to carry than the

M249 5.56mm "SAW" Light Machine Gun

larger 240B machine gun. While the 240B is nine pounds heavier, the 240B gunner has an assistant and an ammo bearer to carry the bulk of the gun's ammunition. A SAW gunner must carry all his rounds, somewhere between six hundred and a thousand, in addition to his usual, heavy rucksack. The SAWs also tend to be the most ancient, abused, and poorly maintained weapons in Ranger School and can barely be counted on to fire half the time. Because most SAW gunners have trouble burning through their ammunition, their rucksacks get heavier and heavier with each ammunition resupply. This tempts some of the more unscrupulous rangers to bury ammunition in the ground and pray the RIs do not find it.

Today, my half-rusty SAW comes with just over nine-hundred rounds of ammunition.

Things could always be worse, Goldsmith, at least you are not in a graded position, getting evaluated today.

Around 6:30 a.m. the sun finally starts peeking over the chill, damp-green horizon and illuminates our spartan patrol base, a triangular-shaped hobo encampment with forty-odd rangers. Some of us lie down and pull perimeter security on torn, half-pieces of foam padding while others shave and brush their teeth using metal canteen cups and cold creek water. We rub our hands together and blow into them to bring some feeling into numb fingers. Machine gunners take cat naps resting their cheeks on knuckles and buttstocks. Newton and Leon, as they are prone to do, lie next to each other, cradled in the other's arms for warmth, softly singing Journey's Don't Stop Believin'.

Meanwhile, today's platoon leader, platoon sergeant, squad leaders, and a select group of the Charlie Platoon lieutenants prepare the op order and plan the day's movements and operations. The rest of us, the regular Joes, continue to pull outward security, clean our weapons, and do our best to catch snippets of sleep without getting caught by the RIs. We talk to our battle buddies in low whispers, swapping barracks tales and war stories, and laugh morbidly at our miserable condition.

Planning is more rushed than usual today. By 10:00 a.m., the day's PL issues the op order to the squad leaders. Salvador, our floppy-necked squad leader, briefs us on all the important details.

"We're doing a raid today. Headed that way," he says. "Any questions?"

We have none. Newton and I proceed to sling our oppressively heavy rucksacks onto our backs. With all the SAW ammunition, mine must weigh eighty pounds.

Time to march off into the woods again.

Two Hours Later

Marching is demanding work. After moving a mere one or two klicks, there is intense, constant pain in my knees, back, the bottom of my feet, my sprained left ankle, and just about everywhere else in my young but battered body. Walking here is not a passive activity. We must avoid tripping, falling, and hurting ourselves, as well as making any noise, all while maintaining the proper spacing between us and keeping a constant visual watch on our teammates and leaders who could pass us critical orders at a second's notice. Above all, we must constantly scan the environment around us with our eyes, ears, and noses, looking for signs of enemy insurgents, the Opfor, who want to shoot us and blow us up along the way.

While climbing one steep, muddy hillside I am forced to position my feet at weird sideways angles to gain traction, all while slipping backward every other step. It places a tremendous strain on my twisted ankle, but somehow, I slide my way up to the top. On another hillside, on the descent, I slip, fall, and hit my knee on a rock. "That can't be good for the cellulitis..." I mumble depressively to myself as I struggle painfully to my feet.

Can't stop, gotta keep marching. Another, stronger voice says in my head. *Pick yourself up and keep moving.*

The struggles within each of our own minds are borne in silence. "Noise and light discipline," demands that we march in silence, oftentimes fourteen hours of the day, in daylight or moonlight, until actively engaged by the enemy. We lay in ambushes, conduct recons, and establish patrol bases solely with arm and hand signals, nods of the head, and occasional hurried whispers. On the march, we trip and fall, hurting ourselves, sometimes seriously but somehow, we force ourselves to rise again, without curses, without exclamations, and continue to walk again. The constant silence can be maddening at times, and I find myself craving human conversation.

In a futile, self-defeating effort to cope with the constant pains of the march, my mind selectively bounces around from one body part to another, focusing on one for as long as I can bear it before transferring my focus to another injured site. I move from the large, generalized muscle soreness in my back to the searing, steady pain of the rucksack's straps digging into my shoulders before being drawn to the sharp pain of the blisters on the soles, then onto my knee, and then my hips, rubbed raw by my rucksack's thinly padded kidney pad before, finally, my quadriceps start cramping up in the most painful way imaginable and hijack my entire sensory system.

Everything hurts, all I want to do is stop and rest, but can I cease marching? Can I yell to my comrades, "Hey! Hold on, fellas! Wait for me, let me rest!"

No. The answer is no.

See, this is Mountain Phase of Ranger School. Everybody feels this way. We have places to be, missions to accomplish, Opfor to kill. No one is going to stop for me, just as I would not stop for them, even if they happen to be having the worst day of their lives.

So, one does what one must, and takes another step forward.

Suddenly, the PL raises his open palm into the air, meaning "Halt!" This is followed by a horizontal hand making patting motions, telling the platoon to take a knee and pull security in the short halt. The signals are quickly transmitted throughout the platoon.

Sweet merciful heavens! My cramping legs and battered feet could certainly use a short break. Unfortunately, since we are only taking a knee in the short halt, my eighty-pound rucksack stays on my back, where it has been for the last two hours, and continues to cause me agony. Unless I can find a convenient tree to lean up against, my rucksack straps are going to continue to eat through my shoulders, tug and contort my back, and break down my will to continue. Unfortunately, there are no suitable candidates nearby so I can do nothing but kneel and suffer.

Then Salvador, bless his soul, relays the command to take off our rucks and assume the "long halt" security posture.

Oh, joyous day! I gleefully strip off my rucksack and lie down on my belly on the cold, hard ground. Free of its crushing tyranny, only now can my body rest. The platoon leader must need a long conference with the four squad leaders and the platoon sergeant, but it does not concern me, I am just grateful to have my rucksack off my back, if only for a few minutes.

I deploy the SAW's built-in bipod legs and point the barrel away from the patrol and into the forest. It is time to commune with my friends the spiders and ants again, with the twigs and seeds, rocks and pieces of bark which occupy my little patch of dirt.

I am euphoric for the break from the march, for the moment, but nothing comes free in Ranger School. As the minutes creep by, the bare ground and chill autumn wind sucks away more of my body heat and the sweat covering every inch of my body begins to cool. Before ten minutes have passed, I am miserably cold. The pains of the march are temporarily exchanged for depressing cold, boredom, and the knowledge that the objective is not getting any closer while we lie still on the ground.

Fifteen, twenty minutes pass, and still, we are not moving.

"What the fuck, PL!" I hear Jenson groan ten meters to my left. "Let's get moving!"

The cold makes us miserable, and it also makes us sleepy, irredeemably, impossibly sleepy. Soon, the hardest battle of all is simply staying awake and not passing out into warm, peaceful sleep oblivion. But none of us can afford to do that. If the RIs catch us sleeping during the patrol, it is a near guarantee we will get a major-minus, especially if we lie about it. If any of us collect three or more major-minuses during the phase, for sleeping on the line or any other reason, we will recycle Mountain Phase at a minimum or even face a Day 1 restart, a terrible fate.

I already have at least one major-minus from that incident a few days ago, where I threw my rucksack out of the helicopters before they landed. That was a close call, easily the stupidest thing I have done in Ranger School, and but for the RI's mercy and good humor I should have been kicked out of here on a safety violation that day. I simply cannot risk getting any more major-minuses by doing something stupid like falling asleep on the line.

Must... stay awake, Goldsmith... cannot sleep... think about everything you are going to eat when this is all over, that's right, Goldsmith, peanut butter, cheesecake, sushi... steak... blooming onion..."

"Hey!" I awake with a start to the shouts of an RI. "Wake the FUCK UP, rangers!"

Oh, no! Has the RI caught me sleeping?

"I said wake the fuck up, rangers!"

No, he has not. The RI is yelling at Leon and Newton, who lie face down in the dirt about five meters from my position. He decides to give each of them a major-minus for falling asleep on the line. This is Leon's second one this phase. They do not look happy, especially pale, little Leon who suddenly looks like he wants to vomit.

"Gotta stay awake... the RI is so close... stay, fucking, up, Goldsmith!" I mutter to myself out loud. It is so hard, so unbelievably hard to stay awake in this cold, silent world.

If only we'd move again! I scream internally, fully cognizant that twenty minutes previously I was begging the gods for a break, willing to do anything and everything for a rucksack flop.

Again, my short-term prayers are answered. Salvador returns from the leaders' pow-wow, and orders us to ruck up again. As usual, my pinched nerve shoots electric jolts of pain through my upper back as I throw my rucksack on.

After slowly, silently, and painfully walking another klick, which takes an hour, the lead squad in the platoon runs into four members of the Opfor. They engage in a gun battle, while the rest of us hang back in reserve. We get a short respite, on our knees, rucksack straps digging into our shoulders, while the lead squad fixes, maneuvers on, and destroys the enemy using the standard react to contact battle drill. The RIs are satisfied enough with their performance, they do not drop anyone as a casualty.

Moments later, we stand up and start walking again. We make it a few hundred meters more when the day's RIs halt the platoon.

"Time for the assumption of command, rangers. Time for a new PL and platoon sergeant."

The four squad leaders will stay in their graded positions for twenty-four hours, but the day's first platoon leader and platoon sergeant switch out halfway through the day. The second pair of leaders take command of the platoon during our walk to the objective and will lead us until six a.m. tomorrow morning.

"Ranger Sven, you are the new platoon leader. Ranger Groves, you are the new platoon sergeant. You have ten minutes to get briefed on the mission, change out your equipment, and get this platoon marching again. Roger, PL?"

"Roger, sergeant," Sven, the new platoon leader, responds glumly, as he exchanges weapons and maps with the former platoon leader.

The rest of the platoon takes a knee and suffers under the weight of our rucksacks. Before ten minutes have elapsed, the assumption of command is wrapped up and we are up and moving again, marching forward towards the objective.

We walk for half an hour longer and my watch tells me it is almost two p.m. when something unexpected happens. One of the RIs halts the platoon and orders the platoon leadership to assemble at his position.

"Rangers, there's been a frago," he tells Sven, Salvador, and the other leaders. "A new, time-sensitive and critical mission has come down from battalion headquarters, so listen up!"

The RI describes how the Opfor, our illusive insurgent enemy, has managed to shoot down a helicopter with a man portable surface-to-air missile. Our platoon has been tasked with moving as quickly as possible to the crash site, conveniently located only one klick away, to secure it and retrieve the pilots and crew, dead or alive. It has been reported that Opfor are likely already at the crash site and that additional enemy reinforcements will be moving into the area.

"You need to get to the crash site to rescue any survivors as quickly as possible, meaning you need to get these rangers moving fast. Are you capable of doing that, PL?"

"Roger, Sergeant!" he yells, but even when Sven is motivated his voice is meek and mouse-like.

"Then get moving. Go! Go!"

There is little time for the squad leaders to brief the men. Salvador merely tells us, "There's been a frago. Opfor downed a helicopter about a klick away, we are going to get the pilots."

Sven checks his map and compass one last time, shifts the direction of our march, and orders First Squad to head out. Ten seconds later Sven pumps his fist up and down in the air, the signal to "double-time," or start running. First Squad takes off. My squad is next in line.

This is going to suck.

The platoon's formation slowly disintegrates as we alternatively jog, powerwalk, trip, tumble, and fall our way, armed to the teeth and carrying heavy packs, through a kilometer cross-country movement. The team leaders and squad leaders encourage the stragglers like Bailey and the machine gun teams and do their best to retain some semblance of order in the formation. Humping a SAW, I quickly find myself near the back of the pack, legs aching and lungs burning.

Even at three times our normal pace it takes us twenty minutes to get to the backside of a small hill immediately behind the crash site. Everyone is panting and heaving, taking deep, sucking breaths upon arrival. Sven orders us to drop our rucksacks and prepare our weapons and equipment for a raid as he assembles the platoon leaders for a quick leader's recon of the crash site.

First Squad kicks off a rifleman and a SAW gunner for the S&O or "surveillance and observation" team. They emplace themselves at the top of the hill to provide an overwatch of the entire crash site. From their high vantage point, the S&O team can see scattered helicopter wreckage strewn about in a small, wooded depression below. Half a dozen enemy Opfor wearing a ragtag mixture of uniforms mill about the area, several of them smoking cigarettes. Three of them guard a motionless body lying on the ground.

"We have a visual on one of the pilots, over," the S&O team radios to the PL using a squad Icom radio.

Meanwhile, the first of the platoon's three machine gun teams arrives at the top of the hill, dragging a tripod mounted 240B with them. A few minutes later, all three teams are assembled under the direction of the weapons squad leader, affectionately called "the Weasel," who gives a head nod to the platoon sergeant, letting him know that the big guns are up.

"Support by fire is set, PL, over," the platoon sergeant says into his radio hand mike.

The security squad leader comes over the net. "So is security, PL. Got both ends of the trail into and out of this place sealed off, over."

Sven, the platoon leader, takes a knee behind a sturdy tree trunk along with the two assault squads who have crept up with him up to the edge of the crash site. The downed pilot and the enemy Opfor are no more than fifty meters to their front, but they have managed to creep in silently and unseen. Sven looks to his left and sees the first assault squad, my squad, laying down in the prone in a line stretching out before him. He looks to his right and sees the second assault squad doing the same. He gets head nods from both the squad leaders, meaning, four SAW machine guns and fourteen rifles are ready to rock and roll.

"Weasel," Sven says into his hand mike, "the security and assault squads are set. Tell the gunners to do their best not to shoot near the pilot once this thing starts. Everyone, prepare to execute the raid on my signal."

Everyone and everything is silent for a moment. I am laying down in the dirt, my cheek resting on the top of my left hand, which is wielded to the buttstock of my SAW machine gun. My right pointer finger rests lightly on the trigger. When I breathe in, my cheek rises, just a little bit; when I breathe out, it ever so slightly goes down again. I am ready.

On the top of the hill, the Weasel and the platoon sergeant, closely watched by an RI, pray that the guns will fire without jamming. Each of the three gunners is propped up behind their machine guns, cheeks resting on their hands, fingers on the trigger. The assistant gunners lay next to their gunners, cradling ammo belts in their hands, ready to feed round after round into the big guns while the ammo bearer stands by, ever ready to deliver more.

The Opfor, unaware of our presence, keep puffing away on their cigarettes and look bored. They have no idea what is about to descend upon them.

Sven, the leader of this impromptu POW raid and rescue operation, raises his M4 rifle, peers down his iron sights, and fires off a single round at the closest enemy Opfor.

Thus begins the "mad minute." Three 240B machine guns open up on the hilltop, firing repeated volleys of six-to-nine round bursts into the valley below. They cover the entire objective in murderous plunging fires of 7.62-millimeter bullets, which has all the Opfor still breathing scrambling madly for cover. The SAW machine gunner and rifleman of the S&O team gleefully join in on the fun and shoot their own weapons into the enemy below.

On the assault line, two squads open up with four SAW machine guns, grenade launchers, and rifle fire. The enemy is pinned down by overwhelming firepower, a crossfire of bullets from two different directions. It is a life-or-death struggle, one the Opfor is destined to lose.

After thirty seconds of shooting the volume of fire slackens as one of the 240B machine guns and two of the SAWs, including my own, malfunction and go down. But every other gun keeps blazing away, for ten, twenty, thirty seconds, longer, eager to burn off as much ammo, and thus weight, as possible. None of the Opfor is shooting back any longer, none of them are even moving.

"Shift fire! Shift fire!" Sven finally shouts into his Icom radio, but no one can hear his soft little voice over the din. Everyone keeps firing. Finally, he stands up and starts bellowing at the top of his lungs. "SHIFT FIRE! SHIFT FIRE! SHIFT FIRE!"

Up on the hillside, over the deafening roar of the two remaining machine guns who "talk" or take turns firing six- to nine-round bursts, the Weasel hears and echoes the PL's command.

"Shift fire! Shift fire, damn it!" the Weasel says slapping the gunner's helmets. "Spray the far side of the objective! Don't shoot the pilot!"

The gunners shift their barrels over to the far side of the objective and keep firing.

"Get ready to move, guys," Sven shouts at the two assault squads. Along with everyone else, I rise onto one knee. "Support by fire," he then says into the Icom radio, "cease fire, repeat, cease fire. We are about to assault, over."

"Cease fire! Cease fire!" This time, the Weasel hears Sven over the radio. With the two assault squads about to enter the crash site, it is too dangerous to keep shooting the machine guns any longer. The two working machine guns fall silent.

"Squad leaders," Sven shrilly cries out, "bound your men by fire teams! Push through the objective! ASSAULT!"

Salvador and the other assault squad leader become the new stars of the show, playing their four fire teams like fine instruments. They bound the teams up to and through the objective, half of us firing, the other half advancing, until we push through the crash site and up to the still body of the pilot.

As we pass the dead and lifeless bodies of the Opfor, we quickly check them for life with simulated kicks to the groin. No response means they are dead; if they move, we pump a few more rounds into them. Suddenly, the closest enemy Opfor to the pilot springs to his feet and lets off two three-round bursts with his M4 carbine. He is quickly dispatched by the SAW gunner and the rifleman on the S&O position, firing from the hilltop above, and he falls back to the ground, lifeless.

That threat taken care of, my fire team walks up cautiously to the pilot, weapons at the ready, prepared for anything. This could be a trick, an Opfor just itching to take a few more of us out before we send him to the rebel afterlife. I see a life-sized white-hued manikin, a training dummy with a vaguely human face, dressed in a torn and burned BDU uniform. Our platoon has succeeded in recovering one of the pilots although, at this point, we do not know whether he is dead or alive.

Before we can assess the casualty, we must first secure the objective and make sure there are no more enemy threats waiting to kill us. Suddenly, rifle shots start ringing out again. One of the fire teams in First Squad gets engaged by a two-man Opfor team out in the woods to our front. They hit the dirt and return fire while the other team starts maneuvering into the tree line.

Sven walks up to the pilot and watches the small gunfight off in the distance distractedly, almost in a trance. So much is going on right now. Should he help First Squad, assess the pilot's wounds, something else?

"Well, PL," an RI with an impatient tone appears behind Sven. "What are you doing right now? I think you would be well-advised to check out the casualty. He is the entire fucking reason we came here. Is he alive, is he dead? Is he bleeding, suffering from a head wound, a broken back? What? He obviously needs some help. Do something!"

Sven looks a little shell-shocked. He stares at the lifeless body for several long seconds, before dropping to one knee and taking a simulated pulse on the dummy's neck.

"No, high-speed!" the RI exclaims as he slaps his forehead in frustration. "Have some of your men do it or better yet, get the platoon sergeant over here to do his job. You need to supervise and control this raid until this objective is clear and the mission, if it can be salvaged, is accomplished. Understand, ranger?"

"Roger, Sergeant," Sven says as he looks around frantically for the platoon sergeant before turning to Salvador, taking a knee close by.

"Salvador," Sven says with as much authority as he can muster, "task two of your men with taking care of this pilot. They need to assess and treat his wounds. The rest of us, we need to finish clearing the objective."

Sven dashes off to First Squad's position while Salvador turns to me and says, "Goldsmith, Newton, er..." he motions his free hand awkwardly towards the dummy, "help him out? Okay?"

We both nod yes, happy to pretend to provide medical care to a dummy for a few minutes while the rest of the squad runs around frantically mopping things up.

The rest of the assault squads dispatch the last of the enemy bands before moving through the crash wreckage, past the hastily erected shanty tents of the Opfor, and into the wood line at the far edge of the objective.

"LOA! LOA!" Limit of advance, the team leaders shout as the assault squads form up into a rough semicircular perimeter and face out. Everyone takes a knee, panting and sweating after the recent excitement, ready for an enemy counterattack.

"All right! That's it." The shouts of the RI signal a premature end to our raid. "Come on in, rangers! Bring it on in! It's admin time. Everyone, back to the ORP, let's see those sensitive items while we still have some daylight left."

Our platoon moves quickly back to the ORP, where we left our rucksacks, as the sun starts slipping low towards the horizon. The RIs conduct a rushed "five-poncho layout" to make sure we still have all our weapons and squad equipment before addressing the platoon.

"You rangers have a fun afternoon in front of you. A fun afternoon, maybe evening, too." The RI smiles wickedly at all of us before pulling Sven aside. "See good old Randy here, PL?"

The RI points to the lifeless dummy lying on the ground. Sven nods his head.

"Well, ranger, this brave pilot has been shot multiple times with both machine gun and rifle fire due to your platoon's indiscriminate and excessive fires into the objective. Far as I could tell, no fire control measures were utilized whatsoever other than to spray everything that moves, including friendly forces."

Sven gulps as the RI continues.

"If the raid was better executed, maybe good ol' Randy would be walking out with you guys right now, but no, you all are going to need to carry him out on a stretcher. This brave pilot needs medical attention, and he needs it fast."

"Then he is going to need a medevac, Sergeant," Sven chimes in.

"Good, ranger, so you do have a brain in that head of yours... meaning..."

"RTO! RTO!" Sven shouts. "Come over here!"

The day's radio operator runs over to Sven, hand mike grasped in his palm.

"Call in a nine-line medevac. This airman needs urgent medical attention... Let me see here, line one... location of the pickup site..."

"Pull out your map, ranger." The RI tells them, interrupting him. "Note this grid coordinate, 542130764, your LZ will be there."

"Looks like the LZ will be..." Sven quickly looks over his map, determines the location of the landing zone or "LZ" based on the RI's coordinates, and then scans the terrain features around him. "It looks like the LZ will be on the top of that large hill, over there, one-and-a-half maybe two klicks away. That's where the birds will pick him up."

"Correct, ranger. Those coordinates get you to the top of Hogback Mountain. Get Randy up there before sunset and he just may live. You understand the mission?"

Rangers who are close enough to hear the name "Hogback Mountain" cringe and hang their heads low. Charlie Platoon has summited Hogback Mountain, that bitch of a mountain, before. We climbed up its long, steep slopes on what had to have been the single toughest day of Mountains Techniques Week. Now, we are doing it again, except this time, we must haul a one-hundred-and-seventy-pound dummy along with us.

Sven remembers Hogback Mountain, too, but he has no choice but to nod his head vigorously and say in his usual, submissive way, "I understand the mission, Sergeant."

"Good. Then call in that nine-line medevac, PL, and get this platoon moving to the pickup site." The RI again smiles devilishly. "By my watch, it is now 3:01 p.m. You have two hours to make it there before Randy bleeds out. Let's go, rangers!"

First Squad, the security squad, straps Randy into a "Skedcoe" stretcher, basically a curled blanket made of plastic we drag on the ground. By some unspoken consensus, these poor nine souls have taken it upon themselves to be the primary transporters of our injured airman. Second Squad, my squad, takes lead of the patrol, followed by First Squad with Randy, Third Squad takes the rear, and the PL and his poor radioman dash up and down the formation.

First, Alpha Team of First Squad drags Randy, while Bravo Team humps Alpha Team's rucksacks, in addition to their own load. They struggle like this for one hundred or two hundred meters, then switch out due to exhaustion. Bravo Team may carry Randy another two hundred, maybe three hundred meters more, but then they too need a rest. The rest of the platoon stops and takes a knee when security squad stops and rests.

We are moving slow, too slow, and it is taking forever. Sven talks with the security squad leader during one of their breaks, to see if there is any way we can move faster.

"You want to drag him, PL?"

Sven says nothing and that decides the matter. Five minutes later we are on the move again.

Carrying a half-broken SAW and an eighty-pound rucksack is miserable, but the effort demanded from First Squad to drag Randy cross-country, threading their way through tree trunks, saplings, and bramble, must be soul crushing. I watch as they give it everything they have, one-half of them dragging Randy, the other half carrying the extra weapons and rucksacks. In a way, they seem mad. They refuse to let any of the rest of us help them. They laugh at their labor and truly embrace the suck.

Alpha Team of First Squad finally drags Randy one last, long three-hundred-meter stretch before they drop him, each man in the squad completely spent, at the bottom of Hogback Mountain.

"Where's the goddamn PL?" The RI quizzes the security squad leader, who watches nervously as his men lean over, pant for breath, and abandon all tactical sense.

"Right here, Sergeant." Sven says as he dashes up, his RTO trailing behind him. "I'm right here."

"What is taking so long?" The RI asks him point blank. "You rangers have already wasted an hour just getting here and we haven't even started going uphill yet." The RI points upwards towards the unseen summit of Hogback, somewhere far above us.

"You think the last kilometer was hard," The RI looks dismissively at the exhausted members of First Squad, "you rangers haven't even started."

Sven stands there, silent and doe eyed.

"That means get your men moving, PL! This isn't a GODDAMNED JOKE! You got a brave pilot, an American, a fellow warrior, bleeding to death, and his life is in your hands. If he doesn't get on the medevac bird in an hour, an hour-and-fifteen tops, you'll be the one telling his widow and children he died because a bunch of sorry rangers couldn't get their shit together."

"Roger, Sergeant." Sven sighs, increasingly resigned to receive a "no-go" for his run at platoon leader on what is turning out to be an exceptionally brutal day.

"Security squad leader," Sven sighs again, "pick up that casualty and let's get up Hogback."

It is almost 4:00 p.m., we have not eaten in almost twelve hours, I am severely dehydrated, and every inch of my body is sore, sprained, blistered, and tweaked. Others are in far more terrible shape.

Screw it, let's summit this goddamned mountain!

I take my place near the front of the platoon's formation, pulling security to the front of First Squad, so that they can continue to focus on hauling Randy up the mountain. I do not know how they are doing it because simply placing one foot in front of the other, on the increasingly steep and slick terrain, is difficult. My quadricep muscles ache with lactic acid buildup, my lungs burn and scream out for rest, but we have a mountain to climb, and we are just getting started.

First Squad can no longer just use brute force to pull Randy up the hill, they do not have enough strength left. So, they pull out the ropes in their rucksacks, wrap them around tree trunks, and start using leverage and ratcheting force to slowly drag Randy up the hill.

"Heave..." the security squad leader calls out, abandoning noise discipline.

"Ho!" Three members of security grunt as they fall backwards pulling the ends of the rope with their back and leg muscles. Randy moves a further ten feet up the hill.

"Heave..."

"Ho!" Randy's litter gets snagged on something and only moves another three feet higher.

"Heave..."

"Ho!" The litter gets caught on a root and Randy half falls out of the stretcher.

"Motherfucker!" Two members of First Squad curse in unison.

I am not making much better progress up this mountain than Randy. I stare down at my feet and start counting my steps.

One, two, three, four... five, six... seven, then I must lean over and rest.

One, two, three... four, then I must rest again. Four steps, four measly steps, and I am utterly spent. I want to cry, but it would accomplish nothing.

As the climb continues, I keep falling farther behind the rest of my teammates and find myself slipping from the front to the side of Randy's protective perimeter. Half an hour into the ascent, First Squad is fairly adept at moving Randy up the mountain. Some tie and untie knots, others run loose ropes up the hill to secure them to new tree trunks, others use their raw muscle power to haul up Randy, a few just sherpa extra rucksacks up the slope so that the others can work unhindered. It is brutal, taxing work. All of them slip and fall in the mud, suffer new cuts and bruises, and curse like demons.

But none of them quit.

As time passes, the platoon's orderly protective ring around First Squad and Randy disintegrates. Hardcore stragglers, those rangers happening to have the worst day of their life before we started Hogback, are drifting far, far behind everyone else. Other than First Squad, who works cooperatively, it is each man for himself amongst the rest of the platoon. We all have our weapons, our rucks, and ourselves to haul up this accursed hill. Please, please, please do not ask us to carry any more.

I take five steps, then really struggle to knock out ten, before I must lean over and rest on a small tree sapling. I bend over, one hand on my knee, sucking in air and tugging on my rucksack straps to temporarily relieve the intense stinging pain in my shoulders. Sweat drips into my eyes as my right leg starts cramping up, making me wonder if my legs will soon give out on me entirely.

Of all the days, why did I have to have to be a SAW gunner today?

But self-pity is not going to bring the summit any closer. I keep walking.

Some of the fittest and more lightly equipped rangers in the platoon, about a half-dozen studs, are far ahead of everyone, already halfway up the mountain. I cannot even see some of them anymore. The rest of us continue to suck wind as we haul our burdens up Hogback. I watch rangers in front of me wobble and stumble, lose their footing, and crash violently into tree trunks. I have seen more than one collapse headfirst into the dirt. A few rangers, Bailey among them, lose their rucksacks entirely, and watch helplessly as they roll long distances back down Hogback. Those poor souls must climb back down the mountain, re-cover the lost ground, and still somehow get to the summit.

There is no fucking way I am losing my rucksack. I tell myself as I pull the straps tighter. I would rather break my other ankle before I take one unnecessary step up this accursed rock! If my rucksack starts rolling down the mountain, I assure you that I will still be in it.

After an hour of brutally slow, painful marching, the bulk of the platoon, the security squad, and Randy, are still barely halfway up Hogback.

"It is now 5:00 p.m., rangers!" I can hear the RI shouting at Sven from somewhere high above us. He has been riding Sven since we started our climb, but Sven, to his credit, has taken it well.

"The medevac birds are already on station, waiting for your platoon's arrival! They have a maximum of thirty minutes on station before they have to refuel. Do you know what that means, ranger? Do you?!"

"Yes, Sergeant," says Sven meekly.

"I don't think you do, ranger! That means you have THIRTY FUCKING MINUTES to get Randy to the top of this mountain or I am promise you, I will drop four more rangers, right here, and then we are really going to have a fun night!"

Four more of us getting dropped if we do not get to the top of this bitch by 5:30 p.m.? That means there will be five "Randys" instead of one. That would literally kill all of us.

There is no way we are going to make the RI's time hack. It took us over an hour to climb the first half of Hogback, what makes him think we can do the second half in a fraction of the time? It is an impossible task.

Randy is going to die. I feel sorry for Sven. What a terrible day to be the patrol leader.

First Squad keeps pulling. The rest of us keep walking in silent misery. The RI keeps yelling at Sven. We climb.

Walking up Hogback Mountain is proving to be the most arduous task of my life. I do not even carry my SAW in my hands anymore, it just hangs limply on my chest, held up by my sling, while I utilize both hands to scramble for handholds and catch myself from falling. Meanwhile, I have already drunk all the water easily accessible in my canteens, and there is no way I am digging out more from the bottom of my rucksack.

Meanwhile, First Squad keeps heaving and ho'ing Randy up the hill. It has proven to be an effective method for man-handling his deadweight up a mountain, as evidenced by them being ahead of the stragglers below. Better yet, the ranks of the Randy haulers and rucksack sherpas have recently increased. Some of the fastest rangers have already reached the top, left their rucksacks and weapons at the top with a guard, and returned, selflessly, when they did not have to, to help the rest of us save Randy.

With First Squad's well-honed expertise and the relatively fresh muscles of the new rangers, Randy really starts moving up the mountain.

I continue to pull "security," if you can call it that, on First Squad's left flank. In reality, ninety-nine percent of my focus is on simply keeping one foot moving in front of the other.

Everyone is completely exhausted, a twisted, muddy, awful mess, by the time most of the platoon finally hauls Randy up to the flat topside of Hogback Mountain and sets him beside a fallen tree trunk. We've done it!

Hogback, that cruel bitch, has been conquered by Charlie Platoon, for the second time. We would cheer if we had the energy.

Instead, we establish a security perimeter and mark the helicopter landing zone with VS-17 panels on the ground. Sven and the RTO start radioing in the nine-line medevac to get the birds over to our position, but the RI stops them.

"Don't even bother, rangers. It's 6:16 p.m. The medical air assets left our station forty-five minutes ago and Randy has been dead for half-an-hour for lack of proper medical care."

"Roger, Sergeant." Sven takes the news stoically. Too physically and mentally exhausted to care that he will almost certainly get a "no-go" for the death of Randy, he is just happy he got the platoon up the mountain.

A dozen stragglers continue to filter in over the next twenty minutes. They look terrible, like they just survived something horrific. Some of them drop their rucksacks, flop to the ground, and take deep sucking breaths for several minutes before joining our ever-expanding security ring. Bailey and Fulton are among the last to arrive. Bailey is subtly twitching like a dying cockroach and anxiously muttering gibberish to himself.

"End ex! End ex!" An RI shouts out to all of us. "Bring it in, rangers. We're going admin."

The sky is completely dark now. We pull out our headlamps and do a layout in the chill darkness.

When the short administrative break wraps up the RI tells the entire platoon to gather close around.

"First off, rest in peace, Randy," the RI says as he grabs the handles of Randy's litter and drags him into the brush. "Mortuary affairs will pick him up in the morning."

We all heave a collective sigh of relief, grateful to see the last of poor Randy.

"Second, I want all of you to DRINK WATER! Right now, I mean it, all of you. You look fucking terrible out there, in fact, I don't think I have ever seen such a sorry group of chewed-up pansies in all my years walking this course. You're all fucking pathetic."

The Mountain RIs are some tough sons of bitches, and today's RI is no exception.

"What I should do," the RI continues, "is make you all walk through the woods all night just to instill some pride and respect in you; however, we have somewhere we have to be tonight, so instead, I'm going to give you all a choice…"

ANDREW GOLDSMITH | 177

Ranger School is seldom a democracy, but tonight, we all get a vote. The issue is whether we will walk three klicks cross-country or nine miles on a dirt road to arrive at the company assembly area, where the entire Ranger class will link up and bed down for the night. Knowing how difficult moving cross country at night can be, especially given our rough and sleep-exhausted condition, most of us vote to take the counter-intuitive, but likely easier, nine-mile route.

We redistribute gear and ammo, pull out extra canteens of water, and tighten up our boots and rucksacks straps for what will end up being several hours of furious walking under eighty-pound rucksacks.

The RIs decide this will be a non-tactical march, the better to drive us at a relentless pace on a mostly uphill route. They order those of us in front to keep moving faster while they cruelly taunt and ridicule the platoon's slowest members to keep up. No one is allowed to exchange weapons or packs with anyone else to help alleviate their load. They do not want us to play rangers tonight, they just want us to move quickly.

I hold my own during the march, close to the front of the platoon, with my SAW and a heavy pack full of 800 rounds of rusted, unfired ammunition. I am happy and motivated to be moving briskly on an open road for a change and because there is enough ambient light to see by, I do not need to use my NODs.

Three-and-a-half hours later, delirious, sleep-deprived, and ravenously hungry from nine miles of forced marching, climbing up Hogback with Randy, and the rigors, hazards, sleeplessness, and struggle of the prior five days of the FTX, Charlie Platoon arrives at the company assembly area at 10:30 p.m. This would be an early night for Mountain rangers but, unfortunately, the RIs are not going to let us take advantage of it. We spend the next two-and-half hours improving our fighting positions, digging gun-pits, drawing sector sketches and tying in the ends of our perimeter with the adjoining platoons. Only at 1:00 a.m. are we finally given sanction to eat and sleep while maintaining fifty-percent security, one man up while the other man sleeps.

Leon is my foxhole buddy tonight. We decide on forty-five-minute guard shifts, and I have the first one. I eat my MRE entrée cold and sit up with my legs in my sleeping bag to stay warm. The minutes creep by as I repeatedly fall asleep sitting up and then wake up with a jolt seconds later. Finally, at 1:45 a.m., I nudge and then jostle Leon awake for his guard shift, making him sit up and get out his sleeping bag so that he does not fall back asleep instantly.

I am quite sure Leon will fall asleep through his guard shift and, in a way, I hope he does. I am too tired to care about the consequences, I just need sleep now or I am going to go insane. My eyelids close and instantly I am deeply, soundly asleep.

0402 Hours (04:02 a.m.)
Camp Merrill Training Area
North Georgia Mountains
Day 7 of the Mountains FTX
Hours of Sleep in the Last 48 Hours: 3½ Hours

My eyelids snap open as Leon shakes me vigorously awake. Incredibly, he did not fall asleep on guard last night and even woke me up in time for my second guard shift at 2:30 a.m. It is 4:02 a.m. I only got two forty-five-minute chunks of sleep last night, and like every Mountain morning, I feel terrible.

After our foot check, MRE breakfast, the 6:00 a.m. change of command, and three hours of idly pulling security while the day's leadership plans the mission, McCormick, our squad leader for the day, walks over to my position on the line.

"Goldsmith, how are you doing today, buddy?"

"Pretty good, all things considered, other than the fact that I hear the Crusty Mountain RI is one of our RIs today." I say. "What's going on?"

"I hate to ask this of you, but I need a favor. I need you to be one of my team leaders today. Bravo Team Leader. Can you do it?"

No, damn it! I want to exclaim. Team leader! Can there be a worse position in Mountains?

Being a team leader is worse than carrying a machine gun, worse than being a SAW Gunner, almost worse than being in a graded position. It entails thankless hard work, responsibility, and a myriad number of duties, all at the risk of alienating one's comrades and getting low Peers rankings at the end of the phase. Unlike Darby Phase, a team leader is not a graded position in Mountains, but otherwise, the responsibilities are the same. A team leader is responsible for directly leading the tired, surly, injured, brain-dead regular soldiers that form the bulk of the platoon. They must whip the men into shape and get them to actually accomplish their mission tasks. An effective team leader is proactive, constantly doing something both day and night, and the success, or failure, of the squad leaders, platoon sergeant, and PL ultimately rests on his shoulders.

It is a thankless, demanding task that carries a lot of risk, which is why most soldiers try to dodge the role whenever possible. But I owe McCormick for a dozen small favors. The old man has been kind to me throughout the course, and surely, I think, he would do the same for me if the roles were reversed. Hell, I should be flattered that he thinks I am good enough to do the job, it means he respects and trusts me.

So, although I really do not want to be a team leader, not today, not any day in Ranger School, I put on a brave face and cheerfully exclaim:

"Happy to help out, McCormick. Let's get you a 'go' today!"

"Great! Thanks, Goldsmith. I owe you a big one. We need to work hard to keep the men in line today. Everyone's sucking."

Ain't that the truth?

"First things first," McCormick continues, "we need to send two guys down to the stream to do water resupply. Everyone is low on water, and I don't want anyone going down with heat stroke today. Can you send Leon and Bailey?"

"I don't know, man, I don't think we should send Bailey. He's talking to himself again and nothing seems to be getting through. In fact, he kind of scares me."

"Well, do you want to do it, Goldsmith?"

Up here in Mountains, we get our drinking water from the cool water streams that crisscross our area of operations. To make it safe to drink, we add iodine tablets to our canteens. It makes the water taste a little off, but it is better than getting sick.

Water resupply is an important job. Knowing full well how sloppy everyone is, I really should supervise or even perform this mission critical task myself. That would be the right thing to do. On the other hand, if you want me to collect and carry everyone's empty canteens, dozens of them, and take them one hundred-meters across the woods to the nearest cold-mountain creek, stoop my aching back over the muddy streambank, plunge my hands into ice-cold water, and methodically fill everyone's canteens, if that is what you want me to do, then my answer is...

"No, no thank you. I'll tell Leon and Bailey to do it."

"Good man, Goldsmith." McCormick smiles. "Well, the op order starts in a few minutes, and I have to help the PL finish planning. Troop the line, keep the men busy and awake."

"Roger that, squad leader."

I grab an empty duffel bag and gather up the squad's canteens, about two dozen one-liter and two-liter OD green plastic water bottles. I walk over to Leon and Bailey's fighting position where they are both sleeping. I have to rigorously shake them awake. Bailey is particularly unnerving because he keeps falling back asleep with his eyes open.

"Hey, Bailey! Bailey!" I snap my fingers in front of his face to get his attention. "How are you feeling today, buddy?"

"Mish... hoosh..."

"I'm your team leader for today, OK, pal?" I speak to him like a small child. "You need to listen to me, all right?"

"Misha misha fram all night. All night, reshian!"

Bailey, the outcast bat boy, is doing terrible most days, but today, he is in another world. The sleep deprivation, solitude, lack of food, and the unending abuse to his body has destroyed his higher cognition. He mutters to himself incessantly while staring at the ground or past and through anyone speaking to him. This deep into the Mountains FTX he can execute basic tactical maneuvers on autopilot, but little else, and even then, he requires a lot of shouts, shoves, and tugs from his squad mates.

"Anyway," I turn away from Bailey to address Leon, the more capable of the duo, "it's your guys' turn to go do water resupply, so I am going to need you to..."

Feisty little Leon gives me his trademark death stare.

"... and uh, we kind of need it done right now."

Leon mumbles something that sounds vaguely like "Fuck you."

"What was that?" I ask him.

"Yeah, yeah, Team Leader," Leon assures me. "We'll get it done."

"Misha, fram, fram. Misha fram." Bailey mutters as he stares off into space.

"The squad appreciates it guys, here you go." I thrust the duffel bag with the squad's empty canteens into Leon's hands. "I gotta keep trooping the line. Get one of the other guys in the squad to cover this position while you're gone. I'll be back in a few minutes to help you distribute canteens. Okay?"

"Roger that!" Leon responds with obvious false motivation. Bailey mumbles something. Satisfied that the task will be completed, I walk away.

Now that bossy Goldsmith is gone, Bailey decides he can safely lie down again and fall asleep on his rifle's buttstock. Unfortunately for him, Leon's tiny but sturdy frame pulls him to his feet, shoves the duffel bag into his hands, points him in the general direction of the nearest creek, and gives him a light shove.

"Go fill the squad's canteens, Bailey!" Leon yells at him like a dog. "Hurry up! Get it done!"

"Mishur, mishur... no, no... wi-yo..."

"Goddamn it, Bailey!" Leon shouts. "I said 'Go!'"

Bailey stumbles off into the woods like the village drunkard, dragging the duffel bag with our empty canteens on the ground behind him. He moves forward in a daze, tripping over tree roots and slipping on rocks slick with morning dew.

Within a few minutes, the soles of his boots sink into soft mud. He lifts his head and sees a small stream to his front.

Bailey shakes the canteens out of the duffel bag and dumps them into the mud. Two canteens immediately fall into the creek and slowly drift away in the current. Bailey does not notice. He unscrews the cap of another canteen and plunges it into the freezing water. He fills it up less than halfway before half-screwing on the cap and throwing it back into the empty duffel bag.

The second canteen gets filled up three-quarters of the way before Bailey slips on the muddy streambank plunging his right knee and hands into the chill stream water.

"Fuck!" Bailey cries out as he stands up out of the water. It is the first intelligible word he has spoken all day. "Mishur, fracker...Misha!" Momentarily fully awakened, he angrily screws down the second canteen's cap and throws it into the bag.

Bailey's already numb hands are now stinging painfully from the shock of the chill water. His right leg from the thigh down is soaking wet with fifty-degree creek water. He manages to half fill up a third, fourth, and fifth canteen, his head increasingly drooping with tiredness with each canteen until....

Ker-plunk!

Bailey falls face first into twelve inches of water. The canteen he was filling leaves his hand and drifts down the stream. He leaps out of the water and flops down on the muddy streambank, shocked by the cold, panting, and breathing hard.

Soaking wet, alone, and demoralized, Bailey decides he has had enough of filling everyone else's canteens. If they want water, they can do it themselves. He quickly gathers up the remaining empty canteens scattered on the ground, tosses them into the duffel bag, and slowly starts ambling back to the patrol base.

"Jesus Christ!" Newton exclaims when he first sees Bailey stumble back minutes later, his legs streaked with mud and his uniform completely soaked with stream water.

"You fall in Bailey?" Salvador asks before laughing heartily.

"Risha mash," Bailey mumbles in response, any wakefulness he gained from his cold-water plunge already dissipated. He limps over to my position on the perimeter and dumps the canteen duffel bag at my feet. The bag is streaked with mud and half-soaked through with water.

"Okay," I am not sure what to make of this development. "Thanks, Bailey. Where's Leon?"

"Misha... masha..."

I am not going to get any kind of sensible answer from Bailey, and Leon is probably sleeping back at his position, the bastard.

"Go ahead and get your rucksack ready to go," I tell Bailey. "We are moving out in a few minutes."

"All night," he says to no one in particular before wandering away again.

I pick up the suspiciously light duffel bag and start trooping the line to hand back everyone's canteens. It is quickly apparent that Bailey has only filled a few of them, most of them only half full, and several canteens are missing entirely.

Goddamnit! I am tempted to scream at Bailey, but I know it would not help anything. Besides, this is my own damn fault. I should have supervised the water resupply, a mundane but critical task. Right now, in our states, I cannot rely on my squad mates to fulfill even the most basic tasks, even ones clearly in their self-interest like drinking water or treating their injuries. I should not have left this water resupply to be fulfilled by a sleepy ranger and the dumbest, most droned-out guy in the squad.

I failed as a leader. I go to break the terrible news to McCormick just as the PL finishes delivering the op order.

"We're fucked, McCormick." I tell him straight up. "The water resupply was botched, and we have almost no water. Averaged out, each man in the squad has less than a canteen-and-a-half. Who knows when we will get another chance to resupply. We've gotta send another team out. I'll take Newton with me and…"

McCormick takes the bad news with a blank face, blinks twice, and deliberates calmly before arriving at a decision. "No time, Goldsmith. The platoon is moving out in five mikes. We're just going to have to suck it up and make it work. Evenly distribute the water so that everyone has the same amount and keep a close eye on everyone during the march. If we come to any streams, and the RIs aren't watching, we'll resupply on the march."

"Roger," I tell McCormick, knowing that this is not good. My legs start cramping just thinking about the day's impending water shortage. Fucking Bailey! I want to scream again. But there's no time to properly curse my hapless squad mate. The platoon leader orders us to throw our rucksacks on our backs and to get ready to start walking.

My squad is Assault Two squad today, so we walk in the back of the platoon formation. After the first squad moves a mere one hundred meters into the woods, and before my squad even leaves the assembly area, the platoon is rapidly called to a halt by the shouts of the infamous Crusty Mountain RI.

"Halt! Halt, rangers! What in the FLYING FUCK do you think you are doing? Everyone, bring it in! I said BRING IT IN!"

Fifty meters in front of us, the Crusty Mountain RI starts screaming at Green, the day's first platoon leader. The veins on the RI's neck and forehead are bulging out of his skin and he is holding something behind his back. I walk up in time to hear poor Green's response.

"I… uh? What's wrong, Sergeant?" Green is genuinely stumped. The mission has barely started, he has not had any time to make any mistakes yet.

"You tell me, PL?" The RI stares daggers at Green, expecting a response.

Green just shrugs his shoulders.

"For one, it's because you fucking amateurs are walking in file instead of wedge formation," the RI says sternly, "which ends now, you understand? But mostly, it's because of this…"

The Crusty Mountain RI raises a two-hundred-round linked belt of rusty, dirt-covered SAW machine gun blanks above his head and shakes it furiously.

Oh no! I gasp, along with all the other men in the platoon watching the spectacle.

"Oh, that's right, shitbags! One of you high-speed motherfuckers thought you could bury some extra ammo at the assembly area. You know, just lighten your load at the expense of combat effectiveness. But what you didn't realize is that if I was able to find this prize in less than thirty seconds of examining the sloppy overnight position you all left behind, then your hungry, supply-constrained enemy who lives and dies in these woods is certainly going to find it, use these rounds on you, and kill your fellow rangers!"

Green hangs his head low. This is not his fault, some unknown ranger certainly acted alone, but as the leader, he must take the brunt of the RI's fury.

"So, congratulations, PL, you just killed your fucking buddies."

We are screwed. I wonder which asshole did this to us.

The RI can read our minds. In a calm, steady voice, he says, "Now, which one of you dumbasses want to take responsibility for this?"

There is nothing but the sound of crickets from Charlie Platoon.

"Huh? Any takers? No? That's what I thought... THEN DUMP YOUR RUCKSACKS NOW, MOTHERFUCKERS! Let's see what else you've lost or buried since you've been out here. That's right, NOW! Yeah, PL, I'm talking to you, too! Dump it!"

We have not walked for five minutes, and we are already doing a layout on the march? Suddenly, I break out into a cold sweat and feel a lump in my stomach. What if the RI realizes that my squad has barely any water?

"One wet weather top, rangers, hold them up!"

Just knowing I must ration my water makes my throat parched. I need to conserve what I have, and, as a leader, I may even have to share some of my water with my teammates if they really need it.

"Seven t-shirts, count them, seven. I don't care how nasty they are, pull them out!"

Fortunately, after laying us out for ten minutes, the Crusty Mountain RI grows bored.

"You're lucky we're pressed for time today. You have two minutes to pack up, tie everything down, and be ready to move again! PL, if I find any more buried ammo from this platoon, today or any other day, you are all getting 'no-go's,' you understand me?"

Green, shaken, nods his assent while Jenson, the ranger who in fact did bury the ammo, heaves a huge sigh of relief.

I didn't get caught this time, the weasel thinks.

"Back to tactical, rangers. Move out!"

What is on the operational menu for today? "Movement to Contact," otherwise known as walking through enemy territory to bait them into attacking you, so that you can maneuver on and destroy them. Movement to contact is relatively simple, a routine task for a ranger platoon, especially when we are dispatching raggedy teams of no more than two or three Opfor at a time.

The only problem is, before we can clear an area, we first must get there, the hard way, with foot power. Today, we have four NAIs, or Named Areas of Interest, to clear during daylight hours.

Today, the seventh day of the Mountain FTX, is a rough one to be a leader. This deep into the FTX, everyone is haggard, braindead, sorely in need of motivation, nutrition, and above all, sleep. I have a tough crew of Joes to lead, cajole, and occasionally threaten with physical violence: rock-solid, but surly Newton, Bailey the zombie, and sleepy, feisty little Leon. All of them require different leadership styles, all of them present unique challenges.

Just like every other day in Mountains, we walk for a long time through the woods, taking a knee every fifteen or twenty minutes while the platoon leader checks his map or prepares to cross a trail. All of us sweat and strain under our heavy packs, rise up again, walk for a while, halt for a while again, walk through NAI #1, get shot at by the Opfor, conduct a react to contact battle drill, walk for a while, take a knee, walk for a while, take a knee again, walk for a while longer, walk through NAI #2, get shot at by the Opfor, conduct a react to contact battle drill, walk for a while again...

The whole time, the Crusty Mountain RI rides Green, the day's first platoon leader, giving him no slack.

"You better get this platoon moving, PL!"

"Roger, Sergeant."

"The platoon's formation looks like dog shit!"

"Roger, Sergeant."

"You've hit the first two NAIs late. At this rate, it is highly unlikely we will make it to the patrol base before dawn."

"Roger, Sergeant." What else can he say?

As we approach NAI #3 the RI halts us.

"Halt this platoon," he tells Green. "I've seen enough. You are hereby relieved of duty as the platoon leader. Time for another ranger to assume command."

"Let's see, here... " everyone's favorite RI rummages around in his shirt pocket for his notepad. "Fulton, Ranger Fulton, step right up. You are the new platoon leader and, Brown, Ranger Brown, you are the new platoon sergeant."

Floppy-necked Fulton, the formerly unflappable green beret, sighs deeply before rising from a knee and trotting over to the RI and the outgoing PL. He and Green exchange weapons, maps, and night vision devices; all the while, Fulton's head is slumped pathetically forward on his chest, as usual.

"What the fuck is wrong with your neck, son?" the RI teases Fulton.

"Muscles gave out, Sergeant," Fulton says flatly, "Rucksack palsy. You know how it is."

"I guess I thought a 'snake eater' like you would hold up a little better out here."

"Me too, Sergeant." Fulton responds sadly, "Me too."

We keep walking. We have been drinking water sparingly, to our detriment, but by now, each man in my squad has less than a quart of water. We are all thirsty, many of us have cramps and other symptoms of dehydration. Somehow, we have not passed any suitable streams to refill our canteens and the only thing on every ranger's mind is: how far is it to the next NAI?

Newton especially asks me this question relentlessly.

"I don't know, Newton," I reply after his twentieth query. "McCormick didn't have time to properly brief me."

"Yeah, yeah," he says dejectedly. Even a stud like Newton is sucking today.

A few hours into the march, everyone in the squad is thirsty, in varying stages of dehydration, and most of us are completely out of water. But we keep walking, what else can we do? We cannot complain to the RIs about the situation, it might lead to McCormick failing his patrol or even being recycled or expelled from Ranger School on a safety violation. The repercussions would probably extend to me and Dale, the team leaders, as well.

It is unspoken among us because by now everyone knows the deal. What happens in the squad, stays in the squad, and no one snitches on anybody about anything to the RIs.

Nobody.

So, the squad sucks it up and drives on. We march all day on twisted ankles, through heat cramps, our backs screaming, two of us, including Fulton the PL, without working necks, but we manage to clear both NAI #3 and NAI #4 by our six-p.m. deadline, just as the sun starts going down.

The RI tells us to go admin and directs us to walk towards a small open area. It is there my squad sees a very welcome sight. It is a "water buffalo," a 400-gallon steel tank filled with drinkable water, resting off to the side of a main trail.

It's a Ranger School miracle.

"Fill up your canteens, rangers. All of them!" the RI barks at us. "None of you fuckers are going down on my watch!"

He certainly does not have to tell anyone in my squad twice. We cheer silently with parched mouths and stiff quadricep muscles as we pull out our one- and two-liter canteens. McCormick slaps me on the back joyously and Newton personally helps Bailey fill all his canteens.

The RI conducts a five-poncho layout in the fast-fading light of dusk.

"Sit down on your rucksacks and listen up, rangers," he tells the platoon as the layout finishes. "There has been a frago, a change of mission. Instead of going straight to the patrol base, you will now execute an ambush at, you better be writing this down, PL..." The RI glares at Fulton, whose chin is buried in his chest. "...at grid coordinates 76345889..."

An ambush?! Tonight? After doing movement to contacts ceaselessly, all day? It figures, it would be too easy for us to simply walk in pitch blackness for another three to five hours before calling it a night around midnight at the patrol base. No, let's set up a night ambush first.

"PL," the Crusty Mountain RI turns to Fulton, "have your men mount their night vision devices and have the team leaders double check to make sure everything is tied down really good. You are all droning and look like shit out there. I don't want anyone losing anything tonight."

"Wilco, Sergeant."

"Get it done! And lord almighty," the RI points at half my squad, still busy filling canteens at the water buffalo, "how fucking long does it take to do a water resupply? It's like all your canteens were empty."

The RI breaks his chain of thought to glance approvingly up at the increasingly cloud-covered, wind-swept, dark night sky.

"I'd start moving quickly if I were you, PL." He tells Fulton. "The ambush site is a ways off still, and the weatherman is predicting rain tonight..."

2101 Hours (9:01 p.m.)
Camp Merrill Training Area
North Georgia Mountains
Night 7 of Mountains FTX
Hours of Sleep in the Last 65 Hours: 3½ Hours

We have been walking in moon-lit darkness for two hours, seeing the nighttime world through our NODs. I see nothing but green, dark green, light green, hazy green, smoky green, staticky green—just green, green, and more green. Whether on the march or sitting still, I see a blurry, green nightmare world of shadows that plays tricks on my eyes and gives me a headache. I am so sick of the color green, I so desperately want to see other colors. More than that, I want to close my eyes and sleep, I want to rip the suffocating, fogged-up lenses of the NODs off my face, toss them far into the woods, and free myself from their torment.

It has stiff competition, but walking long distances at night with NODs, under a heavy pack, following and, even worse, leading droned-out Mountain rangers, is easily the worst part of Ranger School.

Just like my infantry unit back home, most of us wear the clunky, binocular "PVS 7-Bravos," while a select few leaders in each squad have

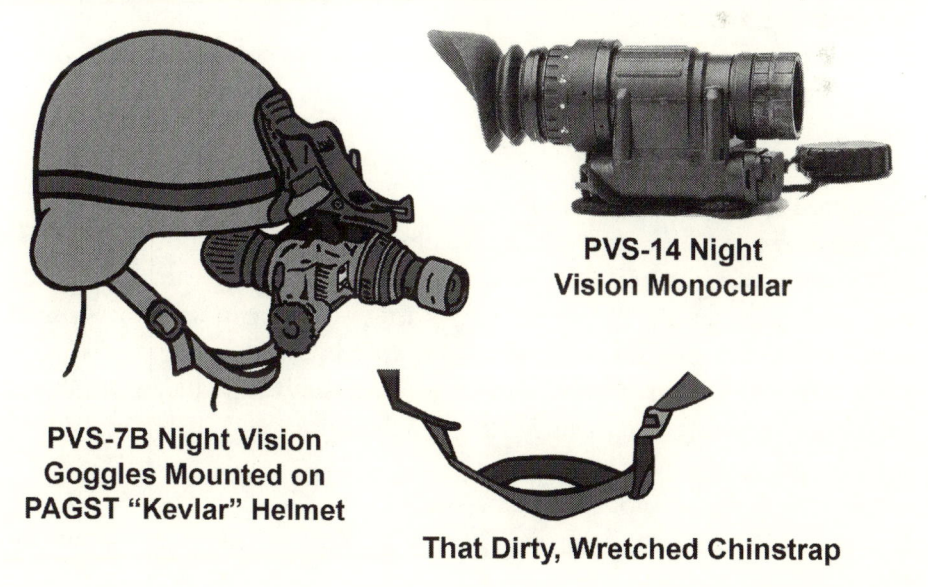

PVS-14 Night Vision Monocular

PVS-7B Night Vision Goggles Mounted on PAGST "Kevlar" Helmet

That Dirty, Wretched Chinstrap

ANDREW GOLDSMITH | 189

"PVS Fourteens," which are lighter and monocular, leaving one eye free for normal vision.

Like most nights, I am stuck wearing the larger seven-bravos. This is unfortunate because even for an experienced infantryman like myself, who has spent hundreds if not thousands of hours walking, driving, and shooting at night with NODs, I still find the experience difficult, unpleasant, and even dangerous. At night, I stumble and fall more than in the daytime, aggravating old injuries and creating new ones. This is especially true when walking through thick woods, on steep terrain, with unseen vines and roots entangling and tripping you at any moment.

The NODs are perched several inches in front of our faces and supported by "rhino" mounts attached to the front of our loose-fitting, 1990s-era Kevlar paratrooper helmets. The one-and-a-half pound, unbalanced weight of the PVS 7-Bravos causes increased strain to our neck muscles the longer we wear them. As evidenced by Fulton and Salvador, this weight can cripple the necks of formerly strong men.

NODs are awkwardly weighted to the front, but they also cause our loose-fitting helmets to sway from side-to-side with each step on the march. The top of my head is sore, hair pulled, and flesh rubbed raw from the webbing on the underside of the helmet sliding endlessly back and forth across my scalp all night. The NODs and rhino mount also get tangled up in vines and tree branches causing our heads to snap to the side as our bodies keep moving forward.

The only thing securing the unwieldy amalgamation of night vision, rhino mount, and helmet to our heads is a single dirt and sweat stained, OD green chinstrap, a grimy little thing which rubs itself ceaselessly side-to-side and back-and-forth along my raw, torn-up, weather-beaten chin.

Rub. Rub. Rub. Rub. Rub. Rub.

Forget what I said before about walking at night with NODs being the worst part of Mountains. If you want to pinpoint and laser-target the absolute worst thing about Ranger School, it is this. The relentless, unstoppable, inevitable, and dreadful rub of the dirty, sweaty, nasty, black, grimy, rough-sewn, blood and tear-soaked chinstrap on my poor, tortured chin. If I could banish any of the myriad pains of Ranger School from my life forever, surely, it would be this.

Rub. Rub. Rub. Rub. Rub. Rub.

To any normal man, this would be a minor annoyance, but I am no normal man, I am an abused and impoverished Mountain ranger, and here in the darkness of the forest night, the non-stop rubbing is like Chinese water torture, slowly driving me insane.

Rub. Rub. Rub. Rub. Rub. Rub.

Constant rubbing, first on my chin, and then on my scalp. Then I trip and fall but catch myself on a tree sapling. I have to stop and rub the condensation from the lenses of my fogged-up NODs for the twentieth time and then dash forward to catch up with everyone. By the time I get there, the platoon leader has halted everyone to get a headcount to make sure we have not lost anyone since the last headcount two hundred meters ago. And all the while...

Rub. Rub. Rub. Rub. Rub. Rub.

Nothing but constant rubbing, unceasing pain, feelings of revulsion, and ever-increasing irrational rage.

What the fuck are we doing?!? I scream inside my head. Let's move faster, goddamnit!

Our slow nighttime pace also drives me crazy. We always move at a crawl at night, slower than any non-ranger would ever imagine. What really slows us down are the frequent stops for two, five, even ten minutes at a time.

Fulton halts the platoon, again, and tells us all to take a knee. Sitting still, I get relief from the constant rubbing, but our rucksacks are still on, and the longer we sit here the more my back feels like it is on fire. Fulton, the back of his Kevlar helmet tied to his rucksack frame to hold up his limp, floppy head, staggers past my position to consult with McCormick.

How far the mighty have fallen. With his floppy neck, Fulton makes for a pitiful, even contemptible sight, especially under the green glow of NODs. Motherfucker still owes me a wheat snack bread, too, I invariably catch myself muttering.

Eventually, we get up and start walking again, with no explanation forthcoming of why the stop was needed.

As the hour nears ten p.m., half of the platoon cannot even be bothered to take a knee in the short halt any longer. Dreading the inevitable and painful rising up again and resenting the frequent stops, they opt to stand and awkwardly sway like punch-drunk boxers. They are completely and utterly spent, without the strength to rise again if they kneel down in the dirt.

Newton and Leon are in this camp, and no amount of pleading from me, McCormick, or even Fulton, the platoon leader, is sufficient to get them to bend the knee.

Occasionally, I hear a lot team leaders whispering, "Take a knee," to their troops in the darkness. "Fuck you!" is the most common response.

We rise and start moving again, for five minutes or so, until the next short halt is called.

Rub. Rub. Rub. Rub. Rub. Rub.

The only thing that could make this night worse is rain.

It starts drizzling on us at 10:30 p.m. at the same time we establish the objective rally point for our ambush. Of course, the RIs do not allow us to put on any rain gear. Twenty minutes later, as we head out to the ambush line, it starts coming down in large, fat droplets.

"Misha masha misha!" Bailey yells at the sky.

For once, we all understand what he is saying.

Fulton, the PL, moves with my squad and the other assault squad towards the last covered and concealed position overlooking the "kill zone," a curved section of trail one hundred meters to our front. Meanwhile, the security squad emplaces two teams at the far ends of the trail while the Weasel and the platoon sergeant emplace the machine guns on a small rock outcropping off to our right.

The assault force lies down behind a small rise in the ground with a good, unobstructed view of the kill zone, where we will concentrate our fires and annihilate the unsuspecting enemy. Everyone radios that they are in position within ten minutes and just before 11:00 p.m. the ambush is officially set. By now, even in our diminished states, setting up a platoon ambush in total darkness is a mundane affair. Everyone settles in to await the arrival of the enemy as the rain keeps falling.

The waiting is the hard part. We sit and we shiver, and we wait, trying desperately, so desperately hard, to stay awake. It is an impossible task. We are all so tired from walking sixteen hours a day, getting no more than two hours of sleep a night, always carrying an eighty-pound rucksack, or worse. The human body has its limits, and we passed them a long time ago. Our uniforms are soaking wet from the steadily increasing rain and provide no warmth from the near-freezing nighttime temperatures. We almost wish the thermometer would drop a few degrees so dry snow would come down instead of wet rain.

I am still a team leader with responsibilities, so every ten or fifteen minutes I crawl on my hands and knees up and down the ambush line to wake my squad mates and check-in with my squad leader, McCormick, who I also must nudge awake on occasion.

I return to my own spot on the line only to fight a losing battle with my eyelids. I stare endlessly at the exact same spot though my green-tinged NODs. I start seeing ghoulish faces in the wind and rain-swept trees such as I have not seen since the worst nights in Darby. The tree spirits have twisty, swirling, evil-looking faces.

I have never been so tired in my life. Never. Stay up, stay up, stay up! I scream at myself internally before slipping, slipping, slipping into unconsciousness...

Suddenly, I wake with a start, caused by my forehead plummeting towards the muddy ground. Somehow, only two or three minutes have passed since I last checked my watch, and then the cycle repeats.

Stay up, stay up, stay up!

Helplessly, I slip into and out of sleep, getting a minute here, thirty seconds there, before deciding it is time to troop the line again. This time I do not even bother waking up Bailey, or Leon for that matter, I know they will just fall back asleep the second I leave. Newton seems half-awake, which tonight is good enough for me.

I crawl back through the mud to my spot on the line. My watch says it is 11:21, then 11:27, then 11:32. Every passing minute feels like ten minutes, the time spent here on the ambush line feeling like an eternity. In my waking moments, I see little green men moving into and out of the trees, which increasingly is starting to resemble an urban metropolis. Sometimes they point rifles at me, other times they carry spears and swords.

Is that the Opfor? I cannot help but think. Why are they not shooting at us? Maybe I am dreaming all of this, though I certainly feel awake. When I pinch myself and really force myself to focus hard on their outlines, they vanish into the storm, so they must not be real, yet I cannot know for sure.

At times like this, I fear that I am losing my grip on reality and degenerating into a mental wreck like Bailey. I cannot trust my senses anymore. The last thing I want to do is prematurely initiate and ruin our ambush by shooting at non-existent wood spirits. I decide that I will leave it up to others, like Fulton or McCormick, to decide what is real tonight and what isn't.

And that is why, two minutes shy of midnight, when my eyelids dart open and I see three enemy Opfor slowly ambling down the trail, just to the right of my sector of fire, I do not shoot my weapon. I am only sixty percent sure they are real people, and not a hallucination. That leaves a lot of doubt, too much doubt for me to blow an ambush on my own.

Surely, if they are real, I think, other rangers will see them, too, and initiate the ambush.

So, I watch and see how the situation develops.

But nothing happens. Either the rest of the platoon is making the same calculations I am, or they are all dead asleep, because the three apparitions keep walking across the kill zone until they exit on the far side, free to continue on their merry way. I watch the men or spirits, whatever they are, disappear into the woods again.

"RAAANNNGEEEERS!" The unmistakable, throaty roar of the Crusty Mountain RI shatters the evening silence. "WHAT THE FUCK WAS THAT?!?"

Everyone in Charlie Platoon is jolted wide awake.

"WHY DIDN'T YOU INITIATE THE AMBUSH?" Through my NODs, I can see the RI shaking with rage, spittle flying from his mouth, as he storms over to Fulton's position. The RI looms over Fulton, his boots inches from his head. Fulton lies in the dirt and looks upwards as best he can, lifting his forehead with his left hand. He is not a little afraid that the RI may stomp him in a fit of rage and says nothing.

"Huh, PL? Tell me, why didn't you initiate the ambush? What were you doing, PL?"

The way the RI says "PL" makes Fulton cringe and involuntarily release a sob.

"I uh, I uh..."

"TELL ME!" the RI screams at him irately. "Were you sleeping? Were you scared? Can you just not lift that scrawny neck of yours anymore? What the FUCK happened, ranger? My Opfor ambled right past two security positions, the support by fire, the entire motherfucking ambush line... I'm just speechless, ranger. For once in my life, I am speechless."

Fulton lies there quietly, eyes downcast, awaiting his doom.

The Crusty Mountain RI pauses, takes a breath, and resumes his harangue in a calmer voice. "Just tell me one thing, PL, was your entire platoon sleeping on the ambush line, or just you? Because if the whole goddamned platoon was sleeping, I'll recycle every one of them."

"I... I was sleeping, Sergeant," Fulton says without hesitation, "This is on me, and nobody else."

What a terrible, terrible night to be the platoon leader. I suddenly feel great sorrow and pity for Fulton the green beret. He was riding high here, in Ranger School, until his neck gave out, that is. In this moment, I almost forgive him for stealing my wheat snack bread in Darby.

Almost.

"Yeah, I knew you were sleeping, ranger." the RI says distastefully as he looks up to address the entire platoon. "You know what though, rangers," he spits on the ground after saying this last 'ranger,' "you all still owe me an ambush. We're going to run this thing again, and this time, YOU'RE ALL GOING TO STAY AWAKE! You got that, PL, your whole goddamn platoon is going to stay awake! If I catch another ranger sleeping on the ambush line, he is going to be an automatic recycle, I promise you that."

"Roger, Sergeant," Fulton responds lamely and with hollow-sounding words. "We'll get this done."

The Crusty Mountain RI shakes his head distastefully, speaks something unintelligible into his radio and then yells at us "Back to tactical, rangers!" before retreating into the woods behind us.

We are back on the ambush line. My watch says it is now four minutes past midnight, technically a new day in Ranger School, although the current one is far from over. It should be easy to stay awake now. After all, we just received an ass-chewing, been given a rare second chance, and now we know exactly what to expect: three straggly, poorly armed Opfor strolling along the trail, right through our designated kill zone. We do not know exactly when they will be coming back, but odds are, it will be within ten or fifteen minutes, half an hour at most.

I can stay awake for a measly ten or fifteen minutes, even in the rain, even on a miserable night like this...

But it is impossible. After three or four minutes, I awake with a jolt only to find that I was dozing again. Fortunately, I do not see any RIs anywhere. I look up and down the ambush line, everyone I can see has his face in the dirt, resting on his forearms, or pressed peacefully into the buttstock of a machine gun.

I look out into the kill zone and, lo and behold, there it is again, strange figures in the trees. Except this time, I see three goblins escorting some kind of wagon, something big creeping slowly behind them without lights on.

Entranced by the figures, I keep watching them. Suddenly they turn to face the ambush line and start waving at us, waving at me even.

Should I shoot? Are they real? Why doesn't anyone else see this? Are they all sleeping again? I am so tired and delirious from lack of sleep I cannot trust my own senses. I do not want to blow our second shot at the ambush. I will have to defer to my leadership, again, McCormick, Fulton, anyone else but me.

I am just a team leader. I am not getting graded. It is not my place to make that call. Besides, none of this may be real.

The green shadow creatures have stopped waving. They shrug their shoulders and keep sauntering down the trail. Their wagon, which increasingly is starting to resemble a Ford F-150 pickup truck, rolls right into the center of the kill zone.

That is of course, unless I am hallucinating all of this.

"JESUS FUCKING CHRIST, RANGERS!" The Crusty Mountain RI leaps from the bushes behind the ambush line and snatches Fulton's M4 from his grasp.

Pop, pop, pop! The RI shoots three blank rounds into the kill zone before throwing it distastefully back at its owner.

There is one second of silence, two at most, before our training kicks in, and the forty-five rangers of Charlie Platoon wake from their stupors to execute an ambush.

"BRAAK-BRAAK-BRAAK…" the muzzle flashes of the heavy machine guns illuminate the support by fire position off to my right as they sweep the objective with automatic gun fire. They focus the bulk of their fires on the vehicle, which is still slowly moving forward. They are joined by the two dozen rifles, grenade launchers, and light machine guns of the assault squads arrayed on a line parallel to the trail. Together, we devastate the kill zone with a glorious "mad minute" of crossfire.

Now that we are engaged with the Opfor, now that I can smell cordite, and hear the machine guns "talking" to each other, adrenaline courses through my veins and I am wide awake. So is everyone else in my team, even Bailey. Fulton is also back in the game. I watch him elegantly take a knee and direct the fires of the ambush line.

Maybe, just maybe, he and McCormick can still get their "go's" out of this debacle.

By now, the three Opfor pedestrians have dropped lifelessly to the ground. The pickup truck slows to a complete stop, veering slightly off the trail near the far end of the kill zone, its driver presumably "dead."

"Cease fire!" Fulton yells out "Cease fire!" The assault squads stop firing, echo the command, and the machine guns too fall silent.

Fulton tells the two assault squads to get ready to move. We push up off the earth and rise onto one knee, barrels up, weapons ready to fire.

"ASSAULT!" Fulton yells out loud enough for the entire platoon to hear. The two assault squads start bounding their fire teams up to and across the trail. We move past the Opfor dead, simulating striking them in the groin to confirm their lifeless state and kick their weapons away from them. A fire team from Second Squad clears and searches the pickup truck while the rest of us form a security perimeter on the far side of the trail.

Once our actions on the objective are concluded, Fulton withdraws the platoon from the ambush site. The Crusty Mountain RI halts the exercise and gathers us together for an administrative sensitive items check. As we sit on our rucksacks and pull out our weapons and gear with red-lens headlamps, the rain starts coming down harder and the wind picks up.

We have been here long enough to know that this is not going to be just another damp, miserable Mountain night. A real storm is brewing, and we are going to get wet.

The RI harangues us in the rain. For once, he sounds more disappointed than angry.

"Rangers, I... I don't even know where to start. Falling asleep, letting the enemy walk undetected through your kill zone, not once, but twice... I have never seen such a thing, ever."

He takes a moment to simply glare at us in the darkness.

"And that is why," the anger in his voice rises, "I'm going to march you fucking idiots all night! You thought you were tired before... Ha! You know nothing about exhaustion, not yet anyway. Put those rucksacks on your back and let's get this platoon moving, PL! Back to tactical!"

I see a green burst of light through my NODs, the first flash of distant lightning, and the sound of thunder a few seconds later. The rain is pouring down in sheets now, the worst rain we have seen so far in Ranger School. Now we must slip and slide our way through ever deeper mud as we walk towards tonight's ever-distant patrol base.

There is nothing worse than rain, not to a ranger student. The rain amplifies every other misery in this school, the ones already driving us towards the brink of physical and mental destruction. Rain makes us wet, cold, and more liable to get hurt. The water makes our rucksacks heavier, our footing less secure, and the way forward far more difficult and hazardous. In the rain, rangers shut down, especially regular Joes. They can become insubordinate and fail to take basic care of themselves, even when it is in their own best interests.

Rain has the power to darken the mood of even the most stoic ranger. Rain has caused deaths in previous classes. It makes us want to cry; it makes us want to quit.

We walk for another hour and the rain does not stop. Lightning continues to flash through the sky and the pauses before the thunder are grower shorter.

The Crusty Mountain RI suddenly halts the platoon and tells us we are going "admin."

"Gather round and listen up! There is a lightning warning for our area, rangers." The RI yells at us through the downpour. "We are going to change our route a bit and head… that way." The RI calls Fulton over and shows him a clearing on the map about six hundred meters away from our present position.

"You are all going to get into a line and start running, as fast as you can move, until we get there. You got that, PL?"

Running? These guys? In this weather? Fulton thinks, his head sunk low into his chest, but what can he say other than, "Roger, Sergeant."

So, we start running.

Glop! Glop! Glop! Glop! Glop! Glop!

The weight of our bodies combined with our heavy rucksacks drive our boot prints deeply and firmly into the mud. Our NOD-mounted helmets slip-and-slide and move every which way on top of our heads. The outer lenses of the NODs are obscured by rain drops while the inner ones are fogged up with condensation. I run into trees and slip and fall on my face on several occasions. In the process, I re-sprain my twisted ankle but have no choice but to rise, curse the storm, and keep running.

Fifteen minutes later we emerge into a small, slightly sloped clearing, with several small saplings but otherwise devoid of trees. The RI tells us to halt and to form up into ranks by squad.

"Take off your rucks and sit on them, rangers. For safety reasons," the RI says this last part distastefully, "we're going to have to temporarily pause training until this lightning storm passes our immediate area."

This is bad news and it elicits groans from Charlie Platoon. The longer we sit here the longer it will take to get to the patrol base, and the less sleep we are going to get.

Then, as a cruel joke, the Crusty Mountain RI smiles and says, "Go ahead and take out your rain gear, rangers. Your Gore-Tex jackets and pants. Go ahead, put them on."

For the first time in the course, we have permission to actually use our rain gear. Now, when it is pointless. We have already been soaking wet for hours. The damage already done, few of us even bother to move. "It's not an option! GET YOUR GODDAMNED RAIN GEAR ON NOW, RANGERS!"

We don our rain gear, sit on our rucksacks, and wait out the storm. Backs hunched over and shrunk small, we look like muddy, grumpy little turtles. Everyone is in ill humor, each man focusing intently on his own suffering, never a good idea. The leaders have ceased caring for anyone but themselves and have long since resigned themselves to getting 'no-go's' on today's patrol.

"What's the point in fighting destiny?" McCormick says stoically, as he consoles Fulton, his head sunk pitifully into his chest as always, "Sometimes you're dealt a bad hand and there is nothing you can do."

Meanwhile, Bailey keeps mumbling nonsense incessantly and loudly enough for half the platoon to hear.

"Shut the fuck up, Bailey." Newton yells at him, shaking his shoulders. "Quit your mumbling and suffer in silence like the rest of us." But Bailey does not stop.

We sit and wait out the lightning storm for over an hour. We shiver underneath our ponchos, fall asleep sitting up, and feel sorry for ourselves. Finally, close to 2:00 a.m., after the rainfall and wind slackens for a few moments, the RI orders us all to rise to our feet before addressing us.

"The worst of the lightning is past our position, rangers," he says calmly, rainwater dripping from his soft cap. "Therefore, we are going back to tactical."

Meaning we can resume walking in this downpour for another hour or two until we reach the patrol base which, since it is already 2:00 a.m., means we will get no sleep tonight.

"But seeing how you all have wasted so much time today," the shrewd RI must sense an imminent mutiny, "we're going to establish the patrol base right here, where you all are standing, just in case that lightning storm passes by us again."

Some good news finally. We are home for the night.

"You got that PL?" The Crusty Mountain RI says to Fulton. "Let's get his patrol base established, the right way. No finger-drilling either, got it? You rangers are back to tactical, time now!"

And the Crusty Mountain RI walks off again, into the darkness, never to be seen for the rest of the night.

Fulton, the platoon sergeant, and the squad leaders are back in charge of the platoon. According to protocol, we still have to set up the patrol base, establish the security plan, and clean our weapons before we can eat our long-awaited dinner MRE and catch a few minutes of sleep. In short, there is a lot of work to do before we can rest.

But not tonight, not this deep into the Mountain FTX. Not when most of us already have a fairly good idea of whether or not we have a "go." Not after sleeping less than four hours in the last seventy-two, after being starved and brutalized for weeks, and now this accursed downpour. No, it is times like these when rangers shut down, when rangers stop listening to anything but their own selfish wants.

Indeed, at 2:04 a.m. something snaps in all of us. Everyone has had enough of the games, enough of being told what to do, enough of fearing the RIs and the consequences of failing a patrol, enough of Mother Nature hurling herself against us and doing nothing to stop it.

Fuck it, I'm done, the Mountain rangers say, in so many words, and all protocol goes out the window. Rangers team up into small survival groups of two or three and quickly begin constructing rain shelters out of their ponchos in a vain attempt to get dry and comfortable. Others simply plop down in the mud and tear hungrily into their MRE dinner ration, having not eaten anything in the last twenty-one hours. Those rangers who still possess dry clothing throw on as many layers of snivel gear as possible before crawling into damp sleeping bags and going to sleep.

No one establishes fighting positions, emplaces claymores, draws sector sketches, or any of the other dozen-odd tasks that go into establishing a patrol base. Most importantly, no one is cleaning our muddy, rusted, and likely inoperable weapons. No one plans on pulling guard tonight and the security perimeter is non-existent. If the Opfor attack us tonight in any force, we will get overrun and wiped out.

This is not a ranger patrol any longer, this is a gypsy camp, a boy scout jamboree from hell with forty-five droning, hungry, sleepy, useless rangers.

Fulton is one of the few trying to salvage something from the debacle. He ineffectively attempts to rally the platoon sergeant and the squad leaders before pleading with individual men to establish a proper patrol base. It is no use, even the leaders who are getting graded have given up.

"You can't expect us to work in this, can you?" McCormick's response is at least congenial. Other leaders tell Fulton to "fuck off," or that they "got their go," the worst thing a ranger can say to another ranger. Some simply turn their backs on him.

"But we're still getting graded," Fulton responds sensibly. "If we just give up, we're going to fail our patrol."

"Might as well just cut our losses, brother." McCormick pats Fulton on the back of his broken neck. "What are we going to do, bring order to this?"

McCormick lifts Fulton's chin with one hand while he pans around the patrol base with the other. They see a muddy swamp with scattered poncho tarp-style hootch shelters strewn about in random order. Rangers mill about in the rain as if they were on holiday, sleeping, eating, pissing in the wood line. There is no order, it is a scene of absolute chaos.

It looks more like a vagrant camp than a secure overnight base of operations. If the Crusty Mountain RI were seeing this, he would have a heart attack.

"The men are exhausted tonight, and they need rest," McCormick continues. "Who knows what tomorrow will bring. We'll get another chance to get our 'go's'… hopefully." He drifts off to work on his own shelter.

But Fulton is not the only ranger in Charlie Platoon that is still in the fight.

I am dumbfounded by the chaos unfolding in front of me. I have never seen the platoon disintegrate like this, and become worse than children, animals. For the moment I feel completely lucid and wide awake. Oddly detached, I can see the big picture.

And it infuriates me.

This is not how rangers are supposed to act!

Anger and raw fury seethe and surge up from somewhere deep inside of me. I have never been so angry, not when I was bullied in high school, taunted by my drill sergeants in Basic Training, or blown up by the enemy in Iraq. As I coldly watch Fulton try and fail to persuade even a single ranger to do the right thing, even Dale, I feel nothing but contempt for him. Each failure makes him more dejected until he too, looks on the verge of defeat.

His men are building shelters, eating, or already fast asleep in their sleeping bags. It is every man for himself. Fulton eventually gives up and simply plops down in the mud in the middle of our camp.

"They're all just giving up," Fulton mutters to himself as heavy rainfall pours down on him. "Giving up, just like that..."

Not all of us, Fulton, I think to myself as I watch him, not all of us. Everyone else may have thrown in the towel, may have scrambled to secure a dry piece of land and a quick meal before snatching some sleep, but I am still here, and I'm not going anywhere.

I am a fucking ranger.

Driven insane by furious anger I trade my carbine for Leon's SAW and a 200-round drum of ammunition. I extend the bipod legs, throw it on the cold, mud and rain-soaked ground, and plop down behind it. Half my body is lying in an inch-deep puddle of water but I make no effort to avoid it.

I peer intently down the sights of the machine gun, pulling security on behalf of all my fellow rangers, hoping and praying that some Opfor or even the goddamned Crusty Mountain RI himself will walk up upon us. Anger warms my body; wrath fuels my brain; I feel deliriously energized with demonic energy. Sleep be damned, only the weak need sleep!

It should almost be a rule: when you are utterly exhausted, starved, injured, and have nothing left... you can always run off hate.

Fulton sits in his own rain puddle and snivels somewhere behind me. I find him contemptible. He's weak and has given up like everyone else, I think to myself. Pathetic.

Damn this rain and damn this sorry lot of men. These are supposed to be green berets, Airborne Rangers, and the toughest future infantry officers, what the hell are they doing? All I see are a bunch of self-interested savages. I have never seen anything like this, not while training with my mechanized infantry unit and certainly not in Iraq. Has Mountains truly brought us this low?

Screw everyone here, shame on me for volunteering for this stupid school, fuck the Tab, nothing but a stupid piece of fabric anyways, and damn every Hollywood war movie that convinced me to join the Army in the first place. While we're at it, damn warmth and comfort, food and sleep, rest, weekends, I don't need any of it. I am going to keep doing the right thing, I am going to lie in this puddle and pull security all night. I am going to shoot anyone who dares attack us.

Because I'll sleep when I'm dead.

Fulton rises sullenly from his rain puddle and begins walking around his non-existent perimeter. That is when he almost steps on me. He lightly chuckles when he sees me lying belly down behind a machine gun, unsheltered, in a muddy pool of water.

"Goldsmith! Hey!" he says to me. "I almost didn't see you there. What are you doing in the mud?"

"Pulling security!" I say abruptly through clenched teeth, "Doing my job, PL."

"Well, I appreciate it, buddy, but everyone else is already under shelter. You might as well do the same. You can't help me now."

The nerve of this guy. I am tempted to stand up and shout in his face, "Where's my wheat snack bread, motherfucker," but I respond differently.

"This isn't about you, PL. This is about doing what's right. This is about not being weak; this is about having standards and always pulling security and, and..." anger flares up inside me and gives me another temporary burst of energy.

"Goldsmith," Fulton coolly interrupts my tirade, "you know you're pointing your machine gun directly into our own headquarters position, right?"

"Well," I stare up from my puddle with a murderous glint in my eyes, "you better tell them to fuckin' move then." I drop my eyes to my gunsights again.

"Okay then..." Fulton sees that there is no point in reasoning with me. Everyone else has succumbed to weakness; I have succumbed to blinding rage.

"I guess," Fulton says softly, "you just try to stay dry, all right, Goldsmith? You know, I am starting to think that everyone else is right. It is time to call it a night." He is suddenly at peace with writing this terrible day off and starting anew tomorrow.

But not me, not yet. "You do that, PL!" I say coldly, and Fulton, his head sunk into his chest, walks away to build a poncho shelter.

I stay in the mud, peering into my sights, fuming with anger. One thing I know for sure, the rain has infected the other rangers with pure, unadulterated weakness. I alone remain, resolute and strong, and I will stay here all night if I must. No one can fault me for being soft, for shirking my load, for spitefully telling some poor soul "I got my go," for allowing that son-of-a-bitch rain god to defeat me. He can go to hell just like everyone else. Let them scamper for shelter, eat in comfort, and rest easily. I will lie in a puddle in the middle of a lightning storm, in near-freezing temperatures. My rage will burn all through the night. I will sleep when I am dead. I am a ranger!

Twenty minutes into my vigil, McCormick trips over me after coming back from taking a piss in the wood line.

"Goldsmith!" he leaps back, surprised, "What are you doing?"

"What needs to be done," I say curtly.

"Oh, yeah? Looks like you are doing an excellent job of it." McCormick smiles and laughs. "Why don't you come inside me and Dale's shelter, it's all set up already, and eat yourself a warm MRE. How does that sound?"

"Got to keep watch, do the right thing... weakness... all alone, always..." It sounds great, but pride and anger compel me to ramble off a dozen different reasons for why I cannot join McCormick.

"Come on, Goldsmith... Get up! Get up, you big oaf." One of the kindest pairs of hands I have ever felt help me to my feet.

Deliriously, I mumble my assent. I allow McCormick to guide me into the veritable hootch mansion he and Dale have constructed out of several rain ponchos. I do not know how they did it, but their hootch is spacious, sturdy, warm, and does a fantastic job keeping the rain out.

"Thank you for letting me in," I tell Dale.

"Don't mention it Goldsmith," he says like a gracious host, "get dry, get warm, take off your boots, eat your MRE, get some sleep, okay. Make yourself at home, okay."

I change into the driest set of clothing I own and, for the first time in days, I am truly warm, inside, and out. All three of us slowly, gracefully eat our dinner MREs, relishing every bite, not dropping a single crumb. Warmed up and with some calories in our bellies, I regain my faculties and exchange pleasantries with my two new officer friends. We laugh and tell stories as I hang my wet clothes on the sides of the hootch to dry. I even take my time unpacking my damp sleeping bags and laying them out carefully on the ground.

The pitter-patter of the rain drops grows steadily fainter until the rain is merely a drizzle. Inside this gentle shelter I am warm and safe. The rain cannot touch me, I am with people who care for me, there is no hunger, discomfort, or approaching dawn.

Content, I lay my head down to sleep, for what I hope is forever...

"WAKE THE FUCK UP, RANGERS!"

0401 Hours (04:01 a.m.)
Camp Merrill Training Area
North Georgia Mountains
Day 8 of the Mountain FTX
Hours of Sleep in the Last 72 Hours: 3½ Hours

"It's four o'clock, rangers. Time to rise and shine."

No, no. It cannot be possible.

"I said, get up, rangers! You all move like nuns fuck!"

No. No. No. No. No. No. NOOOOOOOOOOOO!

How can this be? My eyes were closed for mere seconds before the Crusty Mountain RI's shouts shattered my peace.

McCormick and Dale also look momentarily bewildered in their sleeping bags, but then McCormick shrugs his shoulders and states the obvious.

"Guess we're getting no sleep tonight."

This cannot be. I am still in denial. Can it really be 4:00 a.m. in the morning?

I look at my watch and indeed the RI speaks the truth. It is 4:01 a.m. now. I got literally no sleep last night.

I barely have the strength to whimper, which is good, because Ranger School has no sympathy. Tears and despair will not get me through this day, or the next, they will not help me survive, so I have no time for them. I put on a brave smile and get moving.

Thank the heavens, the rainfall has slackened, but it is still coming down in a light drizzle. Damp clothing and the pre-dawn, chill, Georgia mountain autumn air causes me to shiver uncontrollably as I slide out of my sleeping bag. I put on one boot and then slip the second one carefully over a sprained ankle. I tie up the laces with the side of my thumb and my ring finger, the least cracked and bloody of all my fingertips. Fulton, in charge again, orders us to push out the perimeter into something resembling a patrol base.

I help McCormick and Dale break down their hootch mansion before taking up my new spot on the line with Bailey. When the medics show up at 5:00 a.m. to do their foot checks we get to eat our MRE breakfast. I thoroughly enjoy my vacuum-sealed breakfast omelet MRE. The meal is disliked, even hated by many rangers, but I actually like it because you can throw all the extras in the meal into the entrée to make one giant, soft, and easy to eat slop. I also like it because I am hungry enough to eat a dead pigeon right now.

Salvador is describing some truly hilarious and obscene bat boy sexual escapade involving himself, Newton, and the wife of a Colonel when the roar of the Crusty Mountain RI shatters the moment's serenity.

"Yesterday's team leaders, from every squad," he growls, "gather on me! C'mon, LET'S GO!"

Any smile I may have been wearing disappears immediately. Like the other seven team leaders from yesterday, my eyes go wide and my heart pounds in my chest.

What devilry is this? What could he possibly want with all the team leaders?

Eight unfortunates rise and glumly walk over to the RI's position in the center of the patrol base.

"Take a knee and gather close, rangers." We take a knee and hesitantly slide closer to the RI.

"Yesterday was a fucking debacle. You and your men moved like pond water all day and the leadership completely lost all control of the platoon on several occasions. Every single graded leader, every single one: both PLs, the platoon sergeants, and all four squad leaders, they're all getting 'no-go's.' And do you rangers know why?"

We stay silent, but we can all guess the answer. A few of us nod our heads up and down like abused animals who know their place in a cruel, unjust world.

"They are all getting 'no-go's,'" the RI continues, "because you team leaders fucked them. You couldn't control the men, you couldn't keep them awake on the ambush line, you finger-drilled your rehearsals, you sleep-walked through establishing security, you were sloppy, and you half-assed every goddamned thing! In short, your inability to step up and lead your teams directly caused their failure…"

Thank heavens team leader is not a graded position in Mountains, we all think.

"… and that's why I'm all giving all of you…" he weighs our sins in the balance, "two major-minuses."

Two major-minuses! Holy shit! Two major-minuses added to my prior major-minus for that unfortunate helicopter rucksack incident last week means I will be facing a disciplinary review board at the end of the FTX. Anyone seeing the board has a good chance of recycling, even if they pass patrols and Peers.

Accordingly, I am screwed. Did I endure all this mountain suffering for nothing? Will I have to do this wretched Mountain Phase over again all because I agreed to be McCormick's team leader yesterday?

"Give me your roster numbers, rangers," the RI whips out a small notebook, "and then get the fuck out of my sight. You all disgust me."

I give the Crusty Mountain RI my roster number and amble slowly back to my fighting position. Strangely, I am not as dejected as I should be. For one, there is a good chance the RI is bluffing, playing mind games with us to increase the stress and hope we crack when he has no intention of actually giving us the major-minuses. Further, I know there was very little I could have done to improve the men's performance yesterday. We are all such a mess right now, so broken down, tired and hungry, that it is amazing our bodies and minds function at all.

And if I do have three major-minuses right now, whether unjustly or rightfully earned, then so be it. That day of reckoning, if it ever comes, will be at the conclusion of this field exercise, back in civilization, back at Camp Merrill. It will not affect my destiny today, and surviving today is all that matters.

I rejoin Bailey on the perimeter. I am consoled by the fact that the RI changeover is completed, and I will not have to hear the Crusty Mountain RI's bark for at least another twenty-four hours.

The day's new leadership has been appointed and, again, I am fortunate not to be among them. The squads have rotated and today my squad is "support by fire," meaning we hump the three big machine guns, the M240Bs, in three-man teams. Of course, since I was absent during weapon selection, I get stuck carrying the big gun. It is waiting for me, propped up on my rucksack, 49.7 inches long and weighing 27.6 pounds, mud-encrusted and rusty from last night's rain, and draped with a one-hundred round starter ammunition belt.

"Damn it," is all I can manage to mutter. No sleep last night, two undeserved major-minuses, and I have to be the M240B gunner? This day is starting out great, and it's barely 5:30 a.m.

I feel chewed up and spit out, but then again, I always feel this way up here.

So really, it is just another day in Mountains.

2230 Hours (10:30 p.m.)
Camp Merrill Training Area
North Georgia Mountains
Night 8 of the Mountain FTX
Hours of Sleep in the Last 90 Hours: 3½ Hours

> ***Droning, verb*** *– definition: After a prolonged period of sleep deprivation, the condition of no longer being able to cognitively function while still having to shoot, move, and communicate as a ranger. See also: sleepwalking, zombie.*

Droning. When a ranger is next-level tired, so mentally, physically, and spiritually beat down by existence, so numbed to the same, monotonous sensory inputs, that his higher thinking faculties cease and he turns into a living, breathing zombie. Droning rangers can go through the motions. They can walk, they can talk, they can carry a rucksack, they might even be able to execute an assault, but they will do it all half-asleep and about as stupidly as you can possibly imagine. Droning tends to come out at night, under NODs, when one has been walking so long, so relentlessly, ploddingly slow, that one just keeps walking, even while sleeping and vividly dreaming.

Droning rangers exhibit odd behavior. They lose the ability to think and take care of themselves. They turn into gibbering, mumbling wrecks like Bailey and walk off in random directions into the woods. They see goblins in the trees, fall asleep under bushes, and cause the whole platoon to halt and search for them when they become lost rangers.

Nothing can rouse a droning ranger, not for long anyways. The only cure is sleep, and that is something in desperately short supply around here.

This is another night where I count my lucky stars that I am not a leader. Today started out well enough, despite not sleeping the night before. It was a typical day of planning and marching. We cleared the day's last objective hours ago, before sunset, and have been marching to the patrol base ever since.

> **Sleep Deprivation**
>
> Arguably the greatest stressor in Ranger School, and a major one in combat, sleep deprivation dumbs you down by impairing your attention, reasoning, alertness, concentration, and problem-solving abilities. Sleep deprivation can cause accidents, make you more emotional, especially irritable, increase your appetite, feel like intoxication, and even cause impotence. Moreover, as this ranger can tell you, after days and days with almost no sleep, a person can suffer hallucinations, auditory distortions, and paranoia. Interestingly, sleep deprivation triggers "microsleeps," which last for less than a second to half-a-minute, where a person falls asleep regardless of what they are doing, whether that is marching in the middle of the night or talking to an angry RI. As cult leaders know, if you make people go long enough without sleep, you can turn them into mindless, droning zombies who cannot think for themselves and who must be led and cajoled like small children.

But as darkness falls, and the days and weeks of sleep deprivation, injury, and want make themselves felt again, whatever force is keeping our ranger platoon functioning simply evaporates.

We start droning.

It is hard work humping a rucksack and carrying the big machine gun. I am awake and semi-conscious in bits and pieces, when someone yells at me, grabs my collar, or when I run into the ranger in front of me. Repeatedly, I catch myself sliding inexorably into slumberland, slip, slip, slipping until … I wake with a start when my chin drops hard to my chest or I trip over some object on the march.

I shake my head side-to-side, causing the chin strap to rub painfully against my chin, in a futile attempt to stay awake. The jolts of pain and anger wake me just enough to walk forward another ten or twenty meters before sleep overwhelms me again.

More than ever before, the forest itself tries to drag us down and consume us. Tree branches, vines, entangling bushes, stumps, roots, holes, and deadfall grasp, scrape, and wind themselves amongst us, slowing our progress, injuring us, and even snatching our weapons out of our hands. Some droning rangers do not even notice that their weapons are gone. Earlier tonight, Leon caught Bailey with his hands empty, his M4 carbine dragging by its tie-down strings in the dirt behind him. Leon spots him doing it yet again, picks up the carbine, and thrusts it into his hands.

"Hold your goddamn weapon in your hands, Bailey! You hear me."

"Misha-musha. Whoosh," Bailey murmurs softly.

"Wake-up, motherfucker!" You hear me?" Leon grabs Bailey's collars and tries to shake him awake.

"Mumph-mumph…" Bailey adds. "Muh-shooosh."

"Wake up, Bailey!" Slap, slap! Leon literally tries to slap some sense into Bailey. "Wake up!"

Yet, incredibly, Bailey sleeps through it all. Leon pushes him away, satisfied that he is at least carrying his weapon again, for the moment, before Leon too starts droning.

The rest of us are not doing much better. We limp forward like blind, stumbling drunks, dragging ourselves forward by inertia, and little else. We don't know and we don't care who is guiding us.

Just after 11:00 p.m., after sleep marching for hours, we arrive at the base of a steep hill. The platoon is ordered to a halt. Hopeful whispers that we are finally near the site of tonight's patrol base travel up and down the line.

But then, remarkably, the members of Charlie Platoon fall back into a stupor. There is no difference between leaders and men, no one issues any orders or does anything. Everyone, everyone is just mindlessly droning. Forty-five of us just stand there and sway, eighty-pound rucksacks on little stick legs, swinging back and forth in the wind, falling in and out of sleep, standing up like cattle.

For ten minutes we just stand there and sway, until finally, one of the RIs loses it.

"What the fuck are you doing, rangers!" He shrieks at us. "Get the patrol base reconned and established, NOW! Where is the PL... ? PL! P-motherfucking-L! Get your ass up here."

No one in the platoon responds. Few of us can even be bothered to lift our heads to glance to our right or left, let alone figure out where the boss is. We just keep swaying on our feet. Most of us say, "I'm not the PL," in our heads, add "glad I'm not that guy," and then fall asleep on our feet again.

The sad fact is, tonight's platoon leader, White, an officer from some other squad, is droning just as badly as any other ranger in Charlie Platoon. Nothing short of firing a machine gun next to his head will wake him from his stupor.

One of his squad mates, finally realizing what is going on, rushes over to him and bodily shakes him, "Wake up! Wake up, man! The RI is asking for you White, and boy, is he angry. Go! Go!"

White's buddy has to practically push him to the RIs position before he retreats back into the darkness to stand and sway with everyone else again.

"Are you the PL?" the RI asks White.

White does not understand the question and stands there silently with a blank face.

"Are you the fucking platoon leader?"

Ranger White weighs this interesting query for several seconds but cannot quite grasp what the RI is saying.

"Jesus Christ!" The RI runs his right hand over his face, inhales deeply to calm his steadily rising fury, but cannot contain the explosion of rage.

"PL, you have thirty fucking minutes to get this patrol base reconned and established. Do you understand me? You need to light a fire under your ass and every other ranger out here and get them moving. You all can be sleeping in an hour, or walking all night, it's entirely up to you."

"Yesh, yesh... Sergeant..." Sleep does sound mighty sweet to White right about now. For three, four, then five seconds, he stands there and sways peacefully just thinking about it.

"GET... MOVING... NOW!" The RI yells so loud in White's face it finally wakes him up. He scurries off to rally the rest of the men.

The next few minutes are a blur. Unknown hands and voices start herding us up the hill, pushing us, prodding us, yelling at us to move higher and to move quickly. I am so delirious and tired at this point, I only experience reality in jarring flashes. All I know is, the way forward is dark and steep, faceless people keep shouting at me, and I keep losing my footing and sliding back down the hill.

"Where are we going?" I frustratedly ask the men around me as faceless hands keep pushing us forward and tree branches scratch my face and eyes. Prickly thorns scratch my legs and thighs and the terrain grows ever steeper. No one answers me.

It is hard to tell whether I am dreaming or awake. I must be dreaming, I decide because sane, alert men would never try to establish a patrol base on such a steep and inhospitable slope. We are going to have to tie ourselves to trees tonight to make sure we do not roll down the hill. Who is taking us up here, anyways? Hopefully not the green goblins I keep seeing in the trees.

"What is this place, fucking Mordor?" Newton exclaims out loud, getting lunatic chuckles in response.

The going keeps getting steeper and I cannot see anything through either my NODs or the naked eye. We plunge straight through brackish bushes that entangle our boots and scratch our calves and dry, scratchy tree branches that crack and snap as our faces break through them. I take two steps forward, grab onto a tree sapling, and pull myself up just a little bit more, only to have to bend over and rest and struggle to catch my breath again. I grow increasingly anxious and concerned about where we are going and how there is no conceivable way men can sleep at a place like this.

"Here," some unfamiliar voice tells me where the terrain is particularly tough, "set up right here."

"What? Here?" I say in disbelief. "In this patch of thorns? Impossible."

I do not know who is giving me orders, but I do see Salvador, my assistant gunner, next to me complying and taking the rucksack off his back.

"Shhh! Quiet!" The voice tells me. "Set up here. This is where we are going to spend the night."

"Impossible!" I throw my hands up in despair, "No one can set up anything here. It's nothing but rocks, thorns, and tree roots. I just want to eat, we haven't slept in days... why, why are we setting up here?"

I sit down in the dirt, rucksack still on my back, clutch my knees together, and hang my helmeted head down low in my lap, defeated. I would cry, had Ranger School left me any tears to shed.

But then the heavens answer my prayers.

Wheeeeeeeeeeeeee-ooooooooooooooooooooo! Booooom!

Wheeeeeeeeeeeeee-ooooooooooooooooooooo! Booooom!

Can it be? Arty sims? Is our base already under enemy attack?

Wheeeeeeeeeeeeee-ooooooooooooooooooooo! BOOOOOOOM!!

Oh, joyous night. It is! The Opfor is launching mortars at us. This means we must leave this wretched place, and quickly. I am so happy I could kiss the ground, but not every ranger in the platoon shares my enthusiasm. Many rangers are enraged that sleep is again getting snatched from their grasp and howl angrily at the small sliver of moon in the sky.

I start jogging downhill though I cannot see five feet in front of me. Again, unseen hands and voices push and prod me. I jog recklessly forward, relying on blind luck to guide and protect me. The longer we run the more my exuberance fades. We still have to get away from the artillery barrage, re-organize the platoon again, walk to the alternate patrol base, and then establish our new patrol base for the night.

No one knows how far away the alternate patrol base is and how long it will take us, in our pitiful, droning condition, to get there. Who knows, maybe the terrain at the new base will be even worse?

It is now past midnight, technically a new day, and we are on the march again. It only takes a few minutes before every ranger is a sleep-marching drone again.

We limp and shuffle our feet another one hundred meters before the first short halt is called. We stop and sway, few of us bothering to take a knee, half asleep for ten minutes, before we start moving again. Nobody knows why we stopped, probably not even the PL.

The sooner we get to where we are going, the better, any damn fool can see that, but for some reason the platoon leader and platoon sergeant keep placing us in the short halt. With each stop, I get increasingly angry, and so does Newton.

"Damn it, White!" Newton hisses at the PL as he walks near our position. "Why the fuck are we stopping, again?"

"Take a knee, Newton," White whispers hurriedly.

Newton just stands there, swaying, and glaring at the platoon leader.

"Just take a knee, Newton. I need to make sure we are going the right way, give me a minute to figure that out, but meanwhile, please take a knee."

Newton is somnolent, swaying back and forth like the rest of us as he shakes his head back and forth, and says, "Nope."

"C'mon, Newton," White whispers to him. "The RIs are watching."

"Maybe they are, maybe they aren't. I don't give a shit. Move on, PL."

"Don't be a buddy fucker." White's tone suddenly grows stern as Newton becomes the embodiment of the thirty other men in the platoon who also refuse to take a knee. "How hard is it to take a knee when we stop, bro? C'mon, I did it for you!"

How hard is it to take a knee, you ask, White? Right now, for some of us, it is the hardest thing in the world to do, requiring all the strength, all the will that we have left. Sure, it's easy enough to go down, but what about rising again? We all know that we will be moving again in three, five, or ten minutes, anyway, so why bother? This late into the march, when our rucksack straps dig painfully deep into our shoulders after being on our backs for twelve hours, it is just too much to ask us to kneel and suffer more.

The only thing we should be doing right now, Ranger White, is moving towards the patrol base, as fast as we possibly can, towards an hour or two of sleep.

And that is why, Newton has nothing to say but, "Fuck you, and fuck taking a knee! Let's get moving, PL!"

The PL, about to have a mutiny on his hands, knows that harsh words and stern measures are not going to work in this situation. He resumes his desperate, pleading tone.

"C'mon, Newton. Please," White says. "Please take a knee. We're all so very tired, but it's what we're supposed to do and the RIs are watching. You would want me to do the same for you, and I have. Please, friend, be a pal and please, just take a knee."

Newton sways back and forth, cracks a single eyelid open, thrusts his pointer finger into White's face and emphatically tells him, "Fuck you! I got my go!" before descending into a standing, swaying sleep stupor again.

White orders us to start walking again. We walk and we drone. I am conscious and awake for only seconds at a time before I descend into liminal darkness again. I cannot tell how long we stop and how long we walk for. My NODs slip and slide on my head, my chinstrap rubs my chin raw, I re-tweak my twisted ankle again, and more rangers head off in odd directions into the wood line.

Finally, after a dozen short halts, minutes or hours later, I cannot tell, Charlie Platoon walks up onto a small goat path ringing the base of a gently rising, lightly forested slope.

I do not know how we did it, but the slurred whispers sent up and down the line indicate that the platoon has managed to arrive at the alternate patrol base.

But remarkably, everyone just stands there, swaying like palm trees in the wind, for one minute, two minutes, five minutes, and more. Again, droning leaders and regular Joes are indistinguishable from each other. No one issues any orders or exercises any command. All forty-five men of the platoon just stand there and sway, doing absolutely nothing.

Then, through the green-tinged blurry view of my NODs, one ranger, then another, and another, drops his rucksack on the ground, lays down next to it, and goes to sleep. All of us, even the leaders being graded, are simply too tired and broken down to care. They are tired of struggling to identify their squad mates' faces in pitch blackness, tired of giving the same orders repeatedly, only to have them ignored, tired of sounding like an asshole, but mostly, supremely frustrated with the impossible task assigned to them: corralling exhausted and demoralized men with nothing left to give.

The scene around me has me mystified. It is as if we are in a sleepy-time fairy realm where mortal man is condemned to eternal slumber. I cannot believe that no one is doing anything, especially now that we are so close to home, so close to a meal and some actual sleep, if only we can get moving, now!

This is so stupid! I tell myself as I watch the last of the standing rangers lay their heads down on their rucks. Someone, anyone needs to do something! What the fuck are the PL, Platoon Sergeant, and the squad leaders even doing right now? Are they just resigned to fail, again, just like last night? Do they want to recycle? Do they want to endure this crucible again?

As my anger rises, precious, energizing adrenaline courses through my veins. I am wide awake now, enraged at my fellow rangers who have called it quits.

Now once again I must harness my last remaining strength, one forged by three long years in the regular infantry, a power available only to those men, those infantrymen, who have known true suffering, and overcome it. Even when one is inexhaustibly tired, in pain, starving, lacking shelter, friendship, motivation, and purpose, when one has been robbed of everything, you always have something left, the raw, furious power of wrathful anger and an abject refusal to quit.

I tap into this power now. It clears my head and I know just what to do. This is not about the Mission any longer, not about killing the Opfor, and not about the platoon leadership getting "go's" on their patrol, no, no longer. This is about survival now, it is about eating an MRE and getting an hour or two of sleep before another brutal, grinding day tomorrow where, who knows, maybe they will make me PL.

Today's leaders have had their chance to shine, to lead, but they have failed us. Nothing is going to happen tonight unless we make it happen, unless I make it happen.

Sometimes a ranger must step up and lead.

I drop my rucksack to the ground and loosen the cord tying my 240B machine gun to my load bearing vest. I swap it out for the M4 carbine of a sleeping ranger next to me. He does not even notice. I grab the only two rangers still standing, Dale and remarkably, Leon, of all people. I tell them to drop their rucksacks and to follow me.

"Hey!" Leon sleepily objects to my orders. "I'm just a team leader today, not the PL or even a squad leader. Why are you making me go on the leader's recon?"

"I was a machine gunner until two minutes ago, Leon. You're going to listen to me and go on this leader's recon so we can set up the patrol base and get some sleep tonight. How does that sound? You want to help me, or do you want to stand here and twiddle your thumbs while I go off and do this on my own?"

Leon wants sleep and an MRE dinner just as badly as I do. He glances at Dale, who shrugs his shoulders, before nodding his assent.

"Where's the patrol base supposed to be?" Dale asks me.

"I don't know. Let's find the PL."

The three of us fan out and look for White, the PL. We lift up the heads of sleeping rangers and peer into their faces looking for our leader.

Where is the goddamn PL? I ask myself as I shake and stare into the faces of four different rangers. Finally, Dale finds him and whistles me over.

"White, there you are... Hey, hey, are you listening!" I snap my fingers in front of his face while I reach into his front pockets to pull out his map. "Where is the patrol base supposed to be? Can you show me on the map? Is it here? Are we close?"

"That way," he points dreamily, first to the North, then to the East, without even looking, "that way, one hundred meters, maybe two. There's a small depression in the ground next to a hill where we should set up."

"That way?" I point towards the northeast.

"Yeah, yeah." He shakes his head up and down eagerly before laying his head back on his rucksack and falling asleep instantly.

"You want to come with us?" I ask White, shaking his shoulders to rouse him. He is the platoon leader after all, this is his graded patrol.

But the motherfucker is already snoring, so we leave him.

The three of us walk up the gentle slope, through a dense section of trees, before the ground slopes down again and then levels out. There, I can see a small grass covered hill, about where the PL told us it would be. Under the glow of NODs, I can see that this site is different from the hellish terrain of the first patrol base. Relatively flat and lacking thorny vines, it is a veritable paradise.

"This the spot?" Leon asks me.

"Even if it isn't," I make a command decision, "this is where we are spending the night. Let's walk the perimeter."

The three of us designate the three apexes of the triangular patrol base, where the machine guns will be set up, and walk the legs between them. There are sufficient large-trunked trees and small rises and dents in the ground to use for cover. The small hill near the center would make a great spot for the command team to pitch their hootches and establish radio communications.

The three of us are satisfied that it will make a great home for the night.

"I'd say the patrol base has been reconned," Dale whispers to me.

"I agree. Let's get the rest of the platoon," I say before leaning in towards Leon. "Dale and I are going to head back to get the rest of the platoon. Can you stay behind and guide us in when we return? I don't want to lose this place and I do not know if I can find it again in the dark."

"Yeah, yeah," he says curtly in response.

"I really don't want to get lost, not now, and I want to get the guys emplaced fast, so please, please," I plead with Leon, knowing his propensity to fall asleep, "stay right here, stay awake, and look for my IR flash in about ten or fifteen minutes, you got that?"

"Aye, aye, Cap'n," Leon responds a little dreamily.

"This is really important, Leon, the whole platoon is counting on you, so please, stand up and stay awake."

"Don't worry, bro, I got this," he assures me, sounding annoyed. "I'm awake now and I'll stay awake. Get the rest of the platoon."

"Awesome. Let's go, Dale!"

It takes us about five minutes to dash through the trees and up and over the hill before we stumble back upon the rest of the platoon. Everyone is lying down and sleeping next to their rucksacks.

"Get up! Wake up! Stand up!" I command them. "You guys want to get some real sleep at the patrol base tonight or what?" On a night like tonight, there is no time for niceties. I needle them in the ribs with my boots, pick up and drop the rucksacks they rest their heads on, anything to get my platoon mates on their feet again.

Unfortunately, most of the men around me, many of them highly trained, hardened combat killers, are now as helpless as newborn babes. I manage to get some men to wake up, stand up, and put on their rucksacks only to have them take them off again and resume sleeping after I pass their position.

"C'mon, guys! The patrol base is already scouted out," I plead with them. "Leon is already there by himself, waiting for us, we just have to get there, and then we can eat, then we can sleep. What do you say?"

After ten minutes of walking up and down the line, after waking up the same guys two, sometimes three times, Charlie Platoon is on its feet again, rucksacks on their backs, swaying like palm trees in the wind.

I run up to the front of the platoon, to First Squad's location, and tell the most alert-looking ranger there to have his squad closely follow me. Dale is going to hang back in the rear to make sure we have everyone and to police up the stragglers. We are not walking in modified fire team wedge formation tonight. No, that would be asking the impossible. Tonight, we are herding ranger sheep. We will keep it simple and walk in ranger file.

I take a deep breath, make a quick prayer that we will not lose anyone, and start leading Charlie Platoon up the hill.

I have already made this trip, barely twenty minutes before, but now I lead forty-four instead of two men. Now the stakes are higher, and I am less sure of my navigational abilities. I feel like we must be getting close to where we left Leon, so I start twisting the knob on my NODs to emit flashes of infrared light, an "IR flash," to identify myself in the darkness. Anyone wearing NODs can see such a signal from some distance away.

But I do not see him or his return signal, even after we walk another fifty, even one hundred meters. I look up, down, and all around me, but he is not there.

Where is Leon? Flash, flash, flash, goes my IR light. I walk ten steps.

Where is Leon? Flash, flash, flash, goes my IR light. I walk five more steps.

Flash, flash, flash… nothing. Goddamn it! Where is that guy? I could have sworn we were getting close. Am I going the right way?

We walk twenty-five meters further. I am really getting nervous that I am getting the whole platoon lost, and worse, that I left Leon out there by himself somewhere, and maybe we will not be able to find him.

I was only supposed to be a machine gunner today, I remind myself. I was only trying to make things better. Did I just make things worse?

Then, as I walk upon the trunk of a broad tree that looks oddly familiar, I nearly trip right over Leon's small, still body. He is sitting up, back leaning against the tree trunk, night vision goggles down over his eyes, and his head sunk into his chest.

I should have known. The bastard fell asleep. Never trust a sleepy ranger.

But I'm not too mad, because at least we found him and I managed to lead the platoon to the patrol base without getting lost. Now it is just a matter of guiding everyone into their positions.

I shake Leon awake and help him to his feet.

"Flash your IR light like a disco ball, Leon, don't let up. Guide the rest of the platoon into our position. Can you do that? We are so close to sleep tonight, Leon, so close…"

The platoon is still a collection of walking zombies. I personally walk

First Squad into their positions on the first leg of the triangular patrol base. I space them the proper distance, tell them to take off their rucks, and to lie down and pull security.

By the time I return, Second and Third Squad, corralled by Dale, are waiting in two separate clumps, along with Leon, who is still awake, and White, the PL, who is still droning as bad as anyone. Dale emplaces Second Squad while I do the same for Third Squad. Within minutes Charlie Platoon officially occupies the patrol base.

The squad leaders, catching a second wind now with the imminent prospect of chow and sleep, put their men to work establishing security while I continue to direct platoon operations. I drag White along with me.

"PL, you might want to set up the Platoon command post right there," I tell him, "On top of that low rise by the grove of trees, it's almost in the center of the patrol base."

"Uh-huh."

"I'm going to double check to make sure the squads are putting out claymores and drawing sector sketches, then I'll check on the guns."

"Roger," White yawns.

"If we work fast, we'll get," I look at my watch, it is already past 2:30 a.m., "maybe an hour-and-fifteen minutes of sleep tonight..."

"Hm-huh, hm-huh..." White says, his eyes slowly closing.

"We gotta work fast though because..."

"Pssst! Pssst! Ranger! Hey you, ranger."

A voice from the bushes interrupts me. I point my finger at my chest naively.

"Yeah, you! Dumbass! Come here, ranger. You and the PL, too. Let's go!" An RI shows himself and beckons us towards a small rise in the center of the patrol base.

"You rangers are a soup sandwich, a complete and utter mess. I do not know if I have ever seen such a sloppy gang of amateurs..."

The RI continues his harsh evaluation as a flood of worry courses through me. I do not know if the RI is going to punish me for usurping the chain of command or for establishing a half-assed patrol base, maybe both. He might blow our platoon out of here, just like the last patrol base, only to have us walk again, until sunrise, to the next one.

Instead, he is kind and merciful.

"No security tonight, rangers. You hear me? No one is pulling security," The RI tells me as my eyes grow wide with astonishment. "That's right, I want all of you to eat your MREs and then bed down immediately. No weapons maintenance, no hygiene, no guard, just eat and go to sleep. It is now..." the RI looks at the glowing face of his watch, "two-forty a.m. in the morning. Wake up is pushed to five a.m. You will all get at least two hours of sleep tonight rangers, that is not an option."

Two hours of guaranteed sleep, without guard? Oh, blessed day. I am so happy I could cry. I am convinced this man is an angel, not a Mountain RI.

"You all have ten minutes to eat your MREs," our benefactor continues, "after that, I want everyone tucked into your fart sacks, for good."

I nod my head dumbly up and down. I think White is sleeping again.

"If I see anyone, and I mean anyone, walking around after three, I swear to fucking God, I will blow you out of this patrol base, drop four of you as casualties, and make you carry each other through the woods all night. Understand, rangers?"

"Roger, Sergeant!" I say excitedly, while I elbow White in the ribs. He comes to, yells out "Roger!" and then stares off into space.

The PL grumbles in response, stares sternly at both of us one second longer, and then dismisses us.

"Now get the fuck out of here, rangers!"

I positively skip away. I can already taste my savory Chili Mac dinner entrée and the sweet oblivion of deep, dark sleep. I dash along the three legs of the patrol base to share the good news. I beseech everyone to eat quickly and go to bed.

The information disseminated, my mission complete, it is now time to enjoy the fruits of my labor. I head back towards the point of our triangular base where my gun team is waiting for me.

"Salvador? Bailey?" I whisper as I come up upon three sleeping figures in sleeping bags. "Is that you guys?"

"No, Goldsmith." I hear Fulton's voice. "Wrong team, they're somewhere else."

I dash down another leg of the patrol base towards a different point of the triangle. "Hey!" I call out to the men lying there. "Salvador, Bailey, it's Goldsmith. Where are you?"

"Not here," Dale's unmistakably deep, monotone responds, "okay."

Shit! Where are these guys? Only one more spot to go, the third and last point. Now, which way did I just come from again? Was it that leg or this leg of the patrol base?

Unsure of exactly where to go next, I run back up to the top of the small hill at the center of the patrol base for a better vantage point. The RI sees me, checks his watch, and then glares at me, so I scurry back down the hill. It is already 2:55 a.m., I have five minutes to find my position and bed down.

I have to get in my sleeping bag, I have to eat my MRE, I have to get to my sleeping bag... I recite over-and-over again in my head. Where is my goddamn position?!

"Bailey? Salvador?"

"Wrong, again, Goldsmith!" It's Fulton. "What's wrong with you? Get the hell out of here, I'm trying to sleep!"

I dash down what I think is a new leg of the base. I trip over some legs and tumble over several men from Second Squad. They curse me for a fool before rolling back over to go to sleep.

I get to the end of the line. "Salvador? Salvador? Is that you?"

"Are you okay, Goldsmith?!"

I ignore Dale and dash off frantically again.

This is bad, this is really bad. I think to myself as my anxiety rises to a fever pitch. Why can't I find my position? If I do not bed down soon, the RI is going to blow us out of here, and if that happens, if I am the cause of us all losing out on precious, life-saving sleep, the other rangers will never forgive me.

All I want to do is eat. All I want to do is sleep. I want them both so bad it hurts. I just need to find my goddamn position.

"Pssst! Bailey? Salvador?"

"No, Goldsmith! Goddamn it! I told you that two minutes ago. Get the fuck out of here, okay! I'm trying to sleep, okay!" It is Dale's voice again, and I have never heard him so angry.

I sit down in the dirt, on the verge of panic. I am pathetic, I think to myself. How dare I call myself a ranger when I cannot even find one of three points of a triangle. I am truly lost. I might as well just lay down right here, cover myself with leaves for warmth, pass out, and hope the RI does not see me. Otherwise, I risk us all getting blown out of here for hours of more walking. This cannot happen, I just can't do it. It would kill me.

Desperate, I start feeling light-headed and dizzy. I force myself to sit up and look around me, desperately searching for a recognizable landmark, but reality is swirling around me. Trees become men, men become rocks and obstacles; everything is green, everything is shadow. I just want to eat; I just want to sleep. I am two years old again and helpless. Tears start welling up in my eyes.

I am about to give up, about to admit defeat, when a sure, strong hand suddenly grips my shoulder and spins me around.

"There you are, Goldsmith, we've been looking for you."

McCormick, is that you? Salvador? Newton?

No, it is none of them, it is Bailey, of all people, and he has his wits about him again.

"C'mon, Goldsmith." He guides me through the trees. "Just a little bit further... yep, yep, yep, over here... Right about... here we are."

Bailey guides me into our gun position. My 240B machine gun rests on its bipods, Salvador is sprawled out in his sleeping bag, already fast asleep. Bailey helps me to take off my rucksack and unpack my sleeping gear.

I eat a cold MRE by red-lens flashlight under a poncho with Bailey. It is a glorious, memorable meal; me and Bailey make small talk and even trade a few items, something I have not done since Darby.

It is now 3:10 a.m. The RIs are gone and there is no sign of life in our ranger camp. Bailey and I are the only rangers left awake. My belly has some food in it, and I am about to get almost two hours of guaranteed sleep. I am ecstatic at the prospect.

Just another day in Mountains, I think to myself dreamily, as I sigh with pleasure and my eyes slam shut.

"Wake the fuck up, rangers!"

Chapter 10: "Down from the Mountains"

Rule #17: Help out your buddies whenever you can.

1503 Hours (03:45 p.m.)
Camp Merrill Training Area
North Georgia Mountains
Day 39 of Ranger School
Last Day of the Mountain FTX

Charlie Platoon descends a steep hill, walking in file down a slick, muddy, goat trail. We enter a green and vibrant looking patch of forest, crawling with ferns and watered by several small streams of cool, sparkling water. Patches of sunlight pierce through the clouds and the forest canopy and illuminate the scene with a warm, golden glow. The day is warm with only a slight cooling breeze and no sign of rain. Mother nature is positively smiling upon us.

Or maybe, I'm hallucinating again.

But everyone else feels it, too. The bat boys have a skip in their step, the officers' backs are straight and proud like they used to be, even Bailey is smiling. The bat boys, who always know these things, have told us that today is the last day of the Mountains FTX.

Rather than give us reason to slack off, the news energizes us, gives us the fuel to continue to push past our limits, through injury, without sleep, to work as a functioning team again. By happy coincidence, today also happens to be Thanksgiving, though that doesn't mean anything to a pack of rangers on patrol.

In short, we are happy and motivated, even though the Crusty Mountain RI has returned to walk with our platoon today, one last time. He is shadowing Sven, the day's second platoon leader, who presumably failed his prior two patrols and is getting one last shot to get his "go."

Though he still wears a permanent scowl, our favorite RI is unusually tame and soft-spoken today. This might be because he is satisfied enough with our performance or, more likely, his calm demeanor is the result of walking with the Sergeant Major today, his boss's boss, a square-jawed, gray-haired, extremely fit "old man" in his forties with combat and skills badges flowing off his uniform. Like us, the Sergeant Major is also smiling.

When the North Georgia Mountains gives you a view like this, it is hard not to enjoy this mountain life. And while I certainly do not enjoy marching all night on hobbled limbs, not sleeping, and slowly starving to death, there are aspects of this life that it will be sad to leave behind, like drinking water directly from cool-watered mountain creeks, sleeping like a dead man under the stars, treasuring each morsel of food I consume, and being at home in the woods with a pack of hardened warriors and, somehow, belonging.

Living up here in the Mountains makes me feel authentic and alive. Food tastes better when you walk and labor all day. Jokes land better when you are suffering. The smallest little reward, the slightest joy, can feel like a godsend. There are things I used to worry and complain about, back in the "real" non-ranger world, which make me ashamed, now that I know how truly trivial they were.

I would like to come out here again someday, I cannot help but think to myself. A day when I am not half-starved, humping a god-awful heavy rucksack, and severely sleep deprived, a day when I could just, enjoy it all.

That day is not today. Today, my rucksack is extra heavy. I have been assigned a non-graded position as a Forward Observer, or FO. My job is to accompany Sven, the platoon leader, as his radioman and to call in simulated, supporting artillery fires. In addition to my usual heavy basic load, I carry a twenty-pound PRC-119 radio, two extra batteries, and an antenna.

My rucksack must weigh close to ninety pounds today, packed tight and near to bursting with clothing, ammo, and gear, but that's okay, because there are also some perks to the FO job. I carry a light weapon, a basic M4 carbine, and other than having to do a radio check every hour, I have few responsibilities other than keeping up with the PL. So, overall, it's not a bad place to be.

And did I mention, this is the last day of the Mountains FTX?

During the change of command an hour ago, Salvador and Sven were appointed to be the platoon sergeant and the PL, respectively, for a third graded patrol. Sven is characteristically wide-eyed and alarmed at being put in the spotlight and Salvador looks glum. His neck muscles are still broken, unable to support the weight of his head, and his chin rests forlornly on his chest. I still do not know how he and Fulton have managed to survive nine days of this FTX in such wretched states.

Salvador knows that this third appointment on the last day of the FTX is a good indicator that he and Sven did not pass their first two patrols. The RIs are giving them one last chance to get it right, or else they are going to recycle and will have to go through Mountains all over again.

The five-klick movement to the objective is uneventful but, at our usual plodding pace, it takes us all day. By four p.m. we are still a klick away and the sun is dipping low in the sky. Sven knows as well as any of us that if we do not hustle, we are going to miss our 4:45 p.m. hit time for the big raid on the enemy command and control center.

So, he orders us to start running.

My lungs are on fire as Charlie Platoon limps into the Objective Rally Point to drop our rucks and grab the weapons and equipment we need for the raid. My watch says it is 4:32, meaning there is no time for a leader's reconnaissance.

All we know, all we need to know, is that the enemy command and control center rests at the top of the heavily forested hill in front of us. We are going to go up there and kill anything that moves.

With only their maps to guide them, Sven and Salvador quickly huddle with the squad leaders for a last-minute briefing before the raid.

Moments later, the security squad and the machine gun teams split off to take their positions. Sven lines up the two assault squads and tells them to start moving up the hill, and quickly. Capitalizing on his long legs, and motivated to get his "go," Sven strides out in front of us all.

"Let's go, guys!" he says in his shrill, effeminate voice. "Take the hill!"

My primary job as the FO is to keep up with Sven, so that he always has communications with higher headquarters, but I have yet to catch my breath after the run to the ORP, so I struggle dearly to keep up. This will become even harder because everyone else in the platoon will get to drop their rucksacks for the raid, but radiomen are forced to keep them on.

Sven and the fleetest members of the assault squads are already close to the top of the hill, but I am a plodding tortoise. Along with a handful of slow-moving SAW gunners and a single machine gun team, I lag at least one hundred meters behind.

They wave us onwards and encourage us to move faster. I strain and labor for breath as my quadriceps and back muscles burn and scream from lactic acid. I alternatively run, walk, crawl, and use my arms to pull myself up on small trees to get, by any means possible, up the steep hill. Ten minutes pass before I finally catch up to Sven and the assault squads' positions.

I flop down on the ground, exhausted, sucking in air and dripping sweat. Sven kneels on one knee in the middle of the two assault squads, who are laid out in a rough skirmish line, still fifty-meters short of the lip to the top of the hill.

Sven checks his watch: it says 4:44 p.m. We just may be able to pull this thing off in time. He keys the hand mike to his Icom radio.

Psssshhh, the radio hisses. "Security squad leader, Weasel, are your guys emplaced?"

Psssshhh, "Security teams are set, over."

Psssshhh "Roger," Sven responds. "Weasel, are your gun teams in place?"

Psssshhh, "Support by fire... " the Weasel pauses to stop his panting and takes a heavy breath, "support by fire is in position."

Psssshhh, "How's the target look?" Sven asks him. "What do you see, over?"

Psssshhh, "Several huts, a satellite dish... lots of Opfor roaming around, at least a half-dozen of them out in the open, one has a machine gun."

"Sounds like fun," Sven purrs, sounding pleased. "The assault squads still have to crest the top of the hill to get to the objective, but we must initiate this raid now. You guys will have to cover the objective with fires until we can get there."

"Prepare to fire on my command," Sven adds. He must have heard that one in a movie once.

And then, like a militant seeking paradise through a glorious death in battle, Sven stands up, bellows out a mighty, mousy war cry, raises the buttstock of his carbine to his shoulder one-handed, shoots off one, two, and then three rounds of M4 blank fire into the sky, and starts charging up the hill.

"Un-fucking believable..." I say out loud, as I suck in one last, deep gasp of air before I chase off after Sven again.

The assault squad leaders also shake their heads in momentary astonishment before ordering their men up the last stretch of the hill. Getting into the spirit, half of the rangers in the assault squads join Sven in yelling and screaming obscenities at the enemy.

Rat-tat-tat-tat-tat-tat! Rat-tat-tat-tat-tat-tat-tat! Rat-tat-tat-tat-tat-tat!

Meanwhile, the three machine guns of the support by fire position are spewing fire from their barrels. They sweep the entire objective with blankets of imaginary lead, the gunners cackling with glee the entire time, doing their best to blow through as much ammo as possible.

I am doing my best to keep up with Sven as we summit the top of the hill, but my exhaustion and heavy rucksack are making that impossible. Running forward blindly, as fast as I can manage, I make it only five, ten, then fifteen meters up the hill before my foot strikes a tree root and my body goes flying headfirst into the air. I land on all fours, my ninety-pound radio rucksack resting on the back of my neck, pinning me to the ground, with my left cheek pressed into the mud and my knees tucked under my body.

I look like a turtle, curled up on all fours with a ninety-pound rucksack crushing my vertebrae. And the unbelievable thing is that, no matter how hard I try, I just can't get up. My rucksack is pinning me like an Olympic wrestler. I am just in too awkward of a position, too weak and winded to beast my way out of this mess, and it is getting increasingly difficult to breathe.

I try rocking forwards and backwards, then side-to-side, but both methods prove futile. I am getting increasingly light-headed from slow airway constriction. I struggle and labor in vain to free myself, but I am truly and pathetically trapped under the weight of my own rucksack.

Some other rangers run past and over me. Nobody stops to help; no one extends a helping hand. Some of them are too far gone to notice or care about anything other than themselves, others find it ridiculous that I am stuck in such a configuration, or even harbor some small resentment against me.

Whatever it is, they have more important things to do than help some fool stuck like a pinned turtle under his ruck. They run up the hill, to the objective on the hilltop above.

Rat-tat-tat-tat-tat-tat! Rat-tat-tat-tat-tat-tat-tat! Rat-tat-tat-tat-tat-tat!

Now I can hear the assault squads adding their own rifle and machine gun fire to the mix.

Bang-bang! Bang-bang! Bang-bang!

Rat-tat-tat-tat-tat-tat! Rat-tat-tat-tat-tat-tat-tat! Rat-tat-tat-tat-tat-tat!

Two more sluggish rangers practically step on me on their lethargic journey up the hilltop. The whole situation suddenly strikes me as being very funny and I can't help but laugh.

Then I see Leon, humping a SAW again, tiredly walking up the hill ten feet to my left.

"Help... help me... please..." I moan out to him, but he simply spits on the ground and keeps ambling up the hill.

The other rangers have abandoned me to my fate: slow asphyxiation by rucksack. They cannot or will not extend a hand to a fallen brother. Again, I start laughing.

Meanwhile, Salvador, today's platoon sergeant, has been watching the scene in astonishment from his position across the hill.

"Goldsmith!" he cries out as he dashes over to help me, ignoring the pain in his own lungs, his limp, useless neck flopping around on his chest as he runs.

Everyone else has left me in the dust, walked over me, or otherwise consigned me to an ignominious ranger death, but not Salvador, the tattooed, streetwise bat boy with a heart of gold. He handily lifts my rucksack off my neck, pulls me to my feet, looks into my eyes, and asks, "You okay, Goldsmith? You all right?"

Now that I am on my feet again, with that damn rucksack off my neck and able to breathe freely, I am more than all right, suddenly I feel great.

Rat-tat-tat-tat-tat-tat! Rat-tat-tat-tat-tat-tat-tat!

And I am missing out on the battle.

I need to get up this hill fast to make up for lost time. I need to be with Sven, the PL, who I can hear frantically yelling out orders. At a moment like this, he needs his Forward Observer.

A savage burst of energy seizes me. I need to be in that fight! My mind shouts at me. My platoon needs me!

"RAAAAWWWRRRR!" I let out a mighty roar that puts Sven's war cry to shame and I run up the hill as fast as my legs will carry me, towards the fight, towards the sound of blank fire.

I am about to crest the lip of the hill and emerge onto the target when a voice stops me.

"Hold up right there, ranger."

I stop mid-stride and turn my head to see the Crusty Mountain RI standing behind me. For the first time in this wretched phase, I just heard him say the word "ranger" without a disdainful tone.

Me? I point to myself soundlessly as I look stupidly in the trees around me.

"Of course, you, you idiot!" Now he sounds more like himself. "Get over here!"

Suspiciously, like a feral cat, I slink over to the RI, who thrusts something out at me, something slim between his thumb and pointer finger.

"Here, ranger, take a piece," he tells me. "With that display, you've earned it."

The crustiest RI in Mountains offers me a stick of Wrigley's Wintergreen gum, his gum. I grasp it firmly, slide it out of the outside packaging, take it out of the wrapper, shove the trash in my pocket, place the stick of gum in my mouth, and start chewing.

The burst of minty flavor is delightful.

Rat-tat-tat-tat-tat-tat! Rat-tat-tat-tat-tat-tat! Rat-tat-tat-tat-tat-tat!

"SHIFT FIRE! SHIFT FIRE! SHIFT FIRE!" I hear the Weasel shouting in a clump of trees off to my left. The machine gun teams echo the command and shift their fires to the back half-portion of the objective. It means the assault squads are fully formed up and are getting ready to bound through the objective.

"Better get moving, ranger."

I nod wordlessly before I run off again, up and over the lip of the hill, to the raid, the final mission of Mountains, screaming my head off. I am motivated, ready to kill.

I feel like a ranger.

I am reunited with Sven as the assault squads start bounding by fire teams through the objective. As the teams approach the three small hootches and a Conex shipping container situated in the middle of the objective, buddy teams break off to search the crude, small structures. Sven and I watch their handiwork from just behind them, slowly ambling forward, and taking a knee when we're still.

The sun comes out from behind some low clouds. It shines warm, welcoming rays onto my neck and shoulders. I've finally caught my breath and, with little to do other than shadow the PL, I have time to inhale deeply and take in the scene around me. I can smell lemony-pine needles, tree sap, and the sulfurous, yet oddly sweet smell of cordite from expended blank ammunition. I watch my platoon mates swirling around, busy, and full of purpose, each singularly occupied in their individual tasks, all the moving pieces working together to create this beautiful thing called a raid.

How can any red-blooded American boy not love this? I realize now that I am fortunate, blessed even, to be here. It is a gorgeous day in the woods and here I am, a mere infantryman, running around in the woods, shooting cap guns at other soldiers with some of the world's most elite warriors. This is a childhood dream personified. I get to play "ranger," for real.

Rat-tat-tat-tat! Rat-tat-tat! Rat-tat!

The machine guns cease firing as the assault squads push through the back half of the objective and into the woods beyond. Between them, the machine guns and assault squads have accounted for eight dead enemy Opfor and, even better, they have found valuable intelligence, including maps and overhead photos. All-in-all, it is a good raid, the Platoon did not look half bad executing it, and Sven is all smiles.

Back at the ORP site, the Crusty Mountain RI conducts a hasty, no-nonsense sensitive items check while the Sergeant Major addresses us.

"You looked good out there, men," he says laconically before walking off and down the hill again.

"I wouldn't go that far," the Crusty Mountain RI says, "but you rangers didn't look too chewed up out there today."

Coming from this man, this is high praise, positively heart-warming to a group of hardened Mountain rangers.

"PL," he continues, "tell your men to get their rucksacks on and then start walking west until you hit a dirt road. We'll be taking that road north, back to camp."

"Roger, Sergeant!" Sven says cheerfully. "You mean Camp Merrill?"

"Yes, PL, we're heading back to Camp Merrill," and then he leans in closer to Sven, "and if you can make these rangers move with a purpose and get us back in time for the Patriots game tonight, you don't have to do it tactically and you don't have to mount your NODs. You just have to walk, quickly. You think you rangers can handle that?"

"Yes, Sergeant," Sven says confidently, "I know we can! All right guys, let's go, let's go! Shoulder your rucksacks and get ready to move out. Do it quickly, we're going back in!"

As small cheers erupt from Charlie Platoon, the Crusty Mountain RI tells everyone to "Shut the fuck up! Maintain noise discipline or I will smoke your asses all night!"

In a way, I am going to miss this place. Mountains is just starting to feel like home.

We walk west for fifteen minutes into the setting sun until we emerge onto a well-worn dirt trail large enough for Humvees to drive on. The platoon takes up a staggered road march formation while Sven orders everyone to keep up the pace, exhaustion and injury be damned. A handful of rangers are sucking and can barely keep up, but most of Charlie Platoon is happy to comply and we merrily march our way back to camp with huge grins on our faces.

I have endured and learned so much up here in the mountains of North Georgia. I am a different person, a tougher, more stoic, and seasoned man, so different from the sniveling pansy who almost quit during Darby one month ago. I have been through some tough times in three years in the infantry, one of those in Iraq, but no matter how dreadful things were there, I always had my buddies and my leaders to rely upon, to take care of me, to share the suck. No matter how bad things were, we had each other, so it was never that bad.

It is different in Ranger School, especially up here in Mountains. Here, I can only rely on one person, myself, and somehow, despite all my fears and anxiety, I have proven up to the task. I can keep up with the best rangers here, I can be relied upon in a tight spot, I can lead when no one else can. I have survived and even thrived during these cold mountain days and nights in conditions where supposedly harder men, Airborne Rangers, and green berets even, have shut down and become useless. I belong here.

What's more, I know where my true limits are, how much misery and suffering I can actually endure, something few men will ever know. I know firsthand that the mind will quit when the body still has miles to go, that a strong will can overcome nearly all obstacles, that with a sense of mission and a meaningful purpose, almost anything is possible.

Quitting Ranger School is unimaginable now. No matter what happens, whether I pass straight through to Florida, recycle Mountains due to Peers, or Day 1 recycle due to excessive major-minuses and safety violations, it does not matter. I am in this Ranger School thing for the duration. I will either earn my Tab or they will have to carry me out on a stretcher.

The sun has just slipped beneath the horizon but as we emerge onto a paved road, we can still see the sign welcoming us back to Camp Merrill by the pale light of dusk. I want to stop and kiss the ground. Instead, I keep power walking behind the man in front of me.

If I am lucky, the next time I pass by this sign will be on a bus, on the way to Florida, where life, compared to here anyways, is supposed to be easy.

As Newton tells me, "It's all downhill once you come out of Mountains."

I am lucky. That night, I get the good news that I am moving onto Florida Phase. I got my go on the very first patrol of the FTX, I passed Peers with middling marks, and as for the three major-minuses I earned during the phase, I have yet to hear anything about them. Apparently, one or both RIs had a change of heart or failed to submit the proper paperwork. Either that, or they were just playing mind games with us.

Dale, McCormick, Newton, and even Sven, the squad's gray man, are also moving onto Florida, but others are not so fortunate. Bailey, Salvador, Leon, Jenson, and even Fulton, the green beret with the palsied neck, have joined my former battle buddy Tobiri as the newest Mountain Recycles. They are doomed to repeat this arduous phase again and, worst of all, they must do so without any rest. That is because the next class, Ranger Class 02-08, begins their Mountain Phase the day after tomorrow, a mere two days after the end of our brutal FTX.

Poor souls. I do not know how my former squad mates can endure a second Mountain Phase of Ranger School in their sorry states. I sincerely doubt I will see any of them ever again.

"Give 'em hell!" I nonetheless tell Salvador as he slaps palms and exchanges bro hugs with the lucky few of us going to Florida. He still must hold up his useless and broken neck with his left hand. For his sake, I pray that it heals soon.

Losing half of our comrades has dampened the joy of the squad's survivors, but honestly, not by much. Ranger School is two-thirds over and the hardest part of the course is in our rear-view mirror. We are heading down from the mountains, off to the beaches and swamps of the Florida panhandle, where life should be comparatively easy.

I got this, I tell myself confidently on the bus to Florida as I pull my patrol cap over my eyes and drift off to sleep. I am going to earn my Tab… nothing but smooth sailing ahead.

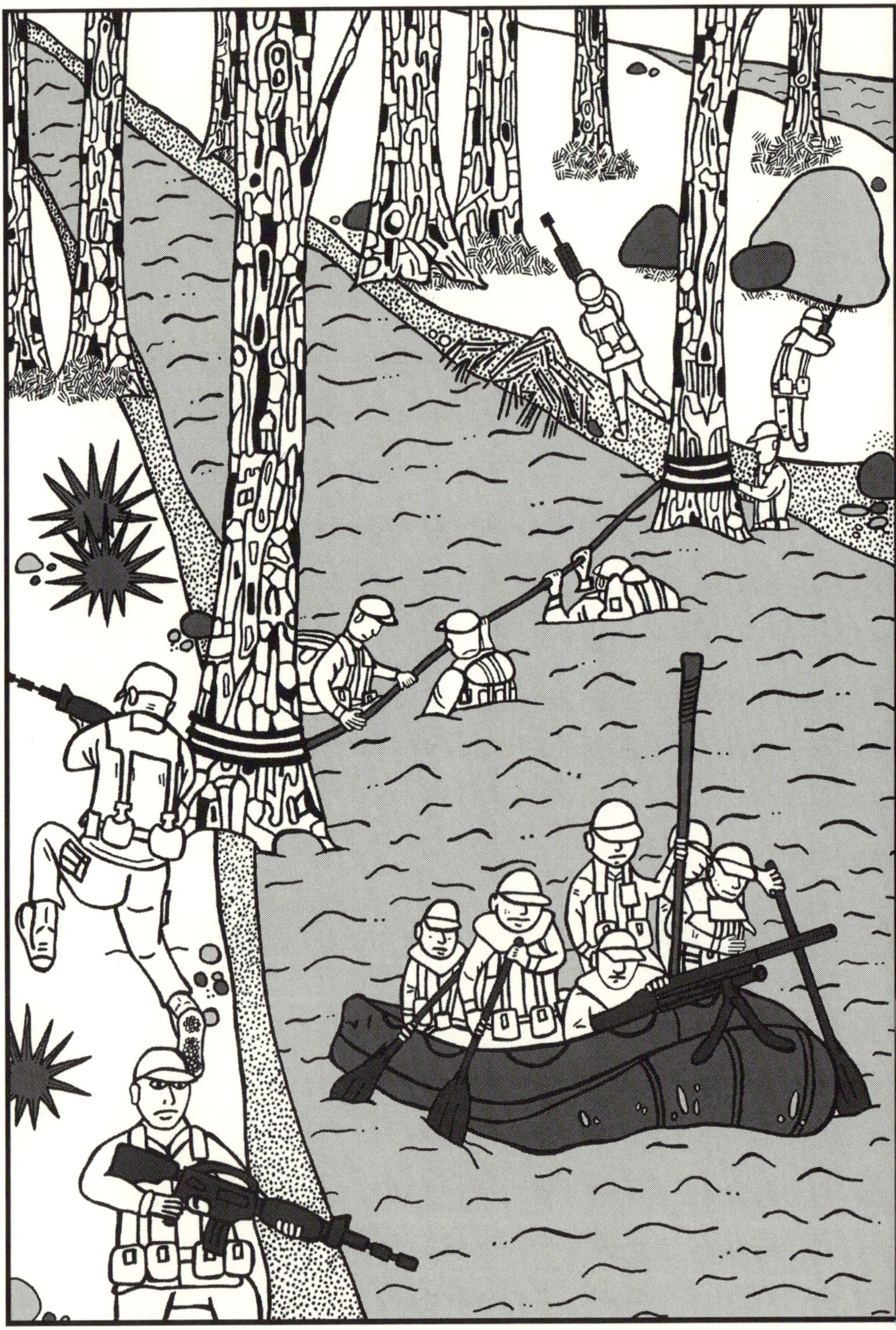

Part III – "Run"
"Swamp" Phase
Camp Rudder, Eglin Air Force Base, Florida
Days 41 – 74

"Once more unto the breach, dear friends, once more."
                                    - William Shakespeare, Henry V.

Rule #18: *Master the rules, so you know when to break them.*

Chapter 11: "Real Rangers Recycle"

Rule #19: Real rangers recycle.

0409 Hours (4:09 a.m.)
December 2007
Charlie Platoon Barracks, Camp Rudder
Eglin Air Force Base, Florida
Day 47 of Ranger School

"Twenty-one days and wake up."

This is how the bat boys count down the days. Chanting it like a mantra when they wake up in the morning or whenever they feel a little down.

"Twenty days and a wake up."

Which is not often, since, for the most part, we like it here at Camp Rudder, home of the third and final phase of Ranger School. Some call it "swamp phase," we just call it "Florida," and compared to Mountains, the place is almost pleasant.

"Nineteen days and a wake up."

We now operate in the far-western corner of the Florida panhandle, in the swamps and pine forests of the inland Emerald Coast, mere miles from the Gulf of Mexico. The weather is warmer, the RIs more laidback, the food more plentiful, and we get a consistent five hours of sleep a night. Moreover, "Florida is flat," as the bat boys are fond of saying, meaning the terrain here is easier to traverse than it was up in Mountains. I can even smell the ocean and hear seagulls cawing off in the distance. It reminds me of home.

The legends are true, everything is better in Florida.

"Eighteen days and a wake up."

The RIs assigned to Charlie Platoon in Florida are chill, almost the polar opposite of the ornery Mountain RIs. One Florida RI in particular, a young and affable staff sergeant, conducts much of our training. He is a solidly built and physically intimidating former bat boy from the deep south with prominent buck teeth in an otherwise red, full, and handsome face. He was a ranger student himself not too long ago, and we can tell he still sympathizes with us. He is eager to share his fieldcraft and knowledge, and even jokes and pals around with us lowly tab-less wonders. He wears his patrol cap in a way none of us have ever seen before, the material pulled back in the rear to make a reverse duckbill. This, along with his buckteeth, makes him an easy target for jokes behind his back, but we all like him.

The Florida RIs have kept us relatively dry during Techniques Week and, so far, there has been no rain. While Alpha and Bravo Platoons train until eleven or twelve at night, in Charlie Company, we are usually back in the barracks by nine. Unlike Darby and Mountains where I was too exhausted to really learn anything during classroom instruction, the training in Florida is mellow, informative, and engaging. We learn about local reptiles, crossing rivers, helicopter extractions, swamp movements, and more, in addition to the obligatory raids and ambushes.

Most importantly of all, the Florida RIs treat us like men with trust and respect. This is the "run" phase of Ranger School, where we are given more freedom to excel or, alternatively, to hang ourselves. Accordingly, few RIs ever yell at us and smokings are rare.

"Seventeen days and a wake up."

We still wake up at 4:00 a.m., every day, we still train long and hard until several hours past sunset, but our bodies are inured to the cold, pain, fatigue, and boredom by now. It is routine for us. Our decimated Mountain squads have also been filled in with a sprinkling of cynical but experienced Florida Recycles. They are eager to teach us how to succeed here in Florida, what to expect, how to game the system, how to be comfortable, even happy, amidst the poverty that is Ranger School.

Our bellies full and our minds rested, the various physical wounds on our bodies we picked up in RAP Week, Darby, and Mountains finally have a chance to heal. Charlie Platoon looks and feels strong again, our morale higher than it has ever been. At night, rather than hitting the pillow the second I can, I find time to chat with my bunkmates or even read the pocket Tao Te Ching I smuggled in here for a precious few minutes. Until now, this was an unthinkable luxury.

I go to bed every night extremely thankful that I am in Charlie Platoon in the last phase of Ranger School. I am on the verge of doing the unthinkable: passing right through Ranger School and earning my Tab in one go. Until now, it was always an impossible dream, a bridge too far, but I can see the end now.

"Sixteen days and a wake up." I say to myself in the morning now, too. "Today we get to cross and float down the Yellow River, and tomorrow, we start the Florida FTX."

Nothing can stop me now.

A few hours later, by the banks of the Yellow River

The Yellow River originates in Alabama, flows through the Florida panhandle, and then empties out into Pensacola Bay. It is ninety-two miles long, has a sandy bottom, brown-colored water, and a swift current. Today, Charlie Platoon must cross it with a bridge made of ropes.

It's cold this morning, the temperature somewhere in the low fifties. I can clearly see my breath and I anticipate that the river water will be shockingly cold. According to the bat boy sages, if the water temperature drops below fifty degrees, the RIs cannot make us cross the river for fear one of us will go hypothermic and die. So ironically, we all pray for freezing cold water.

But we have no such luck.

"Fiddy-point-four degrees, rangers!" The buck-toothed bat boy shouts out with genuine excitement. "Just warm enough to have us a rope bridge crossing of the Yella' River! Happy day, rangers! Let's go, let's go. Security squad, pull those ropes out! Swimmers, get ready to get wet!"

The two swimmers don their life jackets, the rope is tied to the waist of one of them, and they plunge into the water. The current carries them downriver a bit before they manage to reach the far shore about fifty meters away. They tie off the end of the rope to a sturdy tree trunk and pass the signal to the other side.

First Squad, the security squad, gets to work constructing the rope bridge under the watchful eyes of the RIs. Soon enough, the rope bridge is constructed and members of the platoon start crossing.

Assault One squad is the first to go. I am attached to them today as part of a machine gun team, and I carry the big gun. Sooner than I would like, it is my turn to cross. A cold and miserable looking RI, up to his chest in brown river water, beckons me forward.

I take two small steps forward from the bank and drop hip-deep into the Yellow River. The cold, rushing water and swift current takes my breath away and I involuntarily emit a high-pitched squeal. For one second, I sit there motionless, unable to move while my body adjusts to the cold.

"Hurry the fuck up, ranger! Get moving!" the RI snarls at me. He has the worst job of any of us. This poor staff sergeant, apparently the low man on the RI totem pool, must sit in the river the entire crossing. He helps me attach my rucksack and the 240B machine gun to the rope line with carabiners.

"Start walking, ranger! Hand over hand on the rope and pull the gun behind you," he growls out through clenched teeth.

Disoriented by the shock of the chill river water, I blurt out a stupid question, "But what about my rucksack, Sergeant?"

"Ranger, if you waterproofed your rucksack the way we showed you, it will help you float. Now get a fucking move on, genius!"

Fortunately, I waterproofed my rucksack the night before, exactly how the RIs showed me. After tightly shoving most of my rucksack's gear into a wet weather bag I tied a good, tight knot with the drawstring. I then placed that bag into a heavy-duty, contractor's plastic trash bag for a double layer of protection. I smashed out all the air from both bags and then securely tied a second knot in the contractor's bag.

I'm glad I did, because when I lose my footing on the sandy river bottom after a few sideways steps on the rope line, my rucksack bobs in the water, supporting all my weight, and helps to keep my chin and mouth up and out of the river water. Other than my head, the rest of my body is submerged in the river. I drag myself hand over hand to the far shore tugging my machine gun behind me.

I make it safely to the other shore two minutes after first entering the water. I am completely drenched with water and shivering uncontrollably as I lay down behind the 240B machine gun and pull security down the riverbank. The rest of the platoon keeps crossing. It takes an hour for everyone to cross over to the farside.

Then, we have to re-cross the river, which takes another forty minutes, in order to return to our original position on the near bank. As we exit the water for a second time, and after being soaked for almost two hours, the RIs let us open our wet rucksacks to change into dry clothing, if we have any. I am amazed to find that my waterproofing worked and that the inner contents of my rucksack are bone dry after floating twice across the river. Not every ranger is so fortunate.

Less than an hour later I float with most of the Assault One squad down the Yellow River in a black, inflatable Zodiac boat. There are nine rangers in the vessel and an RI. He sits up in the back, looking tall and regal, holding his RI walking stick upright on the deck like a spear. The other rangers paddle while I sit idly by, manning the 240B machine gun, acting as the boat's "air guard." Since the likelihood of the Opfor attacking us in helicopters is next to zero, I get to enjoy a nice float down the Yellow River.

Carrying the big gun has its perks.

We float past white sand beaches, shallows, small whirlpools, and countless tall pine trees. The other rangers are paddling, lost in the typical ranger grind, but along with the RI, I can just sit here peacefully and admire the beautiful, idyllic scenery.

I am actually doing this thing, I reflect, I am about to start the last field training exercise tomorrow. I am on the threshold of finishing this course.

After naively arriving at Ranger School with three weeks preparation, poor equipment, and no idea what I was in for, after almost quitting, yet rising again, I have shown that I can hack it here, that I can "ranger" just as well, if not better, than some of the most elite soldiers in the U.S. Army. I have won the respect of and even become friends with bat boys like Newton and Salvador. I have capably assisted and led seasoned officers like McCormick and young, hard-charging lieutenants like Dale. I have succeeded in this course where others have failed, including several Airborne Rangers and even green berets like Fulton, who is enduring a second hell in Mountain Phase at this very moment.

I have great confidence in each man in my squad and they have earned my trust. McCormick, Dale, Sven, Newton, and the three new Florida Recycles are all good rangers. One-third of the original squad from RAP Week remain, but those who are still here, still standing, are battle-tested and strong, or, at least exceptionally good at blending in and never standing out, like Sven.

We have all suffered so much these last fifty days, watched so many of our comrades fall to the wayside, but I believe, I know, that we will all make it through together.

By making it straight through to Florida, the odds are greatly in my favor that after a little more suffering, a few more sleepless nights, and with a bit of luck, I will earn my Tab, leave this accursed school, and rejoin my comrades in Iraq as a ranger-qualified sergeant.

I cannot wait, but for now, I am just going to enjoy this scenic river float.

After a half-hour of paddling, our boat's RI, a Captain, starts chatting with me.

"You been to Iraq already, ranger?" The RI asks me.

"Yes, sir. Spent last year in Diyala province."

"When are you going over again?"

"My unit is already there, sir," I tell him with a hint of shame in my voice for not being there with them. "I'm looking forward to getting out of this damn school and joining them as soon as possible."

"That's the spirit, ranger," the Captain says approvingly, speaking to me like a real person. "And you'll be there soon enough, but in the meantime, take the time and training you are given here and use it wisely. Learn what you need to learn, do what you need to do, so that you can go back to Iraq, and share it with your men."

"Yes, sir."

Then to the entire boat, motioning with his ornamented walking stick, the RI says, "Take us to the shoreline up there, yes, right there, rangers. I want you all to disembark and form a security perimeter."

We do as the RI orders and pull onto a white, sandy beach. I dismount from the Zodiac boat along with the rangers from Assault One squad. We form a basic, semi-circular perimeter with little effort, and point our weapons outward into a dense grove of pine trees.

"Looks good enough to me, rangers." He tells us. "Back in the boat. Let's turn around and paddle back to the launch site."

Everyone else must paddle even harder up the Yellow River now, but my leisurely cruise is just as pleasant as before. I continue to chat with the RI while enjoying the beautiful scene. At one point a single powerboat filled with loud and intoxicated college students roars past us, going the opposite way. There are girls on the boat, one is even in a bikini. They hoot and holler at us as they roar by. We don't mind.

We make it back to the launch site by one p.m. and back to Camp Rudder by two. The day's training is over. Two RIs form up Charlie Platoon in the dirt and asphalt field in front of the barracks while they take a headcount and tell us what we will be doing the rest of the day.

I stand near the back of the formation with my 240B and do not pay much attention. There is a pleasant-smelling ocean breeze and a warming ray of sunshine beaming squarely on the back of my neck.

I feel good, really good, renewed, light-headed, and euphoric even after today's visit to the river. I feel as ready as I'll ever be to tackle the last FTX of Ranger School.

The RIs designate the first set of leaders for the next day, the PL, the platoon sergeant, and the four squad leaders. I am not among them. The airborne-qualified rangers are jumping into the field exercise tomorrow morning, so they want the leaders to plan the mission and issue the op order tonight at 6:00 p.m.

Charlie Platoon is released to the barracks to plan and prepare for the last ten-day FTX of Ranger School. Tomorrow's leadership and the half-dozen lieutenants who always do more than their fair share of the planning get to work writing the order, preparing the terrain model and, as usual, arguing incessantly over which SOP or standard operating procedure is the right one to utilize in dozens of scenarios. I, like many in the platoon, wisely stay out of their way and instead patch up my equipment and pack my rucksack.

I start to feel light-headed and a little feverish as I put the finishing touches on my gear and tighten down the straps of my rucksack. At five minutes to six, I clamor onto the top of one of the bunk beds that have been arrayed in a semi-circle around the whiteboard at the front of our barracks room. My left knee feels a little stiff, but I shrug it off as I settle in next to Newton, the closest person I have to a friend here, and prepare for two or three hours of sheer op order boredom.

I happily observe that our bunk bed is one of the farthest away from the buck-toothed RI, the only RI supervising the order. It is quickly apparent that he is deeply absorbed in the op order itself and pays little attention to what the members of the audience are doing.

The truth is, I want to stay up for the operations order, I really try to stay awake, but it is impossible. I am just so damn warm and comfortable up here in this bunk, nestled up close with my buddy Newton, who leads the way, as always, by promptly falling asleep the second the op order starts.

There is nothing to worry about, I tell myself as my eyelids slide shut for good. I know this stuff backwards and forwards by now, give me a task and a direction and I will get it done.

I lean my head against Newton's shoulder and instantly descend into deep, dreamless slumber.

Two hours later

I wake from my long nap to the sounds of three-dozen rangers clambering down onto the floor from their bunk beds. The op order is over. I missed the whole thing. Still sitting on the top bunk, I sleepily rub my eyes and stretch my arms up into the sky. I feel great, clear-headed, and rested.

The only problem is, I cannot bend one of my legs. The left knee is immensely swollen, red, mottled, and engorged with hard fluid. It has doubled in size in a few hours and looks grotesque. Not only is it incredibly painful to touch, but it is also so swollen and stiff, I cannot move it, no matter how hard I try.

What madness is this? There is no way I can start the Florida FTX like this. What the hell am I going to do?!

Newton and Dale help get me down off the bed. I wince in pain when I place the slightest amount of body weight on my left leg. I make a futile effort to walk a few normal steps, but I simply cannot bend my knee. It is locked in position with fluid, pus, and whatever the hell it is that is growing inside me.

Newton cursorily examines my knee and shakes his head side-to-side soundlessly. He knows I'm a lost cause.

What is happening to me? I ask the higher powers. Why now when I was so close to getting out of this place?

They do not answer. All I know is, tomorrow is the start of the ten-day field exercise, and after a week of relatively soft living, it is back to the harsh life of the field ranger again. Back to eighty-pound rucksacks, reduced rations, all-day and all-night marches, and little to no sleep.

Right now, I cannot even walk a few steps with only pants and a t-shirt on. I'm fucked.

0630 Hours (6:30 a.m.)
Aid Station, Camp Rudder
Eglin Air Force Base, Florida
Day 48 of Ranger School
Day 1 of Sick Call

"Looks like cellulitis, dear," the pleasant, stout, middle-aged nurse tells me. "A very bad case of cellulitis. The doctor is going to need to examine you to see whether you have to go to the hospital for this."

"Does that mean I'm not going to the field today?" I ask naively.

"You're not going anywhere, kid, not this morning at least," she says confidently as she jots down some notes.

My symptoms: intense swelling, red, warm-feeling skin, inability to move the limb, and pain when I place weight on the limb, make it readily clear that I have cellulitis, a common but potentially serious bacterial infection inside my skin.

"The doctor doesn't come in until eight." The nurse turns off the lights in the almost empty sick bay. "So, in the meantime, get some rest."

"Yes, ma'am," I respond cheerfully. "That is something I can do."

I've had cellulitis before, in the same knee in Darby, but there it was a minor inconvenience at best, a small infection that barely registered among my numerous other aches, pains, and spiritual crises. The medics diagnosed it quickly, gave me seven days of antibiotic pills to take, and before the meds were gone, I was cured, or so it seemed.

It must have been festering this whole time, dormant in Mountains, only to emerge with a vengeance after my plunge into the Yellow River. This time, a few pills are not going to fix me.

And what can I do? No matter how tough and inured to misery I am, no matter how strong my will, I cannot simply power through this sudden affliction, this act of God. I know there is no way I can keep up with a ranger platoon in my condition. I cannot hump an eighty-pound rucksack, conduct a beach landing, carry a casualty, run from a mortar attack, or assault anything. In truth, it is a monumental struggle just to drag myself to the bathroom to relieve myself while standing clumsily on one leg.

I cannot do anything about it, not today, so I might as well let the doctors try to fix me. Maybe they can have me back on my feet in a day or two. Anything is possible. After all, this is Ranger School.

In the meantime, I should utilize this unexpected opportunity to rest. This hospital bed is mighty comfortable compared to a fox hole and since I am the only patient in the aid station, the room is deathly quiet. I am warm, and so long as I do not move my leg, I'm not in much pain.

Still not caught up from the severe sleep deprivation of RAP Week, Darby, and Mountains, and never one to turn down precious slumber, ambrosia to a ranger student, I fall asleep instantly.

Ninety minutes later

"Wake up, Goldsmith. Wake up, soldier."

The doctor, a tall and heavily built Captain in ACU fatigues, shakes my shoulder gently to wake me.

"Yes, sir," I say sleepily as I stretch my neck and open my eyes. "Are you here to fix my knee."

"No promises," he says as he pulls on some latex gloves, "not until we see what we're working with."

He examines his first and only ranger patient of the day. He confirms the nurse's cellulitis diagnosis and has me attempt to move my leg. By now, the knee joint is even more swollen, has an off, zombie-like pallor, and is straight and stiff as a pirate's peg-leg, incapable of bending. I was able to limp on it over to the aid station two hours ago, but there is no way I could walk more than ten feet on it now.

The doctor prescribes a regimen of strong intravenous antibiotics. He has the nurse insert an IV into my arm and advises that if the infection does not improve in a day or two, I will have to go to a larger, better equipped civilian hospital. Otherwise, I could risk serious, even life and limb-threatening health consequences.

This is all fine and dandy, but all I want is my Tab, so I only have one question. "Doctor, am I going to be able to make it back out to the field exercise?"

"That important to you, huh? Well, anything is possible, soldier," the good doctor sighs. "Let's re-evaluate in a day or two. My understanding is that you are allotted three days or seventy-two hours of sick call, maybe we can get you better before then. But until that time, we need to see how the infection responds to the antibiotics and that leg needs to rest."

I must not look satisfied with his answer because the good doctor adds:

"The best thing you can do right now is catch up on your sleep. You think you can do that?"

"Yes, sir, that I can do," I say firmly as the doctor finishes writing his orders and walks out of the room, switching off the lights on his way out.

Again, the room is bathed in semi-darkness. Left to myself in the Aid Station for who knows how long, I have ample time to plan and strategize.

I have a little over seventy hours to get well enough to throw on a rucksack and complete the FTX. Totally possible! I tell myself. I know I can do this! I affirm even stronger. I must! I cry inside, because otherwise, I will recycle.

And this painful eventuality cannot become my reality. I resolve to beat this infection, to utilize my down time here to store up a surplus of sleep, to make it out to the FTX strong and well-rested to lead men, destroy the Opfor, accomplish the mission, and earn my Tab.

This should not be too hard of a problem. I had cellulitis before, and it cleared up rapidly with the proper medicine. Things look bleak right now, but I've already conquered so many, seemingly greater challenges in this place, what's one more obstacle?

I easily and guiltlessly sleep away the entire day, only periodically rousing myself from unconsciousness when the nurse comes to check on the IV lines dripping saline solution and antibiotics into my arm.

I fully awaken just after five p.m., after the rest of the ranger class have already jumped out of airplanes and trudged many miles under a heavy pack through the swampy coastal pine forests of the Florida panhandle. I have not eaten since breakfast, and I am ravenously hungry. I notice an unfamiliar feminine silhouette at the far end of the room. Her back is turned to me as she inventories some supplies.

"Excuse me, uh, nurse?" I say politely, almost timidly. "Do you know how a guy can get some dinner around here?"

"Oh? You're up finally." The nurse, a young woman in army fatigues, turns to face me and walks over to my bed. "We thought you died on us, ranger." She laughs. "How's that knee feeling?"

Honestly with all the sleep, I feel fantastic, especially now that I am in the presence of a goddess. Other than the middle-aged and elderly ladies who work in the chow hall, who are non-sexual, motherly figures to all but the most depraved rangers, this is the first time I am seeing a woman in two months.

And what a woman! She has large, dark-brown eyes, a cute, perfectly sculpted little nose, luscious, dark lips. Her skin is perfectly tanned, olive-colored and unblemished, free of even the slightest speck of dirt. She has shiny, dark-brown hair tied back into an army regulation ponytail. Her loose army fatigues try hard but cannot hide the trim, shapely figure that lies underneath.

Best of all, she does not smell like body odor, she is not encrusted with dirt, swamp water, sweat, blood, or grime, and she does not have a five o'clock shadow. She is a beautiful young woman with the scent of a flower. Her fingers are delicate, her uniform is spotlessly clean, she wears specialist rank, one grade below my own, and her name tag says her name is Birdie, a ridiculous name, Nurse Birdie. I am in love.

The goddess is still standing there, beautiful eyes wide open, awaiting an answer.

"Oh, uh, my knee?" I manage to say lamely. "I'm doing great, but my knee…" I turn my attention to my crippled appendage. It looks even more swollen and inflamed than before. When I try to bend it, it hurts, and does not budge a millimeter.

"I don't think my knee is doing so well," I say sadly. "I don't know why this had to happen now."

"Those antibiotics should start kicking in soon and we'll take good care of you," she tells me confidently. "Hopefully, we can stop the infection from growing any further. Maybe we'll even have you back out there with your boys again. Don't worry so much, ranger."

The way she says "ranger" sends tingles down my spine.

"Trust me," I tell her coolly, "I'm in no hurry to leave this place."

"Good," Nurse Birdie says sweetly, "because you're our only patient right now, and it'll be nice to have someone to take care of for a change."

Could this day get any better?

I wish this moment would last forever, but a hungry ranger must eat, so I get down to business.

"So, Nurse Birdie…"

"You can call me Marie."

What a heavenly name, I think to myself before flashing sad puppy-dog eyes at her and asking the really important question, "So, Marie, how does a guy get some food around here?"

"That's a good question. See, I'm new around here, I have only been here a few weeks. Don't you guys have your own rations or something?"

"No, well uh, not exactly…" This is a bald-faced lie, I have three MREs in my rucksack, my allotted food ration for today and tomorrow, not ten feet away from me. And while I hate lying to sweet Marie, rangers must take care of their stomachs above all else, and it would be nice to have some extra MREs when I do make it out to the field exercise.

"Well, I'm taking my dinner break in the chow hall in about fifteen minutes. I'll bring you back something good. Don't worry, ranger, I'll take care of you."

And she does. Nurse Marie brings me a sumptuous dinner: a double portion of chicken thighs and drumsticks, mounds of mashed potatoes, corn, peas, and carrots, milk, three slices of bread, and all of it soaked in a half-inch layer of thick yellow gravy. Dessert is a piece of chocolate cake. Meanwhile, the other rangers out in the field have nothing to look forward to but vacuum-sealed, preservative-laden, bowel obstructing MREs. They may even get to eat them sometime tonight, at two in the morning, lying around in some mud hole, if they are lucky.

But not me, I am taken care of. I am sopping up gravy with mashed potatoes and licking chicken grease off my fingers, I am lying in a warm bed, seated next to a beautiful young woman, who seems to derive no little joy from taking care of me. I cannot believe the sudden reversal in my fortune.

Maybe this cellulitis thing isn't so bad after all.

"I got a surprise for you, ranger…"

"Yeah?" I suppress the urge to shriek with delight. "Not another needle in my arm, I hope."

"No," she giggles, "not until tomorrow morning, but no, not that." Marie drops her head to my level, glances guiltily behind her to make sure no one else is watching, and then whispers. "But we have to keep this quiet—it'll just be our little secret, okay?"

I nod my head up and down. I do not know if I have ever been happier in my entire life.

"I brought you some ice-cream bars from the chow hall. They're in the freezer. You want one?"

Ice cream, sweet precious ice cream, in Ranger School? Hell yeah, I want it. If I knew recycling was going to be this sweet, if I only knew Nurse Marie was here, waiting for me, I would have recycled a long time ago. Sleep all day, eat ice cream at night, get taken care of by a gorgeous nurse... this is all too good to be true, I must be dreaming.

Marie walks outside of the room to get the ice cream from the freezer. While she is gone, I sit up straighter in bed, brush the crumbs off my bedding, and place my hands in my lap like a good little boy.

Marie comes back with a bar of vanilla ice cream coated in a milk chocolate hard shell. She has the grace and good manners to leave me alone for a few minutes with my precious treat. I gulp it down in six or seven bites before sheepishly calling out to her.

"Marie, you think I could have another one?"

"No, ranger," she chides me playfully, "one is enough. I don't want to spoil you too much."

You'll brook no argument from me, sweet Marie.

"I'll see you tomorrow," she tells me. "I've got some paperwork to do before I clock out for the night."

"Thank you, Marie," I tell her wholeheartedly. "Thank you for, for... everything. You've been so kind to me, so very, very kind. After all I've been through, you've been so..."

"Don't mention it," she interjects coolly. "Now, try to get some sleep so that your knee can heal. I don't know how you're going to do it though; you've practically slept all day."

"Trust me, sleeping is not going to be a problem. Good night, Marie."

And before she can even turn off the lights, belly full and with a grin on my face, I am sound asleep again.

1115 Hours (11:15 a.m.)
Aid Station, Camp Rudder,
Eglin Air Force Base, Florida
Day 49 of Ranger School
Day 2 of Sick Call

"Ranger, you have rhino skin!"

Nurse Marie's latex-gloved left hand holds the top of my wrist as she works hard to push an IV needle and catheter into a vein on the top of my forearm. "I've never known someone so hard to stick. I think I blew another one!"

"Been living pretty rough the last two months," I respond coolly.

"Sheesh, this school sure does a number on you guys. I hear it's pretty hard, is it for real?"

For the last seven weeks and until yesterday, until I met you, Marie, I have not known true peace, rest, or a full stomach. There has not been a day without pain, self-doubt, struggle, and seeing the best and worst of myself and my fellow man. I live with the constant anxiety of being recycled or thrown out of this school tab-less, a complete failure, someone who failed to measure up to the ranger standard. This place has robbed me of any residual pride or shame as I can now defecate in pits in front of a dozen other men without a trace of awkwardness. My once invincible twenty-two-year-old body has been bent and broken and beat-down as never before in my life, far worse than anything I have ever experienced in three years in the infantry and during a combat tour to Iraq. I have eagerly eaten out of the garbage, marched countless miles while dreaming, and suffered from repeated delusions and hallucinations involving fantastic, impossible creatures in the trees.

"It's pretty damn hard." What more can I say, unless you have been here, you wouldn't understand. I change the subject while she keeps probing for a new usable vein.

"How long have you been working here, Marie?"

"Oh, only since a week or two before your class came in. This aid station was short-staffed, and they needed some temporary help, only for a month or so, until your class graduates. When you guys finish, I'm done, too."

Destiny brought us together, Marie.

"Well," I tell her, "I'm glad you're here."

"Ugh! The veins in your right arm are all blown to the wrist. Want to try the top of your left hand?"

"It's not important where you stick me, wherever is easiest for you." In this aid station, chivalry isn't dead.

"Oh, you rangers are sooooo tough." She teases me as she walks around to the other side of my hospital bed, grasping a new needle.

I don't fear the needle, not when you hold it, Marie.

"No, really, tell me," Marie pauses, holding the needle poised above the ripest-looking vein on my left hand, "is this school as hard as they say it is?"

This is nice. Unlike most women, unlike most people in general, she genuinely wants to know.

"Marie, I can honestly say it's the hardest thing I've ever done, probably ever will do."

"Have you deployed?"

"Spent a year in Iraq, in the infantry, running patrols, doing missions. I'm going back with my boys again for another year, maybe longer, as soon as I finish this course."

Marie nods her head knowingly. "I've been to Afghanistan, got back a few months ago," she says without offering more. "So, you're telling me this school is harder than Iraq?"

"Yes." I only have to think about it for a second. "Absolutely."

"You guys are all crazy, you know that? You actually volunteer to come to places like this and torture yourselves, all for no good reason. Why do you do it? Why do any of you guys put yourself through it?"

"Do what? This? You mean Ranger School? Iraq? Afghanistan?"

"Yes. Any of it, all of it?"

I do not have a ready answer, not one she would understand anyways, so I tell her, "We do it for the Tab."

Nurse Marie shakes her head, laughs resignedly, re-aims the IV needle above my left hand, and says, "You ready?"

I nod my head up and down. Yes. Pierce me, Marie.

The needle tip pushes into and then pierces my skin at a forty-five-degree angle. A small squirt of blood leaks out the backside of the cannula and splashes onto my forearm. Nurse Marie drops the angle of the needle to about thirty-degrees and expertly slides the catheter into my vein before withdrawing the needle again.

I exhale, realizing I have been holding my breath the entire time. It was a good stick, quick and relatively painless. Nurse Marie secures the catheter to the back of my hand with medical tape and starts working the IV apparatus constantly pumping three kinds of antibiotics into my bloodstream.

"We'll get you back out there with your boys soon, you crazy ranger. Now, hurry up and heal. I'll bring you some lunch in an hour."

You are a sweet, blessed angel, Marie.

"I'll get back out there, but trust me, I am in no hurry."

0605 Hours (6:05 a.m.)
Aid Station, Camp Rudder
Eglin Air Force Base, Florida
Day 51 of Ranger School
Day 3 of Sick Call

"Ranger, you have less than an hour of remaining sick time," some RI I have never seen before tells me as he reads off a clipboard. "Are you ready to come out to the field?"

It is my fourth morning in the sick bay. I have spent seventy-one hours here. I am still the only patient and the other rangers have already spent three entire days out in the bush. Meanwhile, I have been lying around, getting fat, and sleeping away the days like a newborn infant.

"I can't... my knee, it's still... grotesque." My response comes out weak and uncertain.

"What was that, ranger?" The RI raises his voice and looks me in the eyes. "Speak up!"

"I can't, Sergeant," I respond a little more firmly. "My knee can't bear any weight still, I just, I just couldn't do what it takes out there, Sergeant."

It is the truth. My knee is as swollen and painful as it ever was. Last night I collapsed in the bathroom while urinating because I placed the slightest amount of weight on it. I am still on non-stop IV drip antibiotics and the doctor has yet to rule out sending me to the real, civilian hospital.

I cannot walk to the bathroom, let alone strap on an eighty-pound rucksack and move through a swamp. I cannot raid, I cannot dig a fighting position, I would be completely and utterly useless. Truth is, I would not last an hour out there, my comrades would literally have to carry me through the remaining seven days of the field exercise. I can't do that to them.

"You understand that if you don't come out to the field in the next hour, you are going to recycle this phase?"

I nod my head up and down, meekly assenting. "I understand, Sergeant."

"Then consider yourself recycled, ranger." The RI dashes off something on his clipboard. "When you're healthy enough to walk out of this place, report to Sergeant First Class Williams, he's in charge of the Recycles. There are four of you now. He'll oversee you until the next class starts up, which, because of Christmas Exodus, is going to be a while."

And with that, the RI executes an about face and walks out of the aid station, leaving me alone with my sorrow, pity, and self-scorn.

I am a Recycle now.

All day I think about the other rangers in my class, struggling out there in the field, no doubt facing some of the greatest challenges of this course without me. They are suffering now, while I live in relative luxury, but in a week, they will return, many of them with a Tab. They will be done with this school, moving on with their life and re-joining their brothers in arms, while I will be stuck here in Purgatory, a worthless Recycle.

Who knows if my knee will even heal and, if it does, who is to say I'll be able to walk on it carrying an eighty-pound rucksack and a machine gun? Assuming it does heal, knowing the Army, I will have to spend days, weeks potentially, doing stupid, time-wasting work details like picking up cigarette butts, painting rocks, and moving furniture and supplies from one shipping container to another. Eventually, I will have to join a new class of rangers, men who do not know nor trust me, go through another Florida Techniques Week, and then pass the FTX. After all that hassle and time, there is still no guarantee my cellulitis will not flare up again or that some other terrible Ranger School tragedy will not strike me down.

Psssh! I thought I could earn a Tab. What hubris!

I cannot sleep now because I have already slept too much these last three days. Now that I am finally caught up on my sleep, my biggest problem will be insomnia.

In the long daylight hours, there is nothing to do in the aid station. There is nothing to read, no magazines, no novels, no military manuals even, nothing. There is no work to do, no one to talk to, so I stare up at the ceiling, daydream, and sulk. I self-analyze and make great and heartfelt vows of temperance, industry, and charity.

I have run out of sympathy and Nurse Marie treats me differently now that I am a Recycle. Nothing is ever said, but she does not sit and chat with me any longer. Bringing me food from the chow hall has become a chore for her, the portions she brings grow increasingly smaller and lacking in extras like milk, peanut butter, and bread slices. Needless to say, there is no more ice cream.

I do not blame her. I used to be a wounded ranger, recovering my strength to undertake an impossible mission, but now, I am just a patient, an invalid, a Recycle.

After a few days of eating well, sleeping away the day, and lying around doing nothing I have put a lot of weight back on. The time indoors has caused my skin to lose the glow of the sun. I lie in my own stale sweat, and I have not bathed in over a week because it is still too painful to stand on my own two feet.

"You might want to take a shower tonight, ranger," are the only words Nurse Marie speaks to me on the sixth day of my sojourn at the aid station. It is more of an order than a suggestion. The magic between us is clearly gone. This place does not feel like a home and refuge any longer.

With nothing to do and no one to talk to, I go stir-crazy. Feeling both anger and sorrow for myself, I interrogate myself mercilessly through the long, sleepless hours of the night.

Why now, you worthless Recycle? Why did you have to break down now? I ask myself for the thousandth time.

"I don't know! This wasn't my fault! I was doing good, until this happened."

You wanted this to happen. You wanted your body to quit. You're still nothing but a useless, fucking quitter, like you were in Darby!

"No, I didn't want this to happen! I swear, I was ready to finish this thing. I am stronger, tougher than I was back then."

Then why couldn't you finish this damn thing?!

And so on, and so on, until the sun rises again in the morning.

2301 Hours (11:01 p.m.)
Aid Station, Camp Rudder
Eglin Air Force Base, Florida
Day 4 of being a Florida Recycle
Day 7 in the Sick Bay

It is late at night in the aid station. The lights are off, but the darkness is lightly illuminated by the artificial glow of display screens and LED lights on medical equipment. Like every other night, I cannot sleep. I lie there and make the usual promises to my future self to live a full and virtuous life, and in particular, to never be idle or waste a single moment ever again.

Suddenly, the light switches are thrown and every overhead light in the large room comes on. Two RIs walk onto the middle of the floor. One of them is the amiable bucktoothed RI from Charlie Platoon.

"Now, I know there is an ice machine in here somewhere... where is it?" he says.

"There it is!" the other RI exclaims.

"Let's fill 'er up!"

The RIs are in a hurry to fill their cooler with ice and for several moments do not even realize I am in the room. I cough to make my presence known.

The buck-toothed RI turns with a start to face me. "Oh! Didn't know anyone was in here. You must be our ranger from Charlie Platoon who recycled a few days ago."

"Yes, Sergeant. It's me, the Recycle."

"You know, ranger, I was supposed to grade your patrol the other day."

"Roger." I sigh, imagining for a moment that I was with my platoon, still in the running for my Tab. "Instead, I'm here, a failure."

"What's wrong with you, ranger?" he asks me.

"Cellulitis in my knee, Sergeant—" and then I add self-piteously, "my body just quit on me."

"No, I didn't mean that, ranger, I meant, what is wrong with your attitude?" The RI stares me straight in the eyes and bores into me with his intense, open-eyed stare. "Don't be so down on yourself. Shit happens, ranger. Nothing you can do about it sometimes. Besides, there's nothing wrong with recycling, just a chance to spend some more time here and learn even more."

"But I almost made it straight through, Sergeant." And then I laugh out loud, "Imagine that? Me, a mediocre infantryman, and I almost made it straight through."

"Almost? Almost don't mean shit! You either make it through or you try, and try, and try again. It's that simple. You understand, ranger?"

"I guess, Sergeant..." I say halfheartedly.

"Buck up, ranger! There is no shame to recycling, in fact, and here's a secret, between me and you," the RI leans in closer to me, "only real rangers recycle."

The RI stands there regally, as if he said something very profound, awaiting my response.

"What do you mean?"

"What I just said, that only real rangers recycle. Some of the best team and squad leaders I had in the Ranger Regiment recycled, real leaders, real men, they recycled. Some good officers, too. Hell, I recycled when I came through, twice, and hey, Johnson, didn't you recycle, too?"

The other RI nods his head up and down silently as he shovels handfuls of ice into his cooler.

"Know this, Ranger School will let you finish when it's good and ready, when it's done with you, when you have learned the lessons you need to learn, when you've earned it, and not a single moment sooner. You understand now, ranger?"

"I guess so, Sergeant." I am starting to warm up to the idea, but I am still a little skeptical. Up until now, I have always thought about recycling as a purely negative event.

"Recycling teaches you something about yourself that those who make it straight through will never know. Just because you somehow passed through a phase doesn't mean you necessarily earned it. Some rangers make it through this course with the aid of blind luck, by being carried by their squad mates, or by gaming the system. Some rangers manage to pass through this entire course without once confronting true failure and, somehow, finding a way to rise above it. But Recycles, they know better than anyone what it means to truly want something, to really want the Tab, and to have the guts and determination to make it a reality, regardless of the cost, and no matter how long it takes. You understand what I'm saying, ranger?"

I nod silently at the RI's sage words.

"You think you're the only one who has suffered here? Everyone struggles in Ranger School, that's the whole point. Short of combat, this is the only way to find out who you really are, who you are capable of becoming. The only question that matters is this: when things are falling apart and nothing is going to plan, can you step up and lead when everyone else just wants to curl up into a ball and die, when they've already quit?"

I have already marched hundreds of miles on blistered feet; slept as little as an hour or two a night for weeks; endured countless layouts, stress tests, and smokings by the RIs; dealt with rain and mud, injury, and hellish terrain; indignity after indignity; and mind game on top of mind game. I have seen the strong preying on the weak and the closest of friends betray each other. My body has prematurely aged and been riddled with cold, hunger, injury, and infection. I have endured the endless solitude of an "everyman" cast adrift in a strange land occupied by savage beasts and hostile tribes. My soul has been constantly tormented with anxiety and self-doubt; my cognition plagued by delusions and hallucinations.

The RI is right. What's a little recycling in the big scheme of things? I ask myself. Nothing, that's what.

"If something is easy, ranger, it means less, in fact, it usually means it's worth absolutely nothing at all." The wise bucktoothed former bat boy RI says, "Ranger School is not easy for anyone, don't let them tell you anything different, but for the Recycles, it's even harder. And guess what? That makes the experience even more valuable."

Yes, yes, I see it now.

"You can fail as a leader in the planning or execution of the mission. You could get lost on patrol, the weather might not cooperate, or sometimes, everyone is just droning. Your squad might hate your guts, for good or bad reasons, and Peer you at the end of the FTX, or maybe, as you know, you might get too sick or injured to physically go on. There are a hundred ways to recycle, but only one way to be a failure, and that is to quit."

"And only one thing to do now, Sergeant."

"What's that, ranger?"

"Earn the Tab," I say firmly. "Do whatever it takes to earn the Tab."

"Exactly, ranger, exactly." He looks pleased. "You learn from your mistakes and then you try and try again, as many times as it takes, until you do it right, or die trying. That is what it means to be a ranger. It's not just jumping out of airplanes, blowing in doors, and shooting terrorists in the face, not just that anyways, being a ranger is knowing that nobody is entitled to anything – if you want something, you have to earn it, the hard way, and failure just can't be an option. Recycles know this better than anyone. They know, that in the end, there is nothing sweeter in this world than wearing the Tab."

The RI thumps the Tab he wears on his left shoulder with the knuckles of his right hand.

"You want it, ranger? Do you want it bad enough?"

"Abso-fucking-lutely, Sergeant," I say with true conviction.

"Good. Then earn the Tab, ranger, it's that simple. In a day, two days, five days, whatever it is, you're going to get out of that hospital bed, do whatever stupid details we tell you to do until the next class starts up, and then you'll get back into the suck again. If you're good enough, if you're lucky enough, you'll finish and earn your Tab, and if you don't, then hell, you'll just try again and again, until we kick you out of this school or you graduate.

Understand, ranger?"

I do.

"When it comes to the Tab, when it comes to the mission, when it comes to life, rangers finish what we started, we do not just go some of the way, we go–"

All the way.

Chapter 12: "Back to School"

There is no gift more valuable than fire, no sight finer than the sun.
— The Havamal

Rule #20: Rangers don't fight fair.
Rule #21: When in doubt, attack!

1301 Hours (01:51 p.m.)
January 2008
Camp Rudder Training Area
Eglin Air Force Base, Florida
Day 60 of Ranger School
Day 1 of the Florida FTX

It is the first day of the Florida FTX, the very first hour even, when every muscle in my legs starts horrendously cramping up. Too soon I realize that despite all my foreknowledge, preparation and planning, during this, my second shot at Florida, I have screwed up once again.

I should have drank more water on leave, I scold myself, and certainly, I should have drank less beer.

Over the course of the last fifteen minutes, first minor and then serious leg cramps have been developing in my legs. Now, every muscle in both legs is flexed, tensed, and locking up. It is increasingly difficult to force my knees to bend so that I can keep walking forward. I walk stiffly and peg-legged, like a pirate, tears streaming out of my eyes because of the pain. My body is no longer conditioned to bear a heavy rucksack load for hours on end, not after four weeks as a Recycle and easy living on leave. My back and leg muscles are soft and unconditioned, the calluses on my feet, hard won in Darby and Mountain phases, have disappeared.

My legs barely function, but I must keep moving. I do my best to ignore the pain, mentally forcing my legs to step off the ground and drive forward, each and every step. I am on the verge of physical collapse and seriously close to calling it quits. The only thing keeping me going is shame, anger, and momentum.

And this is unfortunate, because I am the security squad leader today, getting graded and evaluated by the RIs at this very moment, and with these cramps, my head is barely above water. The enemy Opfor chooses this moment to attack us.

A rag-tag band of three or four of them start shooting at my Alpha Team from a small grove of pine trees set on a small rise about three hundred meters to our front. Positioned near the front of the platoon formation, I can see them popping their heads up to shoot at us with rifle fire.

The entire platoon hits the dirt while the men in my squad get on line and start shooting back at the Opfor. Once I see them all shooting, I turn around and start low crawling on my elbows and knees to our rear, looking for the platoon leader who should be coming up to my position.

"Goldsmith!" Hernandez, the imposing green beret and today's PL, yells at me over the blank fire. His firm, steady voice and striking six-foot-six frame allow me to quickly identify him. "How many of them are there?"

"I saw three or four, five at most." I manage to hiss out through the searing agony in my stiff and spasming legs. "Want my squad to lay down a base of fire for one of the assault squads?"

Hernandez ponders this for a second. He looks at the surrounding terrain and the bulk of the platoon, two squads plus, stretched out almost two-hundred meters behind us.

"Negative." He says decisively. "Leave your Alpha Team and a machine gun as a base of fire and you lead your Bravo Team in an assault up the left flank of that hill. Take them in the side, take them fast, so that we can get moving again. Can you do that, Goldsmith? Can I count on you?"

If I were being honest, I would say no. Not in my condition, not with these cramps. I can barely walk, let alone lead a cross-country running assault against a team of Opfor with a group of men I barely know, suffering from the worst leg cramps I have ever had in my entire life.

But when a badass special forces legend like Sergeant First Class Hernandez asks you to do something, you get it done. My "go" on this patrol, and Hernandez's as well, depends on my ability to clear up this little nuisance and get the platoon moving forward again.

"Of course, Hernandez." I put on a brave grin. "I'll get it done."

Here goes nothing.

Welcome back to Ranger School.

Until these accursed cramps, round two of Florida Phase of Ranger School was going well. After a week of rest and IV-infused antibiotics in the aid station, the cellulitis in my knee cleared up, and the leg was good enough to walk on. After spending another week as a Florida Recycle working in the chow hall, picking up cigarette butts, and emptying storage containers, my knee was back to baseline health. It was then that the rangers in my former class, including Newton, Dale, McCormick, and Sven, returned triumphantly from the FTX, celebrated with beer and pizza at Gatorex, earned their Tabs, and left the course, and my life, forever.

Then something unexpected happened. Unbelievably, I was able to leave, to go back to my childhood home in sunny Southern California, because even a training course as tough as Ranger School shuts down for Christmas or "Exodus" leave for two weeks every year in December. I received the unexpected boon of being able to rest, recuperate, and even have a little fun, as if I were a regular person, in the real world, before undertaking my second and probably last attempt at passing Ranger School.

To prepare for the inevitable deprivation, I ate and slept as much as humanly possible so that, days after the New Year, I returned to the course fat, healthy, and well-rested, about as prepared as I could be for the hunger and sleepless nights to come.

Or so I thought.

Along with Sol and Tobes, two fellow Florida Recycles I have grown close with, I got assigned to Bravo Platoon, one of three platoons making up my

ANDREW GOLDSMITH | 261

new class, Ranger Class 02-08. It was then I quickly learned that the Bravo RIs were not as laid back as Charlie Platoon. They treated us with respect, rarely smoked us, and gave us twenty minutes to eat an MRE, but otherwise, they trained us like the Mountain RIs, from early morning until ten or eleven at night. Moreover, they closely supervised our standard operating procedure sessions to make sure we were not just bullshitting and encouraged us to do endless rehearsals with any leftover down time.

Despite the grind, I was and remain happy with my new platoon. I have joined a tight knit, egalitarian group. They are used to working together, yet at the same time, are eager to embrace and utilize the knowledge and experience of the eight Florida Recycles now added to their ranks. A week into Florida Phase, and after spending every waking moment with each other for days, we are all on friendly and familiar terms. We are one tribe, Bravo Platoon.

Hernandez, the singularly impressive special forces sergeant first class with multiple bullet-wound scars in his check and neck, is the unspoken, universally acknowledged leader. He is intimidating and awe-inspiring, the archetype of a warrior, but also friendly, and easy to talk to.

I have also been reunited with Salvador. His palsied neck somehow managed to heal, and he has struck up a fast friendship with Hernandez. Sol, Tobes, and I remain close after our recent Recycle experience. They were generous enough to share the box of MREs and candy bars they stashed in the ceiling of the Recycle barracks before we left for Exodus. Bailey and Tobiri are also in the new platoon, though not in my squad so I do not talk to them much.

Best of all is my new battle buddy, my assistant machine gunner and near-constant companion, Staff Sergeant Powell. He's a thirty-one-year-old, mechanized infantryman from my sister battalion back home in Colorado. One of the old men of Ranger School, he is of average height with a husky build and a reddish, Irish complexion. He is constantly cracking jokes, usually at the RI's or Ranger School's expense, and without fail, can be found with a dip in his lip, chewing tobacco like the Ranger School students of old, despite the severe consequences if he is caught.

Unlike with Tobiri, my assigned battle buddy who collapsed in Mountains, and my bat boy friends, who will always consider me an outsider, I forge a true bond of brotherhood with Powell. For the first time in Ranger School, I find myself with a genuine ranger buddy, someone I can trust, a friend. It has made things a lot easier.

After all the feasting and rest, after being accepted into a new and highly effective team, and after gaining a partner, I thought this second time through Florida would be a breeze.

But these vicious cramps in the very first hour of the FTX are showing me that I was wrong, terribly wrong about that. My body can still fail me in a hundred different ways, my will and my wits will need to be as strong and sharp as ever if I want to get through this thing, and earn my Tab.

Although I am in excruciating pain and can barely bend my knees, Hernandez needs me to assault an enemy position hundreds of meters to our front. Until I dispatch the enemy, the platoon will be pinned down, useless, the mission delayed and even in danger.

Somehow, I rise onto one knee, rally my Bravo Team, and run through the pain. We take the hill from the Opfor, the RIs do not drop any of us as casualties, and I again thank my lucky stars that these are blanks we are shooting, not real bullets.

The platoon is free to start moving again, towards the objective, and Hernandez is visibly pleased when I see him again.

"Good job, Goldsmith." He tells me laconically before waving us forward again.

It is a great start to the FTX.

Only two-hundred-and-thirty-five more hours to go.

Seven Hours Later

We make it to the objective rally point at dusk and finish laying in our ambush under the cover of darkness. I split my security squad into two teams and order them out to the separate far ends of the dirt trail. I go out with my Bravo Team and settle into our position. They watch the trail and the surrounding woods. I mostly stare one hundred meters away into the "kill zone," a thirty-meter section of trail with a gentle bend marked by three swaying palm trees and a clear field of fire.

And there we sit for three hours—an unbelievably boring, but at the same time tense, three hours. We sit and stare out into nothing in complete darkness, waiting for the enemy to appear by the green glow of our night vision devices. Security squad's main job here is to spot the enemy first and give early warning to the rest of the platoon before the ambush is initiated. If we fail in our job, the ambush could be ruined.

Fortunately, this is the very first night of the FTX, so we are all comparatively fresh. We have little trouble staying awake, something that will certainly not be true in the days to come.

It is after eleven at night when my Alpha Team Leader, who has been faithfully watching the trail, calls in on the platoon radio network.

"Psssshhh. PL, they're coming. Psssshhh. We can see four or five Opfor walking down the trail, headed east, over."

An anxious second or two passes before Hernandez coolly responds. Psssshhh, "I see them, too. Psssshhh. Weasel, gun teams, prepare to initiate the ambush on my command." Hernandez is also wide awake and alert as he kneels behind cover, concealed by foliage, and with the two assault squads arrayed in a line beside him.

The first Opfor guerrilla enters the kill zone, but Hernandez waits and does nothing. A second one enters, walks forward a few steps, pauses, and turns around, before walking forward again. Today's machine gunners, Salvador and Tobes, caress their triggers lovingly, aching to fire them, but still Hernandez waits.

A third, fourth, and finally, the fifth and last of the raggedy Opfor band enters the kill zone. He walks five, ten meters forward, before Hernandez shoots him with a three-round-burst of fire from his M4 carbine, and suddenly, the night sky is lit up by muzzle flashes and deafened by the roar of a half-dozen machine guns.

This pitiful band of Opfor, barely a fire team, does not stand a chance. We tear up their bodies with imaginary bullets and they all drop to the ground within seconds.

We keep firing for a few moments longer. The three palm trees marking the kill zone sway in the breeze, illuminated by flashes of blank fire. It is a beautiful and savage scene. As a member of the security squad, observing the trail into and out of the kill zone, I have little to do other than watch the action.

Hernandez orders the machine guns to cease firing, and the assault squads bound through the objective. They clear the kill zone, set up a perimeter on the far side of the trail, and search the objective. Hernandez then pulls everyone off the ambush site in a phased withdrawal as we simulate blowing up the enemy's weapons and supplies with explosives.

It is the best ambush I have seen in Ranger School. I am very lucky to have gotten a graded patrol on the very first day of the FTX, especially with Hernandez as the platoon leader.

The platoon reunites at the Objective Rally Point to retrieve our rucksacks and begin our night march to the patrol base. This is always a slow, disordered process, and tonight, the enemy chooses this exact moment to counterattack us on multiple fronts, just when we are the most exposed.

Chaos erupts. Half of us have our rucksacks on, the other half are still looking for their gear. The squads are mixed up and, in the darkness and over the sounds of gunfire, it is impossible to figure out who anyone is. Leaders desperately look for their men and men for their leaders. People shout out orders, but no one can hear them.

I'm able to locate my Alpha Team easily enough, but in the din of the blank fire and excessive shouting, it proves impossible to find Bravo Team.

"Where's Bravo Team?" I yell at my Alpha Team Leader, hoping he has some idea of their position.

"Beats me, boss." He shrugs his shoulders. "Just tell me where to shoot."

But I don't know where to shoot, that's the problem. For the moment, I cannot clearly distinguish the muzzle flashes of my fellow rangers from those of the enemy. The last thing I want to do is shoot our own people, some of whom have pushed out into the woods and are returning fire, so I advise Alpha Team to hold their position and not fire at anything unless they are completely sure it is the Opfor.

"I gotta go find Bravo Team!" I yell at the Alpha Team Leader, "I'll be back!"

In the darkness and confusion scattered teams of men fight the Opfor piecemeal while others hunker down and look for their rucksacks. Everyone is shouting, running in different directions. It is absolute chaos.

I run around by myself looking for Bravo Team, but I cannot find them. Just as I am about to despair, I stumble across a lone fire team from one of the assault squads, hunkered down behind their rucksacks in the darkness, sitting out the fire fight.

"Hey!" I yell at them, "Where's your team leader?"

"Right here," a tall bat boy I barely know responds. "Who are you?"

"It's Goldsmith. I'm the security squad leader today. Where's the rest of your squad?"

"Your guess is as good as mine."

Pop. Pop. Pop. Looking out at the spot I left Alpha Team, I can clearly see three Opfor shooting at their position. I watch their muzzle flashes light up in response as they return fire.

"You want to work with us to get these motherfuckers?" I ask the bat boy team leader who is also observing the firefight.

"Let do this!" he responds eagerly as he orders his men to stand up and follow me.

With my impromptu team of reinforcements, I rush back to Alpha Team's position. They may not strictly all be my men, and who knows where my Bravo Team is right now, maybe they're all "dead," but at least I have a full squad again, enough to maneuver on and destroy the enemy shooting at us. Sometimes, in Ranger School, you must adapt, go with the flow, and do the best you can with what you have got.

And when in doubt, in the absence of orders . . .

ATTACK!

I order my teams to start bounding towards the enemy, one battle buddy pair shooting while the other moves closer. My ad hoc squad has never worked together before, but each fire team does a superb job of providing covering fire for the other and sticking to their lane as they dash forward in five- or ten-meter increments.

It does not take long for my squad to move through the Opfor position and shoot down the opposition. The blank fire ceases on our end of the battlefield at the same time as the attack on the other end.

Peace once again restored, the night resumes its silence. I am reunited with Bravo Team, the rest of the platoon re-organizes into their respective squads, and after fifteen minutes of confused searching, we are finally able to locate everyone's rucksacks and get them on our backs.

It is after midnight by the time we are ready to march through the coastal forests again, to our patrol base, three klicks away.

We still have a way to go before this night is over, and I know with near certainty that I will not get more than two hours of sleep tonight, if we are lucky. But despite losing Bravo Team during the madness of the Opfor attack, I remain optimistic about my prospects for getting a "go" on this patrol.

Florida, Part II is looking promising. I tell myself as I tighten my rucksack straps for several hours of night marching.

But things were just getting started.

0012 Hours (12:12 a.m.)
Camp Rudder Training Area
Eglin Air Force Base, Florida
Day 63 of Ranger School
Night 3 of the Florida FTX

Forty-eight-hours later and I feel terrible, beat-down, like complete and utter shit—the way only Ranger School and captivity in a North Korean gulag could make you feel. The last two nights, I have slept a combined total of three hours and after three days of walking all day under a heavy pack, humping a machine gun, digging foxholes, and freezing at night, the deep and insatiable hunger that I have not known since I recycled has returned.

After two days of performing well, cracks start to appear in Bravo Platoon. I see lethargy, selfishness, and even insubordination for the first time. Apparently, no one is immune from the stress and exertion of Ranger School. If borne long enough, it will reduce even the most cohesive and high-performing team to the lowest common denominator, an undisciplined mob of droning, selfish rangers.

Once again, life becomes primordial, a constant struggle to save energy and avoid injury. Once again, we must husband our strength, make shrewd calculations, and withstand hard tradeoffs to survive, pass our patrols, and earn our Tabs.

We arrive at the patrol base after midnight, just like the last two nights. It might just be me starting to hallucinate, but the terrain seems unusual in that small unnatural rises and depressions are scattered throughout the interior and the edges of our triangular patrol base, reminiscent of some kind of bumpy Dr. Seuss-like landscape. Tonight's platoon leader, platoon sergeant, and squad leaders decide to make do with the terrain and emplace the platoon in battle buddy pairs along the triangular perimeter. Powell and I man a machine gun at one of the apexes of the triangle. The PL orders everyone to "dig in for the night."

And in Florida, they really mean "dig in," as in, pull out our foldable shovels or "e-tools" and dig hasty fighting positions and machine gun pits into the cold, hard ground. These are not small holes either. A hasty fighting position is at least the length and width of a man, and a gun pit is much larger. Digging in is a foundational infantry skill, and critical in combat when real bullets and shrapnel are flying, but fortunately for us, it was a task the RIs in Darby and Mountains did not require.

But in Florida, every night when we pull up to the patrol base, we must dig great big holes with our little hand shovels before we can even think about putting on warm clothing, eating an MRE, or getting some sleep. It can take an hour or two for a motivated buddy team to dig a decent-sized hole for two or three people. It always take a while because only one man in a pair can dig at a time; the other must be pulling security in case of enemy attack.

Just part of the life of a Florida ranger.

Honestly, on cold nights like tonight, with temperatures in the forties or lower, I do not mind the digging. It keeps me warm and occupied as other rangers in the platoon settle into the business of establishing the patrol base, including putting out claymores, designating sectors of fire, drawing sector sketches, cleaning the machine guns, and a dozen other tasks that can take an hour, two hours, or even longer.

Me and Powell have been taking turns digging and pulling security, shivering in our drying sweat, for only about thirty minutes when something odd happens, something I have never seen before, only heard about in whispered tones from the bat boys.

I see one, then two, and then three fires appear in rapid succession at various points around our patrol base perimeter. Their flickering flames lighten the night sky and send tendrils of smoke rising into the heavens.

"What are they doing?" I ask Powell as I drop my e-tool and stare at the distant flames. "There is no way they are already done digging their hasties. Do you think the RIs gave them permission to start those fires?"

"Eh!" Powell raises his head slightly behind the gun, turns his head to the side, and ejects a fat wad of tobacco juice and saliva onto the ground. "Who knows?"

"Are they trying to get us blown out of here? What the hell! The patrol base isn't even established yet!"

"Guess the leadership doesn't give a shit tonight." He lets more dip spit fly before asking philosophically. "Can you blame 'em?"

Rumor has it that in Florida, during the winter, the RIs will sometimes let the platoons light small warming fires once the patrol base is established. In Techniques Week, I discounted these legends, believing them to be too good to be true. But after watching the fires burn for ten, then twenty minutes without any obvious alarm or disapproval from the RIs, I know that the speakers were telling the truth.

"Hey," I say to Powell, "I'm getting pretty sore over here, want to take the shovel? Another thirty, maybe forty minutes of digging, and our gun pit ought to be about done then maybe we can light our own..."

A flash of light suddenly flares up behind me. I turn around to find that while I was digging, Powell took it upon himself to build our own fire out of MRE cardboard trash, pine needles, and dozens of small twigs and sapling branches.

"I'm going to find some more fuel, Goldsmith. Our gun pit is deep enough, at least for the night. You should stop digging."

I am not in a leadership position tonight, and other than risking a major-minus, there would be no serious consequences for me if the RIs found our gun pit to be deficient. But still, Powell's suggestion makes me anxious.

"I don't think we should, I mean," I tell Powell nervously, "the patrol base isn't established, at least as far as we know, and... and... what if the RIs find out that we are starting too many fires and what if..."

Part of me is shocked to see such a squared-away platoon openly flaunting Ranger School taboos. Deep in my bones I feel—no, I know—that we will be punished for this: blown out of the patrol base, given major-minuses, smoked, and marched all night.

But Powell, as usual, is heedless of any consequences and lacking in concern. He does not respond to my nervous mumblings and simply walks off somewhere to gather sticks and branches for firewood. Meanwhile, I keep guiltily digging my hole.

More fires pop up around the patrol base, at least a dozen now, and still nothing happens. Eventually, it seems like every battle buddy pair in the

Fire: A Winter Ranger's Best Friend

Bring your lighter!

Fire Provides:
- Warmth
- Hot food and drinks
- Entertainment
- Meditation and rest

USE LOTS OF DEAD DRY TWIGS OR KINDLING FOR QUICK STARTING, FAST-BURNING FIRES

MRE cardboard and paper trash works great too!

platoon has one, and some of them are roaring, emitting thick plumes of strong-smelling smoke.

Finally, I lay down my shovel. I too decide to embrace the night's madness.

The hilly, pock-marked patrol base looks even more other-worldly by the light of the flickering flames. The fire and smoke create an eerie, green, orange, and yellow low-hanging ground mist that swirls around our ankles.

Our light discipline utterly compromised by the warming fires, our noise discipline soon goes along with it. We lose control over our tongues and start talking at normal, even excessively loud volumes, as if we were at a block party back home. The sound of our constant chattering bounces off the trees and low-rising hills around us and can probably be heard half-a-mile away.

Any enemy Opfor within miles would be able to see or smell our position, but we do not care. There is no sign of the day's RIs, and the platoon leadership has clearly condoned the abandonment of our usual duties.

By one a.m., men are freely floating around the perimeter of the patrol base. Those rangers whose positions lack fires abandon their spots on the line to join one; those enjoying small fires abandon those to join larger ones. Powell's fire is one of the biggest and brightest. Five other rangers from who knows where have joined us. They eat snacks from their MREs and warm their hands by the flame like hobos.

Still bewildered by the breakdown in discipline, I ask one of them, "What are you guys doing here? Does your squad leader know where you are?"

"I am the squad leader," one responds casually, before chuckling dementedly to himself.

"Well, what the hell? No one's doing any priorities of work, this patrol base looks and sounds like a gypsy camp. Aren't you worried about getting a 'no-go' on your patrol?"

"Hell, man," he says, sounding almost annoyed, "it's after one in the fucking morning and the PL doesn't seem to care, why should we?" He points off to another roaring bonfire off in the distance. I can just barely make out several dancing shadows that look like gremlins darting amongst the flames. "There he is with a bunch of the bat boys, having a good 'ol time."

"Jesus H. Christ..." I sigh to myself resignedly as I stare into Powell's fire and feel its warming rays on my thighs and chest. Then the realization dawns on me.

Fuck it, no one else cares tonight, so I don't either. I grab my rucksack, open the top flap, and grab my dinner MRE. Besides, if the RIs haven't shut

Ranger Sleep System and "Snivel Gear"

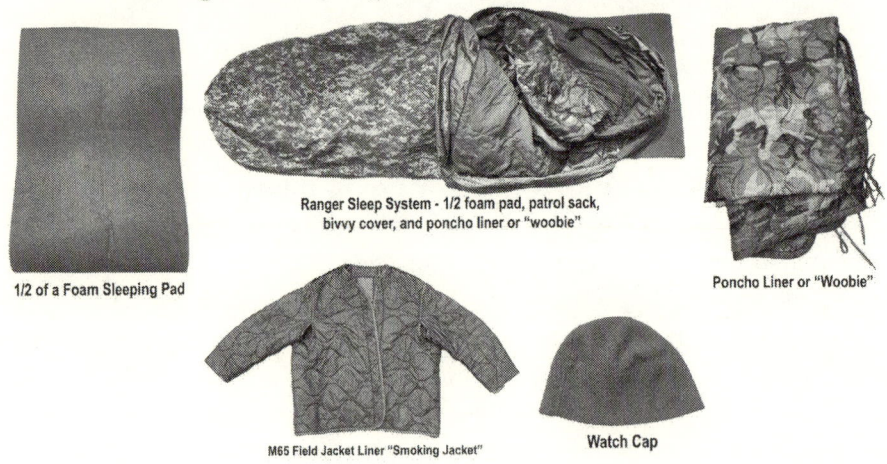

1/2 of a Foam Sleeping Pad

Ranger Sleep System - 1/2 foam pad, patrol sack, bivvy cover, and poncho liner or "woobie"

Poncho Liner or "Woobie"

M65 Field Jacket Liner "Smoking Jacket"

Watch Cap

us down by now, they probably never will. They must be sleeping somewhere in their own camp, oblivious to this madness.

We keep the fires burning most of the night, every ranger in the platoon positively intoxicated by sleep deprivation and fire light. Even stalwart green berets like Hernandez and Tobes have given in. We lose track of time, enjoying ourselves as if we are at a raging high school field party. We laugh and swap war stories from the barracks and training, Iraq and Afghanistan, Darby and Mountains.

By two a.m., men start drifting back to their hootches and sleeping bags, many lying perilously close to still burning fires. Others decide to stay awake long into the night, tending to the flames, happy and content.

At one point, I am pretty sure I see two RIs emerge from the bushes, shake their heads in dismay, and look menacingly towards me and the other rangers around our blaze. I nudge Powell in the ribs, but before I can get his attention, the figures have slipped back into the bushes again. Not sure if I really saw them or not, I keep my mouth shut, so as not to ruin the party.

Later, as I lie down in my sleeping bag, under smoke-obscured starlight, and start drifting off to sleep, I feel light-headed and pleasantly warm. My sleeping bag lies close to our now low-smoldering fire. Powell stirs the coals with a stick, spitting tobacco juice and saliva into the burning slag. He talks to Salvador and some other rangers in a low tone.

I sleep for an hour-and-a-half, but it feels like twenty. No one wakes

anyone up for fireguard tonight.
    We are too far gone.

0203 Hours (2:03 a.m.)
Camp Rudder Training Area
Eglin Air Force Base, Florida
Day 67 of Ranger School
Day 8 of the Florida FTX

"Aaaaahhhhh! Aaaaaaaahhhhhhhh! Aaaaaaaaaaaaahhhhhhhhhhhhhhhhhh!"
    I hiss and growl in muted agony, writhe and twist inside my sleeping bag, as I am awoken yet again from deep slumber by horrendous cramping in my leg muscles. After a minute of intense anguish, the pain and spasms subside enough for me to slightly bend my knees and massage my muscles with cold, stiff hands. After a minute or two of this, the cramps diminish enough to allow me to crawl out of my sleeping bag and stand up.
    How long was I asleep? I ask myself as I rub my eyes and gaze at me and Powell's nearly extinguished warming fire, nothing but small glowing embers and ashes now. Powell is curled up inside his sleeping bag, sleeping soundly, snoring even. As far as I can tell, no one is pulling watch or even tending to their fires in our sector. Everything is dead quiet.
    I look down tiredly at my watch. It tells me it is just past two a.m. in the morning on what is now technically the eighth day of the Florida FTX. I add some MRE cardboard, tree bark, pine needles, and large twigs to the smoldering ashes of our warming fire, blow into it, and watch it quickly roar back to life.
    I stare deeply into the fire, my fire, and I am happy. I really should be sleeping. I have not slept more than an hour or two every night for a week now, sometimes less and, in less than two hours, everyone will be up for another fun-filled day of Ranger School, doing God knows what.
    The night is still pitch black, dawn a long way off. I stare at my dying fire for several long moments, undecided as to whether I should go back to sleep or stare into the flames just a little while longer.
    Suddenly, I hear two rangers talking somewhere off in the distance.
    "You hear about what happened, brother?"

EXAMPLES OF PONCHO SHELTERS OR "HOOTCHES"

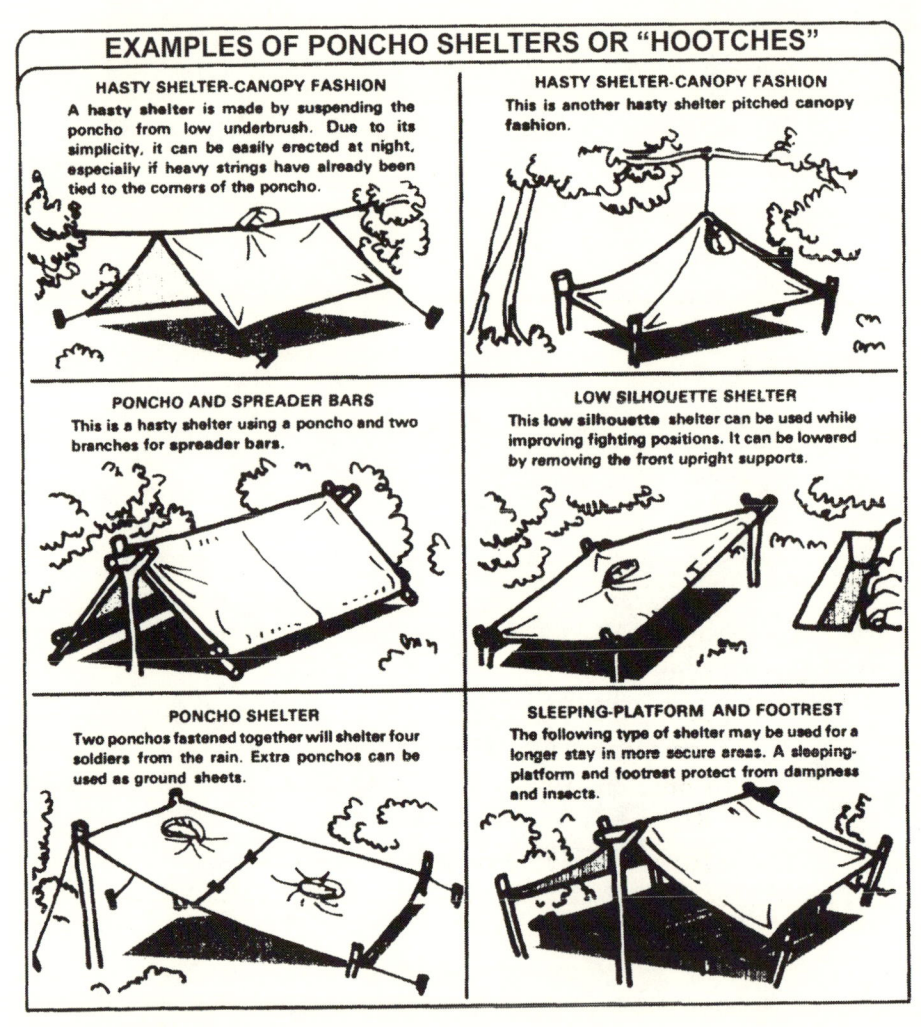

HASTY SHELTER-CANOPY FASHION
A hasty shelter is made by suspending the poncho from low underbrush. Due to its simplicity, it can be easily erected at night, especially if heavy strings have already been tied to the corners of the poncho.

HASTY SHELTER-CANOPY FASHION
This is another hasty shelter pitched canopy fashion.

PONCHO AND SPREADER BARS
This is a hasty shelter using a poncho and two branches for spreader bars.

LOW SILHOUETTE SHELTER
This low silhouette shelter can be used while improving fighting positions. It can be lowered by removing the front upright supports.

PONCHO SHELTER
Two ponchos fastened together will shelter four soldiers from the rain. Extra ponchos can be used as ground sheets.

SLEEPING-PLATFORM AND FOOTREST
The following type of shelter may be used for a longer stay in more secure areas. A sleeping-platform and footrest protect from dampness and insects.

"No. What?"

"The RIs came through our patrol base an hour ago, and guess what? They found the whole platoon sleeping."

"No shit! We're screwed! Hell, what'd they do?"

"I'll tell you what they did. They stole a machine gun from one of the gun pits, detached the grenade launcher from my M16, and then they went back to their RI camp."

"Oh no! We're fucked, man, we're fucked! We gotta get our stuff back, we gotta..."

"Calm down, calm down! It's okay, brother. I waited a few minutes then I

M240B 7.62mm Medium Machine Gun and M122 Tripod

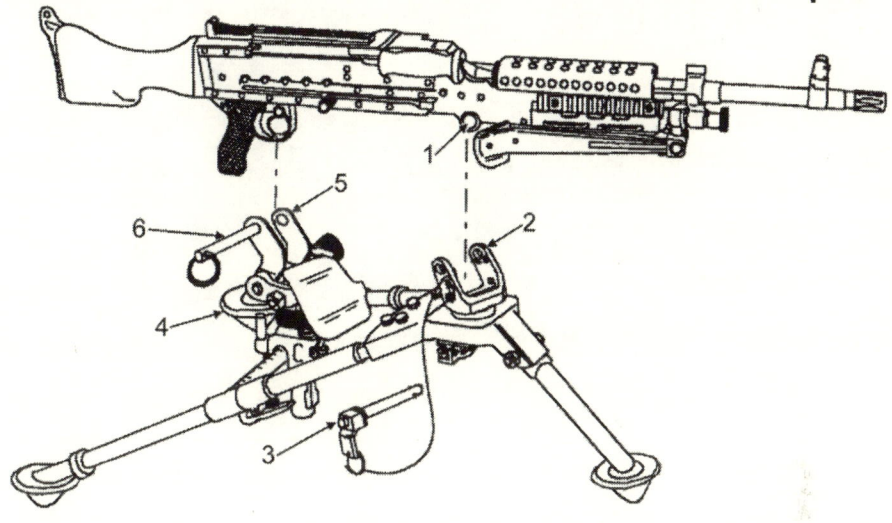

crept down to their camp and found them all sleeping, so I took our machine gun and grenade launcher back, and helped myself to a few of their snacks, right from under their noses."

"Wow! That's incredible, dude. Almost unbelievable!"

"Yeah... it was pretty harrowing, but you know the hardest part was..."

But I am not listening to the two mystery rangers any longer. THE RIs TOOK A MACHINE GUN! The thought chills my blood. Could it have been our machine gun? That hero ranger says he stole it back, but what if they wrote down the serial number?

I hastily pull on my boots and scramble to my feet. I take a few steps into the darkness towards the shallow machine gun pit me and Powell dug a few hours ago. That is where the machine gun should sit, facing outwards, watching the final protective line of one of the three legs of our triangular patrol base.

But I can't find it. I cannot find the machine gun. I was sleeping mere feet from it, but finding the machine gun proves to be difficult. I scramble and grope around in the darkness, feeling for cold, hard steel, but I keep coming up empty. I turn left, walk a few paces, find nothing, and return to where I started. I turn right, walk a few paces, stumble into tree branches and trip and fall over some brush, and still, I find nothing. I walk back towards my warming fire, nothing but smoldering coals, and Powell's sleeping figure, and

The Machine Gun Team — Ammo Bearer aka "Ammo Bitch", Machine Gunner, Assistant Gunner

start again, but after several increasingly frantic moments of searching, I just cannot find it.

Why can't I find our machine gun! My mind screams at me, though I already suspect the answer.

Maybe the RIs did take it!

I fan out and frantically search the surrounding area but even after tripping over several sleeping rangers and their rucksacks, for the life of me, I just cannot find the machine gun.

The damn thing should be less than six feet from where Powell and I are sleeping, a four-foot-long, thirty-pound machine gun mounted on an ungainly, thirty-pound metal tripod, and still, I cannot find it.

The RIs must have it. I think grimly. Must have dragged it off into the woods and back to their camp. I take several steps away from the patrol base and into the surrounding woods, trying to imagine the route they must have taken. It is hard to see by the dim moonlight and I cannot shake the foggy, dream-like feeling clouding my senses.

After several moments of directionless wandering, I suddenly stop, realizing that I am far outside of the patrol base, deep in the woods, and dreadfully alone.

How did I get so far out here and which direction, exactly, did I just come from? With the realization that I could now be lost, a cold jolt of terror shoots through my spine. Where is the patrol base?

But before I can truly panic, my nose detects the unmistakable aroma of wood fires, and the scent instantly calms me. I walk towards a small clearing and look up into the night sky in the general direction of where I just came from. I can see several small plumes of rising smoke, trailing into the air before dispersing, and I know instantly where I can find the patrol base.

Thank the ranger gods for those fires, I think as I trudge back towards our platoon's patch of earth for the night, or I would be off wandering senselessly into the swamps, eaten by an alligator or dying of exposure before the sunrise.

I walk for a minute, and I am back in the patrol base again, stumbling over my own sleeping bag.

Using it as a sure point of reference, I center myself and concentrate.

Focus, Goldsmith, focus. I take a long, deep breath. Powell is right here, the gun pit is there, so the gun should be... right... there.

And miraculously, there it is, ten feet from my sleeping bag and right in front of my face, the 240B, the same one I have been carrying all day, facing out, in the proper position, right where we left it just a few hours before.

The RIs didn't take it! I exclaim to myself exuberantly, clasping my hands together, and staring upwards gratefully towards the sky. Or if they did, at least they brought it back!

But then I see something I would have thought impossible, a terrible, gruesome sight. Someone, some fiend, has sawed off the barrel to the machine gun.

No, no, no, no, no, NO! What is this! What kind of madness is this! I feel like my head is going to explode. Who would do such a thing!

I am instantly in panic mode again. The RIs do not have our machine gun, but someone, them, or somebody else, has sawed off its barrel. There is no way I can explain this, nothing I can do to save myself. One of the big guns has been disabled by the enemy, on my watch, while we slept. I am done, finished, and Powell with me, maybe the rest of the squad, too. There is no coming back from this, no way.

What kind of sadistic motherfucker would bring a hacksaw out to the range and do this to us?!

Seized with terror, no longer capable of dealing with this situation by myself. I rush over to Powell and wake him up in a frenzy.

"Wake up! Wake up! Wake up, Powell! WAKE THE FUCK UP!"

"What?... What!" Powell rubs his eyes but remains lying down in his sleeping bag. "Goldsmith, what do you want!?"

"They did it! The RIs, the Opfor, somebody else... I don't know how, I don't know why, but they did it, they actually did it!"

"What the hell are you talking about?" Powell says bewildered, still not fully awake.

"The barrel, Powell, the machine gun barrel! It's gone, they sawed it off!"

"Go back to sleep, Goldsmith. You're either dreaming or you've gone crazy."

"Look for yourself! It's gone, Powell, it's fucking gone!"

"Can't be. Impossible."

"C'mon on, Powell, if you don't believe me, just look for yourself. C'mon, Powell, LOOK!"

Powell tries to shrug off my frenzied requests, but I am persistent. "All right, Goldsmith, all right. Let's check it out, then."

Powell does not have to go far. He does not even have to leave his sleeping bag. He simply unzips it a bit, sits up, and glances at the machine gun, barely two arms distance away.

"See! See! Look what they've done," I yell at him excitingly before glancing at the gun barrel, "look what... they... did?"

The machine gun is sitting there, right where we left it, and of course, there is nothing wrong with the gun barrel. It is perfectly fine, if not a little dirty, every thing in the right place, including the barrel. There is no sign that anyone tampered with it.

"I … I saw... How is this possible? The RIs, they... they must have put it back..."

"Get some sleep Goldsmith, we have to wake up in an hour. You need it, obviously."

Stupefied, no longer able to trust in my own senses, I do as Powell tells me and I crawl back into my sleeping bag. The moment I close my eyes, I fall instantly asleep.

An hour later, I wake up feeling guilty and ashamed about what I have done. Over the next few hours, while the day's leadership plans the patrol, I surreptitiously ask around about a missing machine gun, but no one has the vaguest idea what I am talking about. I also ask if anyone knows who the ballsy ranger was who undertook the raid to retrieve our stolen items last night. I get nothing but vacant looks and concerned stares.

It is hard to believe I imagined or hallucinated the whole thing, it all seemed so real. Maybe the brave ranger is just being modest about his heroic action or prefers to stay anonymous to avoid getting in trouble.

Or, just maybe, the mystery rangers were forest spirits, trying to lure another hapless victim into the forest. That might be the real reason the Florida RIs let us have fires at night. To guide us back in, if we become lost.

Whatever the case, I should stare into the fire a little less and get more sleep.

1535 Hours (3:35 p.m.)
A beach near Destin, Florida
The Gulf of Mexico
Day 67 of Ranger School
Day 8 of the Florida FTX

"This has got to be the lamest, most overhyped, low-speed, high-drag school in the entire fucking U.S. Army…"

Two squads of rangers sit in the darkness, mostly silent, in the back of a tarped-over five-ton truck, where we have sat for an hour, doing nothing.

"I cannot believe the Army actually tricked me into coming here. I mean, look at me, I'm no spring chicken! Hell, I'm a five-year staff sergeant, I've been getting fucked by the Army for a long time now, and yet, they still got me to volunteer for this?! I should've known better…"

Outside we can hear seagulls cawing and the sounds of passing traffic. It is a beautiful, sunny winter's day on the Gulf Coast of Florida, and we all wish we could get outside and soak up the sun's warming rays. We must be out somewhere in the regular, civilian world, otherwise the RIs wouldn't be hiding us. It is probably a good thing to shield their innocent eyes from our wretched ranger appearances and warped minds.

Powell, my battle buddy, is fired up and ready to rant. We egg him on, eager to break up the monotony.

"Ranger School is so fucking stupid!" he continues. "All they've done from the moment I got here was shit down my throat and make me call it ice cream."

Powell pauses to spit his tobacco juice into a water bottle.

"I can't believe I missed two pre-deployment months with my wife and kids for this. Hell, all my men are in Iraq right now, doing God knows what, probably led by some douchebag, and here I am, locked in the back of a truck like a circus monkey with you smelly, stupid ass clowns, playing cowboys and Indians in the swamps!"

The back of the truck is hooting and hollering now, everyone laughing heartily at what would have been ultra-taboo to say or even think when we all started this course a few months ago.

"And these fucking RIs," Powell starts speaking even louder, "these fucking guys! I don't see a combat patch on hardly any of 'em. What the hell! It's two thousand-and-eight, what rock have these guys been hiding under? I mean, we've only been at war for six or seven fricking years now, I only got, I don't know, two fucking years in Iraq already and about to start a third!"

Several heads nod knowingly. Powell is not the only one in the truck with multiple combat tours.

"I know pimply-faced, cock-sucking first lieutenants, no offense to present company, with more combat experience than these school-house commandos! Hell, they all think they're so high and mighty here, wait until I catch one of these guys out on the street, or in a future unit, I'll show them what's what... I'll... I'll..."

Powell starts flailing his hands around like he is boxing, really getting into his rant when an RI unfurls the tarp flap attached to the five-ton truck's tailgate and pokes his head into the back of the truck.

"What's going on in here, rangers?" he asks us, silent again. "I'm hearing a lot of noise. Keep it down!"

"Roger that, Ser-geant!" Powell yells, sounding extra cheerful and compliant. The rest of us snicker and try to stifle our laughs.

The RI does not say anything as he lets the flap down and re-ties it to the tailgate. The RI is gone for two seconds before Powell goes back to talking smack.

"You RIs aren't as hard as you think you are. There's nothing but pillows and snacks in your rucksacks. Try coming down to a line unit, a regular old infantry company, destined for endless tours to the Sandbox, see how that life suits you!"

Powell keeps us entertained with his internal rage for another fifteen minutes before the tarp flap is reopened and the tailgate is finally dropped by two RIs.

"Get out, rangers!"

Fifteen of us jump out of the back of the truck while three rangers stay back to hand down our rucksacks. After shouldering mine, my eyes adjusted to the light, I take stock of my surroundings.

I am standing on a white-sand beach, close to a major roadway, looking out into a vast expanse of blueish, green saltwater. The sun is shining but starting to hang low in the sky, there is a slight breeze, and the temperature must be in the low sixties, a positively luxurious environment for a ranger. Far off in the distance, close to the horizon, I can see several zodiac boats filled with rangers paddling off towards Santa Rosa Island, the large landmass across the bay.

One of the RIs pulls Hernandez aside to discuss something with him. Hernandez returns to relay the information.

"It's our lucky day, guys. The RIs are short on boats, so we get to wait here for a while until they can bring some back for us."

"You mean more sitting around, Hernandez?" Powell says mockingly. "Imagine that, and in Ranger School."

"Yes, Powell, more sitting around," Hernandez acknowledges, "but it's a gorgeous day and we get to do it in the sun, on a beach, so let's enjoy it."

"Can do, Hernandez, can do," Powell says coolly as he slips in another pinch of Copenhagen Longcut chewing tobacco into his lower lip. He offers some to Hernandez, who also takes a pinch and tucks it into his lip.

We all sit down in the sand and lean on each other's backs, and while away a blissful hour on a warm beach in Florida. Soon enough, we will conduct the culminating mission of the Florida FTX, an amphibious assault across the salty waters of the Santa Rosa Sound to Santa Rosa Island where the entire class will conduct a raid on the Opfor's main base.

As Powell says cynically, "It's going to be some real 'ranger' shit!"

The sun starts to set as the first Zodiac boats come back and get their final checks from the RI boat masters. We load into two boats, a squad in each one, pick up the paddles, and prepare to start rowing.

"Leave those paddles there, rangers," one of the RIs tells us. "There's no time. You lucky sons of bitches get to motor across tonight."

This is great news—we get to enjoy an outboard motor cruise. All of us are uplifted by the news, some rangers even cheer.

"Yeah," the RI says ominously, "the only thing ya'll gonna have to worry about is falling in. The swells are rough tonight, and we're going as fast as the outboards will carry us."

Indeed, it is an eventful crossing, starting at dusk and ending in complete darkness. The zodiac I am not riding in gets hit in the wrong place by a large breaking swell and tosses three rangers overboard. They are fished out of the water quickly enough, but now they are freezing in the wind chill. Four rangers in the front of my boat catch large sea waves to the chest and are soaked through to the skin with cold seawater. They are also miserable.

I am near the back of the boat, carrying a 240B machine gun. I am lucky, I only get soaked from the waist down.

With the outboard motors, it does not take long until we are deposited on the shoreline of Santa Rosa Island. Many of us are soaking wet but there is no time to change into dry clothes. We have less than twenty minutes before the hit time on the Opfor's main base so we must move quickly if we are going to be in position on time.

We dash into the wood line and, foregoing our NODs, run the short distance to the objective by moonlight. We do not have to go far before we see a large, walled enemy compound filled with Conex containers and surrounded by Hesco barrier walls packed with earth. Powell and I join the other machine guns on a small hill raised over and looking into a good portion of the compound. It is a great spot to place plunging machine gun fires on the unaware enemy below.

Powell throws down the tripod and I mount the gun. Together we lay hundreds of rounds of linked 7.62 mm blank ammunition delicately on the ground. We are ready to fire. With the rest of the platoon and the company, we await the command.

The rifle fire of one of the platoon leaders initiates the raid. The machine guns on our hill erupt immediately after. Unfortunately, my wet, semi-rusty machine gun jams twice during the first twenty seconds of firing, but with some remedial action, I'm able to get it up and running again. I fire off a few hundred rounds into the compound, at the dozen or so enemy Opfor I can see running around chaotically below us.

Everyone, an entire company of rangers, keeps firing. My machine jams again, this time seriously. I frantically clear brass and links from the receiver, pulling the charging handle backwards and forwards, while Powell, my assistant gunner, shouts out "Bang! Bang! Bang!" as loud as he can at the Opfor while also laughing wildly.

This is it, I think to myself in a moment of detachment, the culminating exercise of Ranger School, and here I am with a gun that won't fire watching my half-crazed battle buddy yell "bang-bang, I got you," like a small child to our imaginary enemy.

"Bang-bang-bang-bang! You see that, Goldsmith! I got that motherfucker!"

This place isn't so big and bad after all, huh, Goldsmith? And sometimes, it can even be a little fun.

The assault squads rush through the objective below, shooting the few Opfor who remain alive at close range with their rifles and SAW machine guns. From our position on top of the hill, now silent, we can hear them endlessly yelling below. For the moment, we have nothing to do but watch the show.

The raid on the enemy compound completed, the separate platoons of Ranger Class 02-08 retreat from the objective and prepare for the return trip to the mainland.

We still have to walk to and occupy our patrol bases for the night, and there are still two more days in the FTX to go, but there is a positive energy in the air, and everyone can feel it.

We are coming to the end of this damn course.

The finish line is so close we can almost taste it.

0402 Hours (04:02 a.m.)
Camp Rudder Training Area
Eglin Air Force Base, Florida
Day 69 of Ranger School
Day 10, the Last Day, of the Florida FTX

After a wet and miserable night sheltered with forty-four other rangers in a ramshackle abandoned house, I wake with a start. I am brutally cold and wet, my teeth chattering, and my ass is completely numb from sitting in an inch of near-freezing rainwater. My watch says it is just past four in the morning, I have slept for barely an hour, and it is still pitch dark outside, but there is no use trying to go back to sleep, I am simply too cold and uncomfortable.

I stand up and weave my way through a maze of legs and bodies to get out of the house. Once outside, I am pleased to find that the heavy downpour of yesterday has finally subsided. The rain is still coming down, but much lighter than before. However, to compensate for this relative comfort, the winds have picked up considerably and blow rain droplets one way and then another in violent, horizontal gusts of moisture. It is miserable weather.

I am the only ranger outside the house right now. Cold and bored, I do calisthenics and jog around the side yard to try to get warm.

At 4:15 a.m. a single RI appears. Seeing me, he walks over.

"You want to get a fire started, ranger?"

"Hell yeah, I do, Sergeant!" A fire sounds lovely.

"Go ahead then, ranger. Grab some of those pallets over there and stack them together right here."

He motions towards a pile of rain-sodden, chemically treated pinewood pallets stacked up neatly on the side of the house. With numb hands and the help of two other rangers recently emerged from the house, we stack four pallets on top of each other before the RI tells us, "That's good."

The RI liberally splashes the pile with diesel fuel and ignites the whole mess. In the wind and the rain, it takes frequent reapplications of diesel to keep the fire lit, and the flames only really catch after a half-an-hour, but once they do, the warmth they give off is lifesaving.

By 5:00 a.m., Bravo Platoon has a halfway decent, smoky wood pallet fire to stand by as well as an unspoken agreement with last night's RIs that if we keep our mouths shut and do not play grab ass with each other, they will let us slowly dry and thaw ourselves by the fire.

One-by-one, demoralized and half-frozen rangers rise on shaky, cold-cramped legs and step outside to join the increasingly large fire circle outside the house. Acrid, evil-smelling smoke blows into and out of our faces when the wind gusts shift, stinging our eyes, but we do not care. All that matters right now is warmth. No one talks, everyone just extends their body parts towards the flames and slowly comes alive again.

By 6:00 a.m., when the new day's RIs arrive, the majority of Bravo Platoon is outside and crowding around the fire. The RIs designate the poor souls who will be in leadership positions for the day: the PL, platoon sergeant, and the squad leaders. They brief them on the mission and order them to start mission planning inside the house.

"As for the rest of you," he tells the "Joes," the common soldiers of today including myself, "as long as you act like men and don't fuck around, you can all keep staying warm by the fire. In fact, you should build another one."

The regular Joes spend the next few, long, boring, rain-soaked hours crowded together as close to the fires as we can bear. We huddle up close to our buddies, lapping up the warming flames as well as their body heat, focused on only one goal: getting as warm and staying as dry as possible.

A few of us laugh and joke, but most of us are silent, half-asleep on our feet, sometimes nodding off and nearly falling into the flames. We are not a happy bunch, but we consider ourselves blessed in comparison to today's leadership.

The men who have been appointed leaders on this, the last day of the FTX, have almost certainly failed their prior patrols and are being given one last shot to earn their "go's." Otherwise, the handful of rangers like me who have only had one patrol this FTX would be in charge today, not Bailey and Salvador who are now leading patrols for the third time.

It is going to be a challenge to squeeze any kind of performance out of our platoon today, especially in this weather, especially after being beaten down, starved, and sleep deprived these last nine days. This is unfortunate, because without a "go" these rangers will fail this phase and either be recycled or booted out of the course entirely. They all know their chances of passing are slim, all of them are filled with anxiety and self-doubt, but they do their best, along with a handful of selfless lieutenants who help them, to plan and prepare for our final Ranger School mission.

By eleven a.m., the fires have burnt out, the mission has been planned, the gusting winds subside a bit, and the sun burns through the last of the rain and heavy mist. It gives today's leadership hope as we set out for the day. The mission: a good old-fashioned raid on an enemy command and control center.

It doesn't get more ranger than that.

My squad is security squad today and I am a regular Joe. I carry an M4 carbine and an empty AT-4 rocket launcher under the top flap of my rucksack. The day's movement is slow and ponderous, as always, but largely uneventful. Mostly, we just walk. After five hours of walking and just as the sun is starting to set over the horizon, we arrive at the raid site, a rudimentary base composed of three shipping containers, a smoldering fire barrel, a pickup truck, and a skeleton crew of five Opfor.

Security, the machine guns, and the assault squads get into position before Bailey, the PL, initiates the raid by firing off his M4. Following the RIs' instructions to burn through all our ammo, the machine guns and the assault squads fire off hundreds and hundreds of rounds each during an extended mad minute of crossfire. Then the assault teams pick up and begin to rush through the objective.

I sit on a security position overwatching a nearby road. As the assault teams start moving into the base, the truck turns on its engine and starts fleeing the mayhem. Coolly, I place my M4 carbine on the ground, pick up the empty AT-4 launcher tube, simulate preparing it for fire, stand up in the open like Rambo, place it onto my shoulder, take aim at the moving pickup truck, leading it a little bit, and press the fire button.

I shout out, "Shooom-Wooosh," to no one in particular, as I imagine a rocket-propelled warhead leaving the tube and a second later, blasting the moving truck to pieces. One of the RIs might have seen me, or it might have been the hundreds of blank machine gun rounds, but in either case, the truck comes to a complete stop several seconds later and no one exits the vehicle.

Even though this is all make believe, playing "cowboys and Indians" in the woods, pretending to shoot that rocket and taking out that truck felt good—really good—and for the briefest moment, I feel like a badass, like a ranger.

Better than that, as I watch assault mop up the objective, I know in my bones that the FTX is practically over. All we have left is the final nine-kilometer march back to Camp Rudder, something the bat boys have been warning us about since the start of my first Florida Phase.

All I can say, after enduring three months of Ranger School, the pain, the solitude, the hunger, the cold, sadness, betrayal, and sleepless nights, all I can say is: Let's go!

I am fired up. Before we march half-a-klick I take up a 240B machine gun from a grateful platoon-mate and stretch out my strides. My feet feel good, my back is strong, I embrace the march.

Expecting a long, grueling walk, I am pleasantly surprised when we pull up to a pair of five-ton trucks waiting for us on a wide dirt trail after marching for only a mile.

"Climb in, rangers!" one of the RIs shouts at us. "We're going back to camp! I don't know about y'all, but I plan on getting drunk and fucking my woman in a bed tonight. The sooner we get back to camp, the sooner we can make that happen. Let's go rangers, let's go!"

We clamber up onto the back of the trucks with an undeniable feeling of joy. The trucks drive down the trail for a while before turning onto a small, paved road. As we pass another platoon of rangers, the driver slows down to a crawl.

We peer out the side slats of the five tons and cheer our classmates on. They look haggard and remarkably skinny.

"Keep going, Brown!"

"You're close, so close, McCarthy! Just keep moving!"

"See ya at Gatorex tomorrow, sucka!"

But even the marching rangers have smiles on their faces. They know how close to the finish line they are, what's one more little ruck march. I almost wish I were out there marching with them, embracing the suck one last time, rather than riding high on this truck.

But then I turn to my left, where I see Powell's smiling, laughing face. We shake hands and heartily clap each other on the back. Sol, sitting across from us, pulls out a piece of lemon poppyseed pound cake he'd stashed away and breaks it into three pieces for us to share.

I only had one patrol during the FTX, and by now, I know I passed it. I did not earn a single major- or even a minor-minus this phase, and so long as my new squad Peers me well, which I think they will, in the next few hours I will pass Florida Phase of Ranger School. All the misery, all the suffering of this place will be over, and I will have effectively earned my Tab.

"Four more days and a wake up!" The bat boys in my truck start chanting. "Four more days and a wake up!"

All that is left now is four days of wrapping up: cleaning and turning in gear, a bus ride back to Fort Benning, a pass or two, photographs, and graduation rehearsals. Barring some grave misfortune, in five days I will be anything but mediocre, I will be a ranger-tabbed infantryman, on his way to rejoin his brothers in Iraq.

"Four more days and a wake up!" Sol and Powell and I join everyone else. "Four more days and a wake up!"

I made it through. Somehow, through all the suffering, the pain, the doubt, the solitude, the ignorance, the stupidity, and self-sabotage, I made it through.

I am going to wear the Tab.

Chapter 13: "Gatorex"

"Be content with what you have; rejoice in the way things are. When you realize there is nothing lacking, the whole world belongs to you."

– The Tao Te Ching

"[A]fter Ranger training, every day is a holiday and every meal is a banquet!"

– Col. (retired) Ralph Puckett.

Rule #22: Ranger School will humble everyone.
Rule #23: Earn the Tab, every day.

2030 Hours (8:30 p.m.)
Gator Lounge, Camp Rudder
Eglin Air Force Base, Florida
Day 70 of Ranger School

I sit at a picnic table outside the Gator Lounge, playing No Limit Hold 'Em poker with three lieutenants, two bat boys, Tobes the green beret, and an infantryman from 82nd Airborne. Half of us have pizza boxes on our laps, all of us are drinking beer. Yuenglings, Shinerbocks, Budweisers, Heinekens,

I am sipping on my fourth one after eating an entire large pepperoni pizza and several candy bars.

Someone walks up behind me and claps me on the shoulder.

"How ya doing, Goldie?" I can recognize Powell's nasally voice anywhere. "Did you ever think you'd be here, drinking beer in Ranger School, about to wear a Tab?"

"Hell, Powell," I take a swig off my Yuengling before pitching my cards into the center of the table, folding a rotten hand, "you know as well as anyone I've been utterly lost this entire time. I never knew what to expect. So, no, I never thought I would be here."

There is not a single woman here amongst a hundred-plus rangers, but still, I have never been to a better party. Unbelievably, after completing the Florida FTX, the entire Ranger Class, those who passed and those who didn't, get to drink beer and feast on pizza at the Gator Lounge during a glorious nighttime operation called "Gatorex." At this point, most of us, myself included, have earned our Tabs, and barring some unforeseen Act of God, will be graduating Ranger School.

Until this moment, I never knew that beer could taste this good, that conversations could feel so rich, that our past tales of suffering were filled with so much purpose, humor, and meaning. Most of all, I did not know that I could ever feel so close, that I could truly belong, with a group of men such as this.

This Gatorex is a vast improvement on the last one, the one where I was a depressed and forlorn Recycle busing beers and throwing away grease-soaked paper plates for my betters, guys like Newton, Dale, McCormick, and Sven, former squad mates who had earned their Tabs. That night was a rough one, one of the hardest of my life, one where my former brothers no longer spoke to me or even met my gaze.

But now, I am among the conquering heroes.

The glorious night wears on. Starting around 9:00 p.m., the teetotaling rangers and some of the "old guys," in their late twenties and early thirties, begin drifting back to the barracks for some well-deserved rest. But for the rest of us, especially the bat boys, the night is still young.

Unlike most Army-sponsored drinking events, the RIs have placed no absolute limits on our beer consumption. We are "big boys" now, they told us, future Tab-holders, capable of making our own choices, including digging our own graves.

Feisty, little Leon, who weighs less than one-hundred pounds after the ten-day FTX, drinks way too much, his buddies say eight beers, and starts vomiting in the bushes on the side of the Gator Lounge a little after 10:30 p.m.

I am nervous for Leon as I observe an RI coolly watching the scene. I fear his excess might imperil his Tab or, worse than that, spoil the party for all of us.

But the RI is in a benevolent mood.

"Get him out of here!" he tells two of Leon's buddies. "Get him back to the barracks and into bed. Don't let him puke on anything else."

"Roger, Sergeant," they respond glumly.

"And if I see any of you three again this evening, especially him," he points down at Leon's now prostrate figure, lying senseless on the grassy ground, "I'll Day One recycle all your asses! Now go!"

Leon's unrestrained drinking has ended his and his two buddies' Gatorex at 10:37 p.m., but for the rest of us, the party keeps going, at least for a little while.

Soon after, the hour grows late, especially for sleep-deprived rangers fresh from the field. Sleep starts sounding sweeter than more pizza and a bigger buzz. More of us start drifting back to the barracks in ones and twos as the clock ticks closer to midnight. I polish off one final beer, my fifth or sixth, and another half of a pizza as we close out our poker game and distribute the winnings. The night takes on a melancholy air as first Powell, then Sol, Salvador, and Tobes, all say goodbye to get some sleep before our relatively late 5:30 a.m. wake-up tomorrow.

At midnight, I too decide that it is time to go.

I walk the short distance back to the barracks by myself, swinging a sack of candy bars, technically contraband, and whistling a little tune. I too have a smile on my face as I tell myself for the hundredth time tonight: You did it, Goldsmith, you're going to be a ranger!

Yet, there is a sadness mixed in with my joy. It has to do with leaving all of this behind and going back to the "real world," of losing some of the simple things that I have learned to treasure, of never seeing some of these great men, who I endured so much suffering with, ever again.

Only they will ever know what we shared, what we learned, what we did here, in this make-believe-land where we shot blanks at the Opfor, never slept, and learned who we really are as leaders, as men. The others will not believe it, worse than that, they will not care.

Life is simple here in Ranger School. You put on a ruck, you walk all day, you walk all night. It sucked, it was terrible, but I am also going to miss it.

No doubt, in the years to come, I will look back fondly on this place and will treasure the moments that once tormented me, the people I loved, and hated, the experiences that have come to define my life.

But now, at 12:02 p.m., in the immediate moment, there is nothing to do but sleep.

Life is good. I am going to be a ranger.

Nothing but easy times ahead.

1004 Hours (10:04 a.m.)
January 25, 2008
Victory Pond
Fort Benning, Georgia
Day 74 of Ranger School
Ranger Class 02-08 Graduation Day

One hundred-sixty young and old rangers stand in an orderly formation in front of rows of bleachers packed with friends and loved ones. We have straight backs, freshly shaven heads, and huge smiles on our faces. We poke each other in the ribs and stifle the urge to laugh as we watch our families and friends 'ooh' and 'aah' over "Rangers in Action," a live-action demonstration of "ranger" skills put on by the Camp Rogers RIs.

The best parts of Rangers in Action, the Hollywood stuff, the fast roping, jumping out of helicopters, harness extractions, and intense hand-to-hand combat with weapons, we did little to none of here. This is the kind of stuff our recruiters used to trick us into joining the Army in the first place, the kind of things only Ranger Regiment, Green Berets, and Delta Force get to do in their elite units, not things we actually did in Ranger School.

But Rangers in Action has a long and storied tradition, and the families are eating it up. If they want to think we are more badass than we are, let them. They will never understand what truly conspired here, under a heavy rucksack, exposed to the elements, cold, hungry, and tired. Stripped down to our bare essences, we saw Man at his best and his worst. We experienced true horror, and undeniable triumph.

So why not give them a show, even if most of it is a myth? At the very least, it is nice to see the kids, wives, and old folks happy and laughing.

ANDREW GOLDSMITH | 291

10:04 Hours (10:04 a.m.)
January 25, 2008
Victory Pond, Fort Benning, Georgia

But still, as Powell so aptly wiseacres, "What a bunch of crap! We never did any of this stuff! All they did at this school was teach me how to be the world's greatest hobo. I want a refund!"

Even in the chilly January weather, lots of people are in the bleachers to see their soldiers graduate Ranger School. I did not even think to invite anyone because not only is my unit in Iraq and my family on the other side of the country, but I am still in denial that this moment would ever actually come. It always seemed impossible.

Yet here I am.

I do not mind having no one to cheer for me. It's nice to observe the wives and families, the commanders, the bat boy team leaders, and the green beret team members who have turned out to cheer us all on. Powell, whose family is in Colorado and preparing for his imminent departure to Iraq for yet another year, also has no one in attendance. That's okay, too. At least we have each other.

The Rangers in Action demonstration ends and the crowd breaks into applause. A hard-as-woodpecker-lips colonel I barely recognize with white hair and a dozen skill badges gleaming from his chest steps up to the podium to give a short speech about honor, courage, being a ranger, and all that jazz. There is a decent wind blowing and the colonel is not speaking in our direction, but to the audience, so few of us in the formation can even hear what he is saying. It makes it hard to pay attention, especially when Powell keeps cracking jokes.

To take my mind off the boredom and the chill wind, I think about what this course has taught me, a thousand things, really, about tactics and principles and psychology and morality and the true nature of Man. I know already that Ranger School's lessons will take decades to digest, and I may never be able to truly describe the course's deep and lasting impact on my mind, body, and soul.

But I can tell you a few things now, in this immediate moment, as I stand here in formation with some of the finest, most intelligent, meanest, and capable soldiers in the US Army. First, I can tell you that in the most dire of circumstances, the kind that Ranger School specializes in manufacturing, I stood shoulder-to-shoulder, and at times even out-performed, highly-capable and trained green berets; motivated Airborne Ranger Regiment studs; and young, hungry, learned lieutenants who will go on to lead platoons, companies, and ultimately divisions.

I cannot help but feel proud, because after all we have been through together, I have proven I, an ordinary infantryman, belong with them. I can march for days on end, sleep no more than one or two hours a night, climb mountains, and lead an assault. Not only can I survive harsh times with these men but, even and especially when the chips are down, I can lead them.

The first culminating lesson of this course is not to underestimate oneself. If you have an undying, underlying motivating purpose, you can accomplish the seemingly impossible, you can earn your Tab.

The second lesson may be even more important, and it is simple: be humble.

I do not care who you are, Ranger School will be tough and miserable. It will be tough and miserable for a Navy Seal, a green beret badass, a bat boy stud, and the number one graduate of West Point. All these men are mortals, like me, all can and will be broken down to their most humbles selves by the masterclass in pain and deprivation that is Ranger School. I know it because I saw it happen to the good ones, like Hernandez and Salvador, the bad ones, like Fulton and Jenson, and even the ugly ones, like Bailey and Tobiri. Everyone has a limit, no one is invincible, and it is what you do when you hit rock bottom that truly defines who you are.

Ranger School will humble everyone and, indeed, only the humble will survive. It will break you, exhaust you, cause your "friends" to abandon you, leave you completely and utterly alone. It will break you down to the lowest common denominator, reveal the man you really are, and strip you of any meaningless labels or group protections you may have thought you had.

In this state, if you can still complete the mission, well, you deserve to be a ranger.

After this crucible, I know who the men standing next to me are, and they know who I am, more than anyone else in this world maybe, even my brothers in Iraq. There are no secrets between us because we have been through the swamps, climbed mountains, and picked through the trash for tasty morsels, together. We have helped and hurt each other in a hundred different ways. We started this course in our separate tribes, but somewhere along the way, we lost our personas as "bat boys," "green berets," or as "regular infantry grunts." We became, quite simply, rangers.

"You should be proud of the men, the rangers, you see standing here today…"

The colonel is still talking, which gives me more time to reflect on how I got here and, more importantly, how I could help others on the same path. If I had to distill all the lessons of Ranger School down to its principles, its philosophical core, why, if I were to ever write a "Mediocre Infantryman's Guide to Ranger School," I would have to stress the following:

- *Have a purpose for the suffering you will endure. Banish the thought of quitting from your mind by remembering why you came here in the first place.*
- *Be humble. Know that the mighty can fall and never underestimate anyone.*
- *Stay flexible. Seize opportunities as they arise.*
- *Pull your own weight. Do not let the team down, suffer in silence, and do not expect a reward for simply doing your job.*
- *Help your buddies. You owe it to them, and one day they may return the favor. Suffering is also more bearable when it is shared.*
- *Keep a sense of humor. Laughter makes everything better.*
- *Use common sense. Recognize things for what they are, do not overthink things, and don't do dumb shit.*

One final thing I learned, perhaps the most important lesson, is that if you cannot be broken, you will eventually win. The human body, mind, and soul can do more than you ever thought possible. Believe in yourself, test yourself, and you can do great things.

Hell, if even a mediocre infantryman, given a little luck, can become a ranger, so can you, the reader.

I know this, because when I look all around me, at the smiling faces and gaunt cheeks of the graduating Ranger Class of 02-08, I see plenty of men who were not outwardly impressive on Day One, men who are not physical specimens, hardened combat killers, nor archetypal "rangers," men I consistently underestimated throughout the course.

But they are here, nonetheless. Somehow, they made it.

For every Hernandez, Newton, and Dale in Ranger School there is a Bailey, a Tobiri, and that pudgy, goofy transportation officer with coke can glasses and arms the size of soda straws who sailed straight through this course without stopping mostly because you just could not break him.

I am delighted to see Tobiri, my former battle buddy, standing straight and tall in front of his wife in the bleachers. I wrote him off completely after seeing him physically collapse in Mountains, but here he is, by some miracle, physically recovered and caught up with me. He will be going off to lead a combat engineer platoon at his first unit, and he will be doing it wearing a Ranger Tab.

I am also pleased to see ever-mumbling, hopelessly droning Bailey, the most friendless and isolated man in Ranger School. He had an impossibly miserable time here, rougher than anyone, abused and discounted by everybody and especially his fellow bat boys. The sleep deprivation hit him harder than any of us, severely degrading his mental faculties, which honestly, were not that great to begin with. But the guy never gave any thought to quitting, and he could sleepwalk his way through basic combat drills as good as any of us. He is going back to his Ranger Battalion a tabbed Airborne Ranger, a made man, with a new level of self-respect and confidence.

I can also see Salvador, his neck tattoos peeking out from his uniform collar. He was recycled twice in RAP Week for playing with and then killing a snake, then his neck gave out in Mountains causing him to have to go through that terrible, terrible phase twice. He too is graduating with us, along with Leon, the smallest and youngest ranger here, and certainly the one with the foulest mouth. He has recovered from his Gatorex hangover, is wide awake for once, and going back to his Ranger Battalion with a Tab. I have no doubt he will go on to lead teams and then squads of Airborne Rangers in close combat, muzzle-thumping our nation's enemies, while the rest of us sleep soundly in our beds.

If you had told me in Darby that Tobiri, Bailey, Leon, Salvador, and I would all be standing here, earning our Tabs together on the same day, I would have called you a madman.

Yet here we are.

In the end, being a ranger is not about being the guy with the strongest body, rather, it is about being the one with the strongest mind, the greatest will, the clearest purpose, and the willingness to do whatever it takes to complete the mission.

Any mission, no matter how difficult.

"... and before I conclude my remarks," it sounds like the crusty old colonel is finally wrapping up, "I would just like to impart one final lesson to all of you, the Army's newest rangers."

My ears perk up and I turn my gaze from the rangers around me to the old white hair.

"The lesson is this, rangers: You must go out and continue to earn the Tab, not just today, not just tomorrow, but every day, for the rest of your lives. Every... single... day, rangers."

There are a few painful moans and snickers from some of us, but many of us are rapt and paying attention.

"You may think you are done with Ranger School now, but you are wrong. Ranger School has not finished with any of you. In fact, your real challenge is just beginning. Most of you are soon going off to combat, taking charge of a team, a squad, or a platoon. It is then, when you are leading your men through real adversity, when lives are on the line, that you will truly need the lessons learned here."

Many of us are thinking about our buddies, our brothers in Iraq and Afghanistan now. I know I am.

"Now that you wear the Tab, you have the obligation to go back to your units, to your colleagues, friends, and families, and show everyone who a ranger can be, what he can do, and the results he can achieve. You must be physically stronger, mentally tougher, and morally straighter than everyone else in the room. Most of all, you must work harder and fight smarter than everyone else, because, well, that is how you uphold the honor and prestige of the Ranger Tab... and you do it for life... You understand, rangers?"

"HOOOAAAAH!" The assembled rangers shout in unison, genuinely motivated.

"Well then, friends, family members, leaders..." the good colonel's speech comes to its conclusion, "please join us on the field to pin the Tabs on your rangers."

Commanding officers, team leaders, squad leaders, fathers, uncles, wives, brothers, sisters, sons, daughters, and all other manner of relations step down off the bleachers to pin black and yellow Ranger Tabs onto our uniforms. More than a few rangers in the class visibly shed tears of joy. Me and Powell, having no one here in the audience to pin Tabs on us, take turns pinning them on each other.

"Congratulations, ranger!" Powell says with a big, dumb grin as he pins my Tab on my left shoulder.

"Congratulations to you, too, ranger!" I say, as I do the same for him.

"I hereby release all of you from Ranger School. Rejoin your families and your units. Go forth as rangers, to carry on the ranger mission, whatever that may be for each of you." The colonel concludes and dismisses us for good.

"What do you say we get the fuck out of here?" Powell suggests. "I could really go for some Waffle House right about now."

"Me, too," I respond, my stomach growling even though we had a hearty breakfast three hours ago, "let's go."

"Hold on guys! Hold on!" It is Salvador, crouching behind us, trying to hide from someone. "I need a favor. I need you guys to walk shoulder-to-shoulder to the parking lot, I'll be right behind you. Please, walk quickly and try not to let anyone see me, especially if they're wearing a tan beret. Can you guys do that for me?"

As he says this, I see several burly Ranger Regiment corporals and sergeants tossing bat boys, including Leon, Sol, and Bailey, into Victory Pond. I see several others combing the crowd, on the search for newly Tabbed bat boys, who Regimental tradition demands be thrown into the frigid waters, a baptism of sorts as a full-fledged Airborne Ranger.

Seeing that it's January and the pond water freezing, Salvador wants no part of it.

"Screw tradition." He says, "I don't want to get wet. Can you guys help me?"

How could I say no to Salvador? How could I deny anything to the streetwise, heavily tattooed, perennial bat boy Recycle from Brooklyn who earned my trust and never did me wrong? I once regarded him suspiciously and even considered him an enemy, but now, I consider him a faithful friend. I never gave it much thought until now, but I owe Salvador a lot. He has done me a dozen small kindnesses throughout this course, whether that was giving the squad more sleep by purposefully sleeping through guard shifts, not giving me hell for almost quitting, or picking me up off the ground during that last mission in Mountains, when everyone else stepped right over me.

Other than Nurse Birdie and Powell, my ranger buddy, I am going to miss him more than anyone else. He taught me a lot about what it means to be a ranger. So, what do I tell him?

"For you Salvador, anything."

"Eh, why not?" Powell adds as we begin striding out towards the parking lot with mean-looking ranger scowls on our faces. "Although it would be pretty funny to see you tossed in the pond, Salvador."

This is our last mission of Ranger School, escorting Salvador to safety away from the Ranger Regiment team leaders. Somehow, we make it past their sharp eyes and drop off a dry Salvador at the edge of the parking lot.

"Thanks, brothers. I owe you one," Salvador says to us as he waves over a passing gray sedan. "See you later." He says nonchalantly as he hops into the front passenger seat, knowing full well we will never see each other again.

"Well, what do you say, Goldsmith?" Powell turns to me. "Shall we head back to Iraq now?"

Back to Iraq? Back to my platoon, my men, and the mission, hopefully some real combat and lots of enemies to shoot at? That would really be great, a chance to put this Tab to good use.

"Sounds pretty good to me, Powell," I say in all honesty, "pretty damn good."

To a normal person, I must seem crazy, but I am not a normal person. I am a newly Tabbed Ranger in the US Army Infantry, and there is nothing in this world I could possibly want more.

"I mean, why not, Powell," I add, "after all, it can't be any worse than this place."

"Ain't that the fucking truth!"

No matter what life brings next month, next year, or even in the next few decades, somehow, deep in my heart, I know that it will never be as bad as Ranger School.

And if it is, it means I messed up royally.

Rules of Ranger School

Ranger School will suck.
Endure the suffering; earn the Tab.
Do not show up to Ranger School tired, hungry, or alone.
Do not excel; do the bare minimum.
Take care of your feet.
Never volunteer for anything.
Follow the Five Principles of Patrolling.
Ranger School is fucking stupid.
Have a purpose.
Moving forward is better than sitting still.
Don't be a buddy fucker.
Do not be afraid to step up and lead.
You can endure anything for just one day.
Always top off your canteens.
Never trust a sleepy ranger.
Pray there won't be rain.
Help out your buddies whenever you can.
Master the rules, so you know when to break them.
Real rangers recycle.
Rangers don't fight fair.
When in doubt, attack!
Ranger School will humble everyone.
Earn the Tab, every day.

Glossary

Admin, going admin – short for "administrative" - A temporary pause in the mission or "tactical" activities to allow the Ranger Instructors to conduct inspections, layouts, provide instructions, or punish us.

Alpha Team Leader – Along with the Bravo Team Leader, one of two team leaders in a ranger squad; leads and maintains accountability of the individual soldiers in a fire team and reports to the squad leader.

Ambush – A surprise attack from a concealed position on a moving or temporarily halted target. In other words, attacking someone on a road or trail. Along with raids, one of the two main missions performed in Ranger School.

AWOL – acronym for "away without leave" – Deserting your militarily-assigned post whether in training, garrison, or combat.

Bat Boys – Nickname for the privates and specialists from the 75th Ranger Regiment, derived from them being from one of three Ranger Battalions.

Bravo Team Leader – see Alpha Team Leader.

Buddy fucker – The worst thing to be in Ranger School, someone who screws their buddy over for personal gain or just for the hell of it. See also: shitbag.

Chow – Food. Sweet life-sustaining sustenance. Other than sleep, there is nothing finer in this world to a ranger student.

Commando, going commando – Foregoing the wearing of underpants, a common practice in the infantry and Ranger School. Not only does it lighten your rucksack, but it also prevents rashes.

Day One Recycle – Regardless of which phase you are in, having to go back to the very first day of Ranger School to start everything all over again. Generally reserved for serious rules violations, possession of contraband, or repeated failure of a single phase, considered by many ranger students to be a fate worse than death.

Drive-on Tab – A Ranger Tab given to a ranger student by a leader, mentor, or family member who has previously attended and successfully passed Ranger School. Intended to serve as an inspiration when times are tough; a reminder that others have gone through the same suffering as you and that earning the Tab is possible.

Droning – After a prolonged period of sleep deprivation, the condition of no longer being able to cognitively function while still having to shoot, move, and communicate as a ranger. Akin to sleepwalking, droning rangers look, act, and think like zombies.

E-Tool – short for "entrenching tool" - A compact, foldable shovel carried on the rucksack and used by rangers to dig fighting positions and latrines.

Finger-drilling – Going through the motions, but not taking a task seriously, something the Ranger Instructors will not tolerate.

FO - acronym for "forward observer" – One of a ranger platoon's two radiomen; responsible for calling in and coordinating artillery fires. In Ranger School, generally shadows the Platoon Leader and serves as his radioman.

FTX – acronym for "Field Training Exercise" – Realistic, force-on-force training out in the woods, swamps, and mountains where each ranger student is evaluated on his ranger and leadership skills while conducting ranger operations against the Opfor. Each phase of Ranger School has its own FTX which must be passed before moving onto the next one.

Grazing – Eating any sort of food outside of permitted meal times; a serious infraction in Ranger School.

Gray Man – An unassuming, seemingly unimpressive ranger student who manages to skate through the course unseen and off the radar of the

Ranger Instructors. In Ranger School as in life, standouts and strugglers get the most attention so, if you want a quiet, happy experience, it can pay to be mediocre.

Green Beret – Widely used nickname for a US Army Special Forces soldier, derived from their famous green-hued headgear, green berets are specially selected and highly trained soldiers who specialize in unconventional operations, guerilla warfare, and direct-action missions. Oftentimes (but not always) the most skilled, capable, and toughest attendees of Ranger School.

Gypsy Pack – A poorly packed rucksack with items hanging out of it or one with loose, dangling straps. Such a pack makes it easier to lose things, is more easily tangled up in trees and foliage, and is completely unacceptable to the Ranger Instructors.

High-Speed – A motivated, dependable, and capable soldier. Often used sarcastically by Ranger Instructors when addressing students who are anything but high-speed.

Hooah! – The all-purpose Army battle cry, acknowledgment, and filler word; rarely heard at Ranger School, where everyone is too "cool" to say Hooah.

Hootch – also spelled "hooch" – A rudimentary shelter constructed out of one or more poncho tarps.

Hump, humping – To carry a heavy rucksack on your back, the primary thing you will do in Ranger School.

Hygiene – Defecating, brushing one's teeth, shaving, giving oneself a whore bath, or any other personal hygiene tasks.

Joe – A low-ranking, regular soldier in a squad or platoon with no leadership responsibilities, generally a riflemen, grenadier, or machine gunner. Joe's primary jobs are to carry heavy things, stay awake, and follow orders.

Klick – A kilometer in military speak. One klick is approximately 0.6 miles.

Land Nav – short for "land navigation" - Using a map, compass, and terrain association to navigate from point A to point B without the aid of GPS. A critical skill for a ranger hunting guerillas in the woods.

LT – short for "Lieutenant" - the lowest ranking commissioned officers in the US Army. LTs are generally placed in charge of a platoon of soldiers. In Ranger School, most LTs come from various basic officer training courses and report to their first assignment after passing (or failing) Ranger School.

LOM Statement – short for "lack of motivation" statement - A signed statement attesting to one's voluntary quitting of Ranger School. A shameful act, someone who signs an LOM statement can never return to Ranger School, and will never earn the Tab.

Mad Minute – A short period of time, generally a minute, where a squad or platoon's base of fire element and its assaulting element, ideally from a different direction, open fire on an objective in tandem, seeking to shock, immobilize, and damage the enemy with overwhelming fire power before executing the assault.

Major-Minus – short for "Major-Minus Spot Report" - a written citation for doing something seriously wrong in Ranger School, such as falling asleep during a patrol, grazing, or anything else that really pisses off an RI. Earning three or more major-minuses in any phase will likely result in recycling and, in some circumstances, failing Ranger School.

Major-Plus – short for "Major-Plus Spot Report" - Much rarer than its negative counterpart, a major-plus is a written citation for finishing first in a major event at Ranger School or otherwise accomplishing something great. A major-plus cancels out a major-minus.

Medic – also known as "Doc" - The platoon's organic medical care provider, responsible for treating and stabilizing injuries as well as the general hygiene and well-being of the platoon. The medic generally sticks with the Platoon Sergeant on patrol.

Mikes – Military speak for minutes.

Mind Games – When the Ranger Instructors make you do stupid things or demand the impossible in order to mess with your head, get under your skin, and make you quit.

Minor-Minus – short for "Minor-Minus Spot Report" - A minor written citation for doing something mildly bad in Ranger School. Rarer than its more serious counterpart, the major-minus; three minor-minuses add up to one major-minus.

Minor-Plus – short for "Minor-Plus Spot Report" - A minor written citation for doing something good in Ranger School. More common than its weightier counterpart, the Major-Plus, one minor-plus will cancel out a minor-minus and three minor-pluses equals a major-plus.

NODs – acronym for "night optical devices" - Army shorthand for night vision goggles or "NVGs," which is also used by soldiers.

Noise and Light Discipline - Speaking and making as little noise as possible and, at night, using as little light as possible, to stay quiet, unseen, and undetected by the enemy whether on patrol or at the patrol base.

Operation Order or Op Order – the planning format used by Army leaders to inform subordinates how to conduct a military operation. Op orders utilize a five paragraph structure to organize the information and presentation and planning and issuing op orders is practiced extensively throughout Ranger School.

Opfor – short for "Opposing Forces" – Soldiers working for Ranger School who serve as the guerrilla enemy for the ranger students throughout the Ranger School field training exercises.

Peers – short for "Peer Evaluations" – The formal, written reports prepared by ranger students at the end of each phase where each member of the squad is ranked from best to worst, with reasons given why, in order to identify the weakest performing, least popular members of the squad. These rangers risk recycling the phase or even failing Ranger School.

PL – short for "platoon leader" - Responsible for what the platoon accomplishes or fails to accomplish on patrol, including the tactical employment of its weapons, training, administration, personnel management, and logistics. The highest leadership position in both Mountains and Florida phase. In the regular Army, usually a lieutenant or sergeant first class, but in Ranger School, it could be anyone.

Platoon guide – An administrative platoon sergeant position held by a ranger student during garrison and techniques weeks. Responsible for corralling the ranger platoon and communicating RI instructions.

Platoon Sergeant – The senior non-commissioned officer and second-in-command of a platoon. Helps and advises the PL as well as supervises the patrol's administration, logistics, and maintenance operations. In the regular Army, usually a sergeant first class or staff sergeant.

Pog – rhymes with "vogue," acronym for "person other than grunt" –

derogatory term used by infantrymen to refer to non-infantry "support" soldiers. Can be fighting words in the Army.

PT Test – short for "physical training" test - various well-defined tests of physical strength, endurance, and stamina administered to soldiers in Ranger School, and the Army generally. In 2007, the Ranger School PT Test consisted of 49 perfect pushups in two minutes, 59 sit-ups in two minutes, a five-mile run in less than 40 minutes, and six, excruciatingly slow, underhand pull ups.

Rack, rack out – Go to sleep. Derived from "rack," meaning bed or bunk, the place where you sleep.

Raid – A form of attack, usually small scale, involving a swift entry into hostile territory to secure information, kill and confuse the enemy, or destroy enemy installations followed by a planned withdrawal. Along with ambush, one of the two primary missions in Ranger School.

Ranger - multiple usages – 1) A student currently attending Ranger School. 2) A member of the 75th Ranger Regiment. 3) Someone who earned their Ranger Tab. 4) Classically, a ranger was an American light infantry soldier operating on the frontier who was specially trained and equipped to conduct raids, ambushes, and reconnaissance in enemy held territory.

Ranger Regiment, Ranger Battalion – The 75th Ranger Regiment is an elite light infantry and special operations unit consisting of three separate Ranger Battalions, the 1st, 2nd, and 3rd Battalions, and the home of the Bat Boys. Its members wear a Ranger Scroll on the left shoulder of their uniforms in addition to their Ranger Tabs, if they have earned one.

Recon - short for "reconnaissance" – Checking out some location, whether using a map, imagery, or best of all, on the ground and in person, to gather information on it in preparation for an operation or attack.

Recycle, recycling – Failing a phase of Ranger School due to patrol failures, low Peers evaluation rankings, medical problems, or too many major-minuses, and having to go through it again. Many rangers will recycle at least one phase of Ranger School.

RTO – short for "radiotelephone operator" - The squad or platoon's primary radioman, tasked with communicating with higher headquarters, adjacent forces, and close air and indirect fire support.

Rucksack, ruck – A large military hiking backpack worn on the shoulders, generally the Vietnam-era Alice Pack or the more contemporary MOLLE rucksack. Invariably heavy, ranging from as little as thirty-five to as much as one hundred-pounds of clothing, water, ammunition, gear and supplies, the rucksack is the constant companion and bane of the ranger student.

Rucksack Flop – Removing one's rucksack from one's aching back and shoulders and dropping it gratefully onto the ground. A small but significant source of joy to a ranger.

Shitbag – The Army's favorite, all-purpose term for a poorly-performing or unethical soldier.

Smoking, to be Smoked – army slang for "corrective training," or more simply, "punishment" - In lieu of physical violence, the modern Army uses physical exercises, for example: pushups, flutterkicks, jumping jacks, and mountain climbers, in combination with copious amounts of verbal and mental abuse to punish and discipline its soldiers.

Snivel Gear – Cold or wet weather clothing. Referred to as snivel gear presumably because one is a crybaby for wanting to wear it. The wearing of warming/wet weather clothing is tightly controlled and only sparingly allowed in Ranger School.

Squad Leader – The leader of a ranger squad, a maneuver element typically composed of two fire teams of four men each. Responsible for what the squad does or fails to do, the squad leader works closely with the platoon leader and the platoon sergeant to accomplish the ranger mission.

Standard Operating Procedures or "SOP" – The standard way specific tasks are to be done by a ranger squad or platoon.

TA-50 – Army terminology for the standard issue gear issued to soldiers - In Ranger School, TA-50 gear consists of a rucksack, load-bearing vest, ammo pouches, canteen pouches, canteens, and more.

"Take a knee" – While taking a short halt on patrol, rangers are supposed to get down on one knee to minimize their profiles.

Weasel or WSL – short for "Weapons Squad Leader" - The senior squad leader in the platoon, in charge of the two or three machine gun teams and their operators. Generally acknowledged as the easiest graded position in Mountains and Florida phases of Ranger School, it is a highly coveted position.

Wood line – The immediate edge of the woods from one's position; where a ranger urinates and catches a moment of quiet contemplation.

Acknowledgements

It often felt like I was all alone in Ranger School, but I was helped by dozens of strong hands and kind hearts along the way. I could not have earned my Tab or written this book without any of them, but in particular, I would like to thank:

My Attack Company brothers Hunter and Dennis, without either of you I never would have even attempted Ranger School.

First Sergeant "Castle," for giving me a good reason, going back to Iraq with my brothers in arms, to finish Ranger School, at the lowest point in my life.

"Salvador," "Sol," "Powell," "Tobiri," "McCormick," "Nurse Marie," and even "Bailey," without your words of encouragement, small acts of kindness, and dare I say, friendship, I never would have graduated Ranger School.

All my drill sergeants, ranger instructors, team leaders, squad leaders, and platoon leaders, who taught me, the hard way, what it means to be a man, an infantryman, and a ranger.

The entire Double Dagger publishing team and especially my editor Phil Halton for all the support and hard work involved in making this book a reality.

John Spencer, Tim O'Hair, and Colby Allerton for reviewing early drafts of the manuscript and providing invaluable feedback and recommendations.

My wife and children, for allowing me to spend countless hours writing this book and for always listening to my ranger stories. Without your loving support, this story could not have been told.

And finally, I would like to thank everyone I served with in Attack Company, my infantry brothers. You have seen me at my best, and at my worst. We did some amazing things together, impossible things. It was an honor and a privilege to serve with all of you.

"In the absence of orders . . . Attack!"

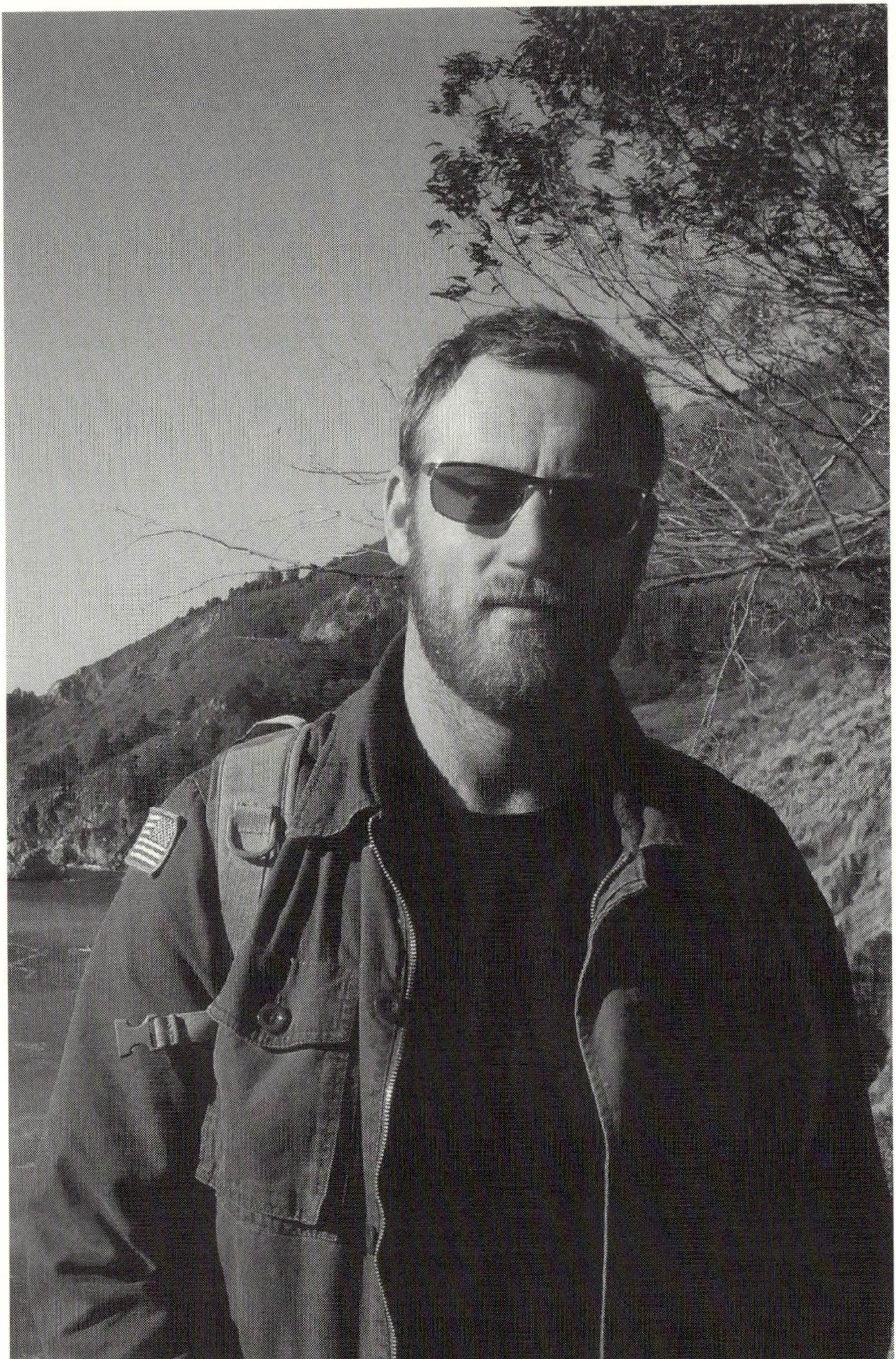

About the Author

Andrew Goldsmith grew up in Los Angeles and joined the US Army infantry at nineteen. After serving two years in Iraq, graduating Ranger School, and attaining the rank of sergeant, Andrew left the Army to study philosophy at the University of Hawaii. Andrew would go on to study law at Pepperdine University School of Law and has been a practicing attorney since 2016. Andrew is also a businessman, a world traveler, endurance athlete, and Gracie jiu jitsu black belt.

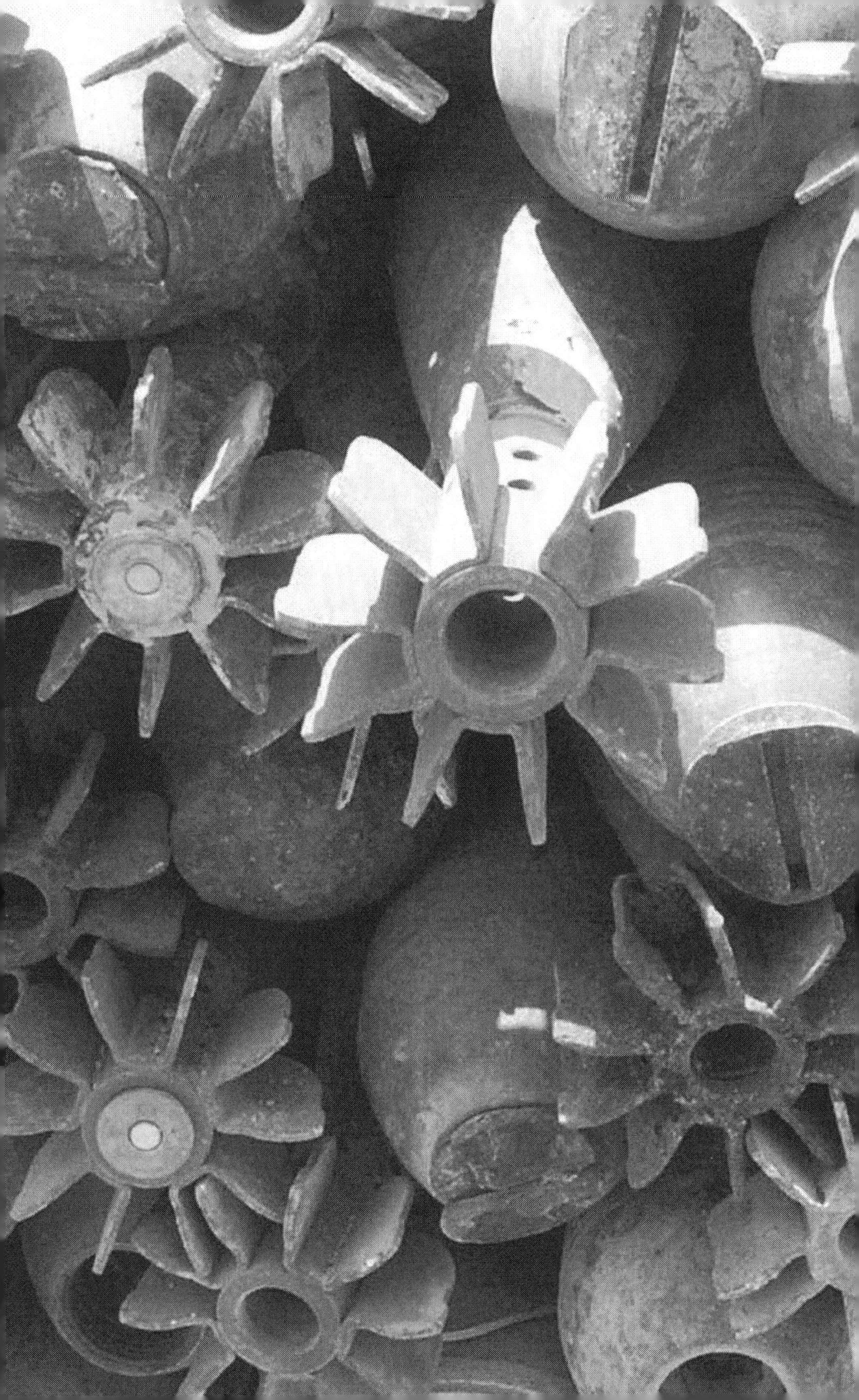

DOUBLE ✝ DAGGER
— www.doubledagger.ca —

Double Dagger Books is Canada's only military-focused publisher. Conflict and warfare have shaped human history since before we began to record it. The earliest stories that we know of, passed on as oral tradition, speak of war, and more importantly, the essential elements of the human condition that are revealed under its pressure.

We are dedicated to publishing material that, while rooted in conflict, transcend the idea of "war" as merely a genre. Fiction, non-fiction, and stuff that defies categorization, we want to read it all.

Because if you want peace, study war.

Made in the USA
Middletown, DE
26 February 2025